Advanced Stochastic Models, Risk Assessment, and Portfolio Optimization

THE FRANK J. FABOZZI SERIES

Advanced Stochastic Models, Risk Assessment, and Portfolio Optimization

The Ideal Risk, Uncertainty, and Performance Measures

SVETLOZAR T. RACHEV
STOYAN V. STOYANOV
FRANK J. FABOZZI

WILEY

John Wiley & Sons, Inc.

ISBN: 978-0-470-05316-4

10 9 8 7 6 5 4 3 2

STR
To my children, Boryana and Vladimir

SVS
To my parents, Veselin and Evgeniya Kolevi, and my brother, Pavel Stoyanov

FJF
To the memory of my parents, Josephine and Alfonso Fabozzi

Contents

Preface

Modern portfolio theory, as pioneered in the 1950s by Harry Markowitz, is well adopted by the financial community. In spite of the fundamental shortcomings of mean-variance analysis, it remains a basic tool in the industry.

Since the 1990s, significant progress has been made in developing the concept of a risk measure from both a theoretical and a practical viewpoint. This notion has evolved into a materially different form from the original idea behind mean-variance analysis. As a consequence, the distinction between risk and uncertainty, which translates into a distinction between a risk measure and a dispersion measure, offers a new way of looking at the problem of optimal portfolio selection.

As concepts develop, other tools become appropriate to exploring evolved ideas than existing techniques. In applied finance, these tools are being imported from mathematics. That said, we believe that probability metrics, which is a field in probability theory, will turn out to be well-positioned for the study and further development of the quantitative aspects of risk and uncertainty. Going one step further, we make a parallel. In the theory of probability metrics, there exists a concept known as an *ideal probability metric*. This is a quantity best suited for the study of a given approximation problem in probability or stochastic processes. We believe that the ideas behind this concept can be borrowed and applied in the field of asset management to construct an *ideal risk measure* that would be ideal for a given optimal portfolio selection problem.

The development of probability metrics as a branch of probability theory started in the 1950s, even though its basic ideas were used during the first half of the 20th century. Its application to problems is connected with this fundamental question: "Is the proposed stochastic model a satisfactory approximation to the real model and, if so, within what limits?" In finance, we assume a stochastic model for asset return distributions and, in order to estimate portfolio risk, we sample from the fitted distribution. Then we use the generated simulations to evaluate the portfolio positions and, finally, to calculate portfolio risk. In this context, there are two issues arising on two different levels. First, the assumed stochastic model should be close to the empirical data. That is, we need a realistic model in the first place. Second, the generated scenarios should be sufficiently many in order to represent a good *approximation* model to the assumed stochastic model. In this way, we are sure that the computed portfolio risk numbers are close to what they would be had the problem been analytically tractable.

This book provides a gentle introduction into the theory of probability metrics and the problem of optimal portfolio selection, which is considered in the general context of risk and reward measures. We illustrate in numerous examples the basic concepts and where more technical knowledge is needed, an appendix is provided.

The book is organized in the following way. Chapters 1 and 2 contain introductory material from the fields of probability and optimization theory. Chapter 1 is necessary for understanding the general ideas behind probability metrics covered in Chapter 3 and ideal probability metrics in particular described in Chapter 4. The material in Chapter 2 is used when discussing optimal portfolio selection problems in Chapters 8, 9, and 10. We demonstrate how probability metrics can be applied to certain areas in finance in the following chapters:

- Chapter 5—stochastic dominance orders.
- Chapter 6—the construction of risk and dispersion measures.
- Chapter 7—problems involving average value-at-risk and spectral risk measures in particular.
- Chapter 8—reward-risk analysis generalizing mean-variance analysis.
- Chapter 9—the problem of benchmark tracking.
- Chapter 10—the construction of performance measures.

Chapters 5, 6, and 7 are also a prerequisite for the material in the last three chapters. Chapter 5 describes expected utility theory and stochastic dominance orders. The focus in Chapter 6 is on general dispersion measures and risk measures. Finally, in Chapter 7 we discuss the average value-at-risk and spectral risk measures, which are two particular families of coherent risk measures considered in Chapter 6.

The classical mean-variance analysis and the more general mean-risk analysis are explored in Chapter 8. We consider the structure of the efficient portfolios when average value-at-risk is selected as a risk measure. Chapter 9 is focused on the benchmark tracking problem. We generalize significantly the problem applying the methods of probability metrics. In Chapter 10, we discuss performance measures in the general framework of reward-risk analysis. We consider classes of performance measures that lead to practical optimal portfolio problems.

Svetlozar T. Rachev
Stoyan V. Stoyanov
Frank J. Fabozzi

Acknowledgments

Svetlozar Rachev's research was supported by grants from the Division of Mathematical, Life and Physical Sciences, College of Letters and Science, University of California–Santa Barbara, and the Deutschen Forschungsgemeinschaft.

Stoyan Stoyanov thanks the R&D team at FinAnalytica for the encouragement and the chair of Statistics, Econometrics and Mathematical Finance at the University of Karlsruhe for the hospitality extended to him.

Lastly, Frank Fabozzi thanks Yale's International Center for Finance for its support in completing this book.

Svetlozar T. Rachev
Stoyan V. Stoyanov
Frank J. Fabozzi

About the Authors

Svetlozar (Zari) **T. Rachev** completed his Ph.D. in 1979 from Moscow State (Lomonosov) University, and his doctor of science degree in 1986 from Steklov Mathematical Institute in Moscow. Currently, he is Chair-Professor in Statistics, Econometrics and Mathematical Finance at the University of Karlsruhe in the School of Economics and Business Engineering. He is also Professor Emeritus at the University of California–Santa Barbara in the Department of Statistics and Applied Probability. He has published seven monographs, eight handbooks and special-edited volumes, and over 250 research articles. His recently coauthored books published by John Wiley & Sons in mathematical finance and financial econometrics include *Fat-Tailed and Skewed Asset Return Distributions: Implications for Risk Management, Portfolio Selection, and Option Pricing* (2005); *Operational Risk: A Guide to Basel II Capital Requirements, Models, and Analysis* (2007); *Financial Econometrics: From Basics to Advanced Modeling Techniques* (2007); and *Bayesian Methods in Finance* (2008). Professor Rachev is cofounder of Bravo Risk Management Group specializing in financial risk-management software. Bravo Group was recently acquired by FinAnalytica, for which he currently serves as chief scientist.

Stoyan V. Stoyanov is the chief financial researcher at FinAnalytica specializing in financial risk management software. He completed his Ph.D. with honors in 2005 from the School of Economics and Business Engineering (Chair of Statistics, Econometrics and Mathematical Finance) at the University of Karlsruhe and is author and coauthor of numerous papers. His research interests include probability theory, heavy-tailed modeling in the field of finance, and optimal portfolio theory. His articles have appeared in the *Journal of Banking and Finance*, *Applied Mathematical Finance*, *Applied Financial Economics*, and *International Journal of Theoretical and Applied Finance*. Dr. Stoyanov has years of experience in applying optimal portfolio theory and market risk estimation methods when solving practical client problems at FinAnalytica.

Frank J. Fabozzi is professor in the practice of finance in the School of Management at Yale University. Prior to joining the Yale faculty, he was a visiting professor of finance in the Sloan School at MIT. Professor Fabozzi is a Fellow of the International Center for Finance at Yale University and is on the Advisory Council for the Department of Operations Research and Financial Engineering at Princeton University. He is the editor of the *Journal of Portfolio Management*. His recently coauthored books published by John Wiley & Sons in mathematical finance and financial econometrics include *The Mathematics of Financial Modeling and Investment Management* (2004); *Financial Modeling of the Equity Market: From CAPM to Cointegration* (2006); *Robust Portfolio Optimization and Management* (2007); *Financial Econometrics: From Basics to Advanced Modeling Techniques* (2007); and *Bayesian Methods in Finance* (2008). He earned a doctorate in economics from the City University of New York in 1972. In 2002, Professor Fabozzi was inducted into the Fixed Income Analysts Society's Hall of Fame and is the 2007 recipient of the C. Stewart Sheppard Award given by the CFA Institute. He earned the designation of Chartered Financial Analyst and Certified Public Accountant.

CHAPTER 1

Concepts of Probability

1.1   INTRODUCTION

Will Microsoft's stock return over the next year exceed 10%? Will the one-month London Interbank Offered Rate (LIBOR) three months from now exceed 4%? Will Ford Motor Company default on its debt obligations sometime over the next five years? Microsoft's stock return over the next year, one-month LIBOR three months from now, and the default of Ford Motor Company on its debt obligations are each variables that exhibit randomness. Hence these variables are referred to as random variables.[1] In this chapter, we see how probability distributions are used to describe the potential outcomes of a random variable, the general properties of probability distributions, and the different types of probability distributions.[2] Random variables can be classified as either discrete or continuous. We begin with discrete probability distributions and then proceed to continuous probability distributions.

---

[1] The precise mathematical definition is that a random variable is a measurable function from a probability space into the set of real numbers. In this chapter, the reader will repeatedly be confronted with imprecise definitions. The authors have intentionally chosen this way for a better general understandability and for the sake of an intuitive and illustrative description of the main concepts of probability theory. In order to inform about every occurrence of looseness and lack of mathematical rigor, we have furnished most imprecise definitions with a footnote giving a reference to the exact definition.

[2] For more detailed and/or complementary information, the reader is referred to the textbooks of Larsen and Marx (1986), Shiryaev (1996), and Billingsley (1995).

1.2   BASIC CONCEPTS

An *outcome* for a random variable is the mutually exclusive potential result that can occur. The accepted notation for an outcome is the Greek letter ω. A *sample space* is a set of all possible outcomes. The sample space is denoted by Ω. The fact that a given outcome ω_i belongs to the sample space is expressed by $\omega_i \in \Omega$. An *event* is a subset of the sample space and can be represented as a collection of some of the outcomes.[3] For example, consider Microsoft's stock return over the next year. The sample space contains outcomes ranging from 100% (all the funds invested in Microsoft's stock will be lost) to an extremely high positive return. The sample space can be partitioned into two subsets: outcomes where the return is less than or equal to 10% and a subset where the return exceeds 10%. Consequently, a return greater than 10% is an event since it is a subset of the sample space. Similarly, a one-month LIBOR three months from now that exceeds 4% is an event. The collection of all events is usually denoted by $\mathfrak{A}$. In the theory of probability, we consider the sample space Ω together with the set of events $\mathfrak{A}$, usually written as $(\Omega, \mathfrak{A})$, because the notion of probability is associated with an event.[4]

1.3   DISCRETE PROBABILITY DISTRIBUTIONS

As the name indicates, a *discrete random variable* limits the outcomes where the variable can only take on discrete values. For example, consider the default of a corporation on its debt obligations over the next five years. This random variable has only two possible outcomes: default or nondefault. Hence, it is a discrete random variable. Consider an option contract where for an upfront payment (i.e., the option price) of $50,000, the buyer of the contract receives the payment given in Table 1.1 from the seller of the option depending on the return on the S&P 500 index. In this case, the random variable is a discrete random variable but on the limited number of outcomes.

---

[3]Precisely, only certain subsets of the sample space are called events. In the case that the sample space is represented by a subinterval of the real numbers, the events consist of the so-called "Borel sets." For all practical applications, we can think of Borel sets as containing all subsets of the sample space. In this case, the sample space together with the set of events is denoted by $(\mathbb{R}, \mathfrak{B})$. Shiryaev (1996) provides a precise definition.

[4]Probability is viewed as a function endowed with certain properties, taking events as an argument and providing their probabilities as a result. Thus, according to the mathematical construction, probability is defined on the elements of the set $\mathfrak{A}$ (called *sigma-field* or *sigma-algebra*) taking values in the interval $[0, 1]$, $P : \mathfrak{A} \rightarrow [0, 1]$.

TABLE 1.1 Option Payments Depending on the Value of the S&P 500 Index.

If S&P 500 Return Is:	Payment Received By Option Buyer:
Less than or equal to zero	$0
Greater than zero but less than 5%	$10,000
Greater than 5% but less than 10%	$20,000
Greater than or equal to 10%	$100,000

The probabilistic treatment of discrete random variables is comparatively easy: Once a probability is assigned to all different outcomes, the probability of an arbitrary event can be calculated by simply adding the single probabilities. Imagine that in the above example on the S&P 500 every different payment occurs with the same probability of 25%. Then the probability of losing money by having invested $50,000 to purchase the option is 75%, which is the sum of the probabilities of getting either $0, $10,000, or $20,000 back. In the following sections we provide a short introduction to the most important discrete probability distributions: Bernoulli distribution, binomial distribution, and Poisson distribution. A detailed description together with an introduction to several other discrete probability distributions can be found, for example, in the textbook by Johnson et al. (1993).

1.3.1 Bernoulli Distribution

We will start the exposition with the *Bernoulli distribution*. A random variable X is *Bernoulli-distributed* with parameter p if it has only two possible outcomes, usually encoded as 1 (which might represent success or default) or 0 (which might represent failure or survival).

One classical example for a Bernoulli-distributed random variable occurring in the field of finance is the default event of a company. We observe a company C in a specified time interval I, January 1, 2007, until December 31, 2007. We define

$$X = \begin{cases} 1 & \text{if } C \text{ defaults in } I \\ 0 & \text{else.} \end{cases}$$

The parameter p in this case would be the annualized probability of default of company C.

1.3.2 Binomial Distribution

In practical applications, we usually do not consider a single company but a whole basket, $C_1, \ldots, C_n$, of companies. Assuming that all these n companies have the same annualized probability of default p, this leads to a natural generalization of the Bernoulli distribution called *binomial distribution*. A binomial distributed random variable Y with parameters n and p is obtained as the sum of n independent[5] and identically Bernoulli-distributed random variables $X_1, \ldots, X_n$. In our example, Y represents the total number of defaults occurring in the year 2007 observed for companies $C_1, \ldots, C_n$. Given the two parameters, the probability of observing k, $0 \le k \le n$ defaults can be explicitly calculated as follows:

$$P(Y = k) = \binom{n}{k} p^k (1 - p)^{n-k},$$

where

$$\binom{n}{k} = \frac{n!}{(n-k)!k!}.$$

Recall that the factorial of a positive integer n is denoted by $n!$ and is equal to $n(n-1)(n-2) \cdot \ldots \cdot 2 \cdot 1$.

Bernoulli distribution and binomial distribution are revisited in Chapter 4 in connection with a fundamental result in the theory of probability called the *Central Limit Theorem*. Shiryaev (1996) provides a formal discussion of this important result.

1.3.3 Poisson Distribution

The last discrete distribution that we consider is the *Poisson distribution*. The Poisson distribution depends on only one parameter, λ, and can be interpreted as an approximation to the binomial distribution when the parameter p is a small number.[6] A Poisson-distributed random variable is usually used to describe the random number of events occurring over a certain time interval. We used this previously in terms of the number of defaults. One main difference compared to the binomial distribution is that the number of events that might occur is unbounded, at least theoretically. The parameter λ indicates the rate of occurrence of the random events, that is, it tells us how many events occur on average per unit of time.

---

[5] A definition of what independence means is provided in Section 1.6.4. The reader might think of independence as no interference between the random variables.

[6] The approximation of Poisson to the binomial distribution concerns the so-called *rare events*. An event is called *rare* if the probability of its occurrence is close to zero. The probability of a rare event occurring in a sequence of independent trials can be approximately calculated with the formula of the Poisson distribution.

The probability distribution of a Poisson-distributed random variable N is described by the following equation:

$$P(N = k) = \frac{\lambda^k}{k!}e^{-\lambda}, \ k = 0, 1, 2, \ldots$$

1.4 CONTINUOUS PROBABILITY DISTRIBUTIONS

If the random variable can take on any possible value within the range of outcomes, then the probability distribution is said to be a *continuous random variable*.[7] When a random variable is either the price of or the return on a financial asset or an interest rate, the random variable is assumed to be continuous. This means that it is possible to obtain, for example, a price of 95.43231 or 109.34872 and any value in between. In practice, we know that financial assets are not quoted in such a way. Nevertheless, there is no loss in describing the random variable as continuous and in many times treating the return as a continuous random variable means substantial gain in mathematical tractability and convenience. For a continuous random variable, the calculation of probabilities is substantially different from the discrete case. The reason is that if we want to derive the probability that the realization of the random variable lays within some range (i.e., over a subset or subinterval of the sample space), then we cannot proceed in a similar way as in the discrete case: The number of values in an interval is so large, that we cannot just add the probabilities of the single outcomes. The new concept needed is explained in the next section.

1.4.1 Probability Distribution Function, Probability Density Function, and Cumulative Distribution Function

A *probability distribution function* P assigns a probability $P(A)$ for every event A, that is, of realizing a value for the random value in any specified subset A of the sample space. For example, a probability distribution function can assign a probability of realizing a monthly return that is negative or the probability of realizing a monthly return that is greater than 0.5% or the probability of realizing a monthly return that is between 0.4% and 1.0%.

---

[7]Precisely, not every random variable taking its values in a subinterval of the real numbers is continuous. The exact definition requires the existence of a density function such as the one that we use later in this chapter to calculate probabilities.

To compute the probability, a mathematical function is needed to represent the probability distribution function. There are several possibilities of representing a probability distribution by means of a mathematical function. In the case of a continuous probability distribution, the most popular way is to provide the so-called *probability density function* or simply *density function.*

In general, we denote the density function for the random variable X as $f_X(x)$. Note that the letter x is used for the function argument and the index denotes that the density function corresponds to the random variable X. The letter x is the convention adopted to denote a particular value for the random variable. The density function of a probability distribution is always nonnegative and as its name indicates: Large values for $f_X(x)$ of the density function at some point x imply a relatively high probability of realizing a value in the neighborhood of x, whereas $f_X(x) = 0$ for all x in some interval (a, b) implies that the probability for observing a realization in (a, b) is zero.

Figure 1.1 aids in understanding a continuous probability distribution. The shaded area is the probability of realizing a return less than b and greater than a. As probabilities are represented by areas under the density function, it follows that the probability for every single outcome of a continuous random variable always equals zero. While the shaded area

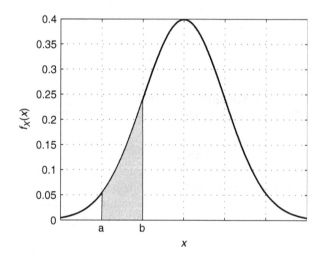

FIGURE 1.1 The probability of the event that a given random variable, X, is between two real numbers, a and b, which is equal to the shaded area under the density function, $f_X(x)$.

in Figure 1.1 represents the probability associated with realizing a return within the specified range, how does one compute the probability? This is where the tools of calculus are applied. Calculus involves differentiation and integration of a mathematical function. The latter tool is called *integral calculus* and involves computing the area under a curve. Thus the probability that a realization from a random variable is between two real numbers *a* and *b* is calculated according to the formula,

$$P(a \leq X \leq b) = \int_a^b f_X(x)dx.$$

The mathematical function that provides the cumulative probability of a probability distribution, that is, the function that assigns to every real value *x* the probability of getting an outcome less than or equal to *x*, is called the *cumulative distribution function* or *cumulative probability function* or simply *distribution function* and is denoted mathematically by $F_X(x)$. A cumulative distribution function is always nonnegative, nondecreasing, and as it represents probabilities it takes only values between zero and one.[8] An example of a distribution function is given in Figure 1.2.

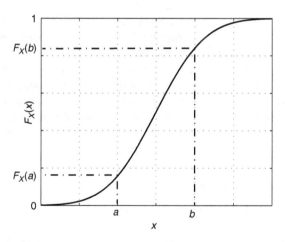

FIGURE 1.2 The probability of the event that a given random variable X is between two real numbers a and b is equal to the difference $F_X(b) - F_X(a)$.

---

[8]Negative values would imply negative probabilities. If F decreased, that is, for some $x < y$ we have $F_X(x) > F_X(y)$, it would create a contradiction because the probability

The mathematical connection between a probability density function f, a probability distribution P, and a cumulative distribution function F of some random variable X is given by the following formula:

$$P(X \leq t) = F_X(t) = \int_{-\infty}^{t} f_X(x)dx.$$

Conversely, the density equals the first derivative of the distribution function,

$$f_X(x) = \frac{dF_X(x)}{dx}.$$

The cumulative distribution function is another way to uniquely characterize an arbitrary probability distribution on the set of real numbers. In terms of the distribution function, the probability that the random variable is between two real numbers a and b is given by

$$P(a < X \leq b) = F_X(b) - F_X(a).$$

Not all distribution functions are continuous and differentiable, such as the example plotted in Figure 1.2. Sometimes, a distribution function may have a jump for some value of the argument, or it can be composed of only jumps and flat sections. Such are the distribution functions of a discrete random variable for example. Figure 1.3 illustrates a more general case in which $F_X(x)$ is differentiable except for the point $x = a$ where there is a jump. It is often said that the distribution function has a point mass at $x = a$ because the value a happens with nonzero probability in contrast to the other outcomes, $x \neq a$. In fact, the probability that a occurs is equal to the size of the jump of the distribution function. We consider distribution functions with jumps in Chapter 7 in the discussion about the calculation of the average value-at-risk risk measure.

1.4.2   The Normal Distribution

The class of *normal distributions*, or *Gaussian distributions*, is certainly one of the most important probability distributions in statistics and due to some of its appealing properties also the class which is used in most applications in finance. Here we introduce some of its basic properties.

The random variable X is said to be normally distributed with parameters μ and σ, abbreviated by $X \in N(\mu, \sigma^2)$, if the density of the random

---

of getting a value less than or equal to x must be smaller or equal to the probability of getting a value less than or equal to y.

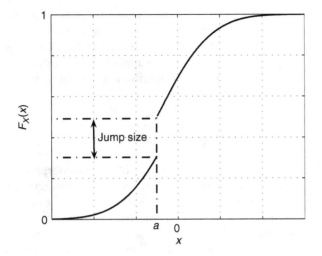

FIGURE 1.3 A distribution function $F_X(x)$ with a jump at $x = a$.

variable is given by the formula,

$$f_X(x) = \frac{1}{\sqrt{2\pi\sigma^2}}e^{-\frac{(x-\mu)^2}{2\sigma^2}}, x \in \mathbb{R}.$$

The parameter μ is called a *location parameter* because the middle of the distribution equals μ and σ is called a *shape parameter* or a *scale parameter*. If $\mu = 0$ and $\sigma = 1$, then X is said to have a *standard normal distribution*.

An important property of the normal distribution is the *location-scale invariance* of the normal distribution. What does this mean? Imagine you have random variable X, which is normally distributed with the parameters μ and σ. Now we consider the random variable Y, which is obtained as $Y = aX + b$. In general, the distribution of Y might substantially differ from the distribution of X but in the case where X is normally distributed, the random variable Y is again normally distributed with parameters and $\tilde{\mu} = a\mu + b$ and $\tilde{\sigma} = a\sigma$. Thus we do not leave the class of normal distributions if we multiply the random variable by a factor or shift the random variable. This fact can be used if we change the scale where a random variable is measured: Imagine that X measures the temperature at the top of the Empire State Building on January 1, 2008, at 6 A.M. in degrees Celsius. Then $Y = \frac{9}{5}X + 32$ will give the temperature in degrees Fahrenheit, and if X is normally distributed, then Y will be too.

Another interesting and important property of normal distributions is their summation stability. If you take the sum of several independent[9] random variables that are all normally distributed with location parameters μ_i and scale parameters σ_i, then the sum again will be normally distributed. The two parameters of the resulting distribution are obtained as

$$\mu = \mu_1 + \mu_2 + \cdots + \mu_n$$

$$\sigma = \sqrt{\sigma_1^2 + \sigma_2^2 + \cdots + \sigma_n^2}.$$

The last important property that is often misinterpreted to justify the nearly exclusive use of normal distributions in financial modeling is the fact that the normal distribution possesses a *domain of attraction*. A mathematical result called the *central limit theorem* states that under certain technical conditions the distribution of a large sum of random variables behaves necessarily like a normal distribution. In the eyes of many, the normal distribution is the unique class of probability distributions having this property. This is wrong and actually it is the class of stable distributions (containing the normal distributions) that is unique in the sense that a large sum of random variables can only converge to a stable distribution. We discuss the stable distribution in Chapter 4.

1.4.3   Exponential Distribution

The exponential distribution is popular, for example, in queuing theory when we want to model the time we have to wait until a certain event takes place. Examples include the time until the next client enters the store, the time until a certain company defaults or the time until some machine has a defect.

As it is used to model waiting times, the exponential distribution is concentrated on the positive real numbers and the density function f and the cumulative distribution function F of an exponentially distributed random variable τ possess the following form:

$$f_\tau(x) = \frac{1}{\beta} e^{-\frac{x}{\beta}}, \ x > 0$$

and

$$F_\tau(x) = 1 - e^{-\frac{x}{\beta}}, \ x > 0.$$

---

[9]A definition of what independent means is provided in section 1.6.4. The reader might think of independence as nointerference between the random variables.

In credit risk modeling, the parameter $\lambda = 1/\beta$ has a natural interpretation as *hazard rate* or *default intensity*. Let τ denote an exponential distributed random variable, for example, the random time (counted in days and started on January 1, 2008) we have to wait until Ford Motor Company defaults. Now, consider the following expression:

$$\lambda(\Delta t) = \frac{P(\tau \in (t, t + \Delta t] | \tau > t)}{\Delta t} = \frac{P(\tau \in (t, t + \Delta t])}{\Delta t P(\tau > t)}.$$

where Δt denotes a small period of time.

What is the interpretation of this expression? $\lambda(\Delta t)$ represents a ratio of a probability and the quantity Δt. The probability in the numerator represents the probability that default occurs in the time interval $(t, t + \Delta t]$ conditional upon the fact that Ford Motor Company survives until time t. The notion of conditional probability is explained in section 1.6.1.

Now the ratio of this probability and the length of the considered time interval can be denoted as a default rate or default intensity. In applications different from credit risk we also use the expressions hazard or failure rate.

Now, letting Δt tend to zero we finally obtain after some calculus the desired relation $\lambda = 1/\beta$. What we can see is that in the case of an exponentially distributed time of default, we are faced with a constant rate of default that is independent of the current point in time t.

Another interesting fact linked to the exponential distribution is the following connection with the Poisson distribution described earlier. Consider a sequence of independent and identical exponentially distributed random variables $\tau_1, \tau_2, \ldots$ We can think of τ_1, for example, as the time we have to wait until a firm in a high-yield bond portfolio defaults. τ_2 will then represent the time between the first and the second default and so on. These waiting times are sometimes called *interarrival times*. Now, let N_t denote the number of defaults which have occurred until time $t \geq 0$. One important probabilistic result states that the random variable N_t is Poisson distributed with parameter $\lambda = t/\beta$.

1.4.4 Student's *t*-distribution

Student's *t*-distributions are used in finance as probabilistic models of assets returns. The density function of the *t*-distribution is given by the following equation:

$$f_X(x) = \frac{1}{\sqrt{\pi n}} \frac{\Gamma((n+1)/2)}{\Gamma(n/2)} \left(1 + \frac{x^2}{n}\right)^{-\frac{n+1}{2}}, \ x \in \mathbb{R},$$

where n is an integer valued parameter called *degree of freedom*. For large values of n, the t-distribution doesn't significantly differ from a standard normal distribution. Usually, for values $n > 30$, the t-distribution is considered as equal to the standard normal distribution.

1.4.5   Extreme Value Distribution

The extreme value distribution, sometimes also denoted as *Gumbel-type extreme value distribution*, occurs as the limit distribution of the (appropriately standardized) largest observation in a sample of increasing size. This fact explains its popularity in operational risk applications where we are concerned about a large or the largest possible loss. Its density function f and distribution function F, respectively, is given by the following equations:

$$f_X(x) = \frac{1}{b} e^{-\frac{x-a}{b} - e^{-\frac{x-a}{b}}}, \; x \in \mathbb{R}$$

and

$$F_X(x) = e^{-e^{-\frac{x-a}{b}}}, \; x \in \mathbb{R},$$

where a denotes a real location parameter and $b > 0$ a positive real shape parameter. The class of extreme value distributions forms a location-scale family.

1.4.6   Generalized Extreme Value Distribution

Besides the previously mentioned (*Gumbel type*) extreme value distribution, there are two other types of distributions that can occur as the limiting distribution of appropriately standardized sample maxima. One class is denoted as the *Weibull-type extreme value distribution* and has a similar representation as the Weibull distribution. The third type is also referred to as the *Fréchet-type extreme value distribution*. All three can be represented as a three parameter distribution family referred to as a *generalized extreme value distribution* with the following cumulative distribution function:

$$F_X(x) = e^{-(1 + \xi \frac{x - \mu}{\sigma})^{-1/\xi}}, \; 1 + \xi \frac{x - \mu}{\sigma} > 0,$$

where ξ and μ are real and σ is a positive real parameter. If ξ tends to zero, we obtain the extreme value distribution discussed above. For positive values of ξ, the distribution is Frechet-type and, for negative values of ξ, Weibull-type extreme value distribution.[10]

---

[10] An excellent reference for this and the following section is Embrechts et al. (1997).

1.5   STATISTICAL MOMENTS AND QUANTILES

In describing a probability distribution function, it is common to summarize it by using various measures. The five most commonly used measures are:

- Location
- Dispersion
- Asymmetry
- Concentration in tails
- Quantiles

In this section we describe these measures and the more general notion of statistical moments. We also explain how statistical moments are estimated from real data.

1.5.1   Location

The first way to describe a probability distribution function is by some measure of central value or location. The various measures that can be used are the mean or average value, the median, or the mode. The relationship among these three measures of location depends on the skewness of a probability distribution function that we will describe later. The most commonly used measure of location is the mean and is denoted by μ or EX or $E(X)$.

1.5.2   Dispersion

Another measure that can help us to describe a probability distribution function is the dispersion or how spread out the values of the random variable can realize. Various measures of dispersion are the range, variance, and mean absolute deviation. The most commonly used measure is the *variance*. It measures the dispersion of the values that the random variable can realize relative to the mean. It is the average of the squared deviations from the mean. The variance is in squared units. Taking the square root of the variance one obtains the *standard deviation*. In contrast to the variance, the mean absolute deviation takes the average of the absolute deviations from the mean. In practice, the variance is used and is denoted by σ^2 and the standard deviation σ. General types of dispersion measures are discussed in Chapter 6.

1.5.3   Asymmetry

A probability distribution may be symmetric or asymmetric around its mean. A popular measure for the asymmetry of a distribution is called its *skewness*. A negative skewness measure indicates that the distribution is

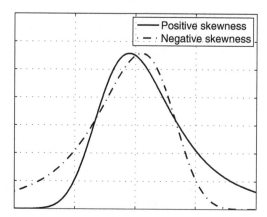

FIGURE 1.4 The density graphs of a positively and a negatively skewed distribution.

skewed to the left; that is, compared to the right tail, the left tail is elongated (see Figure 1.4). A positive skewness measure indicates that the distribution is skewed to the right; that is, compared to the left tail, the right tail is elongated (see Figure 1.4).

1.5.4   Concentration in Tails

Additional information about a probability distribution function is provided by measuring the concentration (mass) of potential outcomes in its tails. The tails of a probability distribution function contain the extreme values. In financial applications, it is these tails that provide information about the potential for a financial fiasco or financial ruin. The fatness of the tails of the distribution is related to the peakedness of the distribution around its mean or center. The joint measure of peakedness and tail fatness is called *kurtosis*.

1.5.5   Statistical Moments

In the parlance of the statistician, the four measures described above are called *statistical moments* or simply *moments*. The mean is the first moment and is also referred to as the *expected value*. The variance is the *second central moment*, skewness is a rescaled *third central moment*, and kurtosis is a rescaled *fourth central moment*. The general mathematical formula for the calculation of the four parameters is shown in Table 1.2.

The definition of skewness and kurtosis is not as unified as for the mean and the variance. The skewness measure reported in Table 1.2 is the so-called *Fisher's skewness*. Another possible way to define the measure is

TABLE 1.2 General Formula for Parameters.

Parameter	Discrete Distribution	Continuous Distribution
Mean	$EX = \sum_i x_i P(X = x_i)$	$EX = \int_{-\infty}^{\infty} x f_X(x) dx$
Variance	$\sigma^2 = E(X - EX)^2$	$\sigma^2 = E(X - EX)^2$
Skewness	$\zeta = \dfrac{E(X - EX)^3}{(\sigma^2)^{3/2}}$	$\zeta = \dfrac{E(X - EX)^3}{(\sigma^2)^{3/2}}$
Kurtosis	$\kappa = \dfrac{E(X - EX)^4}{(\sigma^2)^4}$	$\kappa = \dfrac{E(X - EX)^4}{(\sigma^2)^4}$

the *Pearson's skewness*, which equals the square of the Fisher's skewness. The same holds true for the kurtosis, where we have reported the *Pearson's kurtosis*. *Fishers' kurtosis* (sometimes denoted as *excess kurtosis*) can be obtained by subtracting three from Pearson's kurtosis.

Generally, the moment of order n of a random variable is denoted by μ_n defined as

$$\mu_n = EX^n,$$

where $n = 1, 2, \ldots$ For a discrete probability distribution, the moment of order k is calculated according to the formula

$$\mu_n = \sum_i x_i^n P(X = x_i),$$

and in the case of a continuous probability distribution, the formula is

$$\mu_n = \int_{-\infty}^{\infty} x^n f_X(x) dx.$$

The centered moment of order n is denoted by m_n and is defined as

$$m_n = E(X - EX)^n,$$

where $n = 1, 2, \ldots$. For a discrete probability distribution, the centered moment of order n is calculated according to the formula

$$m_n = \sum_i (x_i - EX)^n P(X = x_i),$$

and in the case of a continuous probability distribution, the formula is

$$m_n = \int_{-\infty}^{\infty} (x - EX)^n f_X(x) dx.$$

1.5.6 Quantiles

Not only are the statistical moments described in the previous section used to summarize a probability distribution, but also a concept called α-*quantile*. The α-quantile gives us information where the first α% of the distribution are located. Given an arbitrary observation of the considered probability distribution, this observation will be smaller than the α-quantile q_α in α% of the cases and larger in $(100 - \alpha)$% of the cases.[11]

Some quantiles have special names. The 25%-, 50%- and 75%-quantile are referred to as the *first quartile*, *second quartile*, and *third quartile*, respectively. The 1%-, 2%-, ..., 98%-, 99%-quantiles are called *percentiles*. As we will see in Chapters 6, the α-quantile is closely related with the value-at-risk measure ($VaR_\alpha(X)$) commonly used in risk management.

1.5.7 Sample Moments

The previous sections have introduced the four statistical moments mean, variance, skewness, and kurtosis. Given a probability density function f or a probability distribution P we are able to calculate these statistical moments according to the formulae given in Table 1.2. In practical applications however, we are faced with the situation that we observe realizations of a probability distribution (e.g., the daily return of the S&P 500 index over the last two years), but we don't know the distribution which generates these returns. Consequently, we are not able to apply our knowledge about the calculation of statistical moments. But, having the observations $r_1, \ldots, r_k$, we can try to estimate the *true moments* out of the sample. The estimates are sometimes called *sample moments* to stress the fact that they are obtained out of a sample of observations.

The idea is simple. The empirical analogue for the mean of a random variable is the average of the observations:

$$EX \approx \frac{1}{k} \sum_{i=1}^{k} r_i.$$

---

[11]Formally, the α-quantile for a continuous probability distribution P with strictly increasing cumulative distribution function F is obtained as $q_\alpha = F^{-1}(\alpha)$.

TABLE 1.3 Calculation of Sample Moments.

Moment	Sample Moment
Mean	$\bar{r} = \dfrac{1}{k} \displaystyle\sum_{i=1}^{k} r_i$
Variance	$s^2 = \dfrac{1}{k} \displaystyle\sum_{i=1}^{k} (r_i - \bar{r})^2$
Skewness	$\hat{\zeta} = \dfrac{\frac{1}{k}\sum_{i=1}^{k}(r_i - \bar{r})^3}{(s^2)^{3/2}}$
Kurtosis	$\hat{\kappa} = \dfrac{\frac{1}{k}\sum_{i=1}^{k}(r_i - \bar{r})^4}{(s^2)^2}$

For large k, it is reasonable to expect that the average of the observations will not be far from the mean of the probability distribution. Now, we observe that all theoretical formulae for the calculation of the four statistical moments are expressed as *means of something*. This insight leads to the expression for the sample moments, summarized in Table 1.3.[12]

This simple and intuitive idea is based on a fundamental result in the theory of probability known as the *law of large numbers*. This result, together with the central limit theorem, forms the basics of the theory of statistics.

1.6 JOINT PROBABILITY DISTRIBUTIONS

In the previous sections, we explained the properties of a probability distribution of a single random variable; that is, the properties of a univariate distribution. An understanding of univariate distributions allows us to analyze the time series characteristics of individual assets. In this section, we move from the probability distribution of a single random variable

---

[12]A hat on a parameter (e.g., $\hat{\kappa}$) symbolizes the fact that the true parameter (in this case the kurtosis κ) is estimated.

(univariate distribution) to that of multiple random variables (multivariate distribution). Understanding multivariate distributions is important because financial theories such as portfolio selection theory and asset-pricing theory involve distributional properties of sets of investment opportunities (i.e., multiple random variables). For example, the theory of efficient portfolios covered in Chapter 8 assumes that returns of alternative investments have a joint multivariate distribution.

1.6.1 Conditional Probability

A useful concept in understanding the relationship between multiple random variables is that of conditional probability. Consider the returns on the stocks of two companies in one and the same industry. The future return X on the stocks of company 1 is not unrelated to the future return Y on the stocks of company 2 because the future development of the two companies is driven to some extent by common factors since they are in one and the same industry. It is a reasonable question to ask, what is the probability that the future return X is smaller than a given percentage, e.g. $X \leq -2\%$, on condition that Y realizes a huge loss, e.g. $Y \leq -10\%$? Essentially, the conditional probability is calculating the probability of an event provided that another event happens. If we denote the first event by A and the second event by B, then the conditional probability of A provided that B happens, denoted by $P(A|B)$, is given by the formula,

$$P(A|B) = \frac{P(A \cap B)}{P(B)},$$

which is also known as the *Bayes formula*. According to the formula, we divide the probability that both events A and B occur simultaneously, denoted by $A \cap B$, by the probability of the event B. In the two-stock example, the formula is applied in the following way,

$$P(X \leq -2\% | Y \leq -10\%) = \frac{P(X \leq -2\%, Y \leq -10\%)}{P(Y \leq -10\%)}. \tag{1.1}$$

Thus, in order to compute the conditional probability, we have to be able to calculate the quantity

$$P(X \leq -2\%, Y \leq -10\%),$$

which represents the joint probability of the two events.

1.6.2 Definition of Joint Probability Distributions

A portfolio or a trading position consists of a collection of financial assets. Thus, portfolio managers and traders are interested in the return on a portfolio or a trading position. Consequently, in real-world applications, the interest is in the joint probability distribution or joint distribution of more than one random variable. For example, suppose that a portfolio consists of a position in two assets, asset 1 and asset 2. Then there will be a probability distribution for (1) asset 1, (2) asset 2, and (3) asset 1 and asset 2. The first two distributions are referred to as the marginal probability distributions or marginal distributions. The distribution for asset 1 and asset 2 is called the *joint probability distribution.*

Like in the univariate case, there is a mathematical connection between the probability distribution P, the cumulative distribution function F, and the density function f of a multivariate random variable (also called a *random vector*) $X = (X_1, \ldots, X_n)$. The formula looks similar to the equation we presented in the previous chapter showing the mathematical connection between a probability density function, a probability distribution, and a cumulative distribution function of some random variable X:

$$P(X_1 \leq t_1, \ldots, X_n \leq t_n) = F_X(t_1, \ldots, t_n)$$

$$= \int_{-\infty}^{t_1} \ldots \int_{-\infty}^{t_n} f_X(x_1, \ldots, x_n) dx_1 \ldots dx_n.$$

The formula can be interpreted as follows. The joint probability that the first random variable realizes a value less than or equal to t_1 and the second less than or equal to t_2 and so on is given by the cumulative distribution function F. The value can be obtained by calculating the volume under the density function f. Because there are n random variables, we have now n arguments for both functions: the density function and the cumulative distribution function.

It is also possible to express the density function in terms of the distribution function by computing sequentially the first-order partial derivatives of the distribution function with respect to all variables,

$$f_X(x_1, \ldots, x_n) = \frac{\partial^n F_X(x_1, \ldots, x_n)}{\partial x_1 \ldots \partial x_n}. \tag{1.2}$$

1.6.3 Marginal Distributions

Beside this joint distribution, we can consider the above mentioned marginal distributions, that is, the distribution of one single random variable X_i. The marginal density f_i of X_i is obtained by integrating the joint density over all variables which are not taken into consideration:

$$f_{X_i}(x) = \int_{-\infty}^{\infty} \cdots \int_{-\infty}^{\infty} f_X(x_1, \ldots, x_{i-1}, x, x_{i+1}, \ldots, x_n) dx_1 \ldots dx_{i-1} dx_{i+1} \ldots dx_n$$

1.6.4 Dependence of Random Variables

Typically, when considering multivariate distributions, we are faced with inference between the distributions; that is, large values of one random variable imply large values of another random variable or small values of a third random variable. If we are considering, for example, X_1, the height of a randomly chosen U.S. citizen, and X_2, the weight of this citizen, then large values of X_1 tend to result in large values of X_2. This property is denoted as the *dependence of random variables* and a powerful concept to measure dependence will be introduced in a later section on copulas.

The inverse case of no dependence is denoted as *stochastic independence*. More precisely, two random variables are *independently distributed* if and only if their joint distribution given in terms of the joint cumulative distribution function F or the joint density function f equals the product of their marginal distributions:

$$F_X(x_1, \ldots, x_n) = F_{X_1}(x_1) \ldots F_{X_n}(x_n)$$

and

$$f_X(x_1, \ldots, x_n) = f_{X_1}(x_1) \ldots f_{X_n}(x_n).$$

In the special case of $n = 2$, we can say that two random variables are said to be independently distributed, if knowing the value of one random variable does not provide any information about the other random variable. For instance, if we assume in the example developed in section 1.6.1 that the two events $X \leq -2\%$ and $Y \leq -10\%$ are independent, then the conditional probability in equation (1.1) equals

$$P(X \leq -2\% | Y \leq -10\%) = \frac{P(X \leq -2\%)P(Y \leq -10\%)}{P(Y \leq -10\%)}$$

$$= P(X \leq -2\%).$$

Indeed, under the assumption of independence, the event $Y \leq -10\%$ has no influence on the probability of the other event.

1.6.5 Covariance and Correlation

There are two strongly related measures among many that are commonly used to measure how two random variables tend to move together, the covariance and the correlation. Letting:

σ_X denote the standard deviation of X.

σ_Y denote the standard deviation of Y.

σ_{XY} denote the covariance between X and Y.

ρ_{XY} denote the correlation between X and Y.

The relationship between the correlation, which is also denoted by ρ_{XY} = corr(X, Y), and covariance is as follows:

$$\rho_{XY} = \frac{\sigma_{XY}}{\sigma_X \sigma_Y}.$$

Here the *covariance*, also denoted by $\sigma_{XY} = \text{cov}(X, Y)$, is defined as

$$\sigma_{XY} = E(X - EX)(Y - EY)$$
$$= E(XY) - EXEY.$$

It can be shown that the correlation can only have values from -1 to $+1$. When the correlation is zero, the two random variables are said to be *uncorrelated*.

If we add two random variables, $X + Y$, the expected value (first central moment) is simply the sum of the expected value of the two random variables. That is,

$$E(X + Y) = EX + EY.$$

The variance of the sum of two random variables, denoted by σ_{X+Y}^2, is

$$\sigma_{X+Y}^2 = \sigma_X^2 + \sigma_Y^2 + 2\sigma_{XY}.$$

Here the last term accounts for the fact that there might be a dependence between X and Y measured through the covariance. In Chapter 8, we consider the variance of the portfolio return of n assets which is expressed by means of the variances of the assets' returns and the covariances between them.

1.8.6 Multivariate Normal Distribution

In finance, it is common to assume that the random variables are normally distributed. The joint distribution is then referred to as a multivariate normal distribution.[13] We provide an explicit representation of the density function of a general multivariate normal distribution.

Consider first n independent standard normal random variables $X_1, \ldots, X_n$. Their common density function can be written as the product of their individual density functions and so we obtain the following expression as the density function of the random vector $X = X_1, \ldots, X_n$:

$$f_X(x_1, \ldots, x_n) = \frac{1}{(\sqrt{2\pi})^n} e^{-\frac{x'x}{2}},$$

where the vector notation $x'x$ denotes the sum of the components of the vector x raised to the second power, $x'x = \sum_{i=1}^{n} x_i^2$.

Now consider n vectors with n real components arranged in a matrix A. In this case, it is often said that the matrix A has a $n \times n$ dimension. The random variable

$$Y = AX + \mu, \tag{1.3}$$

in which AX denotes the $n \times n$ matrix A multiplied by the random vector X and μ is a vector of n constants, has a general multivariate normal distribution. The density function of Y can now be expressed as[14]

$$f_Y(y_1, \ldots, y_n) = \frac{1}{(\pi |\Sigma|)^{n/2}} e^{-\frac{(y-\mu)'\Sigma^{-1}(y-\mu)}{2}},$$

where $|\Sigma|$ denotes the determinant of the matrix Σ and Σ^{-1} denotes the inverse of Σ. The matrix Σ can be calculated from the matrix A, $\Sigma = AA'$. The elements of $\Sigma = \{\sigma_{ij}\}_{i, j=1}^{n}$ are the covariances between the components of the vector Y,

$$\sigma_{ij} = \text{cov}(Y_i, Y_j).$$

Figure 1.5 contains a plot of the probability density function of a two-dimensional normal distribution with a covariance matrix,

$$\Sigma = \begin{pmatrix} 1 & 0.8 \\ 0.8 & 1 \end{pmatrix}$$

---

[13]The joint distribution of a random vector $X = (X_1, \ldots, X_n)$ is called a *multivariate normal distribution* if any linear combination $a_1 X_1 + \cdots + a_n X_n$ of its components is normally distributed. It is not sufficient that only the marginals are normally distributed.

[14]In order for the density function to exist, the joint distribution of Y must be nondegenerate (i.e., the matrix Σ must be positive definite).

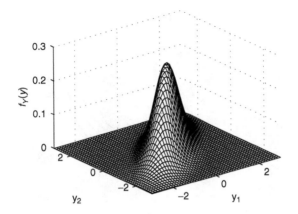

FIGURE 1.5 The probability density function of a two-dimensional normal distribution.

and mean $\mu = (0, 0)$. The matrix A from the representation given in formula (1.3) equals

$$A = \begin{pmatrix} 1 & 0 \\ 0.8 & 0.6 \end{pmatrix}.$$

The correlation between the two components of the random vector Y is equal to 0.8, $\text{corr}(Y_1, Y_2) = 0.8$ because in this example the variances of the two components are equal to 1. This is a strong positive correlation, which means that the realizations of the random vector Y clusters along the diagonal splitting the first and the third quadrant. This is illustrated in Figure 1.6, which shows the contour lines of the two-dimensional density function plotted in Figure 1.5. The contour lines are ellipses centered at the mean $\mu = (0, 0)$ of the random vector Y with their major axes lying along the diagonal of the first quadrant. The contour lines indicate that realizations of the random vector Y roughly take the form of an elongated ellipse as the ones shown in Figure 1.6, which means that large values of Y_1 will correspond to large values of Y_2 in a given pair of observations.

1.6.7 Elliptical Distributions

A generalization of the multivariate normal distribution is given by the class of elliptical distributions.[15] We discuss this class because elliptical distributions offer desirable properties in the context of portfolio selection

---

[15]This section provides only a brief review of elliptical distributions. Bradley and Taqqu (2003) provide a more complete introduction to elliptical distributions and their implications for portfolio selection.

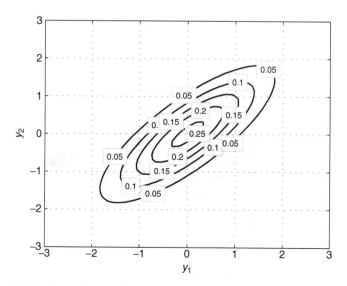

FIGURE 1.6 The level lines of the two-dimensional probability density function plotted in Figure 1.5.

theory. It turns out that in fact it is the class of elliptical distributions where the correlation is the right dependence measure, and that for distributions which do not belong to this family, alternative concepts must be sought.

Simply speaking, an n-dimensional random vector X with density function f is *spherically distributed* if all the level curves,[16] that is, the set of all points where the density function f admits a certain value c, possesses the form of a sphere. In the special case when $n = 2$, the density function can be plotted and the level curves look like circles. Analogously, a n-dimensional random vector X with density function f is *elliptically distributed* if the form of all level curves equals the one of an ellipse.

One can think of elliptical distributions as a special class of symmetric distributions which possess a number of desirable properties. Examples of elliptically distributed random variables include all multivariate normal distributions, multivariate t-distributions, logistic distributions, Lapace distributions, and a part of the multivariate stable distributions.[17] Elliptical

---

[16]The reader interested in outdoor activities such as hiking or climbing as well as geographically interested people might know the concept of level curves from their hiking maps, where the mountains are visualized by there iso-level lines.

[17]For a thorough introduction into the class of ellipitcal distribution, see Fang et al. (1994).

distributions with existing density function can be described by a triple (μ, Σ, g),[18] where μ and Σ play similar roles as the mean vector and the variance-covariance matrix in the multivariate normal setting. The function g is the so-called *density generator*. All three together define the density function of the distribution as:

$$f_X(x) = \frac{c}{\sqrt{|\Sigma|}} g((x - \mu)' \Sigma^{-1}(x - \mu))$$

where c is a normalizing constant. The reader may compare the similarity between this expression and the density function of a multivariate normal distribution.

1.6.8   Copula Functions

Correlation is a widespread concept in modern finance and risk management and stands for a measure of dependence between random variables. However, this term is often incorrectly used to mean any notion of dependence. Actually, correlation is one particular measure of dependence among many. In the world of multivariate normal distribution and more generally in the world of spherical and elliptical distributions, it is the accepted measure.

A major drawback of correlation is that it is not invariant under nonlinear strictly increasing transformations. In general,

$$\mathrm{corr}(T(X), T(Y)) \neq \mathrm{corr}(X, Y),$$

where $T(x)$ is such transformation. One example which explains this technical requirement is the following: Assume that X and Y represent the continuous return (log-return) of two assets over the period $[0, t]$, where t denotes some point of time in the future. If you know the correlation of these two random variables, this does not imply that you know the dependence structure between the asset prices itself because the asset prices (P and Q for asset X and Y, respectively) are obtained by $P_t = P_0 \exp(X)$ and $Q_t = Q_0 \exp(Y)$, where P_0 and Q_0 denote the corresponding asset prices at time 0. The asset prices are strictly increasing functions of the return but the correlation structure is not maintained by this transformation. This observation implies that the return could be uncorrelated whereas the prices are strongly correlated and vice versa.

---

[18]A *triple* or a *3-tuple* is simply the notation used by mathematicians for a group of three elements.

A more prevalent approach that overcomes this disadvantage is to model dependency using copulas. As noted by Patton (2004, p. 3), "The word copula comes from Latin for a 'link' or 'bond,' and was coined by Sklar (1959), who first proved the theorem that a collection of marginal distributions can be 'coupled' together via a copula to form a multivariate distribution." The idea is as follows. The description of the joint distribution of a random vector is divided into two parts:

1. The specification of the marginal distributions.
2. the specification of the dependence structure by means of a special function, called *copula*.

The use of copulas[19] offers the following advantages:

- The nature of dependency that can be modeled is more general. In comparison, only linear dependence can be explained by the correlation.
- Dependence of extreme events might be modeled.
- Copulas are indifferent to continuously increasing transformations (not only linear as it is true for correlations).

From a mathematical viewpoint, a copula function C is nothing more than a probability distribution function on the n-dimensional hypercube $I_n = [0, 1] \times [0, 1] \times \ldots \times [0, 1]$:

$$C : I_n \to [0, 1]$$

$$(u_1, \ldots, u_n) \to C(u_1, \ldots, u_n).$$

It has been shown[20] that any multivariate probability distribution function F_Y of some random vector $Y = (Y_1, \ldots, Y_n)$ can be represented with the help of a copula function C in the following form:

$$F_Y(y_1, \ldots, y_n) = P(Y_1 \leq y_1, \ldots, Y_n \leq y_n) = C(P(Y_1 \leq y_1), \ldots, P(Y_n \leq y_n))$$

$$= C(F_{Y_1}(y_1), \ldots, F_{Y_n}(y_n)),$$

where $F_{Y_i}(y_i)$, $i = 1, \ldots, n$ denote the marginal distribution functions of the random variables Y_i, $i = 1, \ldots, n$.

---

[19]Mikosch (2006), Embrechts and Puccetti (2006), and Rüschendorf (2004) provide examples and further references for the application of copulas in risk management.
[20]The importance of copulas in the modeling of the distribution of multivariate random variables is provided by Sklar's theorem. The derivation was provided in Sklar (1959).

The copula function makes the bridge between the univariate distribution of the individual random variables and their joint probability distribution. This justifies the fact that the copula function creates uniquely the dependence, whereas the probability distribution of the involved random variables is provided by their marginal distribution. By fixing the marginal distributions and varying the copula function, we obtain all possible joint distributions with the given marginals. The links between marginal distributions and joint distributions are useful in understanding the notion of a minimal probability metric discussed in Chapter 3.

In the remaining part of this section, we consider several examples that illustrate further the concept behind the copula function. We noted that the copula is just a probability distribution function and, therefore, it can be characterized by means of a cumulative distribution function or a probability density function. Given a copula function C, the density is computed according to equation (1.2),[21]

$$c(u_1, \ldots, u_n) = \frac{\partial^n C(u_1, \ldots, u_n)}{\partial u_1 \ldots \partial u_n}.$$

In this way, using the relationship between the copula and the distribution function, the density of the copula can be expressed by means of the density of the random variable. This is done by applying the chain rule of differentiation,

$$c(F_{Y_1}(y_1), \ldots, F_{Y_n}(y_n)) = \frac{f_Y(y_1, \ldots, y_n)}{f_{Y_1}(y_1) \ldots f_{Y_n}(y_n)}. \tag{1.4}$$

In this formula, the numerator contains the density of the random variable Y and on the denominator we find the density of the Y but under the assumption that components of Y are independent random variables. Note that the left hand-side corresponds to the copula density but transformed to the sample space by means of the marginal distribution functions $F_{Y_i}(y_i)$, $i = 1, 2, \ldots, n$. The copula density of a two-dimensional normal distribution with covariance matrix,

$$\Sigma = \begin{pmatrix} 1 & 0.8 \\ 0.8 & 1 \end{pmatrix}$$

and mean $\mu = (0, 0)$, is plotted in Figure 1.7. The contour lines of the copula density transformed in the sample space through the marginal distribution

---

[21] The density of a copula function may not exist since not all distribution functions possess densities. In this discussion, we consider only the copulas with a density.

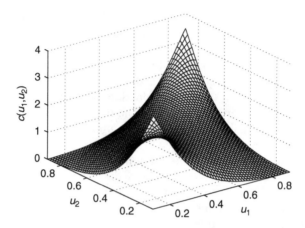

FIGURE 1.7 The copula density of a two-dimensional normal distribution.

functions are given in Figure 1.8. Plots of the probability density function and the contour lines of the probability density function are given in Figures 1.5 and 1.6.

Equation (1.4) reveals that, if the random variable Y has independent components, then the density of the corresponding copula, denoted by c_0, is a constant in the unit hypercube,

$$c_0(u_1, \dots, u_n) = 1$$

and the copula C_0 has the following simple form,

$$C_0(u_1, \dots, u_n) = u_1 \dots u_n.$$

This copula characterizes stochastic independence.

Now let us consider a density c of some copula C. The formula in equation (1.4) is a ratio of two positive quantities because the density function can only take nonnegative values. For each value of the vector of arguments $y = (y_1, \dots, y_n)$, equation (1.4) provides information about the degree of dependence between the events that simultaneously Y_i is in a small neighborhood of y_i for $i = 1, 2, \dots, n$. That is, the copula density provides information about the *local* structure of the dependence. With respect to the copula density c_0 characterizing the notion of independence, the arbitrary copula density function can be either above 1, or below 1. How is this fact related to the degree of dependence of the corresponding n events? Suppose

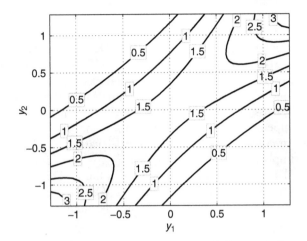

FIGURE 1.8 The contour lines of a copula density of a two-dimensional normal distribution transformed in the sample space.

that for some vector y, the right hand-side of equation (1.4) is close to zero. This means that the numerator is much smaller than the denominator,

$$f_Y(y_1, \ldots, y_n) < f_{Y_1}(y_1) \ldots f_{Y_n}(y_n).$$

As a consequence, the joint probability of the events that Y_i is in a small neighborhood of y_i for $i = 1, 2, \ldots, n$ is much smaller than what it would if the corresponding events were independent. Therefore, this case corresponds to these events being almost disjoint; that is, with a very small probability of occurring simultaneously.

Suppose that the converse holds, the numerator in equation (1.4) is much larger than the denominator and, as a result, the copula density is larger than 1. In this case,

$$f_Y(y_1, \ldots, y_n) > f_{Y_1}(y_1) \ldots f_{Y_n}(y_n),$$

which means that the joint probability of the events that Y_i is in a small neighborhood of y_i for $i = 1, 2, \ldots, n$ is larger than what it would if the corresponding events were independent. Therefore, copula density values larger than 1 mean that the corresponding events are more likely to happen simultaneously.

This analysis indicates that the copula density function provides information about the local dependence structure of a multidimensional random variable Y relative to the case of stochastic independence. Figure 1.8 provides an illustration is the two-dimensional case. It shows the contour lines of the surface calculated according to equation (1.4) for the two-dimensional normal distribution considered in section 1.6.6. All points that have an elevation above 1 have a local dependence implying that the events $Y_1 \in (y_1, y_1 + \epsilon)$ and $Y_2 \in (y_2, y_2 + \epsilon)$ for a small $\epsilon > 0$ are likely to occur jointly. This means that in a large sample of observations, we observe the two events happening together more often than implied by the independence assumption. In contrast, all points with an elevation below 1 have a local dependence implying that the events $Y_1 \in (y_1, y_1 + \epsilon)$ and $Y_2 \in (y_2, y_2 + \epsilon)$ for a small $\epsilon > 0$ are likely to occur disjointly. This means that in a large sample of observations we will observe the two events happening less frequently than implied by the independence assumption.

1.7　PROBABILISTIC INEQUALITIES

Some of the topics discussed in the book concern a setting in which we are not aware of the particular distribution of a random variable or the particular joint probability distribution of a pair of random variables. In such cases, the analysis may require us to resort to general arguments based on certain general inequalities from the theory of probability. In this section, we give an account of such inequalities and provide illustration where possible.

1.7.1　Chebyshev's Inequality

Chebyshev's inequality provides a way to estimate the approximate probability of deviation of a random variable from its mean. Its most simple form concerns positive random variables.

Suppose that X is a positive random variable, $X > 0$. The following inequality is known as *Chebyshev's inequality*,

$$P(X \geq \epsilon) \leq \frac{EX}{\epsilon}, \tag{1.5}$$

where $\epsilon > 0$. In this form, equation (1.5) can be used to estimate the probability of observing a large observation by means of the mathematical expectation and the level ϵ. Chebyshev's inequality is rough as demonstrated geometrically in the following way. The mathematical expectation of a positive continuous random variable admits the representation,

$$EX = \int_0^\infty P(X \geq x)dx,$$

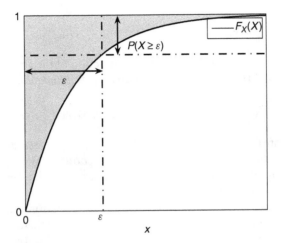

FIGURE 1.9 Chebyshev's inequality, a geometric illustration. The area of the rectangle in the upper-left corner is smaller than the shaded area.

which means that it equals the area closed between the distribution function and the upper limit of the distribution function. This area is illustrated in Figure 1.9 as the shaded area above the distribution function. On the other hand, the quantity $\epsilon P(X \geq \epsilon) = \epsilon(1 - F_X(x))$ is equal to the area of the rectangle in the upper-left corner of Figure 1.9. In effect, the inequality

$$\epsilon P(X \geq \epsilon) \leq EX$$

admits the following geometric interpretation—the area of the rectangle is smaller than the shaded area in Figure 1.9.

For an arbitrary random variable, Chebychev's inequality takes the form

$$P(|X - EX| \geq \epsilon \sigma_X) \leq \frac{1}{\epsilon^2},$$

where σ_X is the standard deviation of X and $\epsilon > 0$. We use Chebyshev's inequality in Chapter 6 in the discussion of dispersion measures.

1.7.2 Fréchet-Hoeffding Inequality

Consider an *n*-dimensional random vector Y with a distribution function $F_Y(y_1, \ldots, y_n)$. Denote by

$$W(y_1, \ldots, y_n) = \max(F_{Y_1}(y_1) + \cdots + F_{Y_n}(y_n) + 1 - n, 0)$$

and by

$$M(y_1, \ldots, y_n) = \min(F_{Y_1}(y_1), \ldots, F_{Y_n}(y_n)),$$

in which $F_{Y_i}(y_i)$ stands for the distribution function of the i-th marginal. The following inequality is known as *Fréchet-Hoeffding inequality*,

$$W(y_1, \ldots, y_n) \leq F_Y(y_1, \ldots, y_n) \leq M(y_1, \ldots, y_n). \tag{1.6}$$

The quantities $W(y_1, \ldots, y_n)$ and $M(y_1, \ldots, y_n)$ are also called the *Fréchet lower bound* and the *Fréchet upper bound*. We apply Fréchet-Hoeffding inequality in the two-dimensional case in Chapter 3 when discussing minimal probability metrics.

Since copulas are essentially probability distributions defined on the unit hypercube, Fréchet-Hoeffding inequality holds for them as well. In this case, it has a simpler form because the marginal distributions are uniform. The lower and the upper Fréchet bounds equal

$$W(u_1, \ldots, u_n) = \max(u_1 + \cdots + u_n + 1 - n, 0)$$

and

$$M(u_1, \ldots, u_n) = \min(u_1, \ldots, u_n)$$

respectively. Fréchet-Hoeffding inequality is given by

$$W(u_1, \ldots, u_n) \leq C(u_1, \ldots, u_n) \leq M(u_1, \ldots, u_n).$$

In the two-dimensional case, the inequality reduces to

$$\max(u_1 + u_2 - 1, 0) \leq C(u_1, u_2) \leq \min(u_1, u_2).$$

In the two-dimensional case only, the lower Fréchet bound, sometimes referred to as the *minimal copula*, represents perfect negative dependence between the two random variables. In a similar way, the upper Fréchet bound, sometimes referred to as the *maximal copula*, represents perfect positive dependence between the two random variables.

1.8   SUMMARY

We considered a number of concepts from probability theory that will be used in later chapters in this book. We discussed the notions of a random variable and a random vector. We considered one-dimensional and multidimensional probability density and distributions functions, which completely characterize a given random variable or random vector. We discussed statistical moments and quantiles, which represent certain characteristics of a random variable, and the sample moments which provide a way of estimating the corresponding characteristics from historical data. In the multidimensional case, we considered the notion of dependence between the components of a random vector. We discussed the covariance matrix versus the more general concept of a copula function. Finally, we described two probabilistic inequalities, Chebychev's inequality and Fréchet-Hoeffding inequality.

BIBLIOGRAPHY

Billingsley, P. (1995). *Probability and measure*, 3rd ed., New York: John Wiley & Sons.

Bradley, B. and M. S. Taqqu (2003). "Financial risk and heavy tails," in *Handbook of Heavy-Tailed Distributions in Finance*, S. T. Rachev, ed. *Elsevier, Amsterdam*, 35–103.

Embrechts, P., C. Klüppelberg and T. Mikosch (1997). *Modeling extremal events for insurance and finance*, Springer.

Embrechts, P., and G. Puccetti (2006). "Bounds for functions of dependent risks," *Finance and Stochastics* 10(3): 341–352.

Fang, K.-T., S. Kotz and K.-W. Ng (1994). *Symmetric multivariate and related distributions*, New York: Marcel Dekker.

Johnson, N. L., S. Kotz and A. W. Kemp (1993). *Univariate discrete distributions*, 2nd ed., New York: John Wiley & Sons.

Larsen, R. J., and M. L. Marx (1986). *An introduction to mathematical statistics and its applications*, Englewed Clifs, NJ: Prentice Hall.

Mikosch, T. (2006). "Copulas—tales and facts," *Extremes* 9: 3–20.

Patton, A. J. (2002). *Application of copular theory in financial econometrics*, Doctoral Dissertation, Economics, University of California, San Diego. Working paper, London School of Economics.

Rüschendorf, L. (2004). "Comparison of multivariate risks and positive dependence," *Journal of Applied Probability* 41(2): 391–406.

Shiryaev, A. N. (1996). *Probability*, New York: Springer.

Sklar, A. (1959). "Fonctions de répartition à n dimensions et leurs marges," *Publications de l'Institut de Statistique de l'Université de Paris* 8: 229–231.

CHAPTER 2

Optimization

2.1 INTRODUCTION

The mathematical theory of optimization has a natural application in the field of finance. From a general perspective, the behavior of economic agents in the face of uncertainty involves balancing expected risks and expected rewards. For example, the portfolio choice problem, which we consider in Chapter 8, concerns the optimal trade-off between risk and reward. We say that a portfolio is *optimal* in the sense that it is the best portfolio among many alternative ones. The criterion that measures the "quality" of a portfolio relative to the others is known as the *objective function* in optimization theory. The set of portfolios among which we are choosing is called the *set of feasible solutions* or the *set of feasible points*. For additional examples on the application of optimization theory to portfolio management, the reader is referred to Fabuzzi et al. (2007).

In optimization theory, we distinguish between two types of optimization problems depending on whether the set of feasible solutions is constrained or unconstrained. If the optimization problem is a constrained one, then the set of feasible solutions is defined by means of certain linear and/or nonlinear equalities and inequalities. These functions are often said to be forming the *constraint set*.

Furthermore, we also distinguish between types of optimization problems depending on the assumed properties of the objective function and the functions in the constraint set, such as *linear problems*, *quadratic problems*, and *convex problems*. The solution methods vary with respect to the particular optimization problem type as there are efficient algorithms prepared for particular problem types.

In this chapter, we describe the basic types of optimization problems and remark on the methods for their solution. For more detailed and/or complementary information, the reader is referred to the books of Boyd and Vandenberghe (2004) and Ruszczyński (2006).

2.2   UNCONSTRAINED OPTIMIZATION

When there are no constraints imposed on the set of feasible solutions, we have an unconstrained optimization problem. Thus, the goal is to maximize or to minimize the objective function with respect to the function arguments without any limits on their values. We consider directly the n-dimensional case; that is, the domain of the objective function f is the n-dimensional space and the function values are real numbers, $f: \mathbb{R}^n \to \mathbb{R}$. Maximization is denoted by

$$\max f(x_1, \ldots, x_n)$$

and minimization by

$$\min f(x_1, \ldots, x_n).$$

A more compact form is commonly used, for example

$$\min_{x \in \mathbb{R}^n} f(x) \tag{2.1}$$

denotes that we are searching for the minimal value of the function $f(x)$ by varying x in the entire n-dimensional space $\mathbb{R}^n$. A solution to equation (2.1) is a value of $x = x^0$ for which the minimum of f is attained,

$$f_0 = f(x^0) = \min_{x \in \mathbb{R}^n} f(x).$$

Thus, the vector x_0 is such that the function takes a larger value than f_0 for any other vector x,

$$f(x^0) \leq f(x), \; x \in \mathbb{R}^n. \tag{2.2}$$

Note that there may be more than one vector x^0 satisfying the inequality in equation (2.2) and, therefore, the argument for which f_0 is achieved may not be unique. If (2.2) holds, then the function is said to attain its *global minimum* at x^0. If the inequality in (2.2) holds for x belonging only to a small neighborhood of x^0 and not to the entire space $\mathbb{R}^n$, then the objective function is said to have a *local minimum* at x^0. This is usually denoted by

$$f(x^0) \leq f(x)$$

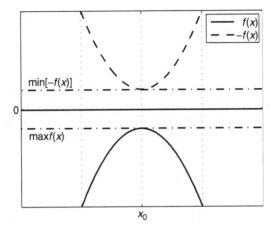

FIGURE 2.1 The relationship between minimization and maximization for a one-dimensional function.

for all x such that $\|x - x^0\|_2 < \epsilon$ where $\|x - x^0\|_2$ stands for the Euclidean distance between the vectors x and x^0,

$$\|x - x^0\|_2 = \sqrt{\sum_{i=1}^{n}(x_i - x_i^0)^2},$$

and ϵ is some positive number. A local minimum may not be global as there may be vectors outside the small neighborhood of x_0 for which the objective function attains a smaller value than $f(x_0)$. Figure 2.2 shows the graph of a function with two local maxima, one of which is the global maximum.

There is a connection between minimization and maximization. Maximizing the objective function is the same as minimizing the negative of the objective function and then changing the sign of the minimal value,

$$\max_{x \in \mathbb{R}^n} f(x) = -\min_{x \in \mathbb{R}^n}[-f(x)].$$

This relationship is illustrated in Figure 2.1. As a consequence, problems for maximization can be stated in terms of function minimization and vice versa.

2.2.1 Minima and Maxima of a Differentiable Function

If the second derivatives of the objective function exist, then its local maxima and minima, often called generically local *extrema*, can be characterized.

Denote by $\nabla f(x)$ the vector of the first partial derivatives of the objective function evaluated at x,

$$\nabla f(x) = \left(\frac{\partial f(x)}{\partial x_1}, \ldots, \frac{\partial f(x)}{\partial x_n} \right).$$

This vector is called the *function gradient*. At each point x of the domain of the function, it shows the direction of greatest rate of increase of the function in a small neighborhood of x. If for a given x, the gradient equals a vector of zeros,

$$\nabla f(x) = (0, \ldots, 0)$$

then the function does not change in a small neighborhood of $x \in \mathbb{R}^n$. It turns out that all points of local extrema of the objective function are characterized by a zero gradient. As a result, the points yielding the local extrema of the objective function are among the solutions of the system of equations,

$$\left| \begin{array}{l} \dfrac{\partial f(x)}{\partial x_1} = 0 \\ \ldots \\ \dfrac{\partial f(x)}{\partial x_n} = 0. \end{array} \right. \tag{2.3}$$

The system of equation (2.3) is often referred to as representing the *first-order condition* for the objective function extrema. However, it is only a necessary condition; that is, if the gradient is zero at a given point in the n-dimensional space, then this point may or may not be a point of a local extremum for the function. An illustration is given in Figure 2.2. The top plot shows the graph of a two-dimensional function and the bottom plot contains the contour lines of the function with the gradient calculated at a grid of points. There are three points marked with a black dot that have a zero gradient. The middle point is not a point of a local maximum even though it has a zero gradient. This point is called a *saddle point* since the graph resembles the shape of a saddle in a neighborhood of it. The left and the right points are where the function has two local maxima corresponding to the two peaks visible on the top plot. The right peak is a local maximum that is not the global one and the left peak represents the global maximum.

This example demonstrates that the first-order conditions are generally insufficient to characterize the points of local extrema. The additional condition that identifies which of the zero-gradient points are points

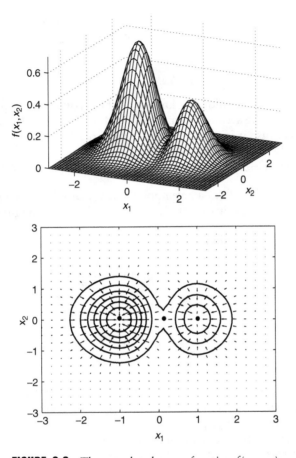

FIGURE 2.2 The top plot shows a function $f(x_1, x_2)$ with two local maxima. The bottom plot shows the contour lines of $f(x_1, x_2)$ together with the gradient evaluated at a grid of points. The middle black point shows the position of the saddle point between the two local maxima.

of local minimum or maximum is given through the matrix of second derivatives,

$$
H = \begin{pmatrix}
\frac{\partial^2 f(x)}{\partial x_1^2} & \frac{\partial^2 f(x)}{\partial x_1 \partial x_2} & \cdots & \frac{\partial^2 f(x)}{\partial x_1 \partial x_n} \\
\frac{\partial^2 f(x)}{\partial x_2 \partial x_1} & \frac{\partial^2 f(x)}{\partial x_2^2} & \cdots & \frac{\partial^2 f(x)}{\partial x_2 \partial x_n} \\
\vdots & \vdots & \ddots & \vdots \\
\frac{\partial^2 f(x)}{\partial x_n \partial x_1} & \frac{\partial^2 f(x)}{\partial x_n \partial x_2} & \cdots & \frac{\partial^2 f(x)}{\partial x_n^2}
\end{pmatrix},
\tag{2.4}
$$

which is called the *Hessian matrix* or just the *Hessian*. The Hessian is a symmetric matrix because the order of differentiation is insignificant,

$$\frac{\partial^2 f(x)}{\partial x_i \partial x_j} = \frac{\partial^2 f(x)}{\partial x_j \partial x_i}.$$

The additional condition is known as the *second-order condition*. We will not provide the second-order condition for functions of n-dimensional arguments because it is rather technical and goes beyond the scope of the book. We only state it for two-dimensional functions.

In the case $n = 2$, the following conditions hold:

■ If $\nabla f(x_1, x_2) = (0, 0)$ at a given point (x_1, x_2) and the determinant of the Hessian matrix evaluated at (x_1, x_2) is positive, then the function has:

— A local maximum in (x_1, x_2) if

$$\frac{\partial^2 f(x_1, x_2)}{\partial x_1^2} < 0 \quad \text{or} \quad \frac{\partial^2 f(x_1, x_2)}{\partial x_2^2} < 0.$$

— A local minimum in (x_1, x_2) if

$$\frac{\partial^2 f(x_1, x_2)}{\partial x_1^2} > 0 \quad \text{or} \quad \frac{\partial^2 f(x_1, x_2)}{\partial x_2^2} > 0.$$

■ If $\nabla f(x_1, x_2) = (0, 0)$ at a given point (x_1, x_2) and the determinant of the Hessian matrix evaluated at (x_1, x_2) is negative, then the function f has a saddle point in (x_1, x_2)

■ If $\nabla f(x_1, x_2) = (0, 0)$ at a given point (x_1, x_2) and the determinant of the Hessian matrix evaluated at (x_1, x_2) is zero, then no conclusion can be drawn.

2.2.2 Convex Functions

In section 2.2.1, we demonstrated that the first-order conditions are insufficient in the general case to describe the local extrema. However, when certain assumptions are made for the objective function, the first-order conditions can become sufficient. Furthermore, for certain classes of functions, the local extrema are necessarily global. Therefore, solving the first-order conditions, we obtain the global extremum.

A general class of functions with nice optimal properties is the class of *convex functions*. Not only are the convex functions easy to optimize but they have also important application in risk management. In Chapter 6, we discuss general measures of risk. It turns out that the property which guarantees that diversification is possible appears to be exactly the convexity property. As a consequence, a measure of risk is necessarily a convex functional.[1]

Precisely, a function $f(x)$ is called a *convex function* if it satisfies the property: For a given $\alpha \in [0, 1]$ and all $x^1 \in \mathbb{R}^n$ and $x^2 \in \mathbb{R}^n$ in the function domain,

$$f(\alpha x^1 + (1 - \alpha)x^2) \le \alpha f(x^1) + (1 - \alpha)f(x^2). \qquad (2.5)$$

The definition is illustrated in Figure 2.3. Basically, if a function is convex, then a straight line connecting any two points on the graph lies "above" the graph of the function.

There is a related term to convex functions. A function f is called *concave* if the negative of f is convex. In effect, a function is concave if it

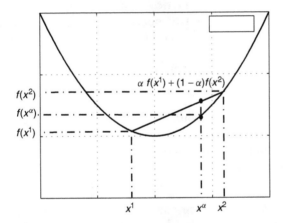

FIGURE 2.3 Illustration of the definition of a convex function in the one-dimensional case. Any straight line connecting two points on the graph lies "above" the graph. On the plot, $x_\alpha = \alpha x^1 + (1 - \alpha)x^2$

[1] A *function* in mathematics can be viewed as a rule assigning to each element of a set D a single element of a set C. The set D is called the *domain* of f and the set C is called the *codomain* of f. A *functional* is a special kind of a function that takes other functions as its argument and returns numbers as output; that is, its domain is a set of functions. For example, the definite integral can be viewed as a functional because it assigns a real number to a function—the corresponding area below the function graph. A risk measure can also be viewed as a functional because it assigns a number to a random variable. Any random variable is mathematically described as a certain function the domain of which is the set of outcomes Ω. Chapter 1 provides more details on the theory of probability.

satisfies the property: For a given $\alpha \in [0,1]$ and all $x^1 \in \mathbb{R}^n$ and $x^2 \in \mathbb{R}^n$ in the function domain,

$$f(\alpha x^1 + (1 - \alpha)x^2) \geq \alpha f(x^1) + (1 - \alpha)f(x^2).$$

We use convex and concave functions in the discussion of the efficient frontier in Chapter 8.

If the domain D of a convex function is not the entire space $\mathbb{R}^n$, then the set D satisfies the property,

$$\alpha x^1 + (1 - \alpha)x^2 \in D \qquad (2.6)$$

where $x^1 \in D, x^2 \in D$, and $0 \leq \alpha \leq 1$. The sets that satisfy equation (2.6) are called *convex sets*. Thus, the domains of convex (and concave) functions should be convex sets. Geometrically, a set is convex if it contains the straight line connecting any two points belonging to the set. Rockafellar (1997) provides detailed information on the implications of convexity in optimization theory.

We summarize several important properties of convex functions:

- Not all convex functions are differentiable. If a convex function is two times continuously differentiable, then the corresponding Hessian defined in equation (2.4) is a positive semidefinite matrix.[2]
- All convex functions are continuous if considered in an open set.
- The sublevel sets

$$L_c = \{x : f(x) \leq c\}, \qquad (2.7)$$

where c is a constant, are convex sets if f is a convex function. The converse is not true in general. Section 2.2.3 provides more information about non-convex functions with convex sublevel sets.

- The local minima of a convex function are global. If a convex function f is twice continuously differentiable, then the global minimum is obtained in the points solving the first-order condition,

$$\nabla f(x) = 0.$$

- A sum of convex functions is a convex function:

$$f(x) = f_1(x) + f_2(x) + \ldots + f_k(x)$$

is a convex function if $f_i, i = 1, \ldots, k$ are convex functions.

---

[2]A matrix H is a *positive semidefinite matrix* if $x'Hx \geq 0$ for all $x \in \mathbb{R}^n$ and $x \neq (0, \ldots, 0)$.

A simple example of a convex function is the linear function,

$$f(x) = a'x, \ x \in \mathbb{R}^n$$

where $a \in \mathbb{R}^n$ is a vector of constants. In fact, the linear function is the only function that is both convex and concave. In finance, if we consider a portfolio of assets, then the expected portfolio return is a linear function of portfolio weights, in which the coefficients equal the expected asset returns.

As a more involved example, consider the following function,

$$f(x) = \tfrac{1}{2}x'Cx, \ x \in \mathbb{R}^n \tag{2.8}$$

where $C = \{c_{ij}\}_{i,j=1}^n$ is a $n \times n$ symmetric matrix. In portfolio theory, the variance of portfolio return is a similar function of portfolio weights. In this case, C is the covariance matrix. The function defined in (2.8) is called a *quadratic function* because writing the definition in terms of the components of the argument X, we obtain

$$f(x) = \frac{1}{2}\left(\sum_{i=1}^n c_{ii}x_i^2 + \sum_{i \neq j} c_{ij}x_i x_j\right)$$

which is a quadratic function of the components $x_i, i = 1, \ldots, n$. The function in (2.8) is convex if and only if the matrix C is positive semidefinite. In fact, in this case the matrix C equals the Hessian matrix, $C = H$. Since the matrix C contains all parameters, we say that the quadratic function is defined by the matrix C.

Figures 2.4 and 2.5 illustrate the surface and contour lines of a convex and nonconvex two-dimensional quadratic functions. The contour lines of the convex function are concentric ellipses and a sublevel set L_c is represented by the points inside some ellipse. The convex quadratic function is defined by the matrix,

$$C = \begin{pmatrix} 1 & 0.4 \\ 0.4 & 1 \end{pmatrix}$$

and the nonconvex quadratic function is defined by the matrix,

$$C = \begin{pmatrix} -1 & 0.4 \\ 0.4 & 1 \end{pmatrix}.$$

A property of convex functions is that the sum of convex functions is a convex function. As a result of the preceding analysis, the function

$$f(x) = \lambda x'Cx - a'x, \tag{2.9}$$

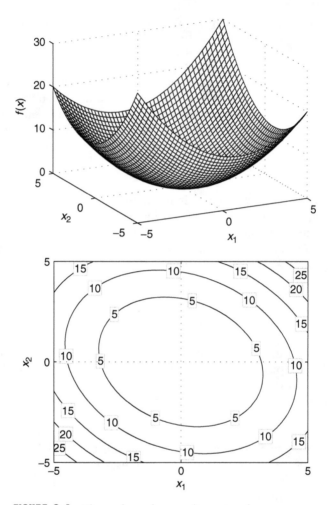

FIGURE 2.4 The surface of a two-dimensional convex quadratic function $f(x) = \frac{1}{2}x'Cx$ and the corresponding contour lines.

where $\lambda > 0$ and C is a positive semidefinite matrix, is a convex function as a sum of two convex functions. We will consider functions similar to equation (2.9) in Chapter 8 in the discussion of the mean-variance efficient frontier. Let us use the properties of convex functions in order to solve the unconstrained problem of minimizing the function in (2.9),

$$\min_{x \in \mathbb{R}^n} \lambda x'Cx - a'x$$

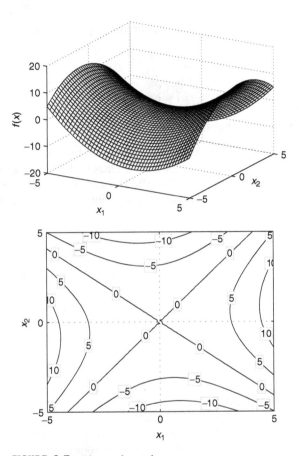

FIGURE 2.5 The surface of a nonconvex two-dimensional quadratic function $f(x) = \frac{1}{2}x'Cx$ and the corresponding contour lines. The point $(x_1, x_2) = (0, 0)$ is a saddle point.

This function is differentiable and we can search for the global minimum by solving the first-order conditions,[3]

$$\nabla f(x) = 2\lambda Cx - \mu = 0.$$

---

[3]In calculating the derivatives, we use the following rules in matrix form,

and
$$\begin{aligned} f(x) = c'x &\implies \nabla f(x) = c \\ f(x) = x'Cx &\implies \nabla f(x) = 2Cx. \end{aligned}$$

The validity of these rules can be directly checked by computing the components of the gradient.

Therefore, the value of x minimizing the objective function equals

$$x^0 = \frac{1}{2\lambda} C^{-1} \mu,$$

where C^{-1} denotes the inverse of the matrix C.

2.2.3 Quasiconvex Functions

Besides convex functions, there are other classes of functions with convenient optimal properties. An example of such a class is the class of *quasiconvex functions*. Formally, a function is called quasiconvex if all sublevel sets defined in (2.7) are convex sets. Alternatively, a function $f(x)$ is called quasiconvex if, $f(x^1) \geq f(x^2)$

implies $f(\alpha x^1 + (1 - \alpha)x^2) \leq f(x^1),$

where x^1 and x^2 belong to the function domain, which should be a convex set, and $0 \leq \alpha \leq 1$. A function f is called *quasiconcave* if $-f$ is quasiconvex.

An illustration of a two-dimensional quasiconvex function is given in Figure 2.6. The top plot shows the graph of the function and the bottom plot illustrates the contour lines. A sublevel set is represented by all points inside some contour line. From a geometric viewpoint, the sublevel sets corresponding to the plotted contour lines are convex because any of them contains the straight line connecting any two points belonging to the set. Nevertheless, the function is not convex, which becomes evident from the surface on the top plot. It is not guaranteed that a straight line connecting any two points on the surface will remain "above" the surface.

Several properties of the quasiconvex functions are summarized below.

- Any convex function is also quasiconvex. The converse is not true, which is demonstrated in Figure 2.6.
- In contrast to the differentiable convex functions, the first-order condition is not necessary and sufficient for optimality in the case of differentiable quasiconvex functions.[4]
- It is possible to find a sequence of convex optimization problems yielding the global minimum of a quasiconvex function. Boyd and Vandenberghe (2004) provide further details. Its main idea is to find

---

[4]There exists a class of functions larger than the class of convex functions but smaller than the class of quasiconvex functions, for which the first-order condition is necessary and sufficient for optimality. This is the class of *pseudoconvex* functions. Mangasarian (2006) provides more detail on the optimal properties of pseudoconvex functions.

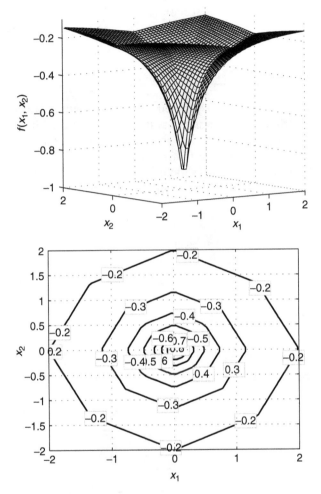

FIGURE 2.6 An example of a two-dimensional quasiconvex function $f(x_1, x_2)$ and its contour lines. Even though the sublevel sets are convex, $f(x_1, x_2)$ is not a convex function.

the smallest value of c for which the corresponding sublevel set L_c is nonempty. The minimal value of c is the global minimum, which is attained in the points belonging to the sublevel set L_c.

- Suppose that $g(x) > 0$ is a concave function and $f(x) > 0$ is a convex function. Then the ratio $g(x)/f(x)$ is a quasiconcave function and the ratio $f(x)/g(x)$ is a quasiconvex function.

Quasiconvex functions arise naturally in risk management when considering optimization of performance ratios. This topic is covered in Chapter 10.

2.3 CONSTRAINED OPTIMIZATION

In constructing optimization problems solving practical issues, it is very often the case that certain constraints need to be imposed in order for the optimal solution to make practical sense. For example, long-only portfolio optimization problems require that the portfolio weights, which represent the variables in optimization, should be nonnegative and should sum up to one. According to the notation in this chapter, this corresponds to a problem of the type,

$$\min_{x} \ f(x)$$
$$\text{subject to} \ \ x'e = 1 \tag{2.10}$$
$$x \geq 0,$$

where:

f(x) is the objective function.

$e \in \mathbb{R}^n$ is a vector of ones, $e = (1, \ldots, 1)$.

$x'e$ equals the sum of all components of x, $x'e = \sum_{i}^{n} x_i$.

$x \geq 0$ means that all components of the vector $x \in \mathbb{R}^n$ are nonnegative.

In problem (2.10), we are searching for the minimum of the objective function by varying x only in the set

$$\mathbf{X} = \left\{ x \in \mathbb{R}^n : \begin{array}{c} x'e = 1 \\ x \geq 0 \end{array} \right\}, \tag{2.11}$$

which is also called the *set of feasible points* or the *constraint set*. A more compact notation, similar to the notation in the unconstrained problems, is sometimes used,

$$\min_{x \in \mathbf{X}} f(x)$$

where $\mathbf{X}$ is defined in equation (2.11).

We distinguish between different types of optimization problems depending on the assumed properties for the objective function and the constraint set. If the constraint set contains only equalities, the problem is easier to handle analytically. In this case, the method of Lagrange multipliers is applied. For more general constraint sets, when they are formed by both equalities and inequalities, the method of Lagrange multipliers is generalized by the *Karush-Kuhn-Tucker conditions* (KKT conditions). Like the first-order conditions we considered in unconstrained optimization problems, none of the two approaches leads to necessary and sufficient conditions for constrained optimization problems without further assumptions. One of the most general frameworks in which the KKT conditions are necessary and sufficient is that of *convex programming*. We have a convex programing problem if the objective function is a convex function and the set of feasible points is a convex set. As important subcases of convex optimization, *linear programming* and convex *quadratic programming* problems are considered.

In this section, we describe first the method of Lagrange multipliers, which is often applied to special types of mean-variance optimization problems in order to obtain closed-form solutions. Then we proceed with convex programming that is the framework for reward-risk analysis. The mentioned applications of constrained optimization problems is covered in Chapters 8, 9, and 10.

2.3.1 Lagrange Multipliers

Consider the following optimization problem in which the set of feasible points is defined by a number of equality constraints,

$$\min_{x} \ f(x)$$
$$\text{subject to } h_1(x) = 0$$
$$h_2(x) = 0$$
$$\cdots$$
$$h_k(x) = 0. \tag{2.12}$$

The functions $h_i(x), i = 1, \dots, k$ build up the constraint set. Note that even though the right-hand side of the equality constraints is zero in the classical formulation of the problem given in equation (2.12), this is not restrictive. If in a practical problem the right-hand side happens to be different than zero, it can be equivalently transformed, for example,

$$\{x \in \mathbb{R}^n : v(x) = c\} \quad \Longleftrightarrow \quad \{x \in \mathbb{R}^n : h_1(x) = v(x) - c = 0\}.$$

In order to illustrate the necessary condition for optimality valid for (2.12), let us consider the following two-dimensional example:

$$\min_{x \in \mathbb{R}^2} \ \tfrac{1}{2} x'Cx$$
$$\text{subject to } x'e = 1, \tag{2.13}$$

where the matrix is

$$C = \begin{pmatrix} 1 & 0.4 \\ 0.4 & 1 \end{pmatrix}.$$

The objective function is a quadratic function and the constraint set contains one linear equality. In Chapter 8, we see that the mean-variance optimization problem in which short positions are allowed is very similar to (2.13). The surface of the objective function and the constraint are shown on the top plot in Figure 2.7. The black line on the surface shows the function values of the feasible points. Geometrically, solving problem (2.13) reduces to finding the lowest point of the black curve on the surface. The contour lines shown on the bottom plot in Figure 2.7 imply that the feasible point yielding the minimum of the objective function is where a contour line is tangential to the line defined by the equality constraint. On the plot, the tangential contour line and the feasible points are in bold. The black dot indicates the position of the point in which the objective function attains its minimum subject to the constraints.

Even though the example is not general in the sense that the constraint set contains one linear rather than a nonlinear equality, the same geometric intuition applies in the nonlinear case. The fact that the minimum is attained where a contour line is tangential to the curve defined by the nonlinear equality constraints in mathematical language is expressed in the following way: The gradient of the objective function at the point yielding the minimum is proportional to a linear combination of the gradients of the functions defining the constraint set. Formally, this is stated as

$$\nabla f(x^0) - \mu_1 \nabla h_1(x^0) - \cdots - \mu_k \nabla h_k(x^0) = 0. \tag{2.14}$$

where $\mu_i, i = 1, \ldots, k$ are some real numbers called *Lagrange multipliers* and the point x^0 is such that $f(x^0) \leq f(x)$ for all x that are feasible. Note that if there are no constraints in the problem, then (2.14) reduces to the first-order condition we considered in unconstrained optimization. Therefore, the system of equations behind (2.14) can be viewed as a generalization of the first-order condition in the unconstrained case.

The method of Lagrange multipliers basically associates a function to the problem in (2.12) such that the first-order condition for unconstrained optimization for that function coincides with (2.14). The method of Lagrange multiplier consists of the following steps.

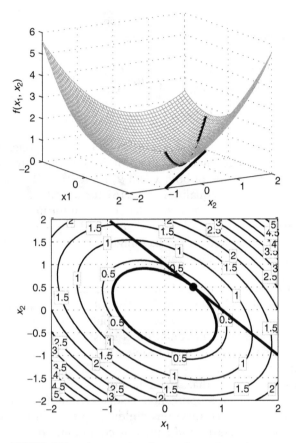

FIGURE 2.7 The top plot shows the surface of a two-dimensional quadratic objective function and the linear constraint $x_1 + x_2 = 1$. The black curve on the surface shows the objective function values of the points satisfying the constraint. The bottom plot shows the tangential contour line to the constraint.

1. Given the problem in (2.12), construct the following function:

$$L(x, \mu) = f(x) - \mu_1 h_1(x) - \cdots - \mu_k h_k(x) \qquad (2.15)$$

where $\mu = (\mu_1, \ldots, \mu_k)$ is the vector of Lagrange multipliers. The function $L(x, \mu)$ is called the *Lagrangian* corresponding to problem (2.12).

2. Calculate the partial derivatives with respect to all components of x and μ and set them equal to zero as follows:

and
$$\frac{\partial L(x, \mu)}{\partial x_i} = \frac{\partial f(x)}{\partial x_i} - \sum_{j=1}^{k} \mu_j \frac{\partial h_j(x)}{\partial x_i} = 0, \quad i = 1, \ldots, n$$
$$\frac{\partial L(x, \mu)}{\partial \mu_m} = h_m(x) = 0, \quad m = 1, \ldots, k. \tag{2.16}$$

Basically, the system of equations (2.16) corresponds to the first-order conditions for unconstrained optimization written for the Lagrangian as a function of both x and μ, $L : \mathbb{R}^{n+k} \to \mathbb{R}$.

3. Solve the system of equalities in (2.16) for x and μ. Note that even though we are solving the first-order condition for unconstrained optimization of $L(x, \mu)$, the solution (x^0, μ^0) of (2.16) is not a point of local minimum or maximum of the Lagrangian. In fact, the solution (x^0, μ^0) is a saddle point of the Lagrangian.

The first n equations in (2.16) make sure that the relationship between the gradients given in (2.14) is satisfied. The following k equations in (2.16) make sure that the points are feasible. As a result, all vectors x solving (2.16) are feasible and the gradient condition is satisfied in them. Therefore, the points that solve the optimization problem (2.12) are among the solutions of the system of equations in (2.16).

This analysis suggests that the method of Lagrange multipliers provides a necessary condition for optimality. Under certain assumptions for the objective function and the functions building up the constraint set, (2.16) turns out to be a necessary and sufficient condition. For example, if $f(x)$ is a convex and differentiable function and $h_i(x), i = 1, \ldots, k$ are affine functions,[5] then the method of Lagrange multipliers identifies the points solving (2.12). Figure 2.7 illustrates a convex quadratic function subject to a linear constraint. In this case, the solution point is unique.

2.3.2 Convex Programming

The general form of convex programming problems is the following:

$$\min_{x} f(x)$$
$$\text{subject to } g_i(x) \leq 0, \quad i = 1, \ldots, m$$
$$h_j(x) = 0, \quad j = 1, \ldots, k, \tag{2.17}$$

---

[5] A function $h(x)$ is called *affine* if it has the form $h(x) = a + c'x$, where a is a constant and $c = (c_1, \ldots, c_n)$ is a vector of coefficients. All linear functions are affine.

where:

f(x) is a convex objective function.

$g_1(x), \dots, g_m(x)$ are convex functions defining the inequality constraints.

$h_1(x), \dots, h_k(x)$ are affine functions defining the equality constraints.

Generally, without the assumptions of convexity, problem (2.17) is more involved than (2.12) because besides the equality constraints, there are inequality constraints. The KKT condition, generalizing the method of Lagrange multipliers, is only a necessary condition for optimality in this case. However, adding the assumption of convexity makes the KKT condition necessary and sufficient.

Note that, similar to problem (2.12), the fact that the right-hand side of all constraints is zero is nonrestrictive. The limits can be arbitrary real numbers.

Consider the following two-dimensional optimization problem;

$$\min_{x \in \mathbb{R}^2} \tfrac{1}{2} x' C x$$
$$\text{subject to} \quad (x_1 + 2)^2 + (x_2 + 2)^2 \leq 3 \qquad (2.18)$$

in which

$$C = \begin{pmatrix} 1 & 0.4 \\ 0.4 & 1 \end{pmatrix}.$$

The objective function is a two-dimensional convex quadratic function and the function in the constraint set is also a convex quadratic function. In fact, the boundary of the feasible set is a circle with a radius of $\sqrt{3}$ centered at the point with coordinates $(-2, -2)$. The top plot in Figure 2.8 shows the surface of the objective function and the set of feasible points. The shaded part on the surface indicates the function values of all feasible points. In fact, solving problem (2.18) reduces to finding the lowest point on the shaded part of the surface. The bottom plot shows the contour lines of the objective function together with the feasible set that is in gray. Geometrically, the point in the feasible set yielding the minimum of the objective function is positioned where a contour line only touches the constraint set. The position of this point is marked with a black dot and the tangential contour line is given in bold.

Note that the solution points of problems of the type (2.18) can happen to be not on the boundary of the feasible set but in the interior. For example, suppose that the radius of the circle defining the boundary of the feasible set in (2.18) is a larger number such that the point $(0, 0)$ is inside the feasible

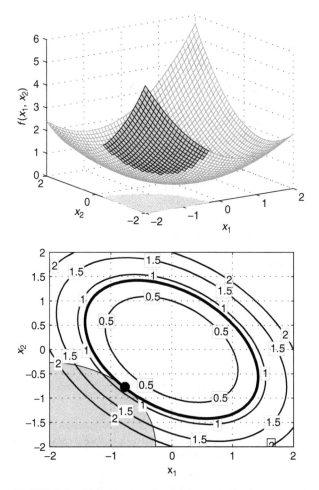

FIGURE 2.8 The top plot shows the surface of a
two-dimensional convex quadratic function and a convex
quadratic constraint. The shaded section on the surface
corresponds to the feasible points. The bottom plot shows
the tangential contour line to the feasible set.

set. Then, the point $(0, 0)$ is the solution to problem (2.18) because at this
point the objective function attains its global minimum.

In the two-dimensional case, when we can visualize the optimization
problem, geometric reasoning guides us to finding the optimal solution
point. In a higher dimensional space, plots cannot be produced and
we rely on the analytic method behind the KKT conditions. The KKT

conditions corresponding to the convex programming problem (2.17) are the following:

$$\nabla f(x) + \sum_{i=1}^{m} \lambda_i \nabla g_i(x) + \sum_{j=1}^{k} \mu_j \nabla h_j(x) = 0$$

$$g_i(x) \leq 0 \quad i = 1, \ldots, m$$

$$h_j(x) = 0 \quad j = 1, \ldots, k$$

$$\lambda_i g_i(x) = 0, \quad i = 1, \ldots, m$$

$$\lambda_i \geq 0, \quad i = 1, \ldots, m. \tag{2.19}$$

A point x^0 such that (x^0, λ^0, μ^0) satisfies (2.19) is the solution to problem (2.17). Note that if there are no inequality constraints, then the KKT conditions reduce to (2.16) in the method of Lagrange multipliers. Therefore, the KKT conditions generalize the method of Lagrange multipliers.

The gradient condition in (2.19) has the same interpretation as the gradient condition in the method of Lagrange multipliers. The set of constraints,

and
$$g_i(x) \leq 0 \quad i = 1, \ldots, m$$
$$h_j(x) = 0 \quad j = 1, \ldots, k$$

guarantee that a point satisfying (2.19) is feasible. The next conditions,

$$\lambda_i g_i(x) = 0, \quad i = 1, \ldots, m,$$

are called *complementary slackness conditions*. If an inequality constrain is satisfied as a strict inequality, then the corresponding multiplier λ_i turns into zero according to the complementary slackness conditions. In this case, the corresponding gradient $\nabla g_i(x)$ has no significance in the gradient condition. This reflects the fact that the gradient condition concerns only the constraints satisfied as equalities at the solution point.

Important special cases of convex programming problems include linear programming problems and convex quadratic programming problems which we consider in the remaining part of this section.

2.3.3 Linear Programming

Optimization problems are said to be *linear programming problems* if the objective function is a linear function and the feasible set is defined by linear equalities and inequalities. Since all functions are linear, they are also convex, which means that linear programming problems are also convex problems. The definition of linear programming problems in standard form is the following:

$$\min_{x} \ c'x$$
$$\text{subject to} \ Ax \le b$$
$$x \ge 0, \tag{2.20}$$

where A is a $m \times n$ matrix of coefficients, $c = (c_1, \ldots, c_n)$ is a vector of objective function coefficients, and $b = (b_1, \ldots, b_m)$ is a vector of real numbers. As a result, the constraint set contains m inequalities defined by linear functions. The feasible points defined by means of linear equalities and inequalities are also said to form a *polyhedral set*. In practice, before solving a linear programming problem, it is usually first reformulated in the standard form given in (2.20).

Figure 2.9 shows an example of a two-dimensional linear programming problem that is not in standard form as the two variables may become negative. The top plot contains the surface of the objective function, which is a plane in this case, and the polyhedral set of feasible points. The shaded area on the surface corresponds to the points in the feasible set. Solving problem (2.20) reduces to finding the lowest point in the shaded area on the surface. The bottom plot shows the feasible set together with the contour lines of the objective function. The contour lines are parallel straight lines because the objective function is linear. The point in which the objective function attains its minimum is marked with a black dot.

A general result in linear programming is that, on condition that the problem is bounded, the solution is always at the boundary of the feasible set and, more precisely, at a vertex of the polyhedron. Problem (2.20) may become unbounded if the polyhedral set is unbounded and there are feasible points such the objective function can decrease indefinitely. We can summarize that, generally, due to the simple structure of (2.20), there are three possibilities:

1. The problem is not feasible, because the polyhedral set is empty.
2. The problem is unbounded.
3. The problem has a solution at a vertex of the polyhedral set.

From computational viewpoint, the polyhedral set has a finite number of verices and an algorithm can be devised with the goal of finding a vertex solving the optimization problem in a finite number of steps. This is the basic idea behind the *simplex method*, which is an efficient numerical approach to solving linear programming problems. Besides the simplex algorithm, there are other more contemporary methods such as the *interior point method* for example.

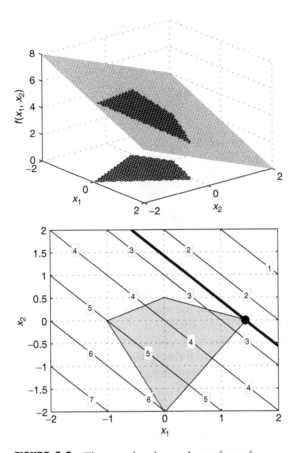

FIGURE 2.9 The top plot shows the surface of a linear function and a polyhedral feasible set. The shaded section on the surface corresponds to the feasible points. The bottom plot shows the tangential contour line to the feasible set.

The application of linear programming in practice is immense. A few classes of practical problems that are solved by the method of linear programming include the *transportation problem*, the *transshipment problem*, the *network flow problem*, and so on. Dantzig (1998) provides an excellent background on the theory and application of linear programing.

2.3.4 Quadratic Programming

Besides linear programming, another class of problems with simple structure is the class of *quadratic programming problems*. It contains optimization problems with a quadratic objective function and linear equalities and inequalities in the constraint set,

$$\min_{x} \ c'x + \tfrac{1}{2}x'Hx$$
$$\text{subject to } \ Ax \leq b, \tag{2.21}$$

where:

$c = (c_1, \ldots, c_n)$ is a vector of coefficients defining the linear part of the objective function.

$H = \{h_{ij}\}_{i,j=1}^{n}$ is an $n \times n$ matrix defining the quadratic part of the objective.

$A = \{a_{ij}\}$ is a $k \times n$ matrix defining k linear inequalities in the constraint set.

$b = (b_1, \ldots, b_k)$ is a vector of real numbers defining the right-hand side of the linear inequalities.

In optimal portfolio theory, mean-variance optimization problems in which portfolio variance is in the objective function are quadratic programming problems. We consider such problems in Chapter 8.

From the point of view of optimization theory, problem (2.21) is a convex optimization problem if the matrix defining the quadratic part of the objective function is positive semidefinite. In this case, the KKT conditions can be applied to solve it.

2.4 SUMMARY

In this chapter, we considered selected topics from optimization theory that form the background needed to understand optimal portfolio selection problems covered in Chapters 8, 9, and 10. The material is divided into two parts: unconstrained optimization and constrained optimization. Concerning unconstrained optimization, we state the necessary first-order condition and consider the classes of convex functions and quasiconvex functions. In constrained optimization, we start with the method of Lagrange multipliers and then focus on the general framework of convex programming. As special cases of convex optimization problems, we consider linear programming and convex quadratic programming.

BIBLIOGRAPHY

Boyd, S., and L. Vandenberghe (2004). *Convex optimization*, Cambridge: Cambridge University Press.

Dantzig, George (1998). *Linear programming and extensions*, Princeton, NJ: Princeton University Press.

Fabozzi, F.J., P.N. Kolm, D. Pachamanova, and S.M. Focardi (2007). *Robust Fortfolio Management*, New Jersey: John Wiley & Sons.

Mangasarian, O. (2006). "Pseudo-convex functions," in *Stochastic optimization models in finance*, 2006 edition, W. Ziemba and G. Vickson (eds.), Singapore: World Scientific, pp. 23–32.

Rockafellar, R.T. (1997). *Convex analysis*, Princeton, NJ: Princeton University Press.

Ruszczyński, A. (2006). *Nonlinear optimization*, Princeton, NJ: Princeton University Press.

CHAPTER 3

Probability Metrics

3.1 INTRODUCTION

The development of the theory of probability metrics started with the investigation of problems related to limit theorems in probability theory. The limit theorems take a very important place in probability theory, statistics, and all their applications. A well-known example by nonspecialists in the field is the celebrated *Central Limit Theorem* (CLT) but there are many other limit theorems, such as the generalized CLT, the maxstable CLT, functional limit theorems, and so on. Without delving into the details, the applicability of the limit theorems stems from the fact that the limit law can be regarded as an approximation to the stochastic model considered and, therefore, can be accepted as an approximate substitute. The central question arising is how large an error we make by adopting the approximate model. This question can be investigated by studying the distance between the limit law and the stochastic model and whether it is, for example, sum or maxima of *independent identically distributed* (i.i.d.) random variables makes no difference as far as the universal principle is concerned.

Generally, the theory of probability metrics studies the problem of measuring distances between random quantities. On one hand, it provides the fundamental principles for building probability metrics—the means of measuring such distances. On the other, it studies the relationships between various classes of probability metrics. The second realm of study concerns problems that require a particular metric, while the basic results can be obtained in terms of other metrics. In such cases, the metrics relationship is of primary importance.

Certainly, the problem of measuring distances is not limited to random quantities only. In its basic form, it originated in different fields of mathematics. Nevertheless, the theory of probability metrics was developed due to the need of metrics with specific properties. Their choice is very often dictated by the stochastic model under consideration and to a large extent determines the success of the investigation. Rachev (1991) provides more details on the methods of the theory of probability metrics and its numerous applications in both theoretical and more practical problems.

Note that there are no limitations in the theory of probability metrics concerning the nature of the random quantities. This makes its methods fundamental and appealing. Actually, in the general case, it is more appropriate to refer to the random quantities as random *elements*. They can be random variables, random vectors, random functions or random elements of general spaces. For instance, in the context of financial applications, we can study the distance between two random stocks prices, or between vectors of financial variables building portfolios, or between entire yield curves which are much more complicated objects. The methods of the theory remain the same, no matter the nature of the random elements.

In this chapter, we start with a gentle introduction to the problem of measuring distances between random variables. We include examples with discrete distributions which build up intuition for the continuous case. Then we proceed with the classification of primary, simple, and compound metrics. The appendix to this chapter contains a more technical treatment of some of the questions under consideration. We limit the discussion to the one-dimensional variables only.

3.2 MEASURING DISTANCES: THE DISCRETE CASE

How can we measure the distance between two random quantities? This is the question we partial answer in this and subsequent sections. We start with random quantities having discrete distributions as the examples are very clear and help prepare for the more complicated continuous case. The discussion is divided into three sections with increasing complexity.

Throughout section 3.2, we do not comment on the axiomatic structure of probability metrics and the definition of the classes of *primary*, *simple*, and *compound* metrics. This discussion starts in section 3.3 and a few topics are further developed in the appendix to this chapter.

Important topics discussed in section 3.2:

- Examples of metrics defined on sets of characteristics of discrete distributions
- Examples of metrics based on the cumulative distribution function of discrete random variables

- Examples of metrics defined on the joint probability of discrete random variables
- Minimal and maximal distances

3.2.1 Sets of Characteristics

Consider a pair of unfair dice and label the elements of the pair *die X* and *die Y*. The probabilities of each die faces are provided in Table 3.1. In the case of die X, the probability of face 1 is higher than 1/6, which is the probability of a face of a fair die, and the probability of face 3 is less than 1/6. The probabilities of die Y have similar deviations from those of a fair die.

We can view the pair of dice as an example of two discrete random variables. We adopt the shorthand notation X for die X and Y for die Y. Clearly, the two discrete random variables have different distributions and, also, different characteristics, such as the mean and higher moments. Therefore, we can compare the two random variables in terms of the differences in some of their characteristics, if these characteristics have special meaning for us. For example, let us choose the mathematical expectation. It is easy to calculate,

$$EX = \sum_{i=1}^{6} ip_i = 40/12$$

and

$$EY = \sum_{i=1}^{6} iq_i = 44/12.$$

The distance between the two random variables, $\mu(X, Y)$, may be computed as the absolute difference between the corresponding mathematical expectations,

$$\mu(X, Y) = |EX - EY| = 4/12.$$

TABLE 3.1 The Probabilities of the Faces of Die X and Die Y.

Die X face	1	2	3	4	5	6
Probability, p_i	3/12	2/12	1/12	2/12	2/12	2/12
Die Y face	1	2	3	4	5	6
Probability, q_i	2/12	2/12	2/12	1/12	2/12	3/12

In a similar way, we may add another characteristic to the mathematical expectation, or consider it separately. For instance, this could be the second moment,

$$EX^2 = \sum_{i=1}^{6} i^2 p_i = 174/12 \quad \text{and} \quad EY^2 = \sum_{i=1}^{6} i^2 q_i = 202/12.$$

If we add it to the mathematical expectation, for the distance we obtain

$$\mu(X, Y) = |EX - EY| + |EX^2 - EY^2| = 32/12.$$

If we considered a pair of fair dice, these characteristics would coincide and we would obtain that the distance between the two random variables is zero. This is quite understandable as two fair dice cannot be distinguished when considered separately, that is, not in one probability space. However, it is possible to obtain zero deviation between given characteristics in the case of unfair dice. Let us illustrate this with the variance of X and Y. The variance of a random variable Z, DZ, is defined as,

$$DX = E(Z - EZ)^2.$$

It is easier to calculate the variance not directly through the definition but making use of a formula that arises directly from the definition,

$$DZ = E(Z - EZ)^2 = EZ^2 - (EZ)^2.$$

In this way, we can take advantage of the already calculated quantities. The variance of X equals

$$DX = EX^2 - (EX)^2 = \frac{174}{12} - \left(\frac{40}{12}\right)^2 = \frac{61}{18}$$

and the variance of Y equals

$$DY = EY^2 - (EY)^2 = \frac{202}{12} - \left(\frac{44}{12}\right)^2 = \frac{61}{18}.$$

In effect, we obtain that $DX = DY$. Thus, any attempts to measure the distance between the two random variables in terms of differences in variance will indicate zero distance, even though die X is quite different from die Y.

3.2.2 Distribution Functions

Intuitively, by including more additional characteristics when measuring the distance between two random variables, we incorporate in $\mu(X, Y)$ more information from their distribution functions. When X and Y have discrete distributions, we may try finding out how many characteristics we have to include, so that we can be sure that the entire distribution function of X, $F_X(x) = P(X \leq x)$ agrees to the entire distribution of Y, $F_Y(x) = P(Y \leq x)$, on condition that all selected characteristics agree. For example, let us consider

$$\mu(X, Y) = \sum_{k=1}^{n} |EX^k - EY^k| \qquad (3.1)$$

assuming that X and Y are the two dice considered above but this time we do not know the probabilities p_i and q_i, $i = 1, 6$. How large should n be so that $\mu(X, Y) = 0$ guarantees that the distributions of X and Y agree completely? Since $\mu(X, Y) = 0$ is equivalent to

$$
\begin{vmatrix}
EX = EY \\
EX^2 = EY^2 \\
\ldots \\
EX^n = EY^n
\end{vmatrix}
\quad \Longleftrightarrow \quad
\begin{vmatrix}
\sum_{i=1}^{6} i(p_i - q_i) = 0 \\
\sum_{i=1}^{6} i^2(p_i - q_i) = 0 \\
\ldots \\
\sum_{i=1}^{6} i^n(p_i - q_i) = 0,
\end{vmatrix}
$$

then we need exactly five equations in order to guarantee that $P(X = i) = p_i = P(Y = i) = q_i$, $i = 1, 6$. This is true because there are six differences $p_i - q_i$ in the equations and we need five equations from the ones above plus the additional equation

$$\sum_{i=1}^{6} (p_i - q_i) = 0,$$

which holds because all probabilities should sum up to one.

The reasoning can readily be extended to any pair of discrete random variables, the values of which are finitely many positive integers. For instance, if X and Y are positive integers valued with k outcomes, then we need $k - 1$ equations in order to solve the linear system.

In summary, we have discovered that if a given number of characteristics of two discrete random variables with finitely many outcomes agree, then their distribution functions agree completely. Then, instead of trying to figure out how many characteristics to include in a metric of a given type such as equation (3.1), is it possible to consider ways of measuring the distance between X and Y directly through their distribution function? This question is very reasonable because, using the distribution function, we can calculate the probability of any event. Therefore, if the distribution functions of two random variables coincide, then we have equal corresponding probabilities of any event and we can conclude that they have the same probabilistic properties. In the pair of dice example, all events are described by the set of all possible unions of the outcomes. Actually, the distribution functions $F_X(x)$ and $F_Y(x)$ of die X and die Y are easy to calculate,

$$
F_X(x) = \begin{cases} 0, & [x] < 1 \\ \sum_{i=1}^{[x]} p_i, & [x] \geq 1 \end{cases} = \begin{cases} 0, & x < 1 \\ 3/12, & 1 \leq x < 2 \\ 5/12, & 2 \leq x < 3 \\ 6/12, & 3 \leq x < 4 \\ 8/12, & 4 \leq x < 5 \\ 10/12, & 5 \leq x < 6 \\ 1, & x \geq 6 \end{cases} \qquad (3.2)
$$

and

$$
F_Y(x) = \begin{cases} 0, & [x] < 1 \\ \sum_{i=1}^{[x]} q_i, & [x] \geq 1 \end{cases} = \begin{cases} 0, & x < 1 \\ 2/12, & 1 \leq x < 2 \\ 4/12, & 2 \leq x < 3 \\ 6/12, & 3 \leq x < 4 \\ 7/12, & 4 \leq x < 5 \\ 9/12, & 5 \leq x < 6 \\ 1, & x \geq 6, \end{cases} \qquad (3.3)
$$

where $[x]$ denotes the largest integer smaller than x.

One way to calculate the distance between two discrete *cumulative distribution functions* (c.d.f.s) $F_X(x)$ and $F_Y(x)$ is to calculate the maximal absolute difference between them,

$$
\mu(X, Y) = \max_{x \in \mathbb{R}} |F_X(x) - F_Y(x)|. \qquad (3.4)
$$

In the case of the two dice example, equation (3.4) can be readily computed, $\max_{x \in \mathbb{R}} |F_X(x) - F_Y(x)| = 1/12$. The maximum is attained at any $x \in [1, 3) \cup [4, 6)$.

Another approach is to compute the area closed between the graphs of the two functions. If the area is zero, then due to the properties of the c.d.f.s we can conclude that the two functions coincide. In the two dice example, this can be done by summing the areas of the rectangles formed by the two graphs, see Figure 3.1. One of the sides of the rectangles is always equal to one because the random variables are integer valued. The formula for the total area between the graphs of the two step functions is easy to arrive at,

$$
\mu(X, Y) = \sum_{k=1}^{6} \left| \sum_{i=1}^{k} p_i - \sum_{i=1}^{k} q_i \right|. \qquad (3.5)
$$

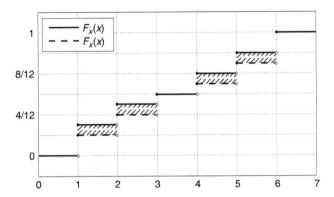

FIGURE 3.1 The plot shows the c.d.f.s of die X and die Y. The area closed between the graphs of the two c.d.f.s is shaded.

Using the probabilities given in Table 3.1, we compute that the $\mu(X, Y) = 4/12$. A formula similar to (3.5) holds in the general case of positive, integer-valued random variables.

A similar approach can be adopted with respect to the quantile function of a random variable Z, or the inverse of the c.d.f. If the inverse c.d.f.s of two random variables coincide, then the distribution functions coincide. As a result, the distance between two random variables can be measured through the distance between the inverse of the c.d.f.s. The inverse $F_Z^{-1}(t)$ of the c.d.f. is defined as

$$F_Z^{-1}(t) = \inf\{x : F_Z(x) \geq t\}.$$

For example, the inverse c.d.f.s of (3.2) and (3.3) are

$$F_X^{-1}(t) = \begin{cases} 1, & 0 < t \leq 3/12 \\ 2, & 3/12 < t \leq 5/12 \\ 3, & 5/12 < t \leq 6/12 \\ 4, & 6/12 < t \leq 8/12 \\ 5, & 8/12 < t \leq 10/12 \\ 6, & 10/12 < t \leq 1 \end{cases} \tag{3.6}$$

and

$$F_Y^{-1}(t) = \begin{cases} 1, & 0 < t \leq 2/12 \\ 2, & 2/12 < t \leq 4/12 \\ 3, & 4/12 < t \leq 6/12 \\ 4, & 6/12 < t \leq 7/12 \\ 5, & 7/12 < t \leq 9/12 \\ 6, & 9/12 < t \leq 1. \end{cases} \tag{3.7}$$

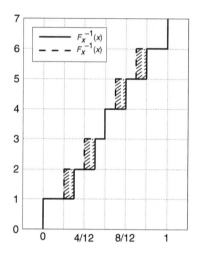

FIGURE 3.2 The plot shows the inverse c.d.f.s of die X and die Y. The area closed between the graphs of the two functions is shaded.

In much the same way as with the c.d.f.s, the distance between the inverse c.d.f.s, and, hence, between the corresponding random variables, can be computed as the maximal absolute deviation between them,

$$\mu(X, Y) = \sup_t |F_X^{-1}(t) - F_Y^{-1}(t)|,$$

or as the area between their graphs. Actually, the area between the graphs of the c.d.f.s and the inverse c.d.f.s is one and the same, therefore formula (3.5) holds. The graphs of the inverse c.d.f.s are shown on Figure 3.2. Compare the shaded areas on Figure 3.1 and Figure 3.2.

3.2.3   Joint Distribution

In the previous two sections, we considered the discrete random variables X and Y separately, without bearing in mind their joint distribution. The two unfair dice we used to illustrate a few basic ways to construct metrics can be dependent in a particular way and we can construct metrics directly using their joint distribution. In this section, we give examples of such metrics and instead of dice, to make things simpler, we use two coins.

First, let us consider a pair of fair coins with joint probabilities as given in Table 3.2. The outcomes are traditionally denoted by zero and one

TABLE 3.2 The Joint Probabilities of
the Outcomes of Two Fair Coins.

		Coin X	
		0	1
Coin Y	0	1/4	1/4
	1	1/4	1/4

and the joint probabilities indicate that the outcomes of the two coins are independent events.

Both coins are fair and, therefore, they are indistinguishable if considered separately, as standalone random mechanisms. If we apply the approach from the previous sections, we conclude that the distance between the two random variables behind the random mechanism is zero. They have the same distribution functions and, consequently, all kinds of characteristics are also the same. In effect, any kind of metric based on the distribution function would indicate zero distance between the two random variables.

Of course, the two random variables are not the same. They only have identical probabilistic properties. For instance, the conditional probability $P(X = 0|Y = 1) = 1/2$, and it follows that the events $\{X = 0, Y = 1\}$ and $\{X = 0, Y = 0\}$ may both occur if we observe realizations of the pair. We conclude that if we would like to measure the distance between the random variables themselves, we need a different approach than the ones described in the previous sections. If the random variables are defined on the same probability space (i.e., if we know their joint distribution), then we can take advantage of the additional information.

One way to calculate the distance between the two random variables is through an absolute moment of the difference $X - Y$, for example,

$$\mu(X, Y) = E|X - Y|. \tag{3.8}$$

A simple calculation shows that $\mu(X, Y) = 1/2$ for the joint distribution in Table 3.2.

From probability theory we know that the joint distribution of a pair of random variables (X, Y) provides a complete description of the probabilistic properties of the pair. We can compute the one-dimensional distribution functions; that is, we know the probabilistic properties of the variables if viewed on a standalone basis, and we also know the dependence between X and Y. If we keep the one-dimensional distributions fixed and change the dependence only, does the distance between the random variables change?

TABLE 3.3 The Joint Probabilities of
the Outcomes of Two Fair Coins
Yielding the Minimal $E|X - Y|$.

		Coin X	
		0	1
Coin Y	0	1/2	0
	1	0	1/2

The answer is yes and we can illustrate it with the metric (3.8) using the joint distribution in Table 3.2. The absolute difference $|X - Y|$ in this case may take only two values: zero and one. Therefore, the mean $E|X - Y|$ can increase or decrease depending on the probabilities of the two outcomes. We have to keep in mind that the one-dimensional probabilities should remain unchanged, that is, the sums of the numbers in the rows and the columns should be fixed to 1/2. Now it is easy to see how the probability mass has to be reallocated so that we obtain the minimal $E|X - Y|$. We have to increase the probability of the outcome $(X = 0, Y = 0)$ and $(X = 1, Y = 1)$ and reduce the probabilities of the other two outcomes. We arrive at the conclusion that the minimal $E|X - Y|$ is attained at the joint distribution given in Table 3.3. The minimal $E|X - Y|$ is called the *minimal metric*.

Note that the minimal $E|X - Y|$ in this case is equal to zero. This is quite reasonable because the joint distribution in Table 3.3 implies that the only possible outcomes are $(X = 0, Y = 0)$ and $(X = 1, Y = 1)$, which means that the two random variables cannot be distinguished. In all states of the world with nonzero probability, they take identical values.

The exercise of finding the maximal $E|X - Y|$ is an alternative to finding the minimal metric. The same reasoning as above shows that now we have to increase the probability of $(X = 0, Y = 1)$ and $(X = 1, Y = 0)$ and reduce the probabilities of the other two outcomes. Finally, we find that the maximal $E|X - Y|$ is attained at the joint distribution given in Table 3.4. The maximal $E|X - Y|$ is called the *maximal distance* because it does not have metric properties. We discuss these questions more deeply in the appendix to this chapter.

Note that in this case the only possible outcomes are $(X = 0, Y = 1)$ and $(X = 1, Y = 0)$ and thus the two random variables are, in a certain sense, maximally distinct; that is, there is not a single state of the world with nonzero probability in which the two random variables take identical values.

TABLE 3.4 The Joint Probabilities of the Outcomes of Two Fair Coins Yielding the Maximal $E|X - Y|$.

		Coin X	
		0	1
Coin Y	0	0	1/2
	1	1/2	0

TABLE 3.5 The Joint Probabilities of the Outcomes Coin U and Coin V.

		Coin U	
		0	1
Coin V	0	3/20	7/20
	1	2/20	8/20

When considering two fair coins, we checked that the minimal $E|X - Y|$ is equal to zero because the two random variables take identical values in all states of the world with nonzero probability and, as a consequence, the realizations of the absolute difference $|X - Y|$ are zero in them. The fact that the minimal $E|X - Y|$ is zero is a consequence of both the dependence, which we tune to minimize $E|X - Y|$, and the one-dimensional distributions. If the one-dimensional distribution of the coins were not the same then we would not obtain a zero distance from the minimal metric. For example, let us consider two coins, coin U and coin V, with joint probabilities as given in Table 3.5.

From the joint probabilities given in Table 3.5, it becomes clear that coin V is fair, while coin U is unfair—the event 0 happens with probability 5/20 and the event 1 with probability 15/20. The same arguments as in the fair-coin example show that the minimal $E|U - V|$ and the maximal $E|U - V|$ are achieved at the joint distributions given in Tables 3.6 and 3.7. The minimal $E|U - V|$ equals 1/4. It cannot equal zero because the one-dimensional distributions are different.

There is a remarkable relationship between minimal metrics and the metrics based on the distribution functions that we considered in the previous section. For example, the metric (3.5) applied to the one-dimensional distributions of the two coins U and V yields exactly 1/4, which is also the

TABLE 3.6 The Joint Probabilities
Yielding Minimal $E|U - V|$.

		Coin U	
		0	1
Coin V	0	1/4	1/4
	1	0	1/2

TABLE 3.7 The Joint Probabilities
Yielding Maximal $E|U - V|$.

		Coin U	
		0	1
Coin V	0	0	1/2
	1	1/4	1/4

value of the minimal $E|U - V|$. At this point, we leave this fact without further comments. We get back to it in the next section.

3.3 PRIMARY, SIMPLE, AND COMPOUND METRICS

The goal of section 3.2 was to introduce the concept of measuring distances between random quantities in the discrete case without giving much theoretical background. Several examples of probability metrics were introduced directly, without showing the underlying axiomatic structure. Important concepts, such as minimal and maximal distances, were only illustrated.

The goal of the current section is to revisit the ideas considered in section 3.2 but at a more advanced level. The examples are constructed with continuous random variables as they were in the discrete case in section 3.2.

Important topics discussed in section 3.3 are:

- Axiomatic construction of probability metrics.
- Distinction between the three classes of primary, simple, and compound metrics.
- Minimal and maximal distances.

3.3.1 Axiomatic Construction

Throughout section 3.2, we used the term *metric* without defining it. Generally, a metric, or a metric function, defines the distance between elements of a given set. Metrics are introduced axiomatically; that is, any function that satisfies a set of axioms is a metric. We give a description of the axiomatic construction of metrics used to measure distances between random quantities in particular. In the appendix to this chapter, we include several remarks on metrics in general.

Generally speaking, a functional,[1] which measures the distance between random quantities, is called a *probability metric*. These random quantities can be of a very general nature. For instance, they can be random variables, such as the daily returns of equities, the daily change of an exchange rate, and the like, or stochastic processes, such as a price evolution in a given period, or much more complex objects such as the daily movement of the shape of the yield curve. We limit the discussion to one-dimensional random variables only. Rachev (1991) provides a more general treatment.

Not any functional can be used to measure distances between random variables. There are special properties that should be satisfied in order for the functional to be called a probability metric. These special properties are the axioms that constitute the building blocks behind the axiomatic construction. They are very natural and intuitive. The first axiom states that the distance between a random quantity and itself should be zero while in general, it is a nonnegative number,

Property 1. $\mu(X, Y) \geq 0$ for any X, Y and $\mu(X, X) = 0$.

Any other requirement will necessarily result in logical inconsistencies.

The second axiom demands that the distance between X and Y should be the same as the distance between Y and X and is referred to as the *symmetry axiom*,

Property 2. $\mu(X, Y) = \mu(Y, X)$ for any X, Y.

---

[1] A *functional* is a function that takes other functions as its arguments and returns a numeric value. Random variables are complicated objects that are viewed as functions defined on a probability space. Any probability metric takes two random variables as arguments and returns a single number that denotes the distance between the two random variables. Therefore, probability metrics are defined as *functionals* rather than functions.

The third axiom is essentially an abstract version of the triangle inequality—the distance between X and Y is not larger than the sum of the distances between X and Z and between Z and Y,

Property 3. $\mu(X, Y) \leq \mu(X, Z) + \mu(Z, Y)$ for any X, Y, Z.

Any functional satisfying Property 1, 2, and 3 is called *probability metric*.

The appendix to this chapter gives a more technical treatment of the axioms and also provides a few caveats.

3.3.2 Primary Metrics

The theory of probability metrics distinguishes between three categories of probability metrics. The principal criterion is contained in the answer to the question: What are the implications for X and Y, provided that they have a zero distance? At first thought, the question may seem redundant. Intuitively, if the distance between X and Y is zero, then they should coincide. This line of thought is fine, but it is incomplete when talking about random elements in general. Suppose that X and Y stand for the random returns of two equities. Then what is meant by X being the same or coincident to Y? It is that X and Y are indistinguishable in a certain sense. This sense could be to the extent of a given set of characteristics of X and Y. For example, X is to be considered indistinguishable to Y if their expected returns and variances are the same. Therefore, a way to define the distance between them is through the distance between the corresponding characteristics, that is, how much their expected returns and variances deviate. One example is

$$\mu(X, Y) = |EX - EY| + |\sigma^2(X) - \sigma^2(Y)|.$$

Such probability metrics are called *primary metrics*, and they imply the weakest form of sameness. Primary metrics may turn out to be relevant in the following situation. Suppose that we adopt the normal distribution to model the returns of two equities X and Y. We estimate the mean of equity X to be larger than the mean of equity Y, $EX > EY$. We may want to measure the distance between X and Y in terms of their variances only because if $|\sigma^2(X) - \sigma^2(Y)|$ turns out to be zero, then, on the basis of our assumption, we conclude that we prefer X to Y. Certainly this conclusion may turn out to be totally incorrect because the assumption of normality may be completely wrong. Section 3.2.1 contains more examples with discrete random variables.

Common examples of primary metrics include:

1. *The engineer's metric.*

$$EN(X, Y) := |EX - EY|,$$

where X and Y are random variables with finite mathematical expectation, $EX < \infty$ and $EY < \infty$.

2. *The absolute moments metric.*

$$MOM_p(X, Y) := |m^p(X) - m^p(Y)|, \ p \geq 1,$$

where $m^p(X) = (E|X|^p)^{1/p}$ and X and Y are random variables with finite moments, $E|X|^p < \infty$ and $E|Y|^p < \infty, p \geq 1$.

3.3.3 Simple Metrics

From probability theory we know that a random variable X is completely described by its cumulative distribution function $F_X(x) = P(X \leq x)$. If we know the distribution function, then we can calculate all kinds of probabilities and characteristics. In the case of equity returns, we can compute the probability of the event that the return falls below a given target or the expected loss on condition that the loss is below a target. Therefore, zero distance between X and Y can imply complete coincidence of the distribution functions $F_X(x)$ and $F_Y(x)$ of X and Y. Of course, this implies complete coincidence of their characteristics and is, therefore, a stronger form of sameness. Probability metrics that essentially measure the distance between the corresponding distribution functions are called *simple metrics*.

In line with the arguments made in section 3.2.2, here we can ask the same question. By including additional characteristics in a primary metric, we include additional information from the distribution functions of the two random variables. In the general case of continuous random variables, is it possible to determine how many characteristics we need to include so that the primary metric turns essentially into a simple metric? In contrast to the discrete case, the question does not have a simple answer. Generally, a very rich set of characteristics ensure that the distribution functions coincide. Such a set is, for example, the set of all moments $Eg(X)$ where the function g is a bounded, real-valued continuous function. Clearly, this is without any practical significance because this set of characteristics is not denumerable; that is, it contains more characteristics than the natural numbers. Nevertheless, this argument shows the connection between the classes of primary and simple metrics.

Common examples of simple metrics are stated in the following:

1. *The Kolmogorov metric.*

$$\rho(X, Y) := \sup_{x \in \mathbb{R}} |F_X(x) - F_Y(x)|, \qquad (3.9)$$

where $F_X(x)$ is the distribution function of X and $F_Y(x)$ is the distribution function of Y. The Kolmogorov metric is also called the *uniform metric*. It is applied in the CLT in probability theory.

Figure 3.3 illustrates the Kolmogorov metric. The c.d.f.s of two random variables are plotted on the top plot and the bottom plot shows the absolute difference between them, $|F_X(x) - F_Y(x)|$, as a function of x. The Kolmogorov metric is equal to the largest absolute difference between the two c.d.f.s. A arrow shows where it is attained.

If the random variables X and Y describe the return distribution of two common stocks, then the Kolmogorov metric has the following interpretation. The distribution function $F_X(x)$ is by definition the probability that X loses more than a level x, $F_X(x) = P(X \leq x)$. Similarly, $F_Y(x)$ is the probability that Y loses more than x. Therefore,

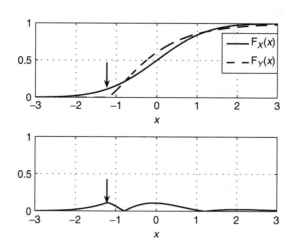

FIGURE 3.3 Illustration of the Kolmogorov metric. The bottom plot shows the absolute difference between the two c.d.f.s plotted on the top plot. The arrow indicates where the largest absolute difference is attained.

the Kolmogorov distance $\rho(X, Y)$ is the maximum deviation between the two probabilities that can be attained by varying the loss level x. If $\rho(X, Y) = 0$, then the probabilities that X and Y lose more than a loss level x coincide for all loss levels.

Usually, the loss level x, for which the maximum deviation is attained, is close to the mean of the return distribution, that is, the mean return. Thus, the Kolmogorov metric is completely insensitive to the tails of the distribution which describe the probabilities of extreme events—extreme returns or extreme losses.

2. *The Lévy metric.*

$$L(X, Y) := \inf_{\epsilon > 0} \{ F_X(x - \epsilon) - \epsilon \le F_Y(x)$$

$$\le F_X(x + \epsilon) + \epsilon, \ \forall x \in \mathbb{R} \} \tag{3.10}$$

The Lévy metric is difficult to calculate in practice. It has important theoretic application in probability theory as it metrizes the weak convergence.

The Kolmogorov metric and the Lévy metric can be regarded as metrics on the space of distribution functions because $\rho(X, Y) = 0$ and $L(X, Y) = 0$ imply coincidence of the distribution functions $F_X(x)$ and $F_Y(x)$.

The Lévy metric can be viewed as measuring the closeness between the graphs of the distribution functions while the Kolmogorov metric is a uniform metric between the distribution functions. The general relationship between the two is

$$L(X, Y) \le \rho(X, Y). \tag{3.11}$$

For example, suppose that X is a random variable describing the return distribution of a portfolio of stocks and Y is a deterministic benchmark with a return of 2.5% ($Y = 2.5\%$). (The deterministic benchmark in this case could be either the cost of funding over a specified time period or a target return requirement to satisfy a liability such as a guaranteed investment contract.) Assume also that the portfolio return has a normal distribution with mean equal to 2.5% and a volatility σ. Since the expected portfolio return is exactly equal to the deterministic benchmark, the Kolmogorov distance between them is always equal to 1/2 irrespective of how small the volatility is,

$$\rho(X, 2.5\%) = 1/2, \quad \forall \, \sigma > 0.$$

Thus, if we rebalance the portfolio and reduce its volatility, the Kolmogorov metric will not register any change in the distance between the portfolio return and the deterministic benchmark. In contrast to the

Kolmogorov metric, the Lévy metric will indicate that the rebalanced portfolio is closer to the benchmark.

3. *The Kantorovich metric.*

$$\kappa(X, Y) := \int_{\mathbb{R}} |F_X(x) - F_Y(x)| dx. \tag{3.12}$$

where X and Y are random variables with finite mathematical expectation, $EX < \infty$ and $EY < \infty$.

The Kantorovich metric can be interpreted along the lines of the Kolmogorov metric. Suppose that X and Y are random variables describing the return distribution of two common stocks. Then, as we explained, $F_X(x)$ and $F_Y(x)$ are the probabilities that X and Y, respectively, lose more than the level x. The Kantorovich metric sums the absolute deviation between the two probabilities for all possible values of the loss level x. Thus, the Kantorovich metric provides aggregate information about the deviations between the two probabilities. This is illustrated on Figure 3.4.

In contrast to the Kolmogorov metric, the Kantorovich metric is sensitive to the differences in the probabilities corresponding to

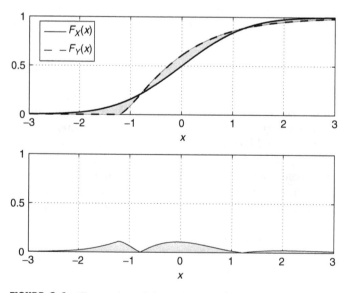

FIGURE 3.4 Illustration of the Kantorovich metric. The bottom plot shows the absolute difference between the two c.d.f.s plotted on the top plot. The Kantorovich metric equals the shaded area.

extreme profits and losses but to a small degree. This is because the difference $|F_X(x) - F_Y(x)|$ converges to zero as the loss level (x) increases or decreases and, therefore, the contribution of the terms corresponding to extreme events to the total sum is small. As a result, the differences in the tail behavior of X and Y is reflected in $\kappa(X, Y)$ but only to a small extent.

4. *The L_p-metrics between distribution functions.*

$$\theta_p(X, Y) := \left(\int_{-\infty}^{\infty} |F_X(x) - F_Y(x)|^p dx \right)^{1/p}, \, p \geq 1, \qquad (3.13)$$

where X and Y are random variables with finite mathematical expectation, $EX < \infty$ and $EY < \infty$.

The financial interpretation of $\theta_p(X, Y)$ is similar to the interpretation of the Kantorovich metric, which appears as a special case, $\kappa(X, Y) = \theta_1(X, Y)$. The metric $\theta_p(X, Y)$ is an aggregate metric of the difference between the probabilities that X and Y lose more than the level x. The power p exercises a very special effect. It makes the smaller contributors to the total sum of the Kantorovich metric become even smaller contributors to the total sum in (3.13). Thus, as p increases, only the largest absolute differences $|F_X(x) - F_Y(x)|$ start to matter. At the limit, as p approaches infinity, only the largest difference $|F_X(x) - F_Y(x)|$ becomes significant and the metric $\theta_\infty(X, Y)$ turns into the Kolmogorov metric. Therefore, if we would like to accentuate on the differences between the two return distributions in the body of the distribution, we can choose a large value of p.

5. *The uniform metric between inverse distribution functions.*

$$\mathbf{W}(X, Y) = \sup_{0 < t < 1} |F_X^{-1}(t) - F_Y^{-1}(t)|, \qquad (3.14)$$

where $F_X^{-1}(t)$ is the inverse of the distribution function of the random variable X.

The uniform metric between inverse distribution functions has the following financial interpretation. Suppose that X and Y describe the return distribution of two common stocks. Then the quantity $-F_X^{-1}(t)$ is known as the *value-at-risk* (VaR) of common stock X at confidence level $(1 - t)100\%$. It is used as a risk measure and represents a loss threshold such that losing more than it happens with probability t. The probability t is also called the *tail probability* because the VaR is usually calculated for high confidence levels, e.g., 95%, 99%, and the corresponding loss thresholds are in the tail of the distribution.

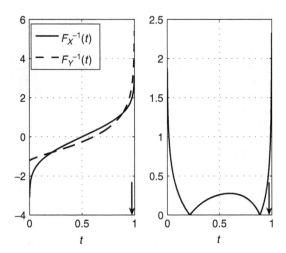

FIGURE 3.5 Illustration of the uniform metric between inverse distribution functions. The right plot shows the absolute difference between the two inverse c.d.f.s plotted on the left plot. The arrow indicates where the largest absolute difference is attained.

Therefore, the difference $F_X^{-1}(t) - F_Y^{-1}(t)$ is nothing but the difference between the VaRs of X and Y at confidence level $(1 - t)100\%$. Thus, the probability metric $\mathbf{W}(X, Y)$ is the maximal difference in absolute value between the VaRs of X and Y when the confidence level is varied. Usually, the maximal difference is attained for values of t close to zero or one that correspond to VaR levels close to the maximum loss or profit of the return distribution. As a result, the probability metric $\mathbf{W}(X, Y)$ is entirely centered on the extreme profits or losses.

Figure 3.5 illustrates this point. Note that the inverse c.d.f.s plotted on Figure 3.5 correspond to the c.d.f.s on Figure 3.3.

6. *The L_p-metrics between inverse distribution functions.*

$$\ell_p(X, Y) := \left(\int_0^1 |F_X^{-1}(t) - F_Y^{-1}(t)|^p dt \right)^{1/p}, \ p \geq 1, \qquad (3.15)$$

where X and Y are random variables with finite mathematical expectation, $EX < \infty$ and $EY < \infty$ and $F_X^{-1}(t)$ is the inverse of the distribution function of the random variable X.

The metric $\ell_1(X, Y)$ is also known as *first difference pseudomoment* as well as the *average metric in the space of distribution functions* because $\ell_1(X, Y) = \theta_1(X, Y)$. Another notation used for this metric is $\kappa(X, Y)$, note that $\theta_1(X, Y) = \kappa(X, Y)$. This special case is called the *Kantorovich metric* because great contributions to the properties of $\ell_1(X, Y)$ were made by Kantorovich in 1940s.

We provide another interpretation of the Kantorovich metric arising from equation (3.15). Suppose that X and Y are random variables describing the return distribution of two common stocks. We explained that the VaRs of X and Y at confidence level $(1 - t)100\%$ are equal to $-F_X^{-1}(t)$ and $-F_Y^{-1}(t)$ respectively. Therefore, the metric

$$\ell_1(X, Y) = \int_0^1 |F_X^{-1}(t) - F_Y^{-1}(t)| dt$$

equals the sum of the absolute differences between the VaRs of X and Y across all confidence levels. In effect, it provides aggregate information about the deviations between the VaRs of X and Y for all confidence levels. This is illustrated on Figure 3.6.

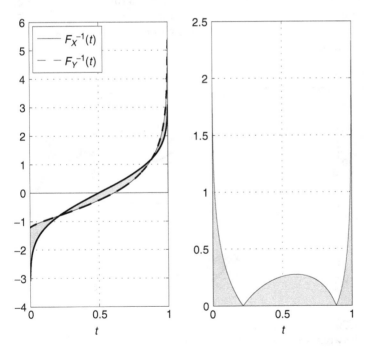

FIGURE 3.6 Illustration of the $\ell_1(X, Y)$ metric. The right plot shows the absolute difference between the two inverse c.d.f.s plotted on the left plot. The $\ell_1(X, Y)$ metric equals the shaded area.

The power p in equation (3.15) acts in the same way as in the case of $\theta_p(X, Y)$. The smaller contributors to the sum in $\ell_1(X, Y)$ become even smaller contributors to the sum in $\ell_p(X, Y)$. Thus, as p increases, only the larger absolute differences between the VaRs of X and Y across all confidence levels become significant in the total sum. The larger differences are in the tails of the two distributions. Therefore, the metric $\ell_p(X, Y)$ accentuates on the deviations between X and Y in the zone of the extreme profits or losses. At the limit, as p approaches infinity, only the largest absolute differences matter and the $\ell_p(X, Y)$ metric turns into the uniform metric between inverse c.d.f.s $\mathbf{W}(X, Y)$.

7. *The uniform metric between densities.*

$$\ell(X, Y) := \sup_{x \in \mathbb{R}} |f_X(x) - f_Y(x)|, \tag{3.16}$$

where $f_X(x) = F'_X(x)$ is the density of the random variable X.

Figure 3.7 illustrates the uniform metric between densities. The densities of two random variables are plotted on the plot and the bottom plot shows the absolute difference between them, $|f_X(x)-f_Y(x)|$, as a function of x. The uniform metric between densities is equal to the largest absolute difference between the two densities. A arrow shows where it is attained.

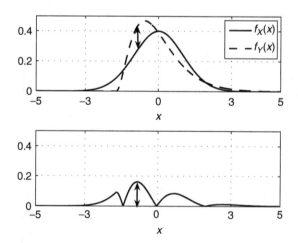

FIGURE 3.7 Illustration of the uniform metric between densities. The bottom plot shows the absolute difference between the two densities plotted on the top plot. The arrow indicates where the largest absolute difference is attained.

The uniform metric between densities can be interpreted through the link between the density function and the c.d.f. The probability that X belongs to a small interval $[x, x + \Delta_x]$, where $\Delta_x > 0$ is small number, can be represented approximately[2] as

$$P(X \in [x, x + \Delta_x]) \approx f_X(x).\Delta_x.$$

Suppose that X and Y are two random variables describing the return distribution of two common stocks. Then the difference between the densities $f_X(x) - f_Y(x)$ can be viewed as a quantity approximately proportional to the difference between the probabilities that X and Y realize a return belonging to the small interval $[x, x + \Delta_x]$,

$$P(X \in [x, x + \Delta_x]) - P(Y \in [x, x + \Delta_x]).$$

Thus, the largest absolute difference between the two density functions is attained at such a return level x that the difference between the probabilities[3] of X and Y gaining return $[x, x + \Delta_x]$ is largest in absolute value.

Just as in the case of the Kolmogorov metric, the value of x for which the maximal absolute difference between the densities is attained is close to the mean return. Therefore, the metric $\ell(X, Y)$ is not sensitive to extreme losses or profits.

8. *The total variation metric.*

$$\sigma(X, Y) = \sup_{\text{all events } A} |P(X \in A) - P(Y \in A)|. \tag{3.17}$$

If the random variables X and Y have densities $f_X(x)$ and $f_Y(x)$, then the total variation metric can be represented through the area closed between the graphs of the densities,

$$\sigma(X, Y) = \frac{1}{2} \int_{-\infty}^{\infty} |f_X(x) - f_Y(x)| dx. \tag{3.18}$$

In financial terms, the interpretation is straightforward. Suppose that X and Y are random variables describing the return distribution of two common stocks. We can calculate the probabilities $P(X \in A)$ and $P(Y \in A)$ where A is an arbitrary event. For example, A can be the event

---

[2]Technically, this is the first-order Taylor series approximation of the distribution function.
[3]This is not a joint probability.

that the loss exceeds a given target x, or that the loss is in a given bound $(x\%, y\%)$, or in an arbitrary unions of such bounds. The total variation metric is the maximum absolute difference between these probabilities. The reasoning is very similar to the one behind the interpretation of the Kolmogorov metric. The principal difference from the Kolmogorov metric is that in the total variation metric, we do not fix the events to be only of the type "losses exceed a given target x." Instead, we calculate the maximal difference by looking at all possible types of events. Therefore, the general relationship[4] between the two metrics is

$$\rho(X, Y) \le \sigma(X, Y). \tag{3.19}$$

The definition in equation (3.17) is useful to arrive at an interpretation but cannot be used to compute the total variation metric in practice. This can be done using the more convenient equation (3.18).

Note that formula (3.5) is an application of $\kappa(X, Y)$ for discrete random variables. In the example in section 3.2 concerning the inverse distribution functions of discrete random variables, we took advantage of the fact that $\ell_1(X, Y) = \kappa(X, Y)$, which is obvious for discrete distributions.

Not all instances of simple metrics involve distribution functions directly such as e.g. $\ell_p(X, Y)$ and the like. Nevertheless, if any of these metrics turn into zero, then it follows that the distribution functions of the corresponding random variables coincide. Other examples of simple metrics are given in the appendix to this chapter.

3.3.4 Compound Metrics

We noted that coincidence of distribution functions is stronger than coincidence of certain characteristics, such as absolute moments. There is a stronger form of identity than the coincidence of distribution functions, which is actually the strongest possible. Consider the case in which no matter what happens, the returns of equity 1 and equity 2 are identical. Hence, we can describe the two random variables as being coincident in each state of the world. As a consequence, their distribution functions are the same because the probabilities of all events of the return of equity 1 are exactly equal to the corresponding events of the return of equity 2. This identity is also known as *almost everywhere identity* because it considers all states of the world that happen with nonzero probability. The probability metrics

---

[4]Compare equations (3.11) and (3.19) in order to see the relationship between the Kolmogorov, the Lévy and the total variation metrics.

that imply the almost everywhere identity are called *compound metrics*. Common examples of compound metrics are stated in the following:

1. *The p-average compound metric.*

$$\mathcal{L}_p(X, Y) = (E|X - Y|^p)^{1/p}, \; p \geq 1, \qquad (3.20)$$

where X and Y are random variables with finite moments, $E|X|^p < \infty$ and $E|Y|^p < \infty, p \geq 1$.

From a financial viewpoint, we can recognize two widely used measures of deviation that belong to the family of the p-average compound metrics. If p is equal to one, we obtain the mean absolute deviation between X and Y,

$$\mathcal{L}_1(X, Y) = E|X - Y|.$$

Suppose that X describes the returns of a stock portfolio and Y describes the returns of a benchmark portfolio. Then the mean absolute deviation is a way to measure how closely the stock portfolio tracks the benchmark. If p is equal to two, we obtain

$$\mathcal{L}_2(X, Y) = \sqrt{E(X - Y)^2}$$

which is a quantity very similar to the tracking error between the two portfolios. The problem of tracking a benchmark is considered in more detail in Chapter 9.

2. *The Ky Fan metric.*

$$\mathbf{K}(X, Y) := \inf\{\epsilon > 0 : P(|X - Y| > \epsilon) < \epsilon\}, \qquad (3.21)$$

where X and Y are real-valued random variables. The Ky Fan metric has an important application in theory of probability as it metrizes convergence in probability of real-valued random variables.

Assume that X is a random variable describing the return distribution of a portfolio of stocks and Y describes the return distribution of a benchmark portfolio. The probability

$$P(|X - Y| > \epsilon) = P\left(\{X < Y - \epsilon\} \bigcup \{X > Y + \epsilon\}\right)$$

concerns the event that either the portfolio will outperform the benchmark by ϵ or it will underperform the benchmark by ϵ. Therefore, the quantity 2ϵ can be interpreted as the width of a performance band.

The probability $1 - P(|X - Y| > \epsilon)$ is actually the probability that the portfolio stays within the performance band, that is, it does not deviate from the benchmark more than ϵ in an upward or downward direction.

As the width of the performance band decreases, the probability $P(|X - Y| > \epsilon)$ increases because the portfolio returns will be more often outside a smaller band. The Ky Fan metric calculates the width of a performance band such that the probability of the event that the portfolio return is outside the performance band is smaller than half of it.

3. *The Birnbaum-Orlicz compound metric.*

$$\Theta_p(X, Y) = \left(\int_{-\infty}^{\infty} \tau^p(t; X, Y) dt \right)^{1/p}, \, p \geq 1, \qquad (3.22)$$

where $\tau(t; X, Y) = P(X \leq t < Y) + P(Y \leq t < X)$.

The function $\tau(t; X, Y)$, which is the building block of the Birnbaum-Orlicz compound metric, can be interpreted in the following way. Suppose that X and Y describe the return distributions of two common stocks. The function argument, t, can be regarded as a performance divide. The term $P(X \leq t < Y)$ is the probability that X underperforms t and, simultaneously, Y outperforms t.[5] If t is a very small number, then the probability $P(X \leq t < Y)$ will be close to zero because the stock X will underperform it very rarely. If t is a very large number, then $P(X \leq t < Y)$ will again be close to zero because stock Y will rarely outperform it. A similar conclusion holds for other term of $\tau(t; X, Y)$ as it only treats the random variables in the opposite way. Therefore, we can conclude that the function $\tau(t; X, Y)$ calculates the probabilities of the relative underperformance or outperformance of X and Y, and has a maximum for moderate values of the performance divide t.

In the case of $p = 1$, the Birnbaum-Orlicz compound metric sums all probabilities of this type for all values of the performance divide t. Thus, it is an aggregate measure of the deviations in the relative performance of X and Y. In fact, it is exactly equal to the mean absolute deviation,

$$\Theta_1(X, Y) = E|X - Y| = \mathcal{L}_1(X, Y).$$

3.3.5 Minimal and Maximal Metrics

From the discussion of the three classes of probability metrics, it becomes apparent that they are interrelated. We noted that they are contained in

---

[5]Note that we consider joint probabilities in contrast to the previous section where we considered probabilities on a standalone basis.

one another. We also noted that primary metrics can be "enriched" so that they turn into simple metrics by the following process. Suppose that we have a list of characteristics which defines the primary metric. Then we start adding additional characteristics which cannot be expressed in any way by means of the ones currently in the list. That is, by enriching the list, we are making our criterion for sameness, or distance, finer and finer. Assume that this process continues indefinitely, until we exhaust all possible characteristics. The primary metric obtained by means of the set of all possible characteristics is actually a simple metric. This is true because the set of all possible characteristics is so rich that by matching it, we end up with coincident distribution functions and therefore the primary metric turns into a simple one.

The theory of probability metrics shows general approaches of passing from one class to another. For instance, assume that we have a compound metric. As we remarked, it is influenced not only by the distribution functions but also by the dependence between the random variables. We can ask the question, is it possible to construct a simple metric on the basis of it? The answer is positive and the simple metric is built by constructing the minimal metric. The process is the following. Choose two random variables X and Y. Compute the distances between all possible random variables having the same distribution as the ones selected using the compound metric. Set the minimum of these distances to be the distance between the random variables X and Y. The result is a simple metric because due to the minimization, we remove the influence on the dependence structure and only the distribution functions remain. In essence, by this process, we associate a simple metric to any compound metric.

The minimal metrics have an important place in the theory of probability metrics and there is notation reserved for them. Denote by μ the selected compound metric. The functional $\hat{\mu}$ defined by the equality

$$\hat{\mu}(X, Y) := \inf\{\mu(\widetilde{X}, \widetilde{Y}) : \widetilde{X} \stackrel{d}{=} X, \ \widetilde{Y} \stackrel{d}{=} Y\} \tag{3.23}$$

is said to be the minimal metric with respect to μ.[6]

Many of the well-known simple metrics arise as minimal metrics with respect to some compound metric. For example, the L_p metrics between distribution functions and inverse distribution functions defined in equations (3.13) and (3.15) are minimal metrics with respect to the p-average compound metric (3.20) and the Birnbaum-Orlicz compound

---

[6]Rachev (1991) provides a mathematical proof that the functional defined by equation (3.23) is indeed a probability metric. This fact is a nontrivial one.

metric (3.22),

$$\ell_p(X, Y) = \hat{\mathcal{L}}_p(X, Y)$$

and

$$\boldsymbol{\theta}_p(X, Y) = \hat{\boldsymbol{\Theta}}_p(X, Y).$$

The Kolmogorov metric (3.9) can be represented as a special case of the simple metric $\boldsymbol{\theta}_p$,

$$\rho(X, Y) = \boldsymbol{\theta}_\infty(X, Y)$$

and, therefore, it also arises as a minimal metric,

$$\rho(X, Y) = \hat{\boldsymbol{\Theta}}_\infty(X, Y).$$

Not all simple metrics arise as minimal metrics. A compound metric such that its minimal metric is equivalent to a given simple metric is called *protominimal* with respect to the given simple metric. For instance, $\boldsymbol{\Theta}_1(X, Y)$ is protominimal to the Kantorovich metric $\kappa(X, Y)$. As we noted, not all simple metrics have protominimal ones and, also, some simple metrics have several protominimal ones.

The definition of the minimal metric (3.23) shows that the compound metric and the minimal metric relative to it are related by the inequality

$$\hat{\mu}(X, Y) \leq \mu(X, Y).$$

We can find an upper bound to the compound metric by a process very similar to finding the minimal metric. We choose two random variables X and Y and compute the distances by means of the compound metric between all possible random variables having the same distribution as the ones selected. Then we set the maximum of these distances to be the needed upper bound. Naturally, this upper bound is called *maximal metric*. It is denoted by

$$\check{\mu}(X, Y) := \sup \{\mu(\tilde{X}, \tilde{Y}) : \tilde{X} \stackrel{d}{=} X, \ \tilde{Y} \stackrel{d}{=} Y\} \qquad (3.24)$$

Thus, we can associate a lower and an upper bound to each compound metric,

$$\hat{\mu}(X, Y) \leq \mu(X, Y) \leq \check{\mu}(X, Y).$$

It turns out that the maximal distance is not a probability metric because the identity property may not hold, $\check{\mu}(X, X) > 0$, as it is an upper bound to the compound metric $\mu(X, Y)$. Functionals that satisfy only Property 2 and Property 3 from the defining axioms of probability metrics are called *moment functions*. Therefore, the maximal metric is a moment function.

We illustrate the notions of minimal and maximal metrics in the next example. Suppose that the pair of random variables (X, Y) has some bivariate distribution with zero-mean normal marginals, $X \in N(0, \sigma_X^2)$, $Y \in N(0, \sigma_Y^2)$. The particular form of the bivariate distribution, or how the two normals are coupled together in a two-dimensional distribution, is insignificant. Let us calculate the minimal and the maximal metrics of the 2-average compound metric $\mathcal{L}_2(X, Y) = (E(X - Y)^2)^{1/2}$. In fact, the compound metric $\mathcal{L}_2(X, Y)$ stands for the standard deviation of the difference $X - Y$. The variance of the difference, σ_{X-Y}^2, can be calculated explicitly,

$$\sigma_{X-Y}^2 = \sigma_X^2 + \sigma_Y^2 - 2\sigma_X\sigma_Y\mathrm{corr}(X, Y),$$

where $\mathrm{corr}(X, Y)$ denotes the correlation coefficient between X and Y. Holding the one-dimensional distributions fixed and varying the dependence model, or the copula function, in this case means that we hold fixed the variances σ_X^2 and σ_Y^2 and we vary the correlation $\mathrm{corr}(X, Y)$. This is true because the one-dimensional normal distributions are identified only by their variances. Recall that the absolute value of the correlation coefficient is bounded by one,

$$-1 \le \mathrm{corr}(X, Y) \le 1,$$

and, as a result, the lower and upper bounds of the variance σ_{X-Y}^2 are

$$\sigma_X^2 + \sigma_Y^2 - 2\sigma_X\sigma_Y \le \sigma_{X-Y}^2 \le \sigma_X^2 + \sigma_Y^2 + 2\sigma_X\sigma_Y.$$

Note that the bounds for the correlation coefficient are not tied to any sort of distributional hypothesis and are a consequence of a very fundamental inequality in mathematics known as the Cauchy-Bunyakovski-Schwarz inequality. As a result, we obtain bounds for the standard deviation of the difference $X - Y$, which is the two-average compound metric,

$$|\sigma_X - \sigma_Y| \le \mathcal{L}_2(X, Y) \le \sigma_X + \sigma_Y.$$

We have followed strictly the process of obtaining minimal and maximal metrics. Therefore, we conclude that, in the setting of the example,

$$\hat{\mathcal{L}}_2(X, Y) = |\sigma_X - \sigma_Y|$$

and

$$\mathcal{L}_2(X, Y) = \sigma_X + \sigma_Y.$$

In fact, the assumption of normality for the one-dimensional distributions is not very limiting. The minimal and the maximal metrics have the above form for other one-dimensional distributions as well.

An example of an explicit expression for a maximal metric is the p-average *maximal distance*

$$\check{\mathcal{L}}_p(X, Y) = \left(\int_0^1 (F_X^{-1}(t) - F_Y^{-1}(1 - t))^p dt \right)^{1/p}, \, p \geq 1 \tag{3.25}$$

where $F_X^{-1}(t)$ is the inverse of the distribution function of the random variable X.

3.4 SUMMARY

In this chapter, we provided a basic introduction into the theory of probability metrics. We illustrated the basic ideas starting from the more simple discrete case and then proceeding to the general case of arbitrary probability distributions. We considered the classes of primary, simple, and compound probability metrics and the construction of minimal and maximal metrics. We gave numerous examples of probability metrics, which were interpreted within the context of finance.

3.5 TECHNICAL APPENDIX

In the field of mathematics, the problem of how to measure distance between various objects, such as vectors, matrices, functions, and the like, is well known, and its importance is well appreciated. Such distances are measured by means of special functions called *metrics*.

The notion of a *metric function*, usually denoted by $\rho(x, y)$, is actually fundamental. It defines the distance between elements of a given set. The most common example is the *Euclidean metric*,

$$\rho(x, y) = \sqrt{\sum_{i=1}^n (x_i^2 - y_i^2)},$$

where $x = (x_1, \ldots, x_n)$ and $y = (y_1, \ldots, y_n)$ are vectors in $\mathbb{R}^n$, which has a very intuitive meaning in the real plane. It calculates the length of the straight line connecting the two points x and y.

Metric functions are defined through a number of axioms. A set S is said to be a *metric space* endowed with the metric ρ if ρ is a mapping from the product $S \times S$ to $[0, \infty)$ having the following properties for each $x, y,$ $z \in S$:

Identity property. $\rho(x, y) = 0 \iff x = y$

Symmetry. $\rho(x, y) = \rho(y, x)$

Triangle inequality. $\rho(x, y) \leq \rho(x, z) + \rho(z, y)$

An example of a metric space is the *n*-dimensional vector space $\mathbb{R}^n$ with the metric

$$\rho(x, y) = ||x - y||_p = \left(\sum_{i=1}^{n} |x_i - y_i|^p \right)^{1/p}, \, p \geq 1.$$

Clearly, the Euclidean metric appears when $p = 2$.

The same ideas behind the definition of a metric function ρ are used in the definition of probability metrics that we discussed in the chapter. However, there are certain peculiarities which arise because the random variables are more complicated objects. In the next section, we comment on the defining properties of probability metrics.

3.5.1 Remarks on the Axiomatic Construction of Probability Metrics

In this section, we include additional remarks on the axioms discussed in the chapter, as well as state relaxations of some of them leading to different notions such as *probability distances*, *semimetrics*, and *quasimetrics*.

The general assumption throughout this section is that the random variables we consider are defined in one and the same probability space $(\Omega, \mathfrak{A}, P)$ and take values on the real line $\mathbb{R}$. There are also additional regularity conditions that we do not mention here. Rachev (1991) considers a much more general setting and provides all necessary technical conditions.

We already noted in section 3.3.1 that the first axiom, called the *identity property*, is a reasonable requirement we cannot do without in the problem of calculating distances. In the theory of probability metrics, we distinguish between two varieties,

ID. $\mu(X, Y) \geq 0$ and $\mu(X, Y) = 0$, if and only if $X \sim Y$.

$\widetilde{ID}.$ $\mu(X, Y) \geq 0$ and $\mu(X, Y) = 0$, if $X \sim Y$.

The notation $X \sim Y$ denotes that X is equivalent to Y. The meaning of *equivalence* depends on the type of metrics. If we consider compound metrics, then the equivalence is in almost sure sense. If we consider simple metrics, then $\sim$ means equality of distribution and, finally, if we consider primary metrics, then $\sim$ stands for equality of some characteristics of

X and Y. The axiom $\widetilde{\text{ID}}$ is weaker than ID. Actually, the primary and the simple probability metrics are semimetrics when considered on the space of pairs of random variables.

The *symmetry axiom* makes sense in the general context of calculating distances between elements of a space,

SYM. $\mu(X, Y) = \mu(Y, X)$.

The third axiom is the *triangle inequality*,

TI. $\mu(X, Y) \leq \mu(X, Z) + \mu(Z, Y)$ for any X, Y, Z.

The triangle inequality is important because it guarantees, together with ID, that μ is continuous in any of the two arguments. This nice mathematical property appears as a result of the consequence of TI,

$$|\mu(X, Y) - \mu(X, Z)| \leq \mu(Z, Y).$$

Observe that if the distance between Z and Y as measured by $\mu(Z, Y)$ is small, so is the left-hand side of the inequality above. That is, intuitively, small deviations in the second argument of the functional $\mu(X, \cdot)$ correspond to small deviations in the functional values. The same conclusion holds for the first argument.

The triangle inequality can be relaxed to the more general form called *triangle inequality with parameter K*,

$\widetilde{\text{TI}}$. $\mu(X, Y) \leq K(\mu(X, Z) + \mu(Z, Y))$ for any X, Y, Z and $K \geq 1$.

Notice that the traditional version TI appears when $K = 1$.

Notice that in the two versions of the triangle inequality, the statement that the inequality holds *for any* X, Y, Z is not very precise. In fact, we are evaluating the functional μ for a pair of random variables, for example (X, Y), and μ shows the distance between the random variables in the pair. The pair cannot be dismantled to its constituents because the random variables X and Y are coupled together by their dependence structure and if μ is a compound functional, then how X and Y are coupled is important. Therefore, the triangle inequality holds for the three pairs (X, Y), (X, Z), and (Y, Z).

As matter of fact, the three pairs cannot be arbitrary. Suppose that we choose the first pair (X, Y) and the second pair (X, Z); that is, we fix the dependence between X and Y in the first pair, and X and Z in the second pair. Under these circumstances, it is obvious that the dependence between

Z and Y cannot be arbitrary but should be consistent with the dependence of the chosen pairs (X, Y) and (X, Z). But then, is there any freedom in the choice of the pair (Z, Y)? Do these arguments mean that by choosing the two pairs (X, Y) and (X, Z) we have already fixed the pair (Z, Y)? It turns out that the pair (Z, Y) is not fixed by the choice of the other two ones. We are free to choose the dependence in the pair (Z, Y) as long as we do not break the following consistency rule:

> *Consistency rule.* The three pairs of random variables (X, Y), (X, Z), and (Z, Y) should be chosen in such a way that there exists a consistent three-dimensional random vector (X, Y, Z) and the three pairs are its two-dimensional projections.

Here is an example illustrating the consistency rule. Choose a metric μ. Suppose that we would like to verify if the triangle inequality holds by choosing three pairs of random variables. The distribution of all pairs is assumed to be bivariate normal with zero mean, $(X, Y) \in N(0, \Sigma_1)$, $(X, Z) \in N(0, \Sigma_2)$, and $(Z, Y) \in N(0, \Sigma_3)$ where the covariance matrices are given by

$$\Sigma_1 = \begin{pmatrix} 1 & 0.99 \\ 0.99 & 1 \end{pmatrix},$$

$$\Sigma_2 = \begin{pmatrix} 1 & 0.99 \\ 0.99 & 1 \end{pmatrix},$$

and

$$\Sigma_3 = \begin{pmatrix} 1 & 0 \\ 0 & 1 \end{pmatrix}.$$

Do these three pairs satisfy the consistency rule? Note that the correlation between X and Y is very strongly positive, $\text{corr}(X, Y) = 0.99$. The correlation between X and Z is also very strongly positive, $\text{corr}(X, Z) = 0.99$. Then, is it possible that Z and Y be independent? The answer is no because, under our assumption, when X takes a large positive value, both X and Y take large positive values, which implies strong dependence between them. The consistency rule states that the dependence between Y and Z should be such that the three pairs can be consistently embedded in a three-dimensional vector. Then, can we find a value for the correlation between Z and Y so that this becomes possible? We can find a partial answer to this question by searching for a consistent three-dimensional normal distribution such that its two dimensional projections are the given bivariate normal distributions. That is, we are free to choose the correlation between Z and Y, $\text{corr}(Z, Y) = \sigma_{ZY}$, on condition that the matrix,

$$\begin{pmatrix} 1 & 0.99 & 0.99 \\ 0.99 & 1 & \sigma_{ZY} \\ 0.99 & \sigma_{ZY} & 1 \end{pmatrix},$$

is a valid covariance matrix, i.e. it should be positive definite. For this particular example, it can be calculated that the consistency condition holds if $\sigma_{ZY} \geq 0.9602$.

Combinations of the defining axioms considered above imply different properties and, consequently, the functionals defined by them have specific names. If a functional μ satisfies:

> ID, SYM and TI. Then μ is called *probability metric*.
>
> $\widetilde{ID}$, SYM, TI. Then μ is called *probability semimetric*.
>
> ID, SYM, $\widetilde{TI}$. Then μ is called *probability distance*.
>
> $\widetilde{ID}$, SYM, $\widetilde{TI}$. Then μ is called *probability semidistance*.

In financial applications in particular, the symmetry axiom is not important and it is better to omit it. Thus, we extend the treatment of these axioms in the same way as it is done in the field of functional analysis. In case the symmetry axiom, SYM, is omitted, then *quasi-* is added to the name. That is, if μ satisfies:

> ID and TI. Then μ is called *probability quasimetric*.
>
> $\widetilde{ID}$, TI. Then μ is called *probability quasisemimetric*.
>
> ID, $\widetilde{TI}$. Then μ is called *probability quasidistance*.
>
> $\widetilde{ID}$, $\widetilde{TI}$. Then μ is called *probability quasisemidistance*.

Note that by removing the symmetry axiom we obtain a larger class in which the metrics appear as symmetric quasimetrics.

3.5.2 Examples of Probability Distances

The difference between probability semimetrics and probability semidistances is in the relaxation of the triangle inequality. Probability semidistances can be constructed from probability semimetrics by means of an additional function $H(x) : [0, \infty) \to [0, \infty)$ that is nondecreasing and continuous and satisfies the following condition:

$$K_H := \sup_{t > 0} \frac{H(2t)}{H(t)} < \infty, \tag{3.26}$$

which is known as *Orlicz's condition*. There is a general result which states that if ρ is a metric function, then $H(\rho)$ is a semimetric function and satisfies the triangle inequality with parameter $K = K_H$. We denote all functions satisfying the properties above and Orlicz's condition (3.26) by $\mathcal{H}$.

In this section, we provide examples of probability distances that are related to the probability metrics stated in the chapter. We show how limit cases are defined, state relationships between some families of probability distances, and mention their application.

Primary Distances

The engineer's distance.

$$\mathbf{EN}(X, Y; H) := H\left(|EX - EY|\right), \quad H \in \mathcal{H}, \qquad (3.27)$$

where the random variables X and Y have finite mathematical expectation, $E|X| < \infty$, $E|Y| < \infty$.

Simple Distances

1. *The Kantorovich distance.*

$$\ell_H(X, Y) := \int_0^1 H(|F_X^{-1}(t) - F_Y^{-1}(t)|)dt, \quad H \in \mathcal{H}, \qquad (3.28)$$

where the random variables X and Y have finite mathematical expectation, $E|X| < \infty$, $E|Y| < \infty$. If we choose $H(t) = t^p$, $p \geq 1$, then $(\ell_H(X, Y))^{1/p}$ turns into the L_p metric between inverse distribution functions, $\ell_p(X, Y)$, defined in (3.15). Note that L_p metric between inverse distribution functions, $\ell_p(X, Y)$, can be slightly extended to

$$\ell_p(X, Y) := \left(\int_0^1 |F_X^{-1}(t) - F_Y^{-1}(t)|^p dt\right)^{1/\min(1,1/p)}, \quad p > 0. \qquad (3.29)$$

Under this slight extension, the limit case $p \to 0$ appears to be the total variation metric defined in (3.17),

$$\ell_0(X, Y) = \sigma(X, Y) = \sup_{\text{all events } A} |P(X \in A) - P(Y \in A)|. \qquad (3.30)$$

The other limit case provides a relation to the uniform metric between inverse distribution functions $\mathbf{W}(X, Y)$ given by (3.14),

$$\ell_\infty(X, Y) = \mathbf{W}(X, Y) = \sup_{0 < t < 1} |F_X^{-1}(t) - F_Y^{-1}(t)|.$$

2. *The Birnbaum-Orlicz average distance.*

$$\theta_H(X, Y) := \int_{\mathbb{R}} H(|F_X(x) - F_Y(x)|)dx, \quad H \in \mathcal{H}, \qquad (3.31)$$

where the random variables X and Y have finite mathematical expectation, $E|X| < \infty$, $E|Y| < \infty$. If we choose $H(t) = t^p$, $p \geq 1$, then $(\theta_H(X, Y))^{1/p}$ turns into the L_p metric between distribution functions, $\theta_p(X, Y)$, defined in (3.13). Note that L_p metric between distribution functions, $\theta_p(X, Y)$, can be slightly extended to

$$\theta_p(X, Y) := \left(\int_{-\infty}^{\infty} |F_X(x) - F_Y(x)|^p dx \right)^{1/\min(1, 1/p)}, \quad p > 0. \qquad (3.32)$$

At limit as $p \to 0$,

$$\theta_0(X, Y) := \int_{-\infty}^{\infty} I\{x : F_X(x) \neq F_Y(x)\}dx, \qquad (3.33)$$

where the notation $I\{A\}$ stands for the indicator of the set A. That is, the simple metric $\theta_0(X, Y)$ calculates the Lebesgue measure of the set $\{x : F_X(x) \neq F_Y(x)\}$.

If $p \to \infty$, then we obtain the Kolmogorov metric defined in (3.9), $\theta_\infty(X, Y) = \rho(X, Y)$.

3. *The Birnbaum-Orlicz uniform distance.*

$$\rho_H(X, Y) := H(\rho(X, Y))$$

$$= \sup_{x \in \mathbb{R}} H(|F_X(x) - F_Y(x)|), \quad H \in \mathcal{H}. \qquad (3.34)$$

The Birnbaum-Orlicz uniform distance is a generalization of the Kolmogorov metric.

4. *The parametrized Lévy metric.*

$$\mathbf{L}_\lambda(X, Y) := \inf\{\epsilon > 0 : F_X(x - \lambda\epsilon) - \epsilon \leq F_Y(x)$$

$$\leq F_X(x + \lambda\epsilon) + \epsilon, \ \forall x \in \mathbb{R}\}. \qquad (3.35)$$

This is a parametric extension of the Lévy metric, $\mathbf{L}(X, Y)$, defined by equation (3.10). The obvious relationship with the Lévy metric is $\mathbf{L}_1(X, Y) = \mathbf{L}(X, Y)$. It is possible to show that the parametric extension $\mathbf{L}_\lambda(X, Y)$ is related to the celebrated Kolmogorov metric, $\rho(X, Y)$, defined by equation (3.9) and the uniform metric between inverse distribution functions, $\mathbf{W}(X, Y)$, given by equation (3.14),

$$\lim_{\lambda \to 0} \mathbf{L}_\lambda(X, Y) = \rho(X, Y)$$

and

$$\lim_{\lambda \to \infty} \lambda \mathbf{L}_\lambda(X, Y) = \mathbf{W}(X, Y).$$

Compound Distances

1. *The H-average compound distance.*

$$\mathcal{L}_H(X, Y) := E(H(|X - Y|)), \quad H \in \mathcal{H}. \tag{3.36}$$

If we choose $H(t) = t^p$, $p \geq 1$, then $(\mathcal{L}_H(X, Y))^{1/p}$ turns into the p-average metric, $\mathcal{L}_p(X, Y)$, defined in equation (3.20). Note that the p-average metric can be slightly extended to

$$\mathcal{L}_p(X, Y) := (E|X - Y|^p)^{1/\min(1,1/p)}, \quad p > 0. \tag{3.37}$$

At the limit, as $p \to 0$, we define

$$\mathcal{L}_0(X, Y) := P(\{w : X(w) \neq Y(w)\}). \tag{3.38}$$

If $p \to \infty$, then we define

$$\mathcal{L}_\infty(X, Y) := \inf\{\epsilon > 0 : P(|X - Y| > \epsilon) = 0\}. \tag{3.39}$$

These limit cases are related to the Ky-Fan distance.

2. *The Ky-Fan distance.*

$$\mathbf{KF}_H(X, Y) := \inf\{\epsilon > 0 : P(H(|X - Y|) > \epsilon) < \epsilon\}, \quad H \in \mathcal{H} \tag{3.40}$$

A particular case of the Ky-Fan distance is the *parametric family of Ky-Fan metrics*

$$\mathbf{K}_\lambda(X, Y) := \inf\{\epsilon > 0 : P(|X - Y| > \lambda\epsilon) < \epsilon\}, \quad \lambda > 0. \tag{3.41}$$

The parametric family $\mathbf{K}_\lambda(X, Y)$ has application in the theory of probability since, for each $\lambda > 0$, $\mathbf{K}_\lambda(X, Y)$ metrizes the convergence in probability. That is, if $X_1, \ldots, X_n, \ldots$ is a sequence of random variables, then

$$\mathbf{K}_\lambda(X_n, Y) \to 0 \quad \Longleftrightarrow \quad P(|X_n - Y| > \epsilon) \to 0, \text{ for any } \epsilon > 0.$$

The parametric family $\mathbf{K}_\lambda(X, Y)$ is related to the p-average compound metric. The following relations hold,

$$\lim_{\lambda \to 0} \mathbf{K}_\lambda(X, Y) = \mathcal{L}_0(X, Y)$$

and

$$\lim_{\lambda \to \infty} \lambda \mathbf{K}_\lambda(X, Y) = \mathcal{L}_\infty(X, Y).$$

Even though the Ky-Fan metrics imply convergence in probability, these two limit cases induce stronger convergence. That is, if $X_1, \ldots,$ $X_n, \ldots$ is a sequence of random variables, then

$$\mathcal{L}_0(X_n, Y) \to 0 \quad \overset{\Rightarrow}{\nLeftarrow} \quad X_n \to Y \text{ "in probability"}$$

and

$$\mathcal{L}_\infty(X_n, Y) \to 0 \quad \overset{\Rightarrow}{\nLeftarrow} \quad X_n \to Y \text{ "in probability."}$$

3. *The Birnbaum-Orlicz compound average distance.*

$$\mathbf{\Theta}_H(X, Y) := \int_{-\infty}^{\infty} H(\tau(t; X, Y)) dt, \quad H \in \mathcal{H}, \qquad (3.42)$$

where $\tau(t; X, Y) = P(X \le t < Y) + P(X < t \le Y)$. If we choose $H(t) = t^p, p \ge 1$, then $(\mathbf{\Theta}_H(X, Y))^{1/p}$ turns into the Birnbaum-Orlicz average metric, $\mathbf{\Theta}_p(X, Y)$, defined in (3.22). Note that the Birnbaum-Orlicz average metric can be slightly extended to

$$\mathbf{\Theta}_p(X, Y) := \left(\int_{-\infty}^{\infty} (\tau(t; X, Y))^p dt \right)^{1/\min(1, 1/p)}, \quad p > 0. \qquad (3.43)$$

At the limit, as $p \to 0$, we define

$$\mathbf{\Theta}_0(X, Y) := \int_{-\infty}^{\infty} I\{t : \tau(t; X, Y) \ne 0\} dt, \qquad (3.44)$$

where $I\{A\}$ is the indicator of the set A. If $p \to \infty$, then we define

$$\mathbf{\Theta}_\infty(X, Y) := \sup_{t \in \mathbb{R}} \tau(t; X, Y). \qquad (3.45)$$

4. *The Birnbaum-Orlicz compound uniform distance.*

$$\mathbf{R}_H(X, Y) := H(\mathbf{\Theta}_\infty(X, Y)) = \sup_{t \in \mathbb{R}} H(\tau(t; X, Y)), \quad H \in \mathcal{H} \qquad (3.46)$$

This is the compound uniform distance of the Birnbaum-Orlicz family of compound metrics.

3.5.3 Minimal and Maximal Distances

We noted that two functionals can be associated to any compound metric $\mu(X, Y)$—the minimal metric $\hat{\mu}(X, Y)$ and the maximal metric $\breve{\mu}(X, Y)$—defined with equations (3.23) and (3.24), respectively. By construction, the relationship between the three functionals is

$$\hat{\mu}(X, Y) \leq \mu(X, Y) \leq \breve{\mu}(X, Y).$$

Exactly the same process as the one described in section 3.3.5 can be followed in order to construct minimal and maximal distances, minimal and maximal semidistances, minimal and maximal quasidistances, and so on. It turns out that the minimal functional

$$\hat{\mu}(X, Y) = \inf\{\mu(\widetilde{X}, \widetilde{Y}) : \widetilde{X} \overset{d}{=} X, \ \widetilde{Y} \overset{d}{=} Y\}$$

is metric, distance, semidistance or quasisemidistance whenever $\mu(X, Y)$ is metric, distance, semidistance or quasisemidistance.[7] The minimization preserves the essential triangle inequality with parameter $K_{\hat{\mu}} = K_{\mu}$ and also the identity property assumed for μ.

In contrast, the maximal functional

$$\breve{\mu}(X, Y) = \sup\{\mu(\widetilde{X}, \widetilde{Y}) : \widetilde{X} \overset{d}{=} X, \ \widetilde{Y} \overset{d}{=} Y\}$$

does not preserve all properties of $\mu(X, Y)$ and, therefore, it is *not* a probability distance. In fact, the maximization does not preserve the important identity property, while the triangle inequality holds with parameter $K_{\breve{\mu}} = K_{\mu}$. As we noted in the chapter, functionals that satisfy properties SYM and $\widetilde{TI}$ and fail to satisfy the identity property are called *moment functions*. Thus the maximal distance is a moment function.

Many simple probability distances arise as minimal semidistances with respect to some compound semidistance. We state the basic relationships between the examples provided in the previous section. If $H \in \mathcal{H}$ is a convex function, then

$$\ell_H(X, Y) = \hat{\mathcal{L}}_H(X, Y),$$

$$\theta_H(X, Y) = \hat{\Theta}_H(X, Y),$$

---

[7] This fact can be seen from the mathematical proof that the minimal distance $\hat{\mu}(X, Y)$ is, indeed, a probability semidistance when $\mu(X, Y)$ is a probability semidistance. Rachev (1991) provides a proof of this fact.

and

$$\rho_H(X, Y) = \hat{\mathbf{R}}_H(X, Y).$$

A very general result, which is used to obtain explicit expressions for minimal and maximal functionals such as $\hat{\mu}(X, Y)$ and $\breve{\mu}(X, Y)$, is the *Cambanis-Simons-Stout theorem*. This theorem provides explicit forms of the minimal and maximal functionals with respect to a compound functional having the general form

$$\mu_\phi(X, Y) := E\phi(X, Y),$$

where $\phi(x, y)$ is a specific function called *quasi-antitone*. The index ϕ is a reminder that the functional has the particular form with the ϕ function. Then for the minimal and the maximal functionals $\hat{\mu}_\phi(X, Y)$ and $\breve{\mu}_\phi(X, Y)$ we have the explicit representations,

$$\hat{\mu}_\phi(X, Y) = \int_0^1 \phi(F_X^{-1}(t), F_Y^{-1}(t))dt \tag{3.47}$$

and

$$\breve{\mu}_\phi(X, Y) = \int_0^1 \phi(F_X^{-1}(t), F_Y^{-1}(1 - t))dt \tag{3.48}$$

The function $\phi(x, y)$ is called quasi-antitone if it satisfies the following property:

$$\phi(x, y) + \phi(x', y') \le \phi(x', y) + \phi(x, y') \tag{3.49}$$

for any $x' > x$ and $y' > y$. This property is related to how the function increases when its arguments increase. Also, the function ϕ should satisfy the technical condition that $\phi(x, x) = 0$. There is another technical condition which is related to the random variables X and Y. The following moments should be finite, $E\phi(X, a) < \infty$ and $E\phi(Y, a) < \infty$, $a \in \mathbb{R}$.

General examples of quasi-antitone functions include:

1. $\phi(x, y) = f(x - y)$ where f is a nonnegative convex function in $\mathbb{R}$, for instance $\phi(x, y) = |x - y|^p$, $p \ge 1$.
2. $\phi(x, y) = -F(x, y)$ where $F(x, y)$ is the distribution function of a two dimensional random variable.

How do we apply the Cambanis-Simons-Stout theorem? There are three steps:

Step 1. Identify the function $\phi(x, y)$ from the particular form of the compound metric.

Step 2. Verify if the function $\phi(x, y)$ is quasi-antitone and whether $\phi(x, x) = 0$. This can be done by verifying first if $\phi(x, y)$ belongs to any of the examples of quasi-antitone functions given above.

Step 3. Keep in mind that whenever we have to apply the result in the theorem for particular random variables (X, Y), then the following moments should satisfy the conditions $E\phi(X, a) < \infty$ and $E\phi(Y, a) < \infty$, $a \in \mathbb{R}$. Otherwise, the corresponding metrics may explode.

Let us see how the Cambanis-Simons-Stout result is applied to the H-average compound distance $\mathcal{L}_H(X, Y)$ defined in (3.36). The compound functional has the general form,

$$\mathcal{L}_H(X, Y) = E(H(|X - Y|)), \quad H \in \mathcal{H}$$

and, therefore, the function $\phi(x, y) = H(|x - y|)$, $x, y \in \mathbb{R}$. Due to the properties of the function H, $\phi(x, x) = H(0) = 0$ and, if we assume additionally that H is a convex function, we obtain that $\phi(x, y)$ is quasi-antitone. Applying the theorem yields the following explicit forms of the minimal and the maximal distance,

$$\hat{\mathcal{L}}_H(X, Y) = \int_0^1 H(|F_X^{-1}(t) - F_Y^{-1}(t)|)dt, \quad H \in \mathcal{H}$$

and

$$\check{\mathcal{L}}_H(X, Y) = \int_0^1 H(|F_X^{-1}(t) - F_Y^{-1}(1 - t)|)dt, \quad H \in \mathcal{H}. \tag{3.50}$$

We tacitly assume that the technical conditions $E(H(|X - a|)) < \infty$ and $E(H(|Y - a|)) < \infty$, $a \in \mathbb{R}$ hold.

Besides the Cambanis-Simons-Stout theorem, there is another method of obtaining explicit forms of minimal and maximal functionals. This method is, essentially, direct application of the celebrated *Fréchet-Hoeffding inequality between distribution functions*,

$$\max(F_X(x) + F_Y(y) - 1, 0) \le P(X \le x, Y \le y)$$

$$\le \min(F_X(x), F_Y(y)). \tag{3.51}$$

We show how this inequality is applied to the problem of finding the minimal distance of the Birnbaum-Orlicz distance defined in equation (3.42).

$$\Theta_H(X, Y) = \int_{-\infty}^{\infty} H(P(X \le t < Y) + P(X < t \le Y))dt$$

$$= \int_{-\infty}^{\infty} H(P(X \le t) + P(Y \le t) - 2P(X \le t, Y \le t)))dt$$

$$\ge \int_{-\infty}^{\infty} H(F_X(t) + F_Y(t) - 2\min(F_X(t), F_Y(t)))dt$$

$$= \int_{-\infty}^{\infty} H(|F_X(t) - F_Y(t)|)dt = \theta_H(X, Y).$$

The inequality follows because we take advantage of the upper bound of the Fréchet-Hoeffding inequality and because H is nondecreasing by assumption.

In fact, the Fréchet-Hoeffding inequality is not unrelated to the Cambanis-Simons-Stout result. The minimal and the maximal functionals are obtained at the upper and the lower Fréchet-Hoeffding bounds and they can also be represented in terms of random variables as

$$\hat{\mu}_\phi(X, Y) = E\phi(F_X^{-1}(U), \ F_Y^{-1}(U)) \tag{3.52}$$

and

$$\check{\mu}_\phi(X, Y) = E\phi(F_X^{-1}(U), \ F_Y^{-1}(1 - U)), \tag{3.53}$$

where U is a uniformly distributed random variable in the interval $(0, 1)$.

BIBLIOGRAPHY

Rachev, S. T. (1991). *Probability Metrics and the Stability of Stochastic Models*, Chichester: John Wiley & Sons.

CHAPTER 4

Ideal Probability Metrics

4.1 INTRODUCTION

Limit theorems in probability theory have a long and interesting history. The first account of a limit result dates back to 1713 when the Swiss mathematician Jacob Bernoulli gave a rigorous proof that the average number of heads resulting from many tosses of a coin converges to the probability of having a head. Later, in 1835, the French mathematician Simeon-Denis Poisson described this result as "The Law of Large Numbers" and formulated an approximation valid in the case of rare events; that is, when the probability of success, or having a head, is small. Nowadays, this result is known as the *approximation of Poisson* to the binomial distribution.

In 1733, the English mathematician Abraham de Moivre published an article in which he calculated approximately the probability of the number of heads resulting from many independent tosses of a fair coin. In this calculation, he used the normal distribution as approximation. In the century that followed, the discovery of de Moivre was almost forgotten. It was rediscovered and extended in 1812 by the French mathematician Pierre-Simon Laplace. This is now known as the *theorem of de Moivre-Laplace* of the normal approximation to the binomial distribution. It has many applications in different areas. In the field of finance, for example, it is the theoretical foundation behind the construction of binomial trees for option pricing.

The theorem of de Moivre-Laplace is a special case of the *Central Limit Theorem* (CLT), but it was not until the beginning of the 20th century that the importance of the CLT was fully recognized. In 1901, the Russian mathematician Aleksandr Lyapunov gave a more abstract formulation and showed that the limit result holds under certain very general conditions known as *Lyapunov's conditions*. Later, other conditions were established that generalized Lyapunov's conditions. A final solution to the problem was given by Bernstein, Lindeberg, and Feller who specified necessary and sufficient conditions for the CLT.

In the past century, the limit theory has been widely extended. For example, the abstract ideas behind the CLT were applied to stochastic processes and it was shown that *Brownian motion* is the limit process in the *Functional Limit Theorem* or *Invariance Principle* about which Jacod and Shiryaev (2002) provide a detailed discussion. Brownian motion is the basic ingredient of the subsequently developed *theory of Ito processes*, which has huge application in finance. The celebrated *Black-Scholes equation* and, in general, derivative pricing, are based on it.

The CLT itself was also extended. Generally, when summing independent and identically distributed *infinite* variance random variables, we do not obtain the normal distribution at the limit but another law. This result is known as the *generalized CLT*. The limit distributions that arise are called the *Lévy alpha-stable distributions* because of the fundamental work of the French mathematician Paul Lévy. The normal distribution is only a special case of the stable distributions. Feller (1971) and Shiryaev (1996) provide further details.

Besides stability with respect to sums of independent and identically distributed random variables, other schemes were also considered. The limit theory of maxstable distributions was developed, which, as the name suggests, studies the limit distribution with respect to maxima of random variables. It has wide application in actuarial mathematics and estimation of operational risk in the field of finance.

From the standpoint of the applications, the limit theorems are appealing because the limit law can be regarded as an approximate model of the phenomenon under study.[1] For example, if we go back to the result of de Moivre-Laplace, the limiting normal distribution can be accepted as an approximate model for calculation of the number of heads in many tosses of a fair coin. In the maxstable scheme, the limiting maxstable distribution can be regarded as an approximate model for the maximum loss a financial institution may face in a given period of time. Certainly, the maximum loss follows a different law, but because of the limit theorem, we can use the maxstable distribution as an approximation. This approach is applicable in estimating operational risk, for example. Similarly, in modeling returns for financial assets, the alpha-stable distributions can be used as an approximate model as they generalize the widely applied normal distribution and are the limiting distribution in the Generalized CLT.

---

[1]Technically, this is known as the *domains of attraction* property.

In summary, in the field of applications we are replacing the phenomenon under study with the limiting distribution. Therefore, an important question arises that concerns the error we make with this replacement. How close is the limiting distribution to the considered phenomenon? The only way to answer this question is to employ the theory of probability metrics. In technical terms, we are looking for a way to estimate the rate of convergence to the limit distribution.

This chapter is organized as follows. We give a brief introduction to the classical CLT and the first attempt to estimate the rate of convergence to the normal distribution—the celebrated *Berry-Esseen result.* Then we give examples of the application of probability metrics to the problem of estimating the convergence rate in the Generalized CLT. They are based on probability metrics called *ideal metrics*, which arise from a modified axiomatic structure. The construction of the ideal metrics is an example of how the set of defining axioms can be modified with the goal of obtaining a metric best suited for the problem under study.

4.2   THE CLASSICAL CENTRAL LIMIT THEOREM

We start with the classical result of de Moivre-Laplace, which shows that the normal distribution can be adopted as a model when we consider the experiment of flipping a fair coin. This is a fairly simplified situation in which we can easily recognize the true merits of the limit theorem. As a next step, we proceed by answering the bigger question of whether the normal distribution can be adopted as a model under more general conditions, what error we could make by adopting it, and when it fails to be an appropriate model.

From the standpoint of the field of finance, these questions are related to the problem of choosing a probabilistic model for financial asset returns distributions and its approximation in pricing options and other derivatives.

4.2.1   The Binomial Approximation to the Normal Distribution

In this section, we consider the simple experiment of flipping an unfair coin. We are interested in calculating the probability that the number of heads resulting from a large number of independent trials belongs to a certain interval, that is, if we toss a coin 10,000 times, then what is the probability that the number of heads is between 6,600 and 7,200, provided that the probability of a head is equal to 2/3?

Let us first derive a simple formula that gives the probability that we obtain exactly a given number of heads. Consider a small number of independent tosses, for example, four. Denote by p the probability that a head occurs in a single experiment, by $q = 1 - p$ the probability that a tail occurs in a single experiment, and by X the random variable indicating the number of heads resulting from the experiment. In this simple setting, the probability that no head occurs is given by

$$P(X = 0) = q \cdot q \cdot q \cdot q = q^4$$

because we multiply the probabilities of the outcomes since we assume independent trials.

The probability that exactly one head occurs is a little more difficult to calculate. If the head occurs on the very first toss, then the probability of the event "exactly one head occurs" is equal to $p \cdot q \cdot q \cdot q = pq^3$. But the head may occur on the second trial. If this is the case, then the corresponding probability is $q \cdot p \cdot q \cdot q = pq^3$. Similarly, if the head occurs on the very last trial, the probability is $q \cdot q \cdot q \cdot p = pq^3$. The probability of the event "exactly one head occurs in a sequence of four independent tosses" is equal to the sum of the probabilities of the events in which we fix the trial when the head occurs. This is because the head may occur either in the first or in the second or in the third, or in the fourth trial,

$$P(X = 1) = 4pq^3.$$

Similar reasoning shows that the probability of the event "exactly two heads occur in a sequence of four independent tosses" equals

$$P(X = 2) = 6p^2q^2$$

as there are six ways to obtain two heads in a row of four experiments. For the other two events, that the heads are exactly three and four, we obtain

and
$$P(X = 3) = 4p^3q$$
$$P(X = 4) = p^4.$$

Note that the power of p coincides with the number of heads, the power of q coincides with the number of tails, and the coefficient is the number of ways the given number of heads may occur in the experiment. In fact, the coefficient can be calculated by means of a formula known as the *binomial coefficient*. It computes the coefficients that appear in front of the unknowns when expanding the expression $(x + y)^n$ in which x and y are the unknowns. For example,

$$\begin{aligned}
(x + y)^4 &= (x + y)^2 \cdot (x + y)^2 \\
&= (x^2 + 2xy + y^2) \cdot (x^2 + 2xy + y^2) \\
&= x^4 + 4x^3y + 6x^2y^2 + 4xy^3 + y^4.
\end{aligned}$$

When the power increases, we need a formula since the direct computation becomes very time consuming. The general formula is given by the equation

$$(x+y)^n = \binom{n}{0}x^n + \binom{n}{1}x^{n-1}y + \binom{n}{2}x^{n-2}y^2 + \cdots$$
$$+ \binom{n}{n-1}xy^{n-1} + \binom{n}{n}y^n \qquad (4.1)$$

in which n is a positive integer and the coefficients $\binom{n}{k}$ and $k = 0, \ldots, n$ are the binomial coefficients. They are calculated through the formula,

$$\binom{n}{k} = \frac{n!}{k!(n-k)!} \qquad (4.2)$$

where the notation $n!$ stands for the product of all positive integers smaller or equal to n, $n! = 1 \cdot 2 \ldots (n-1) \cdot n$.

In the context of the independent tosses of a coin, n stands for the total number of tosses and k denotes the number of heads. Thus the probability of the event "exactly two heads occur in a sequence of four independent tosses" can be written as

$$P(X = 2) = \binom{4}{2}p^2q^2 = \frac{1 \cdot 2 \cdot 3 \cdot 4}{(1 \cdot 2) \cdot (1 \cdot 2)}p^2q^2 = 6p^2q^2.$$

The same reasoning can be used to obtain an equation calculating the probability that k heads occur in a sequence of n independent trials. This probability can only be expressed by means of a binomial coefficient. In order to emphasize the number of trials, we denote the random variable by X_n, where n stands for the number of trials,

$$P(X_n = k) = \binom{n}{k}p^kq^{n-k}, \quad k = 0, 1 \ldots n. \qquad (4.3)$$

The probability distribution defined in equation (4.3) is known as the *binomial distribution*. We can think of it in the following general terms. Replace the tossing of a coin by an experiment in which we identify a certain event as "success." All other events do not lead to success and we say that "failure" occurs. Thus, the binomial distribution gives the probability that exactly k successes occur on condition that we carry out n experiments. The mean value of the binomial distribution equals $EX = np$ and the variance equals $DX = npq$.

TABLE 4.1 The Probability that Exactly k Heads Occur Resulting from 20 Independent Tosses of a Fair Coin.

Number of heads, k	4	7	10	13	16
Probability, $P(X = k)$	0.46%	7.39%	17.62%	7.39%	0.46%

Let us consider the experiment of tossing a fair coin, i.e., $p = q = 1/2$, and fix the number of tosses to 20. What is the probability that exactly four heads occur? We can easily calculate this by means of equation (4.3),

$$P(X_{20} = 4) = \binom{20}{4} \left(\frac{1}{2}\right)^4 \left(\frac{1}{2}\right)^{16} \approx 0.46\%.$$

Table 4.1 gives the corresponding probabilities for other choices of the number of heads. Figure 4.1 graphically displays all probabilities, when the number of heads range from zero to 20.

Note that the probabilities change in a symmetric way around the value mean value $k = 10$, which very much resembles the density of the normal distribution. This similarity is by no means random. As the number of experiments, n, increases, the similarity becomes more and more evident (see Figure 4.2). The limit theorem that proves this fact is known as the *theorem of de Moivre-Laplace*. It states that, for large values of n, the

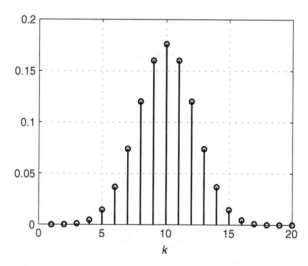

FIGURE 4.1 The probabilities that exactly k heads occur in 20 independent tosses of a fair coin.

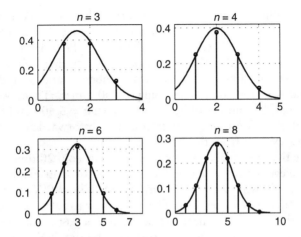

FIGURE 4.2 The probabilities that exactly k heads occur when the number of tosses, n, equals 3, 4, 6 and 8. The smooth curve represents the limiting normal distribution. The quality of the normal approximation improves as the number of tosses increases.

probability that k heads occur equals approximately the density function of a normal distribution evaluated at the value k. The mean value of the normal distribution is np and the standard deviation is $\sqrt{npq}$, in short-hand notation $N(np, npq)$. The density of a normal distribution with mean m and variance σ^2 is given by

$$f(x) = \frac{1}{\sqrt{2\pi\sigma^2}} \exp\left(-\frac{(x-m)^2}{2\sigma^2}\right), \quad x \in \mathbb{R}.$$

Therefore, the limit result[2] states that

$$P(X_n = k) = \binom{n}{k} p^k q^{n-k} \approx \frac{1}{\sqrt{2\pi npq}} \exp\left(-\frac{(k-np)^2}{2npq}\right) \qquad (4.4)$$

for large values of n. In this sense, we can say that the normal distribution can be adopted as an approximate model because the probabilistic properties of the binomial distribution for large values of n are "close" to the probabilistic properties of the normal distribution.

---

[2]In the theory of probability, the limit result is known as the *local* theorem of de Moivre-Laplace.

Are there other indications that the normal distribution can be adopted as an approximate model? The answer is affirmative. Let us consider the question we asked at the beginning of the section. Provided that n is large, what is the probability that the number of heads resulting from independent tosses of an unfair coin is between two numbers a and b? For example, suppose that we toss an unfair coin 10,000 times. Then, what is the probability that the number of heads is between $a = 6,600$ and $b = 7,200$? Any attempt to tackle this question in a straightforward way is doomed. This becomes evident from the following analysis.

Suppose that we independently toss an unfair coin 20 times. The probability of the event that no more than three heads occur can be computed directly in the following way—we sum the probabilities $P(X_{20} = 0)$, $P(X_{20} = 1)$, $P(X_{20} = 2)$, and $P(X_{20} = 3)$. Similarly, in order to calculate the the probability that the number of heads is between $a = 6,600$ and $b = 7,200$ in 10,000 tosses, we have to sum up the probabilities $P(X_{10,000} = k)$ where $6,600 \leq k \leq 7,200$. Apparently, this is not a simple thing to do. The limit result in the theorem of de Moivre-Laplace can be adapted to calculate such probabilities. We can use the limiting normal distribution in order to calculate them,

$$P(a \leq X_n \leq b) \approx \int_a^b \frac{1}{\sqrt{2\pi npq}} \exp\left(-\frac{(x - np)^2}{2npq}\right) dx \qquad (4.5)$$

which means that instead of summing up the binomial probabilities, we are summing up the normal probabilities.[3] The calculation of the right hand-side of (4.5) is easier because it can be represented through the *cumulative distribution function* (c.d.f.) of the normal distribution,

$$P(a \leq X_n \leq b) \approx F(b) - F(a),$$

where $F(x)$ is the c.d.f. of the normal distribution with mean np and variance npq. The c.d.f. of the normal distribution is tabulated and is also available in software packages. In fact, if we assume that $p = 2/3$, then the actual probability, $P(6,600 \leq X_{10,000} \leq 7,200) = 0.9196144$ and, through the corresponding normal distribution, we obtain $F(7,200) - F(6,600) = 0.92135$, which means that we make an error of about 0.17%.

Equation (4.5) has another very important implication. It means that the c.d.f. of the binomial distribution is approximated by the c.d.f. of the corresponding normal distribution,

$$P(X_n \leq b) \approx F(b).$$

---

[3]In the theory of probability, the limit result is known as the *integral* theorem of de Moivre-Laplace.

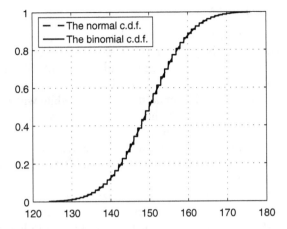

FIGURE 4.3 The binomial c.d.f. resulting from 200 independent tosses of a fair coin and the normal approximation.

This is a very important argument in favor of adopting the normal distribution as an approximate model as it virtually means that the probabilistic properties of the binomial distribution are approximately the same as the ones of the normal distribution. This is illustrated in Figure 4.3, where we plot the c.d.f. of a binomial distribution resulting from 200 independent tosses of a fair coin and the corresponding normal approximation.

The approximations (4.4) and (4.5) have wide application in the field of finance. In particular, generalizations of these results are used in pricing options and other derivatives, the price of which depends on another instrument called *underlying instrument*. The binomial distribution is behind the construction of *binomial trees* employed to evolve the price of the underlying into the future.[4] Deeper theory is necessary for a complete illustration, which goes beyond the scope of the book, but the basic principle is that, as the steps in the tree increase (the number of trials), the binomial path becomes closer to a sample path of the price process of the underlying instrument. Therefore, this technique provides a powerful numerical way to pricing *path-dependent* derivatives. Focardi and Fabozzi (2004) provide more details on the mathematics behind derivative pricing.

---

[4]The binomial approach to option pricing was introduced by Cox et al. (1979), Rendleman and Bartter (1979), and Sharpe (1978).

4.2.2 The General Case

In the previous section, we considered the normal approximation to the binomial distribution when the number of independent trials is large. However, we did not state any limit results but only illustrated them. Usually, the convergence to the normal distribution is derived by means of centered and normalized binomial distributions while we considered the binomial distribution directly. In this setting, it is not possible to obtain a nondegenerate limit as the number of trials approaches infinity because, in this case, the mean value of np and the variance npq explode and the normal approximation $N(np, npq)$, which is well-defined for any finite n, stops making any sense.

The procedure of centering and normalizing a random variable means that we subtract the mean of the random variable and divide the difference by its standard deviation so that the new random quantity has a zero mean and a unit variance. For instance, in the case of the binomial distribution, the random quantity

$$Y_n = \frac{X_n - np}{\sqrt{npq}}$$

has a zero mean and unit variance, $EY_n = 0$ and $DY_n = 1$. Therefore, it makes more sense to consider the limit distribution of Y_n as n approaches infinity because it may converge to a nondegenerate limit distribution as its mean and variance do not depend on the number of trials.

In fact, the approximation in equation (4.5) is an illustration of the limit result

$$\lim_{n \to \infty} P\left(u \le \frac{X_n - np}{\sqrt{npq}} \le v\right) = \frac{1}{\sqrt{2\pi}} \int_u^v e^{-x^2/2}\, dx \qquad (4.6)$$

which means that as the number of trials approaches infinity, the centered and normalized binomial distribution approaches the standard normal distribution $N(0, 1)$. By observing the centered binomial distributions, we can visually compare the improvement in the approximation as the scale is not influenced by n. This is shown on Figure 4.4.

The fact that the centered normal distribution is the limit distribution when the number of independent tosses approaches infinity is truly remarkable. Suppose that in the n-tosses experiment we look at each toss separately. That is, each toss is a random variable that can take only two values—zero with probability q (if a tail occurs), and one with probability p (if a head occurs). Since each toss is a new experiment in itself, we denote these random variables by δ_i where i is the number of the corresponding

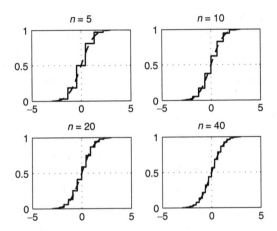

FIGURE 4.4 The centered and normalized binomial c.d.f.s resulting from 5, 10, 20, and 40 independent tosses of a fair coin and the normal approximation.

toss. Thus, if δ_2 takes the value zero, it means that on the second toss, a tail has occurred. In this setting, the random variable X_n describing the number of heads resulting from n independent tosses of a coin can be represented as a sum of the corresponding single-toss experiments,

$$X_n = \delta_1 + \delta_2 + \cdots + \delta_n \qquad (4.7)$$

where the random variables $\delta_i, i = 1, \ldots, n$ are independent and identically distributed (i.i.d.). Therefore, it appears that the limit relation (4.6) concerns a sum of i.i.d. random variables in which the number of summands approaches infinity.

It turns out that the limit relation (4.6) holds true for sums of i.i.d. random variables, just as in (4.7), the distribution of which may be quite arbitrary. They only need to satisfy certain regularity conditions. This result is the celebrated central limit theorem. There are several sets of regularity conditions. In this section, we describe only two of them, as they have vast implications concerning when the normal distribution can be accepted as approximate model.

The Meaning of Summation in Financial Variables Before proceeding with the regularity conditions, let us discuss briefly why summing random variables is important in the context of finance. A huge topic in finance is imposing a proper distributional assumption for the returns of a variable such as stock returns, exchange rate returns, changes in interest rates, and the like. Usually, the distributional hypothesis concerns the logarithmic returns in particular or the changes in the values, which are also known as the *increments*.

Let us consider the price P_t of a common stock. The logarithmic return, or simply the log-return, for a given period (t, T) is defined as

$$r_{(t,T)} = \log \frac{P_T}{P_t}.$$

If the period (t, T) is one month, then $r_{(t,T)}$ is the monthly log-return. We split this period into two smaller periods (t, t_1) and (t_1, T). The log-return of the longer period is actually the sum of the log-returns of the shorter periods,

$$r_{(t,T)} = \log \frac{P_{t_1}}{P_t} + \log \frac{P_T}{P_{t_1}} = r_{(t,t_1)} + r_{(t_1,T)}.$$

In this fashion, we can split further the time interval and we obtain that the log-return of the longer period is the sum of the log-returns of the shorter periods. Thus the monthly log-return is the sum of the daily log-returns. The daily log-returns are the sum of the 10-minute log-returns in one day, and so on. The general rule is that the lower frequency log-returns accumulate the corresponding higher frequency log-returns.

Exactly the same conclusion holds with respect to the increments. Consider an interest rate in a period (t, T). The increments are defined as,

$$\Delta IR_{(t,T)} = IR_T - IR_t$$

which is simply the difference between the interest rate at moment t and T. Splitting the interval into two smaller intervals results in

$$\Delta IR_{(t,T)} = IR_{t_1} - IR_t + IR_T - IR_{t_1} = \Delta IR_{(t,t_1)} + IR_{(t_1,T)},$$

meaning that the increment in the longer period equals the sum of the increments in the smaller period. In this way, the monthly increment equals the sum of the daily increments, and so on.

In effect, the concept that a variable accumulates the effects of other variables is natural in finance. Therefore, it makes sense to adopt a model describing the log-returns of a variable, which describes approximately the probabilistic properties of sums of other variables. This observation makes the limit theorems in probability theory appealing because they show the limit distribution of sums of random variables without the complete knowledge of the distributions of the summands. Nevertheless, there are certain conditions that the summands should satisfy in order for the sum to converge to a particular limit distribution. We continue the discussion of two sets of such conditions.

Two Regularity Conditions Suppose that the random variables $X_1, X_2, \ldots,$ $X_n, \ldots$ are independent and share a common distribution with mean μ and variance σ^2. Consider their sum

$$S_n = X_1 + X_2 + \cdots + X_n. \tag{4.8}$$

The CLT states that the centered and normalized sequence of S_n converges to the standard normal distribution as n approaches infinity on condition that the variance σ^2 is finite. The mean of the sum equals the sum of the means of the summands,

$$ES_n = EX_1 + EX_2 + \cdots + EX_n = n\mu.$$

The same conclusion holds for the variance because the summands are assumed to be independent,

$$DS_n = DX_1 + DX_2 + \cdots + DX_n = n\sigma^2.$$

Thus, subtracting the mean and dividing by the standard deviation, we obtain the statement of the CLT,

$$\lim_{n \to \infty} P\left(u \le \frac{S_n - n\mu}{\sigma\sqrt{n}} \le v\right) = \frac{1}{\sqrt{2\pi}} \int_u^v e^{-x^2/2}\, dx. \tag{4.9}$$

The truly striking implication of the CLT is that the result is, to a large extent, invariant on the distributions of the summands. The distributions only need to be i.i.d. and their variance needs to be finite, $\sigma^2 < \infty$. The common distribution of the summands may be discrete, see equation (4.6) for the binomial distribution, or skewed, or it may have point masses. It really makes no difference. The limit distribution is the standard normal law. This is illustrated on Figure 4.5, which shows the c.d.f.s of the sum of exponential distributions (solid line) converging to the standard normal distribution function (dashed line). The exponential distribution by definition takes only positive values, which means that it is also asymmetric. Figure 4.6 shows the convergence of the corresponding density functions.

Note that the CLT states that the distribution function of the centered and normalized sum converges to the distribution function of the standard normal distribution. Thus, for a large number of summands,

$$P\left(\frac{S_n - n\mu}{\sigma\sqrt{n}} \le v\right) \approx \frac{1}{\sqrt{2\pi}} \int_{-\infty}^v e^{-x^2/2}\, dx.$$

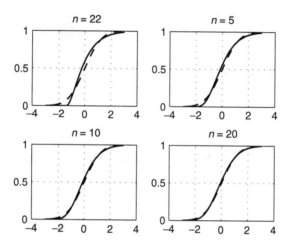

FIGURE 4.5 The c.d.f.s of the centered and normalized sum of exponential distributions (solid line) resulting from 2, 5, 10, and 20 summands and the normal approximation (dashed line).

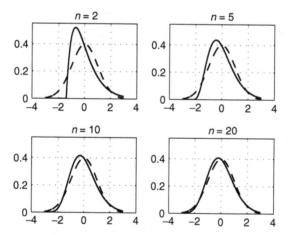

FIGURE 4.6 The density functions of the centered and normalized sum of exponential distributions (solid line) resulting from 2, 5, 10, and 20 summands and the normal approximation (dashed line).

which is the same as saying that the c.d.f of a normal distribution with mean $n\mu$ and variance $n\sigma^2$ is close to the distribution function of the sum S_n. In this sense, we can say that when the number of summands is large, the normal distribution can be accepted as an approximate model because the probabilistic properties of the $N(n\mu, n\sigma^2)$ are close to the probabilistic properties of the corresponding sum.

The fact that the CLT holds when the summands in (4.8) are i.i.d. with finite variance is already a very strong result with far-reaching consequences. Nevertheless, it can be further improved. The assumption of common distribution can be replaced by a different property. It states that as n grows to infinity, the summands should become negligible with respect to the total sum. That is, the contribution of each summand to the sum should become more and more negligible as their number increases; that is, none of the summands should dominate.[5] This property is called *asymptotic negligibility*. Note that the summands need not have a common distribution. Some of them may be discrete random variables, some may have symmetric distribution, others asymmetric. The only conditions they have to satisfy in order for the CLT to hold is, first, they have to be independent and, second, they have to be asymptotically negligible.

Application of the CLT in Modeling Financial Assets   Let us go back to the discussion of the behavior of financial variables. We noted that the daily log-returns accumulate, for example, the 10-minute log-returns. If the daily log-returns appear as a sum of so many short-period log-returns, can we safely assume, on the basis of the CLT, that the distribution of the daily log-return is approximately normal? Such a direct application of the limit result is not acceptable because there are certain conditions which need to be satisfied before we can say that the limit result holds. We have to answer two questions:

1. Is it true that the shorter period log-returns are independent?
2. Are they asymptotically negligible? Is it true that if we sum them up, the total sum is not dominated by any of the summands?

The answer to the first question is negative because of the empirically observed clustering of the volatility effect and the autocorrelations existing in the high-frequency time series. The answer to the second question is also negative. Usually, there are big outliers in the log-returns time series (very large log-returns in absolute value) that dominate the sum and dictate its behavior. They translate into what is known as the *heavy-tailed behavior* of the log-returns time series of stock prices. While the autocorrelations and

---

[5]The appendix to this chapter contains a more precise statement.

the clustering of the volatility can be taken care of by advanced time-series models, the outliers available in the data creep into the residual and, very often, can only be modeled by a nonnormal, heavy-tailed distribution.[6] As a result, we can reject the normal distribution as a realistic approximate model of the log-returns of stock prices. This conclusion has also been verified in a large number of empirical studies.

4.2.3   Estimating the Distance from the Limit Distribution

In the previous section, we stated two sets of conditions which guarantee that the CLT holds. Under these conditions, we can adopt the normal distribution as an approximate model for the sum of random variables (4.8) when the number of summands is large. As we explained, the rationale is that the distribution function of the sum with the number of summands fixed is close to the distribution function of the corresponding normal distribution. We say "the corresponding normal distribution" because its mean and variance should equal the mean and variance of the sum.

We would like to quantify the phenomenon that the two c.d.f.s do not deviate too much. For this purpose, we take advantage of a probability metric which computes the distance between the two c.d.f.s and is, therefore, a simple metric.[7] Such a general treatment is necessary because of the generality of the limit theorem itself. For example, suppose that we would like to fix the number of summands to 20. If the distribution of the summands is symmetric, then we may expect that the sum of 20 terms could be closer to the normal distribution compared to a sum of 20 asymmetric terms. Therefore, we need a way to estimate the error of adopting the limit distribution as a model that is not influenced by the particular distribution of the summands.

This is reasonable from a practical viewpoint as well. Suppose we have reasons to assume that in a given month the daily log-returns of a stock price are roughly independent. There are no outliers in the data that seem homogeneous. Therefore, we can think that the daily log-returns are roughly i.i.d. Thus we can assume that the monthly log-return has, approximately, the normal distribution. If we do not know the distribution of the daily log-returns, we need a more general approach to calculate the error that we make by adopting the normal distribution in terms of the distance between the distribution functions of the sum and the normal law.

---

[6]Rachev et al. (2007) provide more details on the application of time series models in finance.

[7]Chapter 3 discusses the definition and classification of probability metrics.

In the classical setting, when the sum (4.8) consists of i.i.d. summands, there is a result,[8] which states how quickly the distance between the c.d.f. of the centered and normalized sum, and the c.d.f. of the standard normal distribution, decays to zero in terms of the Kolmogorov metric.[9] Denote by $\widetilde{S}_n$ the centered and normalized sum,

$$\widetilde{S}_n = \frac{S_n - n\mu}{\sigma\sqrt{n}} = \frac{X_1 + \cdots + X_n - n\mu}{\sigma\sqrt{n}}.$$

The result states that if $E|X_1|^3 < \infty$, then in terms of the Kolmogorov metric the distance between the two c.d.f.s can be bounded by

$$\rho(\widetilde{S}_n, Z) \le \frac{C \cdot E|X_1|^3}{\sigma^3 \sqrt{n}} \tag{4.10}$$

in which C is an absolute constant that does not depend on the distribution of X_1, $Z \in N(0,1)$, and the Kolmogorov metric ρ is defined as

$$\rho(\widetilde{S}_n, Z) = \sup_{x \in \mathbb{R}} |F_{\widetilde{S}_n}(x) - F_Z(x)|.$$

The right part of the inequality in (4.10) contains a constant C, the third absolute moment $E|X_1|^3$ of the common distribution of the summands and the standard deviation σ. None of these quantities depends on the number of summands. The only term that depends on n is $\sqrt{n}$ in the denominator. The only facts about the common distribution of the summands we have to know are the standard deviation σ and the moment $E|X_1|^3$.

As a result, the "speed" with which the c.d.f. $F_{\widetilde{S}_n}(x)$ approaches $F_Z(x)$ as the number of summands increases, or the *convergence rate*, is completely characterized by $n^{-1/2}$. It is important to note that the convergence in (4.10) cannot be faster under these general conditions.

For practical purposes, we also need the value of the constant C. Currently, its exact value is unknown but it should be in the interval $(2\pi)^{-1/2} \le C < 0.8$. At any rate, an implication of the inequality (4.10) is that the convergence of the c.d.f. of $\widetilde{S}_n$ to the c.d.f. of the standard normal distribution may be quite slow. This is an important observation that we mention in the next section.

---

[8] In the theory of probability, this result is known as the Berry-Esseen theorem.
[9] Chapter 3 provides more background on probability metrics in general and the Kolmogorov metric in particular.

4.3   THE GENERALIZED CENTRAL LIMIT THEOREM

In section 4.2, we considered the classical CLT in which the normal distribution appears as a limit of sums of i.i.d. random variables with finite variance. We discussed the asymptotic negligibility condition that states that as the number of summands grows, none of them should dominate and dictate the behavior of the total sum. A very important question is, what happens if this condition is relaxed; if the summands are so erratic that one of them can actually dominate the others and thus influence the behavior of the entire sum? The normal distribution is not the limit law under these conditions but still there are nondegenerate limit distributions. The limit theorem is a generalization of the CLT and is known as the *Generalized CLT*. The limit distributions are the stable distributions.

    The actual conditions under which the Generalized CLT holds are easy to state. Any properly centered and normalized sum of i.i.d. random variables converges at the limit to a stable distribution. This means that the stable distributions are the *only* distributions that can arise as limits of sums of i.i.d. random variables. This feature makes the stable distributions very attractive for the modeling of financial assets because only they can be used as an approximate model for sums of i.i.d. random variables. Understandably, the normal distribution is a special case of the stable distributions, just as the CLT is a special case of the Generalized CLT. In contrast to the normal distribution, which is symmetric and cannot account for the heavy-tailed nature of the returns of financial variables, the class of nonnormal stable distributions has skewed and heavy-tailed representatives. Because of these differences, stable nonnormal laws are also called *stable Paretian* or *Lévy stable*.[10]

4.3.1   Stable Distributions

The class of the stable distributions is defined by means of their characteristic functions.[11] With very few exceptions, no closed-form expressions are

---

[10] *Stable Paretian* is used to emphasize that the tails of the non-Gaussian stable density have Pareto power-type decay. *Levy stable* is used in recognition of the seminal work of Paul Levy's introduction and characterization of the class of non-Gaussian stable laws.

[11] A characteristic function provides a third possibility (besides the cumulative distribution function and the probability density function) to uniquely define a probability distribution. It is a mapping from the set of real numbers $\mathbb{R}$ into the set of complex numbers $\mathbb{C}$ denoted by $\varphi_X(t) = E^{it X}$, which represents the so-called "Fourier transform" of the distribution of the random variable X. Knowing the

known for their densities and distribution functions. A random variable X is said to have a stable distribution if there are parameters $0 < \alpha \leq 2, \sigma > 0, -1 \leq \beta \leq 1, \mu \in \mathbb{R}$ such that its characteristic function $\varphi_X(t) = Ee^{itX}$ has the following form:

$$\varphi_X(t) = \begin{cases} \exp\{-\sigma^\alpha |t|^\alpha (1 - i\beta \frac{t}{|t|} \tan(\frac{\pi\alpha}{2})) + i\mu t\}, & \alpha \neq 1 \\ \exp\{-\sigma |t|(1 + i\beta \frac{2}{\pi} \frac{t}{|t|} \ln(|t|)) + i\mu t\}, & \alpha = 1, \end{cases} \quad (4.11)$$

where $\frac{t}{|t|} = 0$ if $t = 0$. Zolotarev (1986) and Samorodnitsky and Taqqu (1994) provide further details on the properties of stable distributions.

The parameters appearing in equation (4.11) are the following:

α is called the *index of stability* or the *tail exponent*.

β is a skewness parameter.

σ is a scale parameter.

μ is a location parameter.

Since stable distributions are uniquely determined by the four parameters, the common notation is $S_\alpha(\sigma, \beta, \mu)$.

Figure 4.7 shows several stable densities with different tail exponents and $\beta = 0.6$. All densities are asymmetric but the skewness is more pronounced when the tail exponent is lower. Figure 4.8 shows several stable densities with different tail exponents and $\beta = 0$. All densities are symmetric.

The parameter α determines how heavy the tails of the distribution are. That is why it is also called the *tail exponent*. The lower the tail exponent, the heavier the tails. If $\alpha = 2$, then we obtain the normal distribution. Figure 4.8 illustrates the increase of the tail thickness as α decreases. Thicker tails indicate that the extreme events become more frequent. Due to the important effect of the parameter α on the properties of the stable distributions, they are often called α-*stable* or *alpha stable*.

Apart from the appealing feature that the probabilistic properties of only the stable distributions are close to the probabilistic properties of sums of i.i.d. random variables, there is another important characteristic which is the stability property. According to the stability property, appropriately centered and normalized sums of i.i.d. α-stable random variables is again α-stable. This property is unique to the class of stable laws.

---

characteristic function $\varphi_X(t)$ is mathematically equivalent to knowing the probability density function $f_X(x)$ or the cumulative distribution function $F_X(x)$.

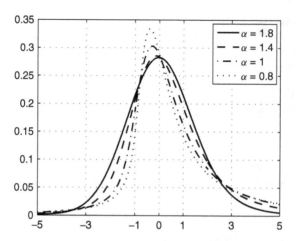

FIGURE 4.7 The density functions of stable laws with parameters $\alpha = 1.8$, 1.4, 1, and 0.8, $\beta = 0.6$, $\sigma = 1$, $\mu = 0$.

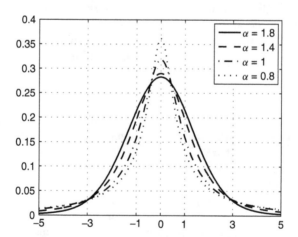

FIGURE 4.8 The density functions of stable laws with parameters $\alpha = 1.8$, 1.4, 1, and 0.8, $\beta = 0$, $\sigma = 1$, $\mu = 0$.

4.3.2 Modeling Financial Assets with Stable Distributions

Let us revisit the problem of modeling the log-return distribution of stock prices started in the previous section. We noted that a major criticism for assuming the normal distribution as a model is that very often there are out-liers in the high-frequency data that dominate in the sum of high-frequency returns or translate into the residuals of a times-series model. These outliers cannot be modeled by the normal distribution. In contrast to the normal distribution, the stable Paretian distributions are heavy-tailed, and they have the potential to describe the heavy-tails and the asymmetry of the empirical data.

The stable Paretian distributions arise as limit distributions of sums of i.i.d. random variables with infinite variance, and their variance is also unbounded. In fact, if $X \in S_\alpha(\sigma, \beta, \mu)$, then the moment $E|X|^p < \infty$ only if $p < \alpha \leq 2$. This means that if we assume a stable Paretian distribution as a model for the log-returns of a price time series, then we assume that the variance of the log-returns is infinite. From a practical viewpoint, this is not a desirable consequence.

Nevertheless, a large number of empirical studies have shown that the stable distributions provide a very good fit to the observed daily log-returns for common stocks in different countries and, thus, the overall idea of using the limit distributions in the Generalized CLT as a probabilistic model has empirical support.[12] As a result, the probabilistic properties of the daily log-returns for common stocks seem to be well approximated by those of the stable distributions. The infinite variance of the stable hypothesis appears as an undesirable consequence. Therefore, it is reasonable to search for distributions close to the stable distributions and, at the same time, have finite variance.

The methods to obtain such distributions concern truncating the tail of the stable law very far away from the center of the distribution. A straightfor-ward approach is to cut the tails of the distribution and to make the random variable defined not on the entire real line but on the interval defined by the two truncation points. Another, more sophisticated approach involves replacing the stable tails very far away from the center of the distribution by the tails of another distribution so that the variance becomes finite. This is the method behind the *smoothly truncated stable distributions* that have been very successfully used in option pricing.[13] The distributions resulting from the tail truncation method are close to the stable distributions as the only dif-ference is the tail behavior very far away from the center of the distribution.

The tail truncation method is reasonable from a practical viewpoint as well—it may not be regarded only as a technical transformation aimed

---

[12]Rachev and Mittnik (2000) provide an extensive review of the application of stable Paretian distributions in finance.

[13]Rachev et al. (2005) provide more details on the application of fat-tailed distribu-tions in finance and, in particular, the smoothly truncated stable distributions.

at taming the infinite variance. On every stock exchange, there are certain regulations according to which trading stops if the market index loses more than a given percentage. In fact, this is a practical implementation of tail truncation because huge losses (very small negative log-returns) usually happen when there is a crisis and in market crashes the market index plunges. Thus, astronomical losses (incredibly small negative log-returns) are not possible in practice.

From the point of view of the limit theorems, the tail truncation results in finite variance, which means that sums of i.i.d. truncated stable distributions converge to the normal distribution. From this perspective, don't we actually assume that it is the normal distribution that drives the properties of the monthly log-returns if the daily log-returns are assumed to follow the truncated stable distribution? This is not the case because the truncated stable distributions converge very slowly to the normal distribution. The c.d.f. of the sum will begin to resemble the normal c.d.f. only when the number of summands becomes really huge.[14] For small and medium number of summands, the density of the sum is actually closer to the density of the corresponding stable distribution. This fact has been established using the theory of probability metrics and is also known as a *prelimit theorem*. Rachev and Mittnik (2000) provide more details on the prelimit theorems and their importance in the applications.

4.4   CONSTRUCTION OF IDEAL PROBABILITY METRICS

The questions addressed in section 4.2.3 arise in the context of the Generalized CLT as well. That is, provided that we fix the number of summands, how close is the sum of i.i.d. variables to the limit distribution? In general, what is the convergence rate? In the literature, there are many results that state the convergence rate in terms of different simple probability metrics, such as the Kolmogorov metric, the total variation metric, the uniform metric between densities, the Kantorovich metric, and the like.[15] In fact, it turned out that probability metrics with special structure have to be introduced in order for exact estimates of the convergence rate to be obtained in limit theorems. These metrics are called *ideal metrics* and their special structure is dictated by the particular problem under study—different additional axioms are added depending on the limit problem. In this respect, they are called ideal because they solve the problem in the best possible way

---

[14]In section 4.2.3, we give an estimate of the speed of convergence in the CLT for i.i.d. random variables, which is not dependent on the distribution of the summands.
[15]See Chapter 3 for definitions and discussion.

due to their special structure. In this section, we describe without delving into details the notion of ideal probability metrics used to obtain exact convergence rates in the Generalized CLT. It appears that the additional axioms have an interesting interpretation from the point of view of finance. This discussion continues in Chapter 9, in the context of the problem of benchmark tracking.

4.4.1 Definition

In Chapter 3, we introduced the axiomatic definition of probability metrics. We briefly repeat the definition discussed in section 3.3.1 of Chapter 3. A probability metric $\mu(X, Y)$ is a functional that measures the "closeness" between the random variables X and Y, satisfying the following three properties:

Property 1. $\mu(X, Y) \geq 0$ for any X, Y and $\mu(X, X) = 0$

Property 2. $\mu(X, Y) = \mu(Y, X)$ for any X, Y

Property 3. $\mu(X, Y) \leq \mu(X, Z) + \mu(Z, Y)$ for any X, Y, Z

The three properties are called the *identity axiom*, the *symmetry axiom*, and the *triangle inequality*, respectively.

The ideal probability metrics are probability metrics that satisfy two additional properties that make them uniquely positioned to study problems related to the Generalized CLT. The two additional properties are the homogeneity property and the regularity property.

Homogeneity Property The *homogeneity property* is:

Property 4. $\mu(cX, cY) = |c|^r \mu(X, Y)$ for any X, Y and constants $c \in \mathbb{R}$ and $r \in \mathbb{R}$.

Basically, the homogeneity property states that if we scale the two random variables by one and the same constant, the distance between the scaled quantities ($\mu(cX, cY)$) is proportional to the initial distance ($\mu(X, Y)$) by $|c|^r$. In particular, if $r = 1$, then the distance between the scaled quantities changes linearly with c.

The homogeneity property has a financial interpretation that is fully developed in section 9.3 of Chapter 9. We briefly remark that if X and Y are random variables describing the random return of two portfolios, then converting proportionally into cash, for example, 30% of the two portfolios results in returns scaled down to $0.3X$ and $0.3Y$. Since the returns of the two portfolios appear scaled by the same factor, it is reasonable to assume that the distance between the two scales down proportionally.

Regularity Property   The *regularity property* is:

> *Property 5.* $\mu(X + Z, Y + Z) \leq \mu(Y, X)$ for any X, Y, and Z independent of X and Y.

The regularity property states that if we add to the initial random variables X and Y one and the same random variable Z independent of X and Y, then the distance decreases.

The regularity property has a financial interpretation, which is also fully developed in section 9.3 of Chapter 9. Suppose that X and Y are random variables describing the random values of two portfolios and Z describes the random price of a common stock. Then buying one share of stock Z per portfolio results in two new portfolios with random wealth $X + Z$ and $Y + Z$. Because of the common factor in the two new portfolios, we can expect that the distance between $X + Z$ and $Y + Z$ is smaller than the one between X and Y.

Any functional satisfying Property 1, 2, 3, 4, and 5 is called an ideal probability metric of order r.

4.4.2   Examples

There are examples of both compound and simple ideal probability metrics. For instance, the p-average compound metric $\mathcal{L}_p(X, Y)$ defined in equation (3.20) in Chapter 3 and the Birnbaum-Orlicz metric $\Theta_p(X, Y)$ defined in equation (3.22) in Chapter 3 are ideal compound probability metrics of order one and $1/p$ respectively. In fact, almost all known examples of ideal probability metrics of order $r > 1$ are simple metrics.

Almost all of the simple metrics discussed in section 3.3.3 in Chapter 3 are ideal:

1. The uniform metric between densities $\ell(X, Y)$ defined in equation (3.16) is an ideal metric of order -1.
2. The L_p-metrics between distribution functions $\theta_p(X, Y)$ defined in equation (3.13) is an ideal probability metric of order $1/p$, $p \geq 1$.
3. The Kolmogorov metric $\rho(X, Y)$ defined in equation (3.9) is an ideal metric of order 0. This can also be inferred from the relationship $\rho(X, Y) = \theta_\infty(X, Y)$.
4. The L_p-metrics between inverse distribution functions $\ell_p(X, Y)$ defined in equation (3.15) is an ideal metric of order 1.
5. The Kantorovich metric $\kappa(X, Y)$ defined in equation (3.12) is an ideal metric of order 1. This can also be inferred from the relationship $\kappa(X, Y) = \ell_1(X, Y)$.

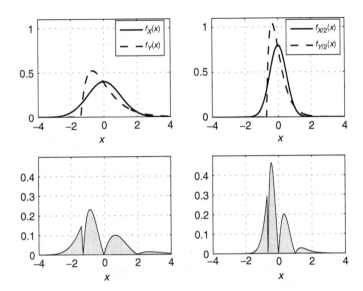

FIGURE 4.9 The left part shows the densities of X and Y and the absolute difference between them. The right part shows the same information but for the scaled random variables $0.5X$ and $0.5Y$.

6. The total variation metric $\sigma(X, Y)$ defined in equation (3.17) is an ideal probability metric of order 0.
7. The uniform metric between inverse c.d.f.s $\mathbf{W}(X, Y)$ defined in equation (3.14) is an ideal metric of order 1.

Let us illustrate the order of ideality, or the homogeneity order, by the ideal metrics $\ell(X, Y)$ and $\sigma(X, Y)$, which are both based on measuring distances between density functions. The left part of Figure 4.9 shows the densities $f_X(x)$ and $f_Y(x)$ of two random variables X and Y. At the bottom of the figure, we can see the absolute difference between the two densities $|f_X(x) - f_Y(x)|$ as a function of x. The upper right plot shows the densities of the scaled random variables $0.5X$ and $0.5Y$. Note that they are more peaked at the means of X and Y. The lower right plot shows the absolute difference $|f_{X/2}(x) - f_{Y/2}(x)|$ as a function of x.

Recall from Section (3.3.3) of Chapter 3 that

$$\ell(X, Y) = \max_{x \in \mathbb{R}} |f_X(x) - f_Y(x)|,$$

which means that the uniform distance between the two densities is equal to the maximum absolute difference. On Figure 4.9 we can see that the maximum between the densities of the scaled random variables is clearly larger than the maximum of the nonscaled counterparts. Actually, it is exactly twice as large,

$$\ell(X/2, Y/2) = 2\ell(X, Y)$$

because of the metric $\ell(X, Y)$ is ideal of order -1.

In section (3.3.3) of Chapter 3 we explained that the total variation metric $\sigma(X, Y)$ can be expressed as one half the area closed between the graphs of the two densities. Since the total variation metric is ideal of order zero,

$$\sigma(X/2, Y/2) = \sigma(X, Y),$$

then it follows that the surface closed between the two graphs is not changed by the scaling. Therefore, the shaded areas on Figure 4.9 are exactly the same.

Suppose that X and Y are random variables describing the return of two portfolios. In line with the interpretation of the homogeneity property, if we start converting those portfolios into cash, then their returns appear scaled by a smaller and smaller factor. Our expectations are that the portfolios should appear more and more alike; that is, when decreasing the scaling factor, the ideal metric should indicate that the distance between the two portfolios decreases. We verified that the metrics $\ell(X, Y)$ and $\sigma(X, Y)$ indicate otherwise. Therefore, in the problem of benchmark tracking that we address in Chapter 9, it makes more sense to consider ideal metrics of order greater than zero, $r > 0$.

Besides the ideal metrics we have listed above, there are others that allow for interesting interpretations:

1. *The Zolotarev ideal metric.*
   Zolotarev's family of ideal metrics is very large. Here we state only one example:

$$\zeta_2(X, Y) = \int_{-\infty}^{\infty} \left| \int_{-\infty}^{x} F_X(t)dt - \int_{-\infty}^{x} F_Y(t)dt \right| dx \qquad (4.12)$$

where X and Y are random variables with equal means, $EX = EY$, and they have finite variances. The metric $\zeta_2(X, Y)$ is ideal of order 2. Zolotarev (1997) provides further details on the properties of the Zolotarev ideal metric.

The Zolotarev ideal metric $\zeta_2(X, Y)$ can be related to the theory of preference relations of risk-averse investors. Risk-averse investors are characterized by the shape of their utility functions—they have concave utility functions. Suppose that X and Y are random variables describing the returns on two investments. Rothschild and Stiglitz (1970) showed that investment X is preferred to investment Y by all risk-averse investors if and only if $EX = EY$ and

$$\int_{-\infty}^{t} F_X(x)\, dx \leq \int_{-\infty}^{t} F_Y(x)\, dx, \quad \forall t \in \mathbb{R}. \tag{4.13}$$

This relation is known as *Rothschild-Stiglitz dominance*. The Zolotarev ideal metric $\zeta_2(X, Y)$ sums up the absolute deviations between the two quantities in inequality (4.13) for all values of t. Therefore, it measures the distance between the investments returns X and Y directly in terms of the quantities defining the preference relation of all risk-averse investors. As a result, we can use it to quantify the preference order. For example, if we know that investment X is preferred to investment Y by all risk-averse investors, we can answer the question of whether X is preferred to Y only to a small degree (if $\zeta_2(X, Y)$ is a small number), or whether X dominates Y significantly (if $\zeta_2(X, Y)$ is a large number).

2. *The Rachev ideal metric.*
   The Rachev family of ideal metrics is also very large. We state only one example. The appendix to this chapter provides further details.

$$\zeta_{s,p}(X, Y) = C_s \left(\int_{-\infty}^{\infty} |E(t - X)_+^s - E(t - Y)_+^s|^p dt \right)^{1/p}, \tag{4.14}$$

where:

  C_s is a constant, $C_s = 1/(s - 1)!$.

  p is a power parameter, $p \geq 1$.

  s takes integer values, $s = 1, 2, \ldots, n, \ldots$.

  $(t - x)_+^s$ is a notation meaning the larger quantity between $t - x$ and zero raised to the power s, $(t - x)_+^s = (\max(t - x, 0))^s$.

  X, Y are random variables with finite moments $E|X|^s < \infty$ and $E|Y|^s < \infty$.

The quantity $E(t - X)_+^s$ appearing in the definition of the metric is also known as the *lower partial moment of order s*. The simple metric $\zeta_{s,p}(X, Y)$ is ideal with order $r = s + 1/p - 1$.

Suppose that X and Y are random variables describing the return distribution of two common-stocks. The quantity $E(t - X)_+$ calculates the average loss of X provided that the loss is larger than the performance level t. Likewise, $E(t - Y)_+$ calculates the average loss of Y larger than t. The absolute difference $|E(t - X)_+ - E(t - Y)_+|$ calculates the deviation between the average loss of X and the average loss of Y for one and the same performance level t.

In the case $p = 1$, the metric

$$\zeta_{1,1}(X, Y) = \int_{-\infty}^{\infty} |E(t - X)_+ - E(t - Y)_+| dt$$

sums up the absolute deviations for all possible performance levels. In this respect, it is an aggregate measure of the deviations between the average losses above a threshold. If $s > 1$, then the metric $\zeta_{s,1}(X, Y)$ sums up the deviations between the lower partial moments for all possible performance levels.

As the power p increases, it makes the smaller contributors to the total sum in $\zeta_{1,1}(X, Y)$ become even smaller in the Rachev ideal metric $\zeta_{1,p}(X, Y)$ defined in (4.14). Thus, as p grows, only the largest absolute differences $|E(t - X)_+ - E(t - Y)_+|$ start to matter. At the limit, as p approaches infinity, only the largest difference $|E(t - X)_+ - E(t - Y)_+|$ becomes significant and the metric $\zeta_{1,p}(X, Y)$ turns into

$$\zeta_{1,\infty}(X, Y) = \sup_{t \in \mathbb{R}} |E(t - X)_+ - E(t - Y)_+|. \tag{4.15}$$

Note that the Rachev ideal metric given in equation (4.15) is entirely concentrated on the largest absolute difference between the average loss of X and Y for a common performance level t.

Similarly, the Rachev ideal metric $\zeta_{s,\infty}(X, Y)$ is calculated to be represented by the expression

$$\zeta_{s,\infty}(X, Y) = C_s \sup_{t \in \mathbb{R}} |E(t - X)_+^s - E(t - Y)_+^s|.$$

It is entirely concentrated on the largest absolute difference between the lower partial moments of order s of the two random variables.

In fact, the Zolotarev ideal metric defined in equation (4.12) appears as a special case of the Rachev ideal metric. The appendix to this chapter gives the Rachev ideal metric in its general form.

In financial theory, the lower partial moments are used to characterize preferences of difference classes of investors. For example, the lower partial moment of order 2 characterizes the investors preferences who are nonsatiable, risk-averse, and prefer positively skewed distributions. Suppose that X and Y describe the return distribution of two portfolios. X is preferred to Y by this class of investors if $EX = EY$ and

$$E(t - X)_+^2 \leq E(t - Y)_+^2, \quad \forall t \in \mathbb{R}.$$

The Rachev ideal metric $\zeta_{2,p}(X, Y)$ quantifies such a preference order in a natural way—if X is preferred to Y, then we can calculate the distance by $\zeta_{2,p}(X, Y)$ and check whether X significantly dominates Y.

Lower partial moments are also used as risk measures in the optimal portfolio selection problem and also a Capital Asset Pricing Model can be built upon them. Bawa (1975) and Bawa and Lindenberg (1977) provide more details.

4.5 SUMMARY

In this chapter, we described the basic results behind the classical Central Limit Theorem and the Generalized Central Limit Theorem. We also motivated the application of the limit distributions as a viable model for asset return distributions. We considered the axiomatic construction of ideal probability metrics for the study of sums of independent and identically distributed random variables and provided a financial interpretation of the new axioms. Finally, we provided two new examples of such metrics—the Zolotarev ideal metric and the Rachev ideal metric.

4.6 TECHNICAL APPENDIX

In this appendix, we provide more details on the conditions related to the CLT. In particular, we remark on the asymptotic negligibility condition mentioned in the chapter and also on the necessary and sufficient condition for the CLT. Concerning the ideal metrics, we state the general forms of the Zolotarev and the Rachev ideal metrics and also the families of the Kolmogorov-Rachev metrics obtained by smoothing other ideal metrics.

4.6.1 The CLT Conditions

The two sets of conditions mentioned in the chapter are *sufficient* conditions. That is, if any of them holds, then the CLT is valid. In the literature, usually the *condition of Lindeberg-Feller* is given as a general sufficient condition for the CLT. However, the Lindeberg-Feller condition is equivalent to the asymptotic negligibility condition, which we discuss below.

The Asymptotic Negligibility Condition In the chapter, we explained that asymptotic negligibility holds if the summands become negligible with respect to the total sum as their number increases. That is, none of the summands dominates and dictates the behavior of the total sum. In this section, we give a more precise formulation of this statement.

Consider a sequence of independent random variables $X_1, X_2, \ldots, X_n,$ $\ldots$ and denote by S_n the sum

$$S_n = X_1 + \cdots + X_n.$$

We do not assume that the distribution of the random variables is the same, meaning that the means and the variances of the random variables may differ. Denote by μ_n the mean of the sum S_n and by σ_n^2 the variance of the sum,

and
$$ES_n = EX_1 + \cdots + EX_n = \mu_n$$
$$DS_n = DX_1 + \cdots + DX_n = \sigma_n^2.$$

The asymptotic negligibility condition holds if

$$\max_{1 \leq j \leq n} P\left(\frac{|X_j - \mu_n|}{\sigma_n} > \delta\right) \longrightarrow 0, \quad n \to \infty \text{ for each } \delta > 0. \qquad (4.16)$$

The asymptotic relation (4.16) can be interpreted in the following way. The standard deviation σ_n describes the variability of the total sum. The ratio $|X_j - \mu_n|/\sigma_n$ compares each of the terms in S_n to the variability of the total sum and, thus, the probability in (4.16) measures the variability of each summand relative to the variability of the sum. Therefore, the asymptotic negligibility condition states that as the number of summands increases indefinitely, the most variable term in S_n is responsible for a negligible amount of the variability of the total sum.

In the Generalized CLT, the condition (4.16) does not hold. In fact, the Lévy stable distributions, which are the limit distributions in the Generalized CLT, satisfy a property that is converse to the asymptotic negligibility condition. It states that the large deviations of a sum of i.i.d. Lévy stable random variables are due to, basically, one summand, x

$$P(Y_1 + \cdots + Y_n > x) \sim P\left(\max_{1 \leq k \leq n} Y_k > x\right),$$

where $Y_1, \ldots, Y_n$ are i.i.d. Lévy stable random variables. That is, the probability that the sum is large is approximately equal to the probability that one of the summands is large. This fact is a manifestation of the fundamental difference between the Lévy stable distributions and the normal distribution.

The Necessary and Sufficient Condition While the asymptotic negligibility condition is very general, it is not a necessary and sufficient condition. The CLT may hold even if it is violated. Next, we formulate the necessary and sufficient condition.

Denote by $\widetilde{S}_n$ the centered and normalized sum,

$$\widetilde{S}_n = Y_1 + \cdots + Y_n = \frac{S_n - \mu_n}{\sigma_n}$$

where the summands $Y_j = (X_j - EX_j)/\sigma_n$. The CLT holds for the centered and normalized sum, $\widetilde{S}_n \overset{d}{\to} Z \in N(0, 1)$, if and only if for every $\epsilon > 0$,

$$\sum_{j=1}^{n} \int_{|x| > \epsilon} |F_{Y_j}(x) - F_{Z_j}(x)||x|\, dx \longrightarrow 0, \qquad n \to \infty, \qquad (4.17)$$

where Z_j has a normal distribution with variance equal to the variance of Y_j,

$$Z_j = \sigma_{Y_j} Z, \quad Z_j \in N\left(0, \sigma_{Y_j}^2\right).$$

Thus, the absolute difference $|F_{Y_j}(x) - F_{Z_j}(x)|$ is between two distribution functions of random variables with equal scales. The expression in (4.17) sums up the deviations between the c.d.f.s of the summands Y_j and the scaled normal distributions $F_{Z_j}(x)$.

The necessary and sufficient condition (4.17) has a more simple form if the random variables $X_1, \ldots, X_n, \ldots$ have equal distribution. Under this assumption, their means and variances are the same, $EX_j = \mu$ and $DX_j = \sigma^2$. Then the sum in (4.17) disappears and we obtain that for every $\epsilon > 0$,

$$\int_{|x| > \epsilon \sqrt{n}} |F_{\widetilde{X}_1}(x) - F_Z(x)||x|\, dx \to 0, \qquad n \to \infty \qquad (4.18)$$

in which $\widetilde{X}_1 = (X_1 - \mu)/\sigma$. Note that as n increases, it is only the integration range that changes in (4.18).

4.6.2 Remarks on Ideal Metrics

We did not specify in the chapter the exact conditions, which need to be satisfied in order for the ideal metrics considered to be finite. In this section, we briefly mention a few general conditions.

Suppose that the probability metric $\mu(X, Y)$ is a simple ideal metric of order r. The finiteness of $\mu(X, Y)$ guarantees equality of all moments up to order r,

$$\mu(X, Y) < \infty \quad \Longrightarrow \quad E(X^k - Y^k) = 0, \quad k = 1, 2, \ldots, n < r.$$

Conversely, if all moments $k = 1, 2, \ldots, n < r$ agree and, in addition to this, the absolute moments of order r are finite, then metric $\mu(X, Y)$ is finite,

$$\begin{aligned} EX^k &= EY^k \\ E|X|^r &< \infty, \\ E|Y|^r &< \infty \end{aligned} \quad \Longrightarrow \quad \mu(X, Y) < \infty,$$

where $k = 1, 2, \ldots, n < r$.

The conditions that guarantee finiteness of the ideal metric μ are very important when investigating the problem of convergence in distribution of random variables in the context of the metric μ.[16] Consider a sequence of random variables $X_1, X_2, \ldots, X_n, \ldots$ and a random variable X that satisfy the conditions,

$$EX_n^k = EX^k, \; \forall n, \; k = 1, 2, \ldots, n < r$$

and

$$E|X|^r < \infty, \; E|X_n|^r < \infty, \; \forall n.$$

For all known ideal metrics $\mu(X, Y)$ of order $r > 0$, given the above moment assumptions, the following holds: $\mu(X_n, X) \to 0$ if and only if X_n converges to X in distribution and the absolute moment of order r converge,

$$\mu(X_n, X) \to 0$$

if and only if

$$X_n \xrightarrow{d} X$$

and

$$E|X_n|^r \to E|X^r|.$$

---

[16]Technically, it is said that the metric μ *metrizes* the convergence in distribution if a sequence of random variables $X_1, \ldots, X_n, \ldots$ converges in distribution to the random variable X, if and only if $\mu(X_n, X) \to 0$ as $n \to \infty$.

This abstract result has the following interpretation. Suppose that X and Y describe the returns of two portfolios. Choose an ideal metric μ of order $3 < r < 4$, for example. The convergence result above means that if $\mu(X, Y) \approx 0$, then both portfolios have very similar distribution functions and also they have very similar means, volatilities, and skewness.

Note that, generally, the c.d.f.s of two portfolios being close to each other does not necessarily mean that their moments will be approximately the same. It is of crucial importance which metric is chosen to measure the distance between the distribution functions. The ideal metrics have this nice property that they guarantee convergence of certain moments. Rachev (1991) provides an extensive review of the properties of ideal metrics and their application.

In the remaining part of the section, we revisit the examples given in the chapter and extend them.

1. *The Zolotarev ideal metric.* In the chapter, we gave only a special case of the Zolotarev ideal metric. The general form of the Zolotarev ideal metric is

$$\zeta_s(X, Y) = \int_{-\infty}^{\infty} \left| F_{s,X}(x) - F_{s,Y}(x) \right| \, dx, \qquad (4.19)$$

where $s = 1, 2, \ldots$ and

$$F_{s,X}(x) = \int_{-\infty}^{x} \frac{(x - t)^{s-1}}{(s - 1)!} dF_X(t) \qquad (4.20)$$

The Zolotarev metric $\zeta_s(X, Y)$ is ideal of order $r = s$. Zolotarev (1997) provides more information.

2. *The Rachev metric.* The general form of the Rachev metric is

$$\zeta_{s,p,\alpha}(X, Y) = \left(\int_{-\infty}^{\infty} \left| F_{s,X}(x) - F_{s,Y}(x) \right|^p |x|^{\alpha p'} \, dx \right)^{1/p'} \qquad (4.21)$$

where $p' = \max(1, p), \alpha \geq 0, p \in [0, \infty]$, and $F_{s,X}(x)$ is defined in equation (4.20). If $\alpha = 0$, then the Rachev metric $\zeta_{s,p,0}(X, Y)$ is ideal of order $r = (s - 1)p/p' + 1/p'$.

Note that $\zeta_{s,p,\alpha}(X, Y)$ can be represented in terms of lower partial moments,

$$\zeta_{s,p,\alpha}(X, Y) = \frac{1}{(s - 1)!} \left(\int_{-\infty}^{\infty} \left| E(t - X)_+^s - E(t - X)_+^s \right|^p |t|^{\alpha p'} \, dt \right)^{1/p'}.$$

The metric defined in equation (4.14) in the chapter arises from the metric in (4.21) when $\alpha = 0$,

$$\zeta_{s,p}(X, Y) = \zeta_{s,p,0}(X, Y).$$

3. *The Kolmogorov-Rachev metrics.* The Kolmogorov-Rachev metrics arise from other ideal metrics by a process known as *smoothing*. Suppose the metric μ is ideal of order $0 \leq r \leq 1$. Consider the metric defined as

$$\mu_s(X, Y) = \sup_{h \in \mathbb{R}} |h|^s \mu(X + hZ, X + hZ) \tag{4.22}$$

where Z is independent of X and Y and is a symmetric random variable $Z \stackrel{d}{=} -Z$. The metric $\mu_s(X, Y)$ defined in this way is ideal of order $r = s$. Note that while (4.22) always defines an ideal metric of order s, this does not mean that the metric is finite. The finiteness of μ_s should be studied for every choice of the metric μ.

For example, suppose that $\mu(X, X)$ is the total variation metric $\sigma(X, Y)$ defined in (3.17) in Chapter 3 and Z has the standard normal distribution, $Z \in N(0, 1)$. We calculate that

$$\sigma_s(X, Y) = \sup_{h \in \mathbb{R}} |h|^s \sigma(X + hZ, X + hZ)$$

$$= \sup_{h \in \mathbb{R}} |h|^s \frac{1}{2} \int_{\mathbb{R}} |f_X(x) - f_Y(x)| \frac{f_Z(x/h)}{h} \, dx$$

$$= \sup_{h \in \mathbb{R}} |h|^s \frac{1}{2} \int_{\mathbb{R}} |f_X(x) - f_Y(x)| \frac{1}{\sqrt{2\pi h^2}} e^{-\frac{x^2}{2h^2}} \, dx. \tag{4.23}$$

in which we use the explicit form of the standard normal density, $f_Z(u) = \exp(-u^2/2)/\sqrt{2\pi}$, $u \in \mathbb{R}$. Note that the absolute difference between the two densities of X and Y in (4.23) is averaged with respect to the standard normal density. This is why the Kolmogorov-Rachev metrics are also called *smoothing metrics*.

The Kolmogorov-Rachev metrics are applied in estimating the convergence rate in the Generalized CLT and other limit theorems. Rachev and Rüschendorf (1998) and Rachev (1991) provide more background and further details on the application in limit theorems.

BIBLIOGRAPHY

Bawa, V. (1975). "Optimal rules for ordering uncertain prospects," *Journal of Financial Economics* 1: 95–121.

Bawa, V., and E. Lindenberg (1977). "Capital market equilibrium in a mean, lower partial moment framework," *Journal of Financial Economics* 5(2): 189–200.

Cox, J., S. Ross, and M. Rubinstein (1979). "Options pricing: a simplified approach," *Journal of Financial Economics* 7: 229–263.

Feller, W. (1971). *An introduction to probability theory and its application*, 2nd ed. New York: John Wiley & Sons.

Focardi, Sergio, and Frank Fabozzi (2004). *The mathematics of financial modeling and investment management*, New York: John Wiley & Sons.

Jacod, J., and A. Shiryaev (2002). *Limit theorems for stochastic processes*, New York: Springer.

Rachev, S., F. Fabozzi, and C. Menn (2005). *Fat-tails and skewed asset return distributions*, New York: John Wiley & Sons.

Rachev, S., and L. Rüschendorf (1998). *Mass transportation problems*, vols. 1 and 2, New York: Springer.

Rachev, S., S. Mittnik, F. Fabozzi, S. Foccardi, and Teo Jasic (2007). *Financial econometrics: From basics to advanced modeling techniques*, New York: Springer.

Rachev, S. T. (1991). *Probability metrics and the stability of stochastic models*, Chichester: John Wiley & Sons.

Rachev, S. T., and S. Mittnik (2000). *Stable Paretian models in finance*, New York: John Wiley & Sons.

Rendleman, R., and B. Bartter (1979). "Two state option pricing," *Journal of Finance* 34(5): 1093–1110.

Rothschild, M., and J. E. Stiglitz (1970). "Increasing risk: A definition," *Journal of Economic Theory* 2(3): 225–243.

Samorodnitsky, G., and M. S. Taqqu (1994). *Stable non-Gaussian random processes*, New York: Chapman & Hall.

Sharpe, W. F. (1978). *Investments*, 1st ed., Englewood Cliffs, NJ: Prentice-Hall.

Shiryaev, A. N. (1996). *Probability*, New York: Springer.

Zolotarev, V. M. (1986). *One-dimensional stable distributions* (Translation of Mathematical Monographs, vol. 65), New York: American Mathematical Society.

Zolotarev, V. M. (1997). *Modern theory of summation of random variable*, New York: Brill Academic Publishers.

5

Choice under Uncertainty

5.1   INTRODUCTION

Agents in financial markets operate in a world in which they make choices under risk and uncertainty. Portfolio managers, for example, make investment decisions in which they take risks and expect rewards. They choose to invest in a given portfolio because they believe it is "better" than any other they can buy. Thus the chosen portfolio is the most preferred one among all portfolios that are admissible for investment. Not all portfolio managers invest in the same portfolio because their expectations and preferences vary.

The theory of how choices under risk and uncertainty are made was introduced by John von Neumann and Oskar Morgenstern in 1944 in *Theory of Games and Economic Behavior*. They gave an explicit representation of investor's perferences in terms of an investor's *utility function*. If no uncertainty is present, the utility function can be interpreted as a mapping between the available alternatives and real numbers indicating the "relative happiness" the investor gains from a particular alternative. If an individual prefers good A to good B, then the utility of A is higher than the utility of B. Thus, the utility function characterizes individual's preferences. Von Neumann and Morgenstern showed that if there is uncertainty, then it is the *expected utility* that characterizes the preferences. The expected utility of an uncertain prospect, often called a *lottery*, is defined as the probability weighted average of the utilities of the simple outcomes. In fact, the expected utility model was first proposed by Daniel Bernoulli in 1738 as a solution to the famous St. Petersburg paradox, but von Neumann and Morgenstern proved that only the expected utility can characterize preferences over lotteries.

The expected utility theory in von Neumann and Morgenstern (1944) defines the lotteries by means of the elementary outcomes and their probability distribution. In this sense, the lotteries can also be interpreted as random variables that can be discrete, continuous, or mixed, and the preference relation is defined on the probability distributions of the random variables. The probability distributions are regarded as *objective*; that is, the theory is consistent with the classical view that, in some sense, the randomness is inherent in nature and all individuals observe the same probability distribution of a given random variable.

In 1954, a decade after the pioneering von Neumann–Morgenstern theory was published, a new theory of decision making under uncertainty appeared. It was based on the concept that probabilities are not objective, rather they are *subjective* and are a numerical expression of the decision maker's beliefs that a given outcome will occur. This theory was developed by Leonard Savage in *The Foundations of Statistics*. Savage (1954) showed that individual's preferences in the presence of uncertainty can be characterized by an expected utility calculated as a weighted average of the utilities of the simple outcomes and the weights are the *subjective* probabilities of the outcomes. The subjective probabilities and the utility function arise as a pair from the individual's preferences. Thus, it is possible to modify the utility function and to obtain another subjective probability measure so that the resulting expected utility also characterizes the individual's preferences. In some aspects, Savage's approach is considered to be more general than the von Neumann-Morgenstern theory.

Another mainstream utility theory describing choices under uncertainty is the state-preference approach of Kenneth Arrow and Gérard Debreu. The basic principle is that the choice under uncertainty is reduced to a choice problem without uncertainty by considering state-contingent bundles of commodities. The agent's preferences are defined over bundles in all states-of-the-world and the notion of randomness is almost ignored. This construction is quite different from the theories of von Neumann–Morgenstern and Savage because preferences are not defined over lotteries. The Arrow-Debreu approach is applied in general equilibrium theories where the payoffs are not measured in monetary amounts but are actual bundles of goods.[1]

In 1992, a new version of the expected utility theory was advanced by Amos Tversky and Daniel Kahneman—the *cumulative prospect theory*. Instead of utility function, they introduce a *value function* that measures the payoff relative to a reference point. Tversky and Kahneman (1992) also introduce a weighting function which changes the cumulative probabilities of the prospect. The cumulative prospect theory is believed to be a superior alternative to the von Neumann-Morgenstern expected utility theory as it resolves some of the puzzles related to it. Nevertheless, the cumulative

---

[1]The equilibrium model was published in Arrow and Debreu (1954).

prospect theory is a *positive theory*, explaining individual's behavior, in contrast to the expected utility theory, which is a *normative theory* prescribing the rational behavior of agents.

The appeal of utility theories stems from the generality in which the choice under uncertainty is considered. On the basis of such general thinking, it is possible to characterize classes of investors by the shape of their utility function, such as nonsatiable investors, risk-averse investors, and so on. Moreover, we are able to identify general rules that a class of investors would follow in choosing between two risky ventures. If all investors of a given class prefer one prospect from another, we say that this prospect *dominates* the other. In this fashion, the first-, second-, and the third-order stochastic dominance relations arise.[2] The stochastic dominance rules characterize the efficient set of a given class of investors; the efficient set consists of all risky ventures that are not dominated by other risky ventures according to the corresponding stochastic dominance relation. Finally, the consequences of stochastic dominance relations are so powerful that any newly formed theory of choice under risk and uncertainty is tested as to whether it is consistent with them.

In this chapter, we briefly describe expected utility theory and the stochastic dominance relations that result. We apply the stochastic dominance relations to the portfolio choice problem and check how the theory of probability metrics can be combined with the stochastic dominance relations.

5.2 EXPECTED UTILITY THEORY

We start with the well-known St. Petersburg Paradox, which is historically the first application of the concept of the expected utility function. As a next step, we describe the essential result of von Neumann–Morgenstern characterization of the preferences of individuals.

5.2.1 St. Petersburg Paradox

St. Petersburg Paradox is a lottery game presented to Daniel Bernoulli by his cousin Nicolas Bernoulli in 1713. Daniel Bernoulli published the solution in 1734 but another Swiss mathematician, Gabriel Cramer, had already discovered parts of the solution in 1728.

---

[2]The theory of stochastic dominance was formulated in the following papers: Hadar and Russel (1969), Hanoch and Levy (1969), Rothschild and Stiglitz (1970), and Whitmore (1970)

The lottery goes as follows. A fair coin is tossed until a head appears. If the head appears on the first toss, the payoff is \$1.[3] If it appears on the second toss, then the payoff is \$2. After that, the payoff increases sharply. If the head appears on the third toss, the payoff is \$4, on the fourth toss it is \$8, and the like. Generally, if the head appears on the n-th toss, the payoff is 2^{n-1} dollars.

At that time, it was commonly accepted that the fair value of a lottery should be computed as the expected value of the payoff. Since a fair coin is tossed, the probability of having a head on the n-th toss equals $1/2^n$,

$$P(\text{First head on trial } n) = P(\text{Tail on trial 1}) \cdot P(\text{Tail on trial 2})$$

$$\cdots \cdot P(\text{Tail on trial } n-1) \cdot P(\text{Head on trial } n) = \frac{1}{2^n}$$

Therefore, the expected payoff is calculated as

$$\text{Expected payoff} = 1 \cdot \tfrac{1}{2} + 2 \cdot \tfrac{1}{4} + \ldots + 2^{n-1} \cdot \tfrac{1}{2^n} + \ldots$$

$$= \tfrac{1}{2} + \tfrac{1}{2} + \ldots + \tfrac{1}{2} + \ldots$$

$$= \infty.$$

This result means that people should be willing to participate in the game no matter how large the price of the ticket. Any price makes the game worthwhile because the expected payoff is infinite. Nevertheless, in reality very few people would be ready to pay as much as \$100 for a ticket.

In order to explain the paradox, Daniel Bernoulli suggested that instead of the actual payoff, the utility of the payoff should be considered. Therefore the fair value is calculated by

$$\text{Fair value} = u(1) \cdot \frac{1}{2} + u(2) \cdot \frac{1}{4} + \ldots + u(2^{n-1}) \cdot \frac{1}{2^n} + \ldots$$

$$= \sum_{k=1}^{\infty} \frac{u(2^{k-1})}{2^n},$$

where the function $u(x)$ is the utility function. The general idea is that the value is determined by the utility an individual gains and not directly by the monetary payoff.

---

[3] Actually, the payoff was in terms of *ducats*—a gold coin used as a trade currency in Europe before World War I.

Daniel Bernoulli considered utility functions with diminishing marginal utility; that is, the utility gained from one extra dollar diminishes with the sum of money one has. In the solution of the paradox, Bernoulli considered logarithmic utility function, $u(x) = \log x$, and showed that the fair value of the lottery equals approximately $2.

The solutions of Bernoulli and Cramer are not completely satisfactory because the lottery can be changed in such a way that the fair value becomes infinite even with their choice of utility functions. Nevertheless, their attempt to solve the problem uses concepts that were later developed into theories of decision making under uncertainty.

5.2.2 The von Neumann–Morgenstern Expected Utility Theory

The St. Petersburg Paradox shows that the naive approach to calculate the fair value of a lottery can lead to counter-intuitive results. A deeper analysis shows that it is the utility gained by an individual that should be considered and not the monetary value of the outcomes. The theory of von Neumann-Morgenstern gives a numerical representation of individual's preferences over lotteries. The numerical representation is obtained through the expected utility, and it turns out that this is the only possible way of obtaining a numerical representation.

We used the term *lottery* in the discussion of the game behind the St. Petersburg Paradox without providing a definition. Technically, a lottery is a probability distribution defined on the set of payoffs. In fact, the lottery in the St. Petersburg Paradox is given in Table 5.1. Generally, lotteries can be discrete, continuous, and mixed. Table 5.1 provides an example of a discrete lottery. In the continuous case, the lottery is described by the *cumulative distribution function* (c.d.f.) of the random payoff. Any portfolio of common stocks, for example, can be regarded as a continuous lottery defined by the c.d.f. of the portfolio payoff. We use the notation P_X to denote the lottery (or the probability distribution), the payoff of which is the random variable X. The particular values of the random payoff (the outcomes) we denote by lower-case letters, x, and the probability that the payoff is below x is denoted by $P(X \leq x) = F_X(x)$, which is in fact the c.d.f.

TABLE 5.1 The Lottery in the St. Petersburg Paradox.

Probability	1/2	1/4	1/8	...	$1/2^n$	...
Payoff	1	2	4	...	2^{n-1}	...

Denote by $\mathcal{X}$ the set of all lotteries. Any element of $\mathcal{X}$ is considered a possible choice of an economic agent. If $P_X \in \mathcal{X}$ and $P_Y \in \mathcal{X}$, then there are the following possible cases:

- The economic agent may prefer P_X to P_Y or be indifferent between them, denoted by $P_X \succeq P_Y$.
- The economic agent may prefer P_Y to P_X or be indifferent between them, denoted by $P_Y \succeq P_X$.
- If both relations hold, $P_Y \succeq P_X$ and $P_X \succeq P_Y$, then we say that the economic agent is indifferent between the two choices, $P_X \sim P_Y$.

Sometimes, for notational convenience, we use $X \succeq Y$ instead of $P_X \succeq P_Y$ without changing the assumption that we are comparing the probability distributions.

A *preference relation* or a *preference order* of an economic agent on the set of all lotteries $\mathcal{X}$ is a relation concerning the ordering of the elements of $\mathcal{X}$, which satisfies certain axioms called the *axioms of choice*. A more detailed description of the axioms of choice is provided in the appendix to this chapter. A numerical representation of a preference order is a real-valued function U defined on the set of lotteries, $U: \mathcal{X} \rightarrow \mathbb{R}$, such that $P_X \succeq P_Y$ if and only if $U(P_X) \geq U(P_Y)$,

$$P_X \succeq P_Y \qquad \Longleftrightarrow \qquad U(P_X) \geq U(P_Y).$$

Thus the numerical representation characterizes the preference order. In fact, we can take advantage of the numerical representation as comparing real numbers is easier than dealing with the preference order directly.

The von Neumann–Morgenstern theory states that if the preference order satisfies certain technical continuity conditions, then the numerical representation U has the form

$$U(P_X) = \int_{\mathbb{R}} u(x)dF_X(x), \tag{5.1}$$

where $u(x)$ is the utility function of the economic agent defined over the elementary outcomes of the random variable X, the probability distribution function of which is $F_X(x)$. Equation (5.1) is actually the mathematical expectation of the random variable $u(X)$,

$$U(P_X) = Eu(X),$$

and for this reason the numerical representation of the preference order is the expected utility.

Note that the preference order is defined by the economic agent; various agents may have different preference orders. In the equivalent numerical representation, it is the utility function $u(x)$ that characterizes U and, therefore, determines the preference order. In effect, the utility function can be regarded as the fundamental building block that describes the agent's preferences.

As we explained, lotteries may be discrete, continuous, or mixed. If the lottery is discrete, then the payoff is a discrete random variable and equation (5.1) becomes

$$U(P_X) = \sum_{j=1}^{n} u(x_j)p_j, \qquad (5.2)$$

where x_j are the outcomes and p_j is the probability that the j-th outcome occurs, $p_j = P(X = x_j)$. The formula for the fair value in the St. Petersburg Paradox given by Daniel Bernoulli has the form of equation (5.2). Thus, the St. Petersburg Paradox is resolved by calculating the fair value through the expected utility of the lottery. If the lottery is such that it has only one possible outcome (i.e., the profit is equal to x with certainty), then the expected utility coincides with the utility of the corresponding payoff, $u(x)$.

5.2.3 Types of Utility Functions

Some properties of the utility function are derived from common arguments valid for investors belonging to a certain category. For example, concerning certain prospects, all investors who prefer more to less are called *nonsatiable*. If there are two prospects, one with a certain payoff of \$100 and another, with a certain payoff of \$200, a nonsatiable investor would never prefer the first opportunity. Therefore, the utility function of any such investor should indicate that the utility corresponding to the first prospect should not be less than the utility of the second one, $u(200) \geq u(100)$. We can generalize that the utility functions of nonsatiable investors should be nondecreasing, and the *nondecreasing property is*

$$u(x) \leq u(y), \text{ if } x \leq y \text{ for any } x, y \in \mathbb{R}.$$

The outcomes x and y can be interpreted as the payoffs of two opportunities without an element of uncertainty, that is, both x and y occur with probability one. If the utility function is differentiable, then the nondecreasing property translates as a nonnegative first derivative, $u'(x) \geq 0$, $x \in \mathbb{R}$.

Other characteristics of investor's preferences can also be described by the shape of the utility function. Suppose that the investor gains a lower utility from a venture with some expected payoff and a prospect with a certain payoff, equal to the expected payoff of the venture; that is, the investor is *risk averse*. Assume that the venture has two possible outcomes—x_1 with probability p and x_2 with probability $1 - p$, $p \in [0, 1]$. Therefore, the expected payoff of the venture equals $px_1 + (1 - p)x_2$. In terms of the utility function, the risk-aversion property is expressed as

$$u(px_1 + (1 - p)x_2) \geq pu(x_1) + (1 - p)u(x_2), \quad \forall x_1, x_2 \text{ and } p \in [0, 1] \quad (5.3)$$

where the left-hand side corresponds to the utility of the certain prospect and the right-hand side is the expected utility of the venture. By definition, if a utility function satisfies (5.3), then it is *concave* and, therefore, the utility functions of risk-averse investors should be concave. That is, concavity $u(x)$ with support on a set S is said to be a concave function if S is a convex set and if $u(x)$ satisfies (5.3) for all $x_1, x_2 \in S$ and $p \in [0, 1]$. If the utility function is twice differentiable, the concavity property translates as a negative second derivative, $u''(x) \leq 0, \forall x \in S$.

A formal measure of absolute risk aversion is the *coefficient of absolute risk aversion*[4] defined by

$$r_A(x) = -\frac{u''(x)}{u'(x)}, \quad (5.4)$$

which indicates that the more curved the utility function is, the higher the risk-aversion level of the investor (the more pronounced the inequality in (5.3) becomes).

Some common examples of utility functions are described as follows.

1. *Linear utility function.*

$$u(x) = a + bx.$$

The linear utility function always satisfies (5.3) with equality and, therefore, represents a risk-neutral investor. If $b > 0$, then it represents a nonsatiable investor.

2. *Quadratic utility function.*

$$u(x) = a + bx + cx^2.$$

If $c < 0$, then the quadratic utility function is concave and represents a risk-averse investor.

3. *Logarithmic utility function.*

$$u(x) = \log x, \qquad x > 0.$$

---

[4]It is also known as the *Arrow-Pratt measure of absolute risk aversion* after the economists Kenneth Arrow and John W. Pratt. See Pratt (1964) and Arrow (1965).

The logarithmic utility represents a nonsatiable, risk-averse investor. It exhibits a decreasing absolute risk aversion since $r_A(x) = 1/x$ and the coefficient of absolute risk aversion decreases with x.

4. *Exponential utility function.*

$$u(x) = -e^{-ax}, \qquad a > 0.$$

The exponential utility represents a nonsatiable, risk-averse investor. It exhibits a constant absolute risk aversion since $r_A(x) = a$ and the coefficient of absolute risk aversion does not depend on x.

5. *Power utility function.*

$$u(x) = \frac{-x^{-a}}{a}, \qquad x > 0, a > 0.$$

The power utility represents a nonsatiable, risk-averse investor. It exhibits a decreasing absolute risk aversion since $r_A(x) = a/x$ and the coefficient of absolute risk aversion decreases with x.

5.3 STOCHASTIC DOMINANCE

In section 5.2.3, we noted that key characteristics of investor's preferences determine the shape of the utility function. For example, all nonsatiable investors have nondecreasing utility functions and all risk-averse investors have concave utility functions. Thus different classes of investors can be defined through the general unifying properties of their utility functions.

Suppose that there are two portfolios X and Y, such that all investors from a given class do not prefer Y to X. This means that the probability distributions of the two portfolios differ in a special way that, no matter the particular expression of the utility function, if an investor belongs to the given class, then Y is not preferred by that investor. In this case, we say that portfolio X dominates portfolio Y with respect to the class of investors. Such a relation is often called a *stochastic dominance relation* or a *stochastic ordering*.

Since it is only a relationship between the probability distributions of X and Y that determines whether X dominates Y for a given class of investors, it appears possible to obtain a criterion characterizing the stochastic dominance, involving only the *cumulative distribution functions* (c.d.f.s) of X and Y. Thus, we are able to identify by only looking at distribution functions of X and Y if any of the two portfolios is preferred by an investor from the class. This section discusses such criteria for three important classes of investors.

5.3.1 First-Order Stochastic Dominance

Suppose that X is an investment opportunity with two possible outcomes—the investor receives \$100 with probability 1/2 and \$200 with probability 1/2. Similarly, Y is a venture with two payoffs—\$150 with probability 1/2 and \$200 with probability 1/2. A nonsatiable investor would never prefer the first opportunity because of the following relationship between the corresponding expected utilities,

$$U(P_X) = u(100)/2 + u(200)/2 \leq u(150)/2 + u(200)/2 = U(P_Y).$$

The inequality arises because $u(100) \leq u(150)$ as a nonsatiable investor by definition prefers more to less.

Denote by $\mathcal{U}_1$ the set of all utility functions representing nonsatiable investors; that is, the set contains all nondecreasing utility functions. We say that the venture X dominates the venture Y in the sense of the *first-order stochastic dominance* (FSD), $X \succeq_{FSD} Y$, if a nonsatiable investor would not prefer Y to X. In terms of the expected utility,

$$X \succeq_{FSD} Y \text{ if } Eu(X) \geq Eu(Y), \text{ for any } u \in \mathcal{U}_1.$$

The condition in terms of the c.d.f.s of X and Y characterizing the FSD order is the following,

$$X \succeq_{FSD} Y \text{ if and only if } F_X(x) \leq F_Y(x), \forall\, x \in \mathbb{R}. \qquad (5.5)$$

where $F_X(x)$ and $F_Y(x)$ are the c.d.f.s of the two ventures.

Figure 5.1 provides an illustration of the relationship between the two c.d.f.s. If X and Y describe the payoff of two portfolios with distribution functions such as the ones plotted in Figure 5.1, then we can conclude that a nonsatiable investor would never invest in Y.

A necessary condition for FSD is that the expected payoff of the preferred venture should exceed the expected payoff of the alternative, $EX \geq EY$ if $X \succeq_{FSD} Y$. This is true because the utility function $u(x) = x$ represents a nonsatiable investor as it is nondecreasing and, therefore, it belongs to the set $\mathcal{U}_1$. Consequently, if X is preferred by all nonsatiable investors, then it is preferred by the investor with utility function $u(x) = x$, which means that the expected utility of X is not less than the expected utility of Y, $EX \geq EY$.

In general, the converse statement does not hold. If the expected payoff of a portfolio exceeds the expected payoff of another portfolio, it does not follow that any nonsatiable investor would necessarily choose the portfolio with the larger expected payoff. This is because the inequality between the

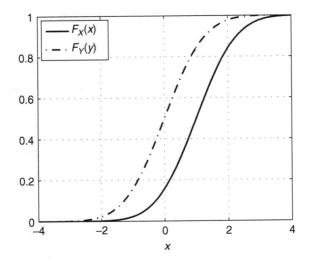

FIGURE 5.1 An illustration of the first-order stochastic dominance condition in terms of the distribution functions, $X \succeq_{FSD} Y$.

c.d.f.s of the two portfolios given in equation (5.5) may not hold. In effect, there will be nonsatiable investors who would choose the portfolio with the larger expected payoff and other nonsatiable investors who would choose the portfolio with the smaller expected payoff. It depends on the particular expression of the utility function such as whether it is a logarithmic or a power utility function.

5.3.2 Second-Order Stochastic Dominance

For decision making under risk, the concept of first-order stochastic dominance is not very useful because the condition in (5.5) is rather restrictive. According to the analysis in the previous section, if the distribution functions of two portfolios satisfy (5.5), then a nonsatiable investor would never prefer portfolio Y. This conclusion also holds for the subcategory of the nonsatiable investors who are also risk-averse. Therefore, the condition in (5.5) is only a sufficient condition for this subcategory of investors but is unable to characterize completely their preferences. This is demonstrated in the following example.

Consider a venture Y with two possible payoffs—$100 with probability 1/2 and $200 with probability 1/2, and a prospect X yielding $180 with probability one. A nonsatiable, risk-averse investor would never prefer

Y to X because the expected utility of Y is not larger than the expected utility of X,

$$Eu(X) = u(180) \geq u(150) \geq u(100)/2 + u(200)/2 = Eu(Y),$$

where $u(x)$ satisfies property (5.3) and is assumed to be nondecreasing. The distribution functions of X and Y do not satisfy (5.5). Nevertheless, a nonsatiable, risk-averse investor would never prefer Y.

Denote by $\mathcal{U}_2$ the set of all utility functions that are nondecreasing and concave. Thus, the set $\mathcal{U}_2$ represents the nonsatiable, risk-averse investors and is a subset of $\mathcal{U}_1$, $\mathcal{U}_2 \subset \mathcal{U}_1$. We say that a venture X dominates venture Y in the sense of *second-order stochastic dominance* (SSD), $X \succeq_{SSD} Y$, if a nonsatiable, risk-averse investor does not prefer Y to X. In terms of the expected utility, $X \succeq_{SSD} Y$ if $Eu(X) \geq Eu(Y)$, for any $u \in \mathcal{U}_2$.

The condition in terms of the c.d.f.s of X and Y characterizing the SSD order is the following,

$$X \succeq_{SSD} Y \iff \int_{-\infty}^{x} F_X(t)dt \leq \int_{-\infty}^{x} F_Y(t)dt, \forall x \in \mathbb{R}, \qquad (5.6)$$

where $F_X(t)$ and $F_Y(t)$ are the c.d.f.s of the two ventures.

Similarly to FSD, inequality between the expected payoffs is a necessary condition for SSD, $EX \geq EY$ if $X \succeq_{SSD} Y$, because the utility function $u(x) = x$ belongs to the set $\mathcal{U}_2$. In contrast to the FSD, the condition in (5.6) allows the distribution functions to intersect. It turns out that if the distribution functions cross only once, then X dominates Y with respect to SSD if $F_X(x)$ is below $F_Y(x)$ to the left of the crossing point. Such an illustration is provided in Figure 5.2.

5.3.3 Rothschild-Stiglitz Stochastic Dominance

In the SSD order, we considered the class of all nonsatiable and risk-averse investors. Rothschild and Stiglitz (1970) introduce a slightly different order by dropping the requirement that the investors are nonsatiable. A venture X is said to dominate a venture Y in the sense of *Rothschild-Stiglitz stochastic dominance* (RSD),[5] $X \succeq_{RSD} Y$, if no risk-averse investor prefers Y to X. In terms of the expected utility, $X \succeq_{RSD} Y$ if $Eu(X) \geq Eu(Y)$, for any concave $u(x)$.

The class of risk-averse investors is represented by the set of all concave utility functions, which contains the set $\mathcal{U}_2$. Thus, the condition in (5.6) is only a necessary condition for the RSD but it is not sufficient to characterize

---

[5]The Rothschild-Stiglitz stochastic dominance order is also called *concave order*.

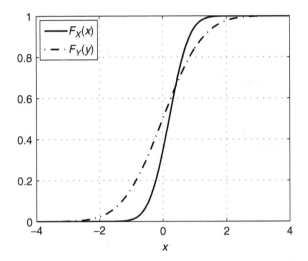

FIGURE 5.2 An illustration of the second-order stochastic dominance condition in terms of the distribution functions, $X \succeq_{SSD} Y$.

the RSD order. If the portfolio X dominates the portfolio Y in the sense of the RSD order, then a risk-averter would never prefer Y to X. This conclusion holds for the nonsatiable risk-averters as well and, therefore, the relation in (5.6) holds as a consequence,

$$X \succeq_{RSD} Y \implies X \succeq_{SSD} Y.$$

The converse relation is not true. This can be demonstrated with the help of the example developed in section 5.3.2. If the portfolio Y pays off \$100 with probability 1/2 and \$200 with probability 1/2, then no risk-averse investor would prefer it to a prospect yielding \$150 with probability one,

$$u(150) = u(100/2 + 200/2) \geq u(100)/2 + u(200)/2 = Eu(Y),$$

which is just an application of the assumption of concavity in (5.3). It is not possible to determine whether a risk-averse investor would prefer a prospect yielding \$150 with probability one or the prospect X yielding \$180 with probability one. Those who are nonsatiable would certainly prefer the larger sum but this is not universally true for all risk-averse investors because we do not assume that $u(x)$ is nondecreasing.

The condition that characterizes the RSD stochastic dominance is the following one,

$$X \succeq_{RSD} Y \iff \begin{cases} EX = EY, \\ \int_{-\infty}^{x} F_X(t)dt \leq \int_{-\infty}^{x} F_Y(t)dt, \forall \; x \in \mathbb{R}. \end{cases} \qquad (5.7)$$

In fact, this is the condition for the SSD order with the additional assumption that the mean payoffs should coincide.

5.3.4   Third-Order Stochastic Dominance

We defined the coefficient of absolute risk aversion $r_A(x)$ in equation (5.4). Generally, its values vary for different payoffs depending on the corresponding derivatives of the utility function. Larger values of $r_A(x)$ correspond to a more pronounced risk-aversion effect.

In section 5.2.3, we noted that a negative second derivative of the utility function for all payoffs means that the investor is risk-averse at any payoff level. Therefore, the closer $u''(x)$ to zero, the less risk-averse the investor since the coefficient $r_A(x)$ decreases, other things held equal. The logarithmic utility function is an example of a utility function exhibiting decreasing absolute risk aversion. The larger the payoff level, the less curved the function is, which corresponds to a closer to zero second derivative and a less pronounced risk-aversion property. An illustration is given in Figure 5.3.

Utility functions exhibiting a decreasing absolute risk aversion are important because the investors they represent favor positive to negative skewness. This is a consequence of the decreasing risk aversion—at higher payoff levels such investors are less inclined to avoid risk in comparison to lower payoff levels at which they are much more sensitive to risk taking. Technically, a utility function with a decreasing absolute risk aversion has a nonnegative third derivative, $u'''(x) \geq 0$, as this means that the second derivative is nondecreasing. A plot of the density graphs of a positively and a negatively skewed distribution is given in Figure 1.4 in Chapter 1.

Denote by $\mathcal{U}_3$ the set of all utility functions that are nondecreasing, concave, and have a nonnegative third derivative, $u'''(x) \geq 0$. Thus, $\mathcal{U}_3$ represents the class of nonsatiable, risk-averse investors who prefer positive to negative skewness. A venture X is said to dominate a venture Y in the sense of *third-order stochastic dominance* (TSD), $X \succeq_{TSD} Y$, if an investor with a utility function from the set $\mathcal{U}_3$ does not prefer Y to X. In terms of the expected utility, $X \succeq_{TSD} Y$ if $Eu(X) \geq Eu(Y)$, for any $u \in \mathcal{U}_3$.

The set of utility functions $\mathcal{U}_3$ is contained in the set of nondecreasing, concave utilities, $\mathcal{U}_3 \subset \mathcal{U}_2$. Therefore, the condition (5.6) for SSD is only

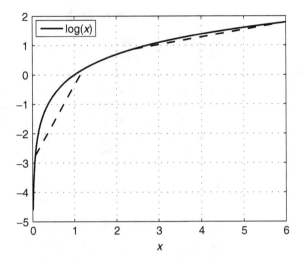

FIGURE 5.3 The graph of the logarithmic utility function, $u(x) = \log x$. For smaller values of x, the graph is more curved while, for larger values of x, the graph is closer to a straight line and thus to risk neutrality.

sufficient in the case of TSD,

$$X \succeq_{SSD} Y \implies X \succeq_{TSD} Y.$$

The condition which characterizes the TSD stochastic dominance is the following one,

$$X \succeq_{TSD} Y \iff E(X - t)_+^2 \leq E(Y - t)_+^2, \forall\, t \in \mathbb{R} \qquad (5.8)$$

where the notation $(x - t)_+^2$ means the maximum between $x - t$ and zero raised to the second power, $(x - t)_+^2 = (\max(x - t, 0))^2$. The quantity $E(X - t)_+^2$ is known as the *second lower partial moment* of the random variable X. It measures the variability of X below a target payoff level t. Suppose that X and Y have equal means and variances. If X has a positive skewness and Y has a negative skewness, then the variability of X below any target payoff level t will be smaller than the variability of Y below the same target payoff level.

At first sight, equation (5.8) has nothing to do with (5.6) and it is not clear that SSD entails TSD. In fact, it is only a matter of algebraic manipulations to show that, indeed, if (5.6) holds, then (5.8) holds as well.

5.3.5 Efficient Sets and the Portfolio Choice Problem

Taking advantage of the criteria for stochastic dominance discussed in the previous sections, we can characterize the *efficient sets* of the corresponding categories of investors. The efficient set of a given class of investors is defined as the set of ventures not dominated with respect to the corresponding stochastic dominance relation. For example, the efficient set of the nonsatiable investors is the set of those ventures which are not dominated with respect to the FSD order. As a result, by construction, any venture which is not in the efficient set will be necessarily discarded by all investors in the class.

The portfolio choice problem of a given investor can be divided into two steps. The first step concerns finding the efficient set of the class of investors which the given investor belongs to. Any portfolio not belonging to the efficient set will not be selected by any of the investors in the class and is, therefore, suboptimal for the investor. Such a class may be composed of, for example, all nonsatiable, risk-averse investors if the utility function of the given investor is nondecreasing and concave. In this case, the efficient set comprises all portfolios not dominated with respect to the SSD order. Note that in this step, we do not take advantage of the particular expression for the utility function of the investor.

Once we have obtained the efficient set, we proceed to the second step in which we calculate the expected utility of the investor for the portfolios in the efficient set. The portfolio that maximizes the investor's expected utility represents the optimal choice of the investor.

The difficulty of adopting this approach in practice is that it is very hard to obtain explicitly the efficient sets. That is why the problem of finding the optimal portfolio for the investor is very often replaced by a more simple one, involving only certain characteristics of the portfolios return distributions, such as the expected return and the risk. In this situation, it is critical that the more simple problem is consistent with the corresponding stochastic dominance relation in order to guarantee that its solution is among the portfolios in the efficient set. Checking the consistency reduces to choosing a risk measure which is compatible with the stochastic dominance relation.

5.3.6 Return versus Payoff

Note that the expected utility theory deals with the portfolio payoff and not the portfolio return. Nevertheless, all relations defining the stochastic dominance orders can be adopted if we consider the distribution functions of portfolio *returns* rather than portfolio *profits*. In the following, we examine the FSD and SSD orders concerning log-return distributions and the connection to the corresponding orders concerning random payoffs. The logarithmic return, or simply the log-return, is a central concept in fundamental theories in finance, such as derivative pricing and modern portfolio theory. Therefore, it makes sense to consider stochastic orders with respect to log-return distributions rather than payoff.

Suppose that P_t is a random variable describing the price of a common stock at a future time t, $t > 0$ where $t = 0$ is present time. Without loss of generality, we can assume that the stock does not pay dividends. Denote by r_t the log-return for the period $(0, t)$,

$$r_t = \log \frac{P_t}{P_0},$$

where P_0 is the price of the common stock at present and is a nonrandom positive quantity. The random variable P_t can be regarded as the random payoff of the common stock at time t, while r_t is the corresponding random log-return. The formula expressing the random payoff in terms of the random log-return is

$$P_t = P_0 \exp(r_t).$$

Even though log-returns and payoffs are directly linked by means of the above formulae, it turns out that, generally, stochastic dominance relations concerning two log-return distributions are not equivalent to the corresponding stochastic dominance relations concerning their payoff distributions.

Consider an investor with utility function $u(x)$ where $x > 0$ stands for payoff. In the appendix to this chapter, we demonstrate that the utility function of the investor concerning the log-return can be expressed as

$$v(y) = u(P_0 \exp(y)), y \in \mathbb{R} \tag{5.9}$$

where y stands for the log-return of a common stock and P_0 is the price at present.[6] Equation (5.9) and the inverse,

$$u(x) = v(\log(x/P_0)), x > 0 \tag{5.10}$$

provide the link between utilities concerning log-returns and payoff.

It turns out that an investor who is nonsatiable and risk-averse with respect to payoff distributions may not be risk-averse with respect to

---

[6]In fact, the correct relationship is a positive linear transform of the function u but this detail is immaterial for the discussion which follows.

log-return distributions. The utility function $u(x)$ representing such an investor has the properties

$$u'(x) \geq 0 \quad \text{and} \quad u''(x) \leq 0, \forall\, x > 0,$$

but it does not follow that the function $v(y)$ given by equation (5.9) will satisfy them. In fact, $v(y)$ also has nonpositive first derivative but the sign of the second derivative can be arbitrary. Therefore, the investor is nonsatiable, but may not be risk-averse with respect to log-return distributions. This is illustrated in Figure 5.4 for the exponential utility function.

Conversely, an investor who is nonsatiable and risk-averse with respect to log-return distributions, is also nonsatiable and risk-averse with concerning payoff distributions. This is true because if $v(y)$ satisfies the corresponding derivative inequalities, so does $u(x)$ given by (5.10). Consequently, it follows that the investors who are nonsatiable and risk-averse on the space of log-return distributions are a subclass of those who are nonsatiable and risk-averse on the space of payoff distributions.

This analysis implies that the FSD order of two common stocks, for example, remains unaffected as to whether we consider their payoff distributions or their log-return distributions,

$$P_t^1 \succeq_{FSD} P_t^2 \qquad \Longleftrightarrow \qquad r_t^1 \succeq_{FSD} r_t^2,$$

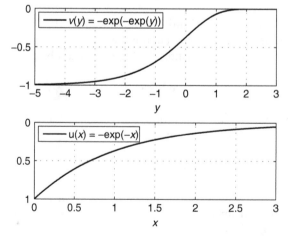

FIGURE 5.4 $u(x)$ represents a nonsatiable and risk-averse investor on the space of payoffs and $v(y)$ is the corresponding utility on the space of log-returns. Apparently, $v(y)$ is not concave.

where P_t^1 and P_t^2 are the payoffs of the two common stocks at time $t > t_0$, and r_t^1 and r_t^2 are the corresponding log-returns for the same period. However, such an equivalence does not hold for the SSD order. Actually, the SSD order on the space of payoff distributions implies the same order on the space of log-return distributions but not vice versa,

$$P_t^1 \succeq_{SSD} P_t^2 \quad \Longrightarrow \quad r_t^1 \succeq_{SSD} r_t^2.$$

In the appendix to this chapter, we demonstrate that the same conclusion holds for the TSD order and, generally, for the n-th order stochastic dominance, $n > 1$. Such kind of relations deserve a closer scrutiny as optimal portfolio problems are usually set in terms of returns and consistency with a stochastic dominance relation implies that the stochastic dominance relation is also set on the space of return distributions, not on the space of payoff distributions. Moreover, in this section we considered only one-period returns. In a multiperiod setting, for example in the area of asset-liability management, matters get even more involved.

Note that these relations are always true if the present values of the two ventures are equal $P_0^1 = P_0^2$. Otherwise they may be violated. Consider, for example, the FSD order of random payoffs. Suppose that P_t^1 dominates P_t^2 with respect to the FSD order, $P_t^1 \succeq_{FSD} P_t^2$. Then, according to the characterization in terms of the c.d.f.s we obtain

$$F_{P_t^1}(x) \leq F_{P_t^2}(x), \quad \forall x \in \mathbb{R}.$$

We can represent this inequality in terms of the log-returns r_t^1 and r_t^2 in the following way:

$$P\left(r_t^1 \leq \log \frac{x}{P_0^1}\right) \leq P\left(r_t^2 \leq \log \frac{x}{P_0^2}\right), \quad \forall x \in \mathbb{R}.$$

In fact, the above inequality implies that $r_t^1 \succeq_{FSD} r_t^2$ if $P_0^1 = P_0^2$. In case the present values of the ventures differ a lot, it may happen that the c.d.f.s of the log-return distributions do not satisfy the inequality $F_{r_t^1}(y) \leq F_{r_t^2}(y)$ for all $y \in \mathbb{R}$, which means that the FSD order may not hold.

5.4 PROBABILITY METRICS AND STOCHASTIC DOMINANCE

The conditions for stochastic dominance involving the distribution functions of the ventures X and Y represent a powerful method to determine if an entire class of investors would prefer any of the portfolios. For example, in order to verify if any nonsatiable, risk-averse investor would not prefer Y to X, we have to verify if condition (5.6) holds. Note that a negative result does not necessarily mean that any such investor would actually prefer Y or be indifferent between X and Y. It may be the case that the inequality between the quantities in (5.6) is satisfied for some values of the argument, and for others, the converse inequality holds. That is, neither $X \succeq_{SSD} Y$ nor $Y \succeq_{SSD} X$ is true. Thus, only a part of the nonsatiable, risk-averse investors may prefer X to Y; it now depends on the particular investor we consider.

Suppose the verification confirms that either X is preferred or the investors are indifferent between X and Y, $X \succeq_{SSD} Y$. This result is only qualitative, there are no indications whether Y would be categorically disregarded by all investors in the class, or the differences between the two portfolios are very small. Similarly, if we know that no investors from the class prefer Y to Z, $Z \succeq_{SSD} Y$, then can we determine whether Z is more strongly preferred to Y than X is?

The only way to approach these questions is to add a quantitative element through a probability metric since only by means of a probability metric can we calculate distances between random quantities.[7] For example, we can choose a probability metric μ and we can calculate the distances $\mu(X, Y)$ and $\mu(Z, Y)$. If $\mu(X, Y) < \mu(Z, Y)$, then the return distribution of X is closer to the return distribution of Y than are the return distributions of Z and Y. On this ground, we can draw the conclusion that Z is more strongly preferred to Y than X is, on condition that we know in advance the relations $X \succeq_{SSD} Y$ and $Z \succeq_{SSD} Y$.

However, not any probability metric appears suitable for this calculation. This is illustrated by the following example. Suppose that Y and X are normally distributed random variables describing portfolio returns with equal means, $X \in N(a, \sigma_X^2)$ and $Y \in N(a, \sigma_Y^2)$, with $\sigma_X^2 < \sigma_Y^2$. Z is a prospect yielding a dollars with probability one. The c.d.f.s $F_X(x)$ and $F_Y(x)$ cross only once at $x = a$ and the $F_X(x)$ is below $F_Y(x)$ to the left of the crossing point because the variance of X is assumed to be smaller than the variance of Y. Therefore, according to the condition in (5.7), no risk-averse investor would prefer Y to X and consequently $X \succeq_{SSD} Y$. The prospect Z provides a nonrandom return equal to the expected returns of X and Y, $EX = EY = a$, and, in effect, any risk-averse investor would rather choose Z from the three alternatives, $Z \succeq_{SSD} X \succeq_{SSD} Y$.

A probability metric with which we would like to quantify the second-order stochastic dominance relation should be able to indicate that, first, $\mu(X, Y) < \mu(Z, Y)$ because Z is more strongly preferred to Y and, second, $\mu(Z, X) < \mu(Z, Y)$ because Y is more strongly rejected than X with

---

[7]Chapter 3 provides more background on probability metrics.

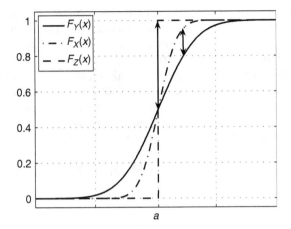

FIGURE 5.5 The distribution functions of two normal distributions with equal means, $EX = EY = a$ and the distribution function of $Z = a$ with probability one. The arrows indicate the corresponding Kolmogorov distances.

respect to Z. The assumptions in the example give us the information to order completely the three alternatives and that is why we are expecting the two inequalities should hold.

Let us choose the Kolmogorov metric,[8]

$$\rho(X, Y) = \sup_{x \in \mathbb{R}} |F_X(x) - F_Y(x)|,$$

for the purpose of calculating the corresponding distances. It computes the largest absolute difference between the two distribution functions. Applying the definition to the distributions in the example, we obtain that $\rho(X, Z) = \rho(Y, Z) = 1/2$ and $\rho(X, Y) < 1/2$. As a result, the Kolmogorov metric is capable of showing that Z is more strongly preferred relative to Y but cannot show that Y is more strongly rejected with respect to Z. Figure 5.5 contains a plot of the c.d.f.s of the three random variables. The arrows indicate where the largest absolute difference between the corresponding c.d.f.s is located. The arrow length equals the Kolmogorov distance.

The example shows that there are probability metrics, which are not appropriate to quantify a stochastic dominance order. The task of finding a suitable metric is not a simple one because the structure of the metric

---

[8]The Kolmogorov metric $\rho(X, Y)$ is introduced in Chapter 3. See equation (3.9).

should be based on the conditions defining the dominance order. Inevitably, we cannot expect that one probability metric will appear suitable for all stochastic orders, rather, a probability metric may be best suited for a selected stochastic dominance relation.

Technically, we have to impose another condition in order for the problem of quantification to have a practical meaning. The probability metric calculating the distances between the ordered random variables should be bounded. If it explodes, then we cannot draw any conclusions. For instance, if $\mu(X, Y) = \infty$ and $\mu(Z, Y) = \infty$, then we cannot compare the investors' preferences.

Concerning the FSD order, a suitable choice for a probability metric is the Kantorovich metric,

$$\kappa(X, Y) = \int_{-\infty}^{\infty} |F_X(x) - F_Y(x)| dx,$$

introduced in section 3.3 of Chapter 3. Note that the condition in (5.5) can be restated as $F_X(x) - F_X(x) \leq 0, \forall x \in \mathbb{R}$. Thus summing up all absolute differences gives an idea how close X is to Y, which is a natural way of measuring the distance between X and Y with respect to the FSD order. The Kantorovich metric is finite as long as the random variables have finite means. We can always count on this assumption if the random variables describe portfolio returns, for example.

The RSD order can also be quantified in a similar fashion. Consider the Zolotarev ideal metric,

$$\zeta_2(X, Y) = \int_{-\infty}^{\infty} \left| \int_{-\infty}^{x} F_X(t) dt - \int_{-\infty}^{x} F_Y(t) dt \right| dx,$$

introduced in section 4.4 of Chapter 4. The structure of this probability metric is directly based on the condition in (5.7), and it calculates in a natural way the distance between X and Y with respect to the RSD order. The requirement that $EX = EY$ in (5.7) combined with the additional assumption that the second moments of X and Y are finite, $EX^2 < \infty$ and $EY^2 < \infty$, represents the needed sufficient conditions for the boundedness of $\zeta_2(X, Y)$. Additional information about ideal metrics is provided in Chapter 4 and its appendix.

Due to the similarities of the conditions (5.6) and (5.8), defining the SSD and the TSD orders and the structure of the Rachev ideal metric defined in (4.14) in section 4.4 of Chapter 4, it is reasonable to expect that the Rachev ideal metric is best suited to quantify the SSD and the TSD orders. The appendix to this chapter contains a generalization of the FSD, SSD, and TSD orders that confirms that the Rachev ideal metric has the appropriate structure to quantify the n-th order stochastic dominance. There are additional assumptions that have to be made for the random variables X and Y ensuring that the Rachev ideal metric is finite. These assumptions are related to the equality of certain moments and are common for all ideal metrics. They can be found in the appendix to Chapter 4.

5.5 SUMMARY

In this chapter, we considered the problem of choice under uncertainty as described by the classical von Neumann–Morgenstern expected utility theory. We also described the most important types of stochastic dominance relations resulting from the theory, which characterize the choices of entire classes of investors. One application of the theory of probability metrics in stochastic dominance relations is to add a quantitative element to their qualitative nature. Instead of knowing only that a venture is preferred to another venture by a whole class of investors, a probability metric is capable of showing if the differences between the two ventures are very small, or one of the two ventures is categorically discarded by the entire class.

Another major point concerning stochastic dominance relations is to take into account if probability distributions of returns or payoffs are considered. Usually, optimal portfolio problems are set in terms of returns and consistency with the SSD order is sought. In such a case, the SSD order concerns distributions of returns, rather than payoffs, and this should be borne in mind when analyzing the solution.

5.6 TECHNICAL APPENDIX

In this appendix, we state the axioms of choice, which are the basis for von Neumann–Morgenstern theory, and we comment on the uniqueness of the expected utility representation of a preference order. The stochastic orders given in the chapter concern the most important classes of investors. We give examples of several others in the appendix. Finally, we briefly mention a parallel between representations of probability metrics known as *dual* and stochastic orders.

5.6.1 The Axioms of Choice

The axioms of choice are fundamental assumptions defining a preference order. In the following, $\mathcal{X}$ stands for the set of the probability distributions of the ventures also known as lotteries, and the notation $P_X \succeq P_Y$ means that the economic agent prefers P_X to P_Y or is indifferent between the two choices. The notation $P_X \succ P_Y$ means that P_X is strictly preferred to P_Y. The axioms of choice are the following:

Completeness. For all $P_X, P_Y \in \mathcal{X}$, either $P_X \succeq P_Y$ or $P_Y \succeq P_X$ or both are true, $P_X \sim P_Y$.

Transitivity. If $P_X \succeq P_Y$ and $P_Y \succeq P_Z$, then $P_X \succeq P_Z$, where P_X, P_Y and P_Z are three lotteries.

Archimedean axiom. If $P_X, P_Y, P_Z \in \mathcal{X}$ are such that $P_X \succ P_Y \succ P_Z$, then there is an $\alpha, \beta \in (0, 1)$ such that $\alpha P_X + (1 - \alpha)P_Z \succ P_Y$ and also $P_Y \succ \beta P_X + (1 - \beta)P_Z$.

Independence axiom. For all $P_X, P_Y, P_Z \in \mathcal{X}$ and any $\alpha \in [0, 1]$, $P_X \succeq P_Y$ if and only if $\alpha P_X + (1 - \alpha)P_Z \succeq \alpha P_Y + (1 - \alpha)P_Z$.

The completeness axiom states that economic agents should always be able to compare two lotteries, that is, two portfolios. They either prefer one or the other, or are indifferent. The transitivity axiom rules out the possibility that an investor may prefer P_X to P_Y, P_Y to P_Z, and also P_Z to P_X. It states that if the first two relations hold, then necessarily the investor should prefer P_X to P_Z. The Archimedean axiom is like a "continuity" condition. It states that given any three distributions strictly preferred to each other, we can combine the most and the least preferred distribution through an $\alpha \in (0, 1)$ such that the resulting distribution is strictly preferred to the middle distribution. Likewise, we can combine the most and the least preferred distribution through a $\beta \in (0, 1)$ so that the middle distribution is strictly preferred to the resulting distribution. The independence axiom claims that the preference between two lotteries remains unaffected if they are both combined in the same way with a third lottery.

The basic result of von Neumann–Morgenstern is that a preference relation satisfies the four axioms of choice if and only if there is a real-valued function, $U: \mathcal{X} \rightarrow \mathbb{R}$, such that:

1. U represents the preference order,

$$P_X \succeq P_Y \qquad \Longleftrightarrow \qquad U(P_X) \geq U(P_Y)$$

for all $P_X, P_Y \in \mathcal{X}$.
2. U has the linear property,[9]

$$U(\alpha P_X + (1 - \alpha)P_Y) = \alpha U(P_X) + (1 - \alpha)U(P_Y)$$

for any $\alpha \in (0, 1)$ and $P_X, P_Y \in \mathcal{X}$.

---

[9]Functions satisfying this property are also called *affine*.

Moreover, the numerical representation U is unique up to a positive linear transform. That is, if U_1 and U_2 are two functions representing one and the same preference order, then $U_2 = aU_1 + b$ where $a > 0$ and b are some coefficients.

It turns out that the numerical representation has a very special form under some additional technical continuity conditions. It can be expressed as

$$U(P_X) = \int_{\mathbb{R}} u(x)dF_X(x)$$

where the function $u(x)$ is the utility function of the economic agent and $F_X(x)$ is the c.d.f. of the probability distribution P_X. Thus the numerical representation of the preference order of an economic agent is the expected utility of X. The fact that U is known up to a positive linear transform means that the utility function of the economic agent is not determined uniquely from the preference order but is also unique up to a positive linear transform.

5.6.2 Stochastic Dominance Relations of Order n

In this chapter, we introduced the first-, second-, and third-order stochastic dominance relations that represent nonsatiable investors, nonsatiable and risk-averse investors, and nonsatiable, risk-averse investors preferring positive to negative skewness. That is, including additional characteristics of the investors by imposing conditions on the utility function, we end up with more refined stochastic orders.

This method can be generalized in the n-th order stochastic dominance. Denote by $\mathcal{U}_n$ the set of all utility functions, the derivatives of which satisfy the inequalities $(-1)^{k+1}u^{(k)}(x) \geq 0$, $k = 1, 2, \ldots, n$ where $u^{(k)}(x)$ denotes the k-th derivative of $u(x)$. For each n, we have a set of utility functions that is a subset of $\mathcal{U}_{n-1}$,

$$\mathcal{U}_1 \subset \mathcal{U}_2 \subset \ldots \subset \mathcal{U}_n \subset \ldots$$

The classes of investors characterized by the first-, second-, and third-order stochastic dominance are $\mathcal{U}_1, \mathcal{U}_2$, and $\mathcal{U}_3$.

Imposing further properties on the derivatives of the utility function requires that we make more assumptions for the moments of the random variables we consider. We assume that the absolute moments $E|X|^k$ and $E|Y|^k$, $k = 1, \ldots, n$ of the random variables X and Y are finite. We say that the portfolio X dominates the portfolio Y in the sense of the n-th order stochastic dominance, $X \succeq_n Y$, if no investor with a utility function in the set $\mathcal{U}_n$ would prefer Y to X,

$$X \succeq_n Y \quad \text{if} \quad Eu(X) \geq Eu(Y), \forall u(x) \in \mathcal{U}_n.$$

Therefore, the first-, second-, and third-order stochastic dominance appear as special cases from the n-th order stochastic dominance with $n = 1, 2, 3$.

There is an equivalent way of describing the n-th order stochastic dominance in terms of the c.d.f.s of the ventures only. The condition is the following one,

$$X \succeq_n Y \qquad \Longleftrightarrow \qquad F_X^{(n)}(x) \leq F_Y^{(n)}(x), \forall x \in \mathbb{R} \qquad (5.11)$$

where $F_X^{(n)}(x)$ stands for the n-th integral of the c.d.f. of X, which can be defined recursively as

$$F_X^{(n)}(x) = \int_{-\infty}^{x} F_X^{(n-1)}(t)dt.$$

An equivalent form of the condition in (5.11) can be derived, which is close to the form of (5.8),

$$X \succeq_n Y \qquad \Longleftrightarrow \qquad E(t - X)_+^{n-1} \leq E(t - Y)_+^{n-1}, \forall t \in \mathbb{R}, \qquad (5.12)$$

where $(t - x)_+^{n-1} = \max(t - x, 0)^{n-1}$. This equivalent formulation clarifies why it is necessary to assume that all absolute moments until order n are finite.

Since, in the n-th order stochastic dominance, we furnish the conditions on the utility function as n increases, the following relation holds,

$$X \succeq_1 Y \quad \Longrightarrow \quad X \succeq_2 Y \quad \Longrightarrow \quad \dots \quad \Longrightarrow \quad X \succeq_n Y,$$

which generalizes the relationship between FSD, SSD, and TSD given in the chapter.

Further on, it is possible to extend the n-th order stochastic dominance to the α-order stochastic dominance in which $\alpha \geq 1$ is a real number and instead of the ordinary integrals of the c.d.f.s, fractional integrals are involved. Ortobelli et al. (2007) provide more information on extensions of stochastic dominance orderings and their relation to probability metrics and risk measures.

5.6.3 Return versus Payoff and Stochastic Dominance

The lotteries in von Neumann–Morgenstern theory are usually interpreted as probability distributions of payoffs. That is, the domain of the utility function $u(x)$ is the positive half-line, which is interpreted as the collection of all possible outcomes in terms of dollars from a given venture. Assume that the payoff distribution is actually the price distribution P_t of a financial asset at a future time t. In line with the von Neumann–Morgenstern theory, the expected utility of P_t for an investor with utility function $u(x)$ is given by

$$U(P_t) = \int_0^\infty u(x)dF_{P_t}(x) \tag{5.13}$$

where $F_{P_t}(x) = P(P_t \le x)$ is the c.d.f. of the random variable P_t. Further on, suppose that the price of the common stock at the present time is P_0. Consider the substitution $x = P_0 \exp(y)$. Under the new variable, the c.d.f. of P_t changes to

$$F_{P_t}(P_0 \exp(y)) = P(P_t \le P_0 \exp(y)) = P\left(\log \frac{P_t}{P_0} \le y\right),$$

which is the distribution function of the log-return of the financial asset $r_t = \log(P_t/P_0)$. The integration range changes from the positive half-line to the entire real line and equation (5.13) becomes

$$U(P_t) = \int_{-\infty}^\infty u(P_0 \exp(y))dF_{r_t}(y). \tag{5.14}$$

On the other hand, the expected utility of the log-return distribution has the form

$$U(r_t) = \int_{-\infty}^\infty v(y)dF_{r_t}(y) \tag{5.15}$$

where $v(y)$ is the utility function of the investor on the space of log-returns which is unique up to a positive linear transform. Note that $v(y)$ is defined on the entire real line as the log-return can be any real number.

Compare equations (5.14) and (5.15). From the uniqueness of the expected utility representation, it appears that (5.14) is the expected utility of the log-return distribution. Therefore, the utility function $v(y)$ can be computed by means of the utility function u,

$$v(y) = a.u(P_0 \exp(y)) + b, \quad a > 0 \tag{5.16}$$

in which the constants a and b appear because of the uniqueness result. Conversely, the utility function $u(x)$ can be expressed via v,

$$u(x) = c.v(\log(x/P_0)) + d, \quad c > 0. \tag{5.17}$$

Note that the two utilities in equations (5.14) and (5.15) are identical (up to a positive linear transform), and this is not surprising. In our reasoning, the investor is one and the same. We only change the way we look at the venture, in terms of payoff or log-return, but the venture is also fixed. As a result, we cannot expect that the utility gained by the investor will fluctuate depending on the point of view.

Because of the relationship between the functions u and v, properties imposed on the utility function u may not transfer to the function v and vice versa. We remark on what happens with the properties connected with the n-th order stochastic dominance given in this appendix. Suppose that the utility function $v(y)$ belongs to the set $\mathcal{U}_n$, i.e., it satisfies the conditions

$$(-1)^{k+1} v^{(k)}(y) \geq 0, \quad k = 1, 2, \ldots, n$$

where $v^{(k)}(y)$ denotes the k-th derivative of $v(y)$. It turns out that the function $u(x)$ given by (5.17) satisfies the same properties and, therefore, it also belongs to the set $\mathcal{U}_n$. This is verified directly by differentiation.

In the reverse direction, the statement holds only for $n = 1$. That is, if $u \in \mathcal{U}_n$, $n > 1$, then the function v given in (5.16) may not belong to $\mathcal{U}_n$, $n > 1$, and we obtain a set of functions to which $\mathcal{U}_n$ is a subset. In effect, the n-th degree stochastic dominance, $n > 1$, on the space of payoffs implies the n-th degree stochastic dominance, $n > 1$, on the space of the corresponding log-returns but not vice versa,

$$P_t^1 \succeq_n P_t^2 \quad \Longrightarrow \quad r_t^1 \succeq_n r_t^2.$$

where P_t^1 and P_t^2 are the payoffs of the two common stocks, for example, at time $t > 0$, and r_t^1 and r_t^2 are the corresponding log-returns for the same period.

Note that this relationship holds if we assume that the prices of the two common stocks at the present time are equal to $P_0^1 = P_0^2 = P_0$. Otherwise, as we demonstrated in the chapter, no such relationship may exist.

5.6.4 Other Stochastic Dominance Relations

There are ways of obtaining stochastic dominance relations other than the n-th order stochastic dominance, which is based on certain properties of investors' utility functions. We borrow an example from reliability theory and adapt it for distributions describing payoffs, losses or returns.[10] The condition defining the order relation is based on the tail behavior of the corresponding distribution.

---

[10]Rachev (1985) and Kalashnikov and Rachev (1990) provide more details on the application of the stochastic order discussed in this section in reliability theory.

Consider the conditional probability

$$Q_X(t, x) = P(X > t + x \mid X > t). \tag{5.18}$$

where $x \geq 0$ and suppose that X describes a random loss. Then equation (5.18) calculates the probability of losing more than $t + x$ on condition that the loss is larger than t. This probability may vary depending on the level t with the additional amount of loss being fixed (x does not depend on t). For example, if $t_1 \leq t_2$, then the corresponding conditional probabilities may be related in the following way,

$$Q_X(t_1, x) \geq Q_X(t_2, x). \tag{5.19}$$

Thus the deeper we go into the tail, the less likely it is to lose additional x dollars provided that the loss is larger than the selected threshold. Conversely, if the inequality is

$$Q_X(t_1, x) \leq Q_X(t_2, x), \tag{5.20}$$

then the further we go into the tail, the more likely it becomes to lose additional x dollars. Basically, the inequalities in (5.19) and (5.20) describe certain tail properties of the random variable X.

Denote by $\overline{F}_X(x) = 1 - F_X(x) = P(X > x)$ the tail of the random variable X. Then, according to the definition of conditional probability, equation (5.18) can be stated in terms of $\overline{F}_X(x)$,

$$Q_X(t, x) = \frac{\overline{F}_X(x + t)}{\overline{F}_X(t)}. \tag{5.21}$$

Denote by $\mathcal{Q}$ the class of all random variables for which $Q_X(t, x)$ is a *nonincreasing* function of t for any $x \geq 0$, and by $\mathcal{Q}^*$ the class of all random variables for which $Q_X(t, x)$ is a *nondecreasing* function of t for any $x \geq 0$. The random variables belonging to $\mathcal{Q}$ satisfy inequality (5.19) and those belonging to $\mathcal{Q}^*$ satisfy inequality (5.20) for any $x \geq 0$.

In case the random variable X has a density $f_X(x)$, then it can be determined whether it belongs to $\mathcal{Q}$ or $\mathcal{Q}^*$ by the behavior of the function

$$h_X(t) = \frac{f_X(t)}{\overline{F}_X(t)}, \tag{5.22}$$

which is known as the *hazard rate function* or the *failure rate function*. If $h_X(t)$ is a nonincreasing function, then $X \in \mathcal{Q}$. If it is a nondecreasing function, then $X \in \mathcal{Q}^*$. In fact, the only distribution that belongs to both classes is the exponential distribution. The hazard rate function of the exponential distribution is constant with respect to t.

In the following, we introduce a stochastic dominance order assuming that the random variables describe random profits. Then we show how the dominance order definition can be modified if the random variables describe losses or returns. Denote by $\Lambda_X(t)$ the transform

$$\Lambda_X(t) = -\log(\overline{F}_X(t)). \tag{5.23}$$

A positive random variable X is said to dominate another positive random variable Y with respect to the Λ transform, $X \succeq_\Lambda Y$, if the random variable $Z = \Lambda_Y(X)$ is such that $Z \in \mathcal{Q}$.

The rationale behind the Λ transform is the following. First, consider the special case $Y = X$. The random variable $Z = \Lambda_Y(X)$ has exactly the exponential distribution because $\overline{F}_Y(X)$ is uniformly distributed. If Y has a heavier tail than X, then Z has a tail, that increases no more slowly than the tail of the exponential distribution and, therefore, $Z \in \mathcal{Q}$. Thus the stochastic order $\succeq_\Lambda$ emphasizes the tail behavior of X relative to Y.

This stochastic order is interesting since it does not arise from a class of utility functions through the expected utility theory and, nevertheless, it has application in finance describing choice under uncertainty. We illustrate this by showing a relationship with SSD.

Suppose that $X \succeq_\Lambda Y$. Then Kalashnikov and Rachev (1990) show that the following condition holds

$$\int_x^\infty \overline{F}_X(t)dt \le \int_x^\infty \overline{F}_Y(t)dt, \quad \forall x \ge 0. \tag{5.24}$$

The converse statement is not true; that is, condition (5.24) does not ensure $X \succeq_\Lambda Y$. Equation (5.24) can be directly connected with SSD. In fact, if (5.24) holds and we assume that the expected payoffs of X and Y are equal, then

$$\int_0^x F_X(t)dt \le \int_0^x F_Y(t)dt, \quad \forall x \ge 0.$$

This inequality means that X dominates Y with respect to RSD and, therefore, with respect to SSD. Thus if we have demonstrated that if $EX = EY$, then

$$X \succeq_\Lambda Y \implies X \succeq_{RSD} Y \implies X \succeq_{SSD} Y. \tag{5.25}$$

Suppose that the random variables describe losses. This interpretation has application in operational risk management where losses are modeled as positive random variables. We modify the stochastic order in the following way. A positive random variable X is said to dominate another positive random variable Y with respect to the Λ transform, $X \succeq_{\Lambda^*} Y$, if the random variable $Z = \Lambda_Y(X)$ is such that $Z \in \mathcal{Q}^*$. In this case, the tail of X is heavier than the tail of Y.

If the random variables describe returns, then the left tail describes losses and the right tail describes profits. The random variable can be decomposed into two terms,

$$X = X_+ - X_-,$$

where $X_+ = \max(X, 0)$ stands for the profit and $X_- = \max(-X, 0)$ denotes the loss. By modifying the stochastic order, we can determine the tail of which of the two components influences the stochastic order. Consider two real valued random variables X and Y describing random returns. The order $\succeq_\Lambda$ compares the tails of the profits X_+ and Y_+, and $\succeq_{\Lambda^*}$ compares the tails of the losses X_- and Y_-.

The stochastic orders $\succeq_\Lambda$ and $\succeq_{\Lambda^*}$ are constructed without considering first a particular class of investors but by imposing directly a condition on the tail of the random variable. There may or may not be a corresponding set of utility functions such that if $Eu(X) \geq Eu(Y)$ for all $u(x)$ in this class, then $X \succeq_\Lambda Y$, for example. Nevertheless, we have demonstrated that the order $\succeq_\Lambda$ is consistent with SSD and is not implied by it. We can generalize by concluding that if practical problems require introducing a stochastic order on the basis of certain characteristics of the profit, the loss or the return distribution, the stochastic order can be defined without seeking first a class of investors which can generate it. In case this question appears important, we can only search for a consistency relation with an existing stochastic order, such as the one in equation (5.25).

BIBLIOGRAPHY

Arrow, J. K. (1965). *Aspects of theory of risk-bearing*, Helsinki: Yrjö Johansson Foundation.

Arrow, J. K., and G. Debreu (1954). "Existence of a competitive equilibrium for a competitive economy," *Econometrica* 22(3): 265–290.

Hadar, J., and W. R. Russell (1969). "Rules for ordering uncertain prospects," *American Economic Review* 59: 25–34.

Hanoch, G., and H. Levy (1969). "The efficiency analysis of choices involving risk," *Review of Economic Studies* 36: 335–346.

Kalashnikov, V., and S. T. Rachev (1990). *Mathematical methods for construction for queueing models*, New York: Wadsworth & Brooks/Cole.

Ortobelli, S., S. T. Rachev, H. Shalit, and F. J. Fabozzi (2007). Risk probability functionals and probability metrics applied to portfolio theory, working paper.

Pratt, J. W. (1964). "Risk aversion in the small and in the large," *Econometrica* 32(2): 122–136.

Rachev, S. T. (1985). *Probability metrics and their applications to the problems of stability for stochastic models*, Doctor of Science Dissertation, Moscow, Steklov Mathematical Institute.

Rothschild, M., and J. E. Stiglitz (1970). "Increasing risk: A definition," *Journal of Economic Theory* 2(3): 225–243.

Savage, L. J. (1954). *The Foundations of Statistics*, New York: John Wiley & Sons.

Tversky, A., and D. Kahneman (1992). "Advances in prospect theory: Cumulative representation of uncertainty," *Journal of Risk and Uncertainty* 5(4): 297–323.

von Neumann, J., and O. Morgenstern (1944). *Theory of games and economic behavior*, Princeton, NJ: Princeton University Press.

Whitmore, G. A. (1970). "Third-degree stochastic dominance," *American Economic Review* 60(3): 457–459.

CHAPTER 6

Risk and Uncertainty

6.1 INTRODUCTION

There has been a major debate on the differences and common features of risk and uncertainty. Both notions are related but they do not coincide. Risk is often argued to be a *subjective* phenomenon involving *exposure* and *uncertainty*.[1] That is, generally, risk may arise whenever there is uncertainty.

While risk is an essential factor in every human decision making, in this chapter we consider it only in the context of investment management. In our context, exposure is identified with monetary loss. Thus investment risk is related to the uncertain monetary loss to which a manager may expose a client. Subjectivity appears because two managers may define the same investment as having different risk—it is a question of personal predisposition.

A major activity in many financial institutions is to recognize the sources of risk, then manage and control them. This is possible only if risk is quantified. If we can measure the risk of a portfolio, then we can identify the financial assets that constitute the main risk contributors, reallocate the portfolio, and, in this way, minimize the potential loss by minimizing the portfolio risk. Even though the recognition that risk involves exposure and uncertainty is illuminating, it appears insufficient in order for risk to be quantified. It merely shows that both uncertainty and monetary loss are essential characteristics. For example, if an asset will surely lose 30% of its value tomorrow, then it is not risky even though money will be lost. Uncertainty alone is not synonymous with risk, either. If the price of an

---

[1]Holton (2004) provides a thorough analysis of the notion of risk. Knight (1921) started the debate about risk and uncertainty.

asset will certainly increase between 5% and 10% tomorrow then there is uncertainty but no risk as there is no monetary loss. As a result, risk is qualified as an *asymmetric phenomenon* in the sense that it is related to loss only.

Concerning uncertainty, it is our assumption that it is an intrinsic feature of the future values of traded assets on the market. If we consider two time instants, the present and a future one, then the inherent uncertainty materializes as a probability distribution of future prices or returns; that is, these are random variables as of the present instant. Investment managers do not know the probabilistic law exactly but can infer it, to a degree, from the available data—they approximate the unknown law by assuming a parametric model and by calibrating its parameters. Uncertainty relates to the probable deviations from the expected price or return where the probable deviations are described by the unknown law. Therefore, a measure of uncertainty should be capable of quantifying the probable positive and negative deviations. In this aspect, any uncertainty measure is symmetric. As an extreme case, consider a variable characterized by no uncertainty whatsoever. It follows that this variable is nonrandom and we know its future value with certainty.

A classical example of an uncertainty measure is *variance*. It equals the average squared deviation from the mean of a distribution—it captures both the upside and the downside deviations from the mean of the distribution. Another measure is the standard deviation, which is the square root of the variance. It is more understandable as it is measured in the same units as the random variable. For instance, if the random variable describes prices, then the standard deviation is measured in dollars; if the random variable describes percentage return, then the standard deviation is measured in percentage points. There are many other measures of uncertainty besides standard deviation, which we discuss in this chapter.

Besides the essential features of risk discussed above, there are other characteristics. For example, investment risk may be *relative*. In benchmark tracking problems, it is reasonable to demand a smaller risk of the strategy relative to a benchmark, that is, smaller potential loss but relative to the loss of the benchmark. If there are multiple benchmarks, then there are multiple relative risks to take into account and strategy construction becomes a multidimensional, or a multicriterion, problem.

Depending on the sources of risk, a financial institution may face *market*, *credit* or *operational risk*.[2] Market risk describes the portfolio exposure to the moves of certain market variables. There are four standard market

---

[2]This distinction is made by the Basel Commettee on Banking Supervision. The Basel Committee consists of representatives from central banks and regulatory authorities

risk variables—equities, interest rates, exchange rates, and commodities. A financial instrument is dependent on those market factors and its price fluctuates as the underlying market factors move. Credit risk arises due to a debtor's failure to satisfy the terms of a borrowing arrangement. Operational risk is defined as the risk of loss resulting from inadequate or failed internal processes, people, and systems. Its contribution to total portfolio risk varies from firm to firm and its management falls under the responsibility of internal auditors.

Apparently, a true functional definition of investment risk is out of reach. Nevertheless, financial institutions have made a lot of effort to model it. Generally, a risk model consists of two parts. First, probabilistic models are constructed for the underlying sources of risk, such as market or credit risk factors, and the portfolio loss distribution is described by means of the probabilistic models. Second, risk is quantified by means of a *risk measure* that associates a real number to the portfolio loss distribution. It is important to recognize that both steps are crucial. Nonrealistic probabilistic models may compromise the risk estimate just as an inappropriate choice for the risk measure may do.

Due to the lack of a functional definition of risk, no perfect risk measure exists. A risk measure captures only some of the characteristics of risk and, in this sense, every risk measure is incomplete. Nonetheless, we believe that it is reasonable to search for risk measures that are ideal for the particular problem under investigation.

In this chapter, we provide several examples of widely used dispersion measures that quantify the notion of uncertainty. A few of their basic features can be summarized into axioms leading to an axiomatic construction of dispersion measures and deviation measures, which are convex dispersion measures. The notion of a probability metric is related to the notion of dispersion. In fact, we demonstrate that probability metrics can be used to generate dispersion measures.

Measures of dispersion are inadequate for quantifying risk. We discuss in detail *value-at-risk* (VaR), its properties, estimation methods, and why it fails to be a true risk measure.

An axiomatic construction of risk measures is possible by setting key characteristics as axioms. We describe this approach in the section devoted to *coherent risk measures* and illustrate the defining axioms depending on

---

of the G10 countries. It has issued two banking supervision Accords, Basel I and Basel II, with the purpose of ensusring that financial institutions retain enough capital as a protection against unexpected losses. In the two accords, a distinction is made between market, credit, and operational risk, and a simple methodology is provided for their quantification.

whether the random variable describes return or payoff. It turns out that the "coherent" properties very much depend on the interpretation of the random variable. If a risk measure is coherent for return distributions, it may not be coherent for payoff distributions.

Finally, we stress the importance of consistency of a true risk measure with the second-order stochastic dominance as it concerns risk-averse investors.

6.2 MEASURES OF DISPERSION

Measures of dispersion can be constructed by means of different descriptive statistics. They calculate how observations in a dataset are distributed, whether there is high or low variability around the mean of the distribution. Intuitively, if we consider a nonrandom quantity, then it is equal to its mean with probability one and there is no fluctuation whatsoever around the mean.

In this section, we provide several descriptive statistics widely used in practice and we give a generalization that axiomatically describes measures of dispersion.

6.2.1 Standard Deviation

Standard deviation is, perhaps, the most widely used measure of uncertainty. It is calculated as the square root of variance, which itself can be regarded as a measure of uncertainty. The standard deviation is usually denoted by σ_X,[3] where X stands for the random variable we consider

$$\sigma_X = \sqrt{E(X - EX)^2} \tag{6.1}$$

in which E stands for mathematical expectation. For a discrete distribution, equation (6.1) changes to

$$\sigma_X = \left(\sum_{k=1}^{n} (x_k - EX)^2 p_k \right)^{1/2},$$

where $x_k, k = 1, \ldots, n$ are the outcomes, $p_k, k = 1, \ldots, n$ are the probabilities of the outcomes, and

$$EX = \sum_{k=1}^{n} x_k p_k$$

---

[3]At times, we will use the notation $\sigma(X)$ instead of σ_X to accentuate that the standard deviation is a functional of the underlying distribution.

is the mathematical expectation. The standard deviation is always a nonnegative number; if it is equal to zero, then the random variable is equal to its mean with probability one and, therefore, it is nonrandom. This conclusion holds for an arbitrary distribution.

In order to see why the standard deviation can measure uncertainty, consider the following simple example. Suppose that X describes the outcomes in a game in which one wins \$1 or \$3 with probabilities equal to 1/2. The mathematical expectation of X, the expected win, is \$2,

$$EX = 1(1/2) + 3(1/2) = 2.$$

The standard deviation equals \$1,

$$\sigma_X = \left((1-2)^2 \frac{1}{2} + (3-2)^2 \frac{1}{2} \right)^{1/2} = 1.$$

In this equation, both the positive and the negative deviations from the mean are taken into account. In fact, all possible values of the random variable X are within the limits $EX \pm \sigma_X$. That is why it is said that the standard deviation is a measure of statistical dispersion, that is, how widely spread the values in a dataset are.

The interval $EX \pm \sigma_X$ covers all the possible values of X only in a few isolated examples. Suppose that X has the normal distribution with mean equal to a, $X \in N(a, \sigma_X)$. Then, the probability of the interval $a \pm \sigma_X$ is 0.683. That is, when sampling from the corresponding distribution, 68.3% of the simulations will be in the interval $(a - \sigma_X, a + \sigma_X)$. The probabilities of the intervals $a \pm 2\sigma_X$ and $a \pm 3\sigma_X$ are 0.955 and 0.997 respectively. Figure 6.1 provides an illustration for the standard normal case.

The probabilities in this example are specific for the normal distribution only. Actually, in the general case when the distribution of the random variable X is unknown, we can obtain bounds on the probabilities by means of *Chebyshev's inequality*,

$$P(|X - EX| > x) \le \frac{\sigma_X^2}{x^2}, \tag{6.2}$$

provided that the random variable X has a finite second moment, $E|X|^2 < \infty$. With the help of Chebyshev's inequality, we calculate that the probability of the interval $EX \pm k\sigma_X, k = 1, 2, \ldots$ exceeds $1 - 1/k^2$,

$$P(|X - EX| \le k\sigma_X) \ge 1 - 1/k^2.$$

If we choose $k = 2$, we compute that $P(X \in EX \pm 2\sigma_X)$ is at least 0.75. Table 6.1 contains the corresponding bounds on the probabilities computed for several choices of k.

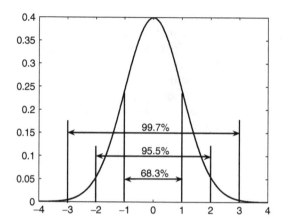

FIGURE 6.1 The standard normal density and the probabilities of the intervals $EX \pm \sigma_X$, $EX \pm 2\sigma_X$, and $EX \pm 3\sigma_X$, where $X \in N(0,1)$, as a percentage of the total mass.

TABLE 6.1 The Values $p_k = 1 - 1/k^2$ Provide a Lower Bound for the Probability $P(X \in EX \pm k\sigma_X)$ When the Distribution of X is Unknown.

k	1.4	2	3	4	5	6	7
p_k	0.5	0.75	0.889	0.94	0.96	0.97	0.98

6.2.2 Mean Absolute Deviation

Even though the standard deviation is widely used, it does not provide the only way to measure uncertainty. In fact, there are important cases where it is inappropriate—there are distributions for which the standard deviation is infinite. An example of an uncertainty measure also often used, which may be finite when the standard deviation does not exist, is the *mean absolute deviation* (MAD). This measure is defined as the average deviation in absolute terms around the mean of the distribution,

$$MAD_X = E|X - EX|, \tag{6.3}$$

where X is a random variable with finite mean. For a discrete distribution, equation (6.3) becomes

$$MAD_X = \sum_{k=1}^{n} |x_k - EX| p_k,$$

where x_k, $k = 1, \ldots, n$, are the outcomes and p_k, $k = 1, \ldots, n$, are the corresponding probabilities. It is clear from the definition that both the positive and the negative deviations are taken into account in the MAD formula. Similar to the standard deviation, the MAD is a nonnegative number and if it is equal to zero, then X is equal to its mean with probability one.

The analysis made for the standard deviation can be repeated for the MAD without any modification. Therefore, the MAD and the standard deviation are merely two alternative measures estimating the uncertainty of a random variable. There are distributions, for which one of the quantities can be expressed from the other. For example, if X has a normal distribution, $X \in N(a, \sigma_X^2)$, then

$$MAD_X = \sigma_X \sqrt{\frac{2}{\pi}}.$$

Thus, for the normal distribution case, the MAD is just a scaled standard deviation.

6.2.3 Semistandard Deviation

The semistandard deviation is a measure of dispersion, which differs from the standard deviation and the MAD in that it takes into account only the positive or only the negative deviations from the mean. Therefore, it is not symmetric. The positive and the negative semistandard deviations are defined as

and
$$\sigma_X^+ = (E(X - EX)_+^2)^{1/2}$$
$$\sigma_X^- = (E(X - EX)_-^2)^{1/2}, \tag{6.4}$$

where:

$(x - EX)_+^2$ equals the squared difference between the outcome x and the mean EX if the difference is positive, $(x - EX)_+^2 = \max(x - EX, 0)^2$.

$(x - EX)_-^2$ equals the squared difference between the outcome x and the mean EX if the difference is negative, $(x - EX)_-^2 = \min(x - EX, 0)^2$.

Thus σ_X^+ takes into account only the positive deviations from the mean and it may be called an *upside dispersion measure*. Similarly, σ_X^- takes into account only the negative deviations from the mean and it may be called a *downside dispersion measure*.

As with the standard deviation, both σ_X^- and σ_X^+ are nonnegative numbers which are equal to zero if and only if the random variable equals its mean with probability one.

If the random variable is symmetric around the mean, then the upside and the downside semistandard deviations are equal. For example, if X has a normal distribution, $X \in N(a, \sigma_X^2)$, then both quantities are equal and can be expressed by means of the standard deviation,

$$\sigma_X^- = \sigma_X^+ = \frac{\sigma_X}{\sqrt{2}}.$$

If the distribution of X is skewed,[4] then $\sigma_X^- \neq \sigma_X^+$. Positive skewness corresponds to larger positive semistandard deviation, $\sigma_X^- < \sigma_X^+$. Similarly, negative skewness corresponds to larger negative semistandard deviation, $\sigma_X^- > \sigma_X^+$. Figure 1.4 in section 5.3.4 in Chapter 5 illustrates positive and negative skewness.

6.2.4 Axiomatic Description

Besides the examples considered in section 6.2, measures of dispersion also include *interquartile range* and can be based on *central absolute moments*. The interquartile range is defined as the difference between the 75% and the 25% quantile. The central absolute moment of order k is defined as

$$m_k = E|X - EX|^k$$

and an example of a dispersion measure based on it is

$$(m_k)^{1/k} = (E|X - EX|^k)^{1/k}.$$

The common properties of the dispersion measures we have considered can be synthesized into axioms. In this way, a dispersion measure is called any functional satisfying the axioms. Rachev et al. (2007) provide the following set of general axioms. We denote the dispersion measure of a random variable X by $D(X)$.

Positive shift. $D(X + C) \leq D(X)$ for all X and constants $C \geq 0$.

Positive homogeneity. $D(0) = 0$ and $D(\lambda X) = \lambda D(X)$ for all X and all $\lambda > 0$.

Positivity. $D(X) \geq 0$ for all X, with $D(X) > 0$ for nonconstant X.

---

[4]Symmetric random variables are described through their distribution function; that is, X is symmetric (around zero) if X has the same distribution function as $-X$, $X \stackrel{d}{=} -X$, where the notation $\stackrel{d}{=}$ means equality in distribution. If the mean of the distribution is not zero, then the condition of symmetry changes to $X - EX \stackrel{d}{=} -(X - EX)$, and we say that X is symmetric around the mean.

According to the positive shift property, adding a positive constant does not increase the dispersion of a random variable. According to the positive homogeneity and the positivity properties, the dispersion measure D is equal to zero only if the random variable is a constant. This property is very natural for any measure of dispersion. Recall that it holds for the standard deviation, MAD, and semistandard deviation—all examples we considered in the previous sections.

An example of a dispersion measure satisfying these properties is the *colog measure* defined by

$$\text{colog}(X) = E(X \log X) - E(X)E(\log X),$$

where X is a positive random variable. The colog measure is sensitive to additive shifts and has applications in finance as it is consistent with the preference relations of risk-averse investors.

6.2.5 Deviation Measures

Rockafellar et al. (2006) provide an axiomatic description of dispersion measures which arises as a special case of our approach in section 6.2.4. The axioms of Rockafellar et al. (2006) define convex dispersion measures called *deviation measures*. An interesting link exists between deviation measures and risk measures, which we illustrate in section 6.5 in this chapter. Moreover, the deviation measures can be described by the method of probability metrics. This is noted in Chapter 9.

Besides the axioms given in section 6.2.4, the deviation measures satisfy the property

Subadditivity. $D(X + Y) \leq D(X) + D(Y)$ for all X and Y.

and the positive shift property is replaced by

Translation invariance. $D(X + C) = D(X)$ for all X and constants $C \in \mathbb{R}$.

As a consequence of the translation invariance axiom, the deviation measure is influenced only by the difference $X - EX$. If $X = EX$ in all states of the world, then the deviation measure is a constant and, therefore, it is equal to zero because of the positivity axiom. Conversely, if $D(X) = 0$, then $X = EX$ in all states of the world. The positive homogeneity and the subadditivity axioms establish the convexity property of $D(X)$.

Apparently not all deviation measures are symmetric; that is, it is possible to have $D(X) \neq D(-X)$ if the random variable X is not symmetric.

This is not a drawback of the construction. Quite the opposite, this is an advantage because an investment manager is more attentive to the negative deviations from the mean. Examples of asymmetric deviation measures include the semistandard deviation, σ_X^- defined in equation (6.4). Deviation measures which depend only on the negative deviations from the mean are called *downside deviation measures*. As a matter of fact, symmetric deviation measures can easily be constructed. The quantity $\tilde{D}(X)$ is a symmetric deviation measure if we define it as

$$\tilde{D}(X) := \tfrac{1}{2}(D(X) + D(-X)),$$

where $D(X)$ is an arbitrary deviation measure.

A downside deviation measure possesses several of the characteristics of a risk measure but it is not a risk measure. Here is an example. Suppose that we have initially in our portfolio a common stock, X, with a current market value of \$95 and an expected return of 0.5% in a month. Let us choose one particular deviation measure, D_1, and compute $D_1(r_X) = 20\%$, where r_X stands for the portfolio return. Assume that we add to our portfolio a risk-free government bond, B, worth \$95 with a face value of \$100 and a one-month maturity. The return on the bond equals $r_B = \$5/\$95 = 5.26\%$ and is nonrandom. Our portfolio now consists of equal shares of the common stock and the bond and its return equals $r_p = r_X/2 + r_B/2$. Using the positive homogeneity and the translation invariance axioms from the definition we obtain $D_1(r_p) = D_1(r_X)/2 = 10\%$. Indeed, the uncertainty of the portfolio return r_p decreases twice since the share of the risky stock decreases twice, this is what the deviation measure is informing us about. Intuitively, the risk of r_p decreases more than twice if compared to r_X because half of the new portfolio earns a sure profit of 5.26%. This effect is due to the translation invariance, which makes the deviation measure insensitive to nonrandom profit.

Examples of deviation measures include the standard deviation, the MAD, the semistandard deviation.

6.3 PROBABILITY METRICS AND DISPERSION MEASURES

Probability metrics were introduced in Chapter 3. They are functionals which are constructed to measure distances between random quantities. Thus, every probability metric involves two random variables X and Y, and the distance between them is denoted by $\mu(X, Y)$, where μ stands for the probability metric.

Suppose that μ is a compound probability metric.[5] In this case, if $\mu(X, Y) = 0$, it follows that the two random variables are coincident in all states of the world. Therefore, the quantity $\mu(X, Y)$ can be interpreted as a measure of relative deviation between X and Y. A positive distance, $\mu(X, Y) > 0$, means that the two variables fluctuate with respect to each other and zero distance, $\mu(X, Y) = 0$, implies that there is no deviation of any of them relative to the other.

This idea is closely related to the notion of dispersion; but it is much more profound because we obtain the notion of dispersion measures as a special case by considering the distance between X and the mean of X, $\mu(X, EX)$. In fact, the functional $\mu(X, EX)$ provides a very general notion of a dispersion measure as it arises as a special case from a probability metric, which represents the only general way of measuring distances between random quantities. In the appendix to this chapter, we demonstrate how the family of symmetric deviation measures arises from probability metrics. Stoyanov et al. (2007) consider similar questions and provide a more general treatment.

6.4   MEASURES OF RISK

As we noted in the introduction, risk is related to uncertainty but it is not synonymous with it. Therefore, a risk measure may share some of the features of a dispersion measure but is, generally, a different object.

From a historical perspective, Markowitz (1952) was the first to recognize the relationship between risk and reward and introduced standard deviation as a proxy for risk. The standard deviation is not a good choice for a risk measure because it penalizes symmetrically both the negative and the positive deviations from the mean. It is an uncertainty measure and cannot account for the asymmetric nature of risk, that is, risk concerns losses only. The deficiencies of the standard deviation as a risk measure were acknowledged by Markowitz who was the first to suggest the semistandard deviation as a substitute, Markowitz (1959). In section 6.2.5, we gave an example illustrating why the semistandard deviation, as well as any other deviation measure, cannot be a true risk measures.

In this section, we provide several examples of risk measures. We consider the VaR and we comment on its properties, and different calculation methods. Where possible, the definitions and equations are geometrically interpreted, making the ideas more intuitive and understandable. We also

---

[5]Section 3.3.1 provides more details on primary, simple, and compound probability metrics.

consider the more general family of coherent risk measures which includes the *average value-at-risk* (AVaR) and the *spectral risk measures* as particular representatives. The AVaR and the spectral risk measures are considered in detail in Chapter 7. Finally, we address the question of consistency of a risk measure with a stochastic dominance order and remark on the relationship between risk measures and uncertainty measures.

6.4.1   Value-at-Risk

A risk measure which has been widely accepted since 1990s is the *value-at-risk* (VaR). In the late 1980s, it was integrated by JP Morgan on a firmwide level into its risk-management system. In this system, they developed a service called RiskMetrics which was later spun off into a separate company called *RiskMetrics Group*. It is usually thought that JP Morgan invented the VaR measure. In fact, similar ideas had been used by large financial institutions in computing their exposure to market risk. The contribution of JP Morgan was that the notion of VaR was introduced to a wider audience.

In the mid-1990s, the VaR measure was approved by regulators as a valid approach to calculating capital reserves needed to cover market risk. The Basel Commettee on Banking Supervision released a package of amendments to the requirements for banking institutions allowing them to use their own internal systems for risk estimation. In this way, capital reserves, which financial institutions are required to keep, could be based on the VaR numbers computed internally by an in-house risk management system. Generally, regulators demand that the capital reserve equal the VaR number multiplied by a factor between 3 and 4. Thus regulators link the capital reserves for market risk directly to the risk measure.

VaR is defined as the minimum level of loss at a given, sufficiently high, confidence level for a predefined time horizon. The recommended confidence levels are 95% and 99%. Suppose that we hold a portfolio with a one-day 99% VaR equal to $1 million. This means that over the horizon of one day, the portfolio may lose more than $1 million with probability equal to 1%.

The same example can be constructed for percentage returns. Suppose that the present value of a portfolio we hold is $10 million. If the one-day 99% VaR of the return distribution is 2%, then over the time horizon of one day, we lose more than 2% ($200,000) of the portfolio present value with probability equal to 1%.

Denote by $(1 - \epsilon)100\%$ the confidence level parameter of the VaR. As we explained, losses larger than the VaR occur with probability ϵ. The probability ϵ, we call *tail probability*. Depending on the interpretation of the random variable, VaR can be defined in different ways. Formally, the

VaR at confidence level $(1 - \epsilon)100\%$ (tail probability ϵ) is defined as the negative of the lower ϵ-quantile of the return distribution,

$$VaR_\epsilon(X) = -\inf_x\{x|P(X \le x) \ge \epsilon\} = -F_X^{-1}(\epsilon) \qquad (6.5)$$

where $\epsilon \in (0, 1)$ and $F_X^{-1}(\epsilon)$ is the inverse of the distribution function. If the random variable X describes random returns, then the VaR number is given in terms of a return figure. The definition of VaR is illustrated in Figure 6.2.

If X describes random payoffs, then VaR is a threshold in dollar terms below which the portfolio value falls with probability ϵ,

$$VaR_\epsilon(X) = \inf_x\{x|P(X \le x) \ge \epsilon\} = F_X^{-1}(\epsilon) \qquad (6.6)$$

where $\epsilon \in (0, 1)$ and $F_X^{-1}(\epsilon)$ is the inverse of the distribution function of the random payoff. VaR can also be expressed as a distance to the present value when considering the profit distribution. The random profit is defined as $X - P_0$ where X is the payoff and P_0 is the present value. The VaR of the random profit equals,

$$VaR_\epsilon(X - P_0) = -\inf_x\{x|P(X - P_0 \le x) \ge \epsilon\} = P_0 - VaR_\epsilon(X)$$

in which $VaR_\epsilon(X)$ is defined according to (6.6) since X is interpreted as a random payoff. In this case, the definition of VaR is essentially given by equation (6.5).

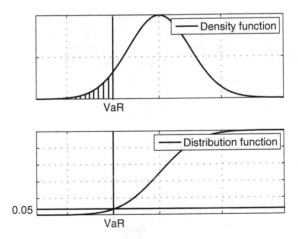

FIGURE 6.2 The VaR at 95% confidence level of a random variable X. The top plot shows the density of X, the marked area equals the tail probability, and the bottom plot shows the distribution function.

According to the definition in equation (6.5), VaR may become a negative number. If $VaR_\epsilon(X)$ is a negative number, then this means that at tail probability ϵ we do not observe losses but profits. Losses happen with even smaller probability than ϵ. If for any tail probability $VaR_\epsilon(X)$ is a negative number, then no losses can occur and, therefore, the random variable X bears no risk as no exposure is associated with it. In this chapter, we assume that random variables describe either random returns or random profits and we adopt the definition in equation (6.5).

We illustrate one aspect in which VaR differs from the deviation measures and all uncertainty measures. As a consequence of the definition, if we add to the random variable X a nonrandom profit C, the resulting VaR can be expressed by the VaR of the initial variable in the following way

$$VaR_\epsilon(X + C) = VaR_\epsilon(X) - C. \qquad (6.7)$$

Thus adding a nonrandom profit decreases the risk of the portfolio. Furthermore, scaling the return distribution by a positive constant λ scales the VaR by the same constant,

$$VaR_\epsilon(\lambda X) = \lambda VaR_\epsilon(X). \qquad (6.8)$$

It turns out that these properties characterize not only VaR. They are identified as key features of a risk measure. We will come back to them in section 6.4.4.

Consider again the example developed in section 6.2.5. Initially, the portfolio we hold consists of a common stock with random monthly return r_X. We rebalance the portfolio so that it becomes an equally weighted portfolio of the stock and a bond with a nonrandom monthly return of 5.26%, $r_B = 5.26\%$. Thus the portfolio return can be expressed as

$$r_p = r_X(1/2) + r_B(1/2) = r_X/2 + 0.0526/2.$$

Using equations (6.7) and (6.8), we calculate that if $VaR_\epsilon(r_X) = 12\%$, then $VaR_\epsilon(r_p) \approx 3.365\%$, which is by far less than 6%—half of the initial risk. Recall from section 6.2.5 that any deviation measure would indicate that the dispersion (or the uncertainty) of the portfolio return r_p would be twice as smaller than the uncertainty of r_X.

A very important remark has to be made with respect to the performance of VaR and, as it turns out, of any other risk measure. It is heavily dependent on the assumed probability distribution of the variable X. An unrealistic hypothesis may result in underestimation or overestimation of true risk. If we use VaR to build reserves in order to cover losses in times of crises, then underestimation may be fatal and overestimation may lead to inefficient use of capital. An inaccurate model is even more dangerous in an optimal portfolio problem in which we minimize risk subject to some constraints. It may adversely influence the optimal weights and not reduce the true risk.

Even though VaR has been largely adopted by financial institutions and approved by regulators, it turns out that VaR has important deficiencies. While it provides an intuitive description of how much a portfolio may lose, generally, it should be abandoned as a risk measure. The most important drawback is that, in some cases, the reasonable diversification effect that every portfolio manager should expect to see in a risk measure is not present; that is, the VaR of a portfolio may be greater than the sum of the VaRs of the constituents,

$$VaR_\epsilon(X + Y) > VaR_\epsilon(X) + VaR_\epsilon(Y), \qquad (6.9)$$

in which X and Y stand for the random payoff of the instruments in the portfolio. This shows that VaR cannot be a true risk measure.

We give a simple example which shows that VaR may satisfy equation (6.9). Suppose that X denotes a bond which either defaults with probability 4.5% and we lose \$50 or it does not default and in this case the loss is equal to zero. Let Y be the same bond but assume that the defaults of the two bonds are independent events. The VaR of the two bonds at 95% confidence level (5% tail probability) is equal to zero,

$$VaR_{0.05}(X) = VaR_{0.05}(Y) = 0.$$

Being the 5% quantile of the payoff distribution in this case, VaR fails to recognize losses occurring with probability smaller than 5%. A portfolio of the two bonds has the following payoff profile: It loses \$100 with probability of about 0.2%, loses \$50 with probability of about 8.6%, and the loss is zero with probability 91.2%. Thus the corresponding 95% VaR of the portfolio equals \$50 and clearly,

$$\$50 = VaR_{0.05}(X + Y) > VaR_{0.05}(X) + VaR_{0.05}(Y) = 0.$$

What are the consequences of using a risk measure that may satisfy property (6.9)? It is going to mislead portfolio managers that there is no diversification effect in the portfolio and they may make the irrational decision to concentrate it only into a few positions. As a consequence, the portfolio risk actually increases.

Besides being sometimes incapable of recognizing the diversification effect, another drawback is that VaR is not very informative about losses beyond the VaR level. It only reports that losses larger than the VaR level occur with probability equal to ϵ but it does not provide any information about the likely magnitude of such losses, for example.

Nonetheless, VaR is not a useless concept to be abandoned altogether. For example, it can be used in risk-reporting only as a characteristic of the portfolio return (payoff) distribution since it has a straightforward interpretation. The criticism of VaR is focused on its wide application by practitioners as a true risk measure which, in view of the deficiencies described above, is not well grounded and should be reconsidered.

6.4.2 Computing Portfolio VaR in Practice

In this section, we provide three approaches for portfolio VaR calculation which are used in practice. We assume that the portfolio contains common stocks which is only to make the description easier to grasp; this is not a restriction of any of the approaches.

Suppose that a portfolio contains n common stocks and we are interested in calculating the daily VaR at 99% confidence level. Denote the random daily returns of the stocks by $X_1, \ldots, X_n$ and by $w_1, \ldots, w_n$ the weight of each stock in the portfolio. Thus the portfolio return r_p can be calculated as

$$r_p = w_1 X_1 + w_2 X_2 + \cdots + w_n X_n.$$

The portfolio VaR is derived from the distribution of r_p. The three approaches vary in the assumptions they make.

The Approach of RiskMetrics The approach of RiskMetrics Group is centered on the assumption that the stock returns have a multivariate normal distribution. Under this assumption, the distribution of the portfolio return is also normal. Therefore, in order to calculate the portfolio VaR, we only have to calculate the expected return of r_p and the standard deviation of r_p. The 99% VaR will appear as the negative of the 1% quantile of the $N(Er_p, \sigma_{r_p}^2)$ distribution.

The portfolio expected return can be directly expressed through the expected returns of the stocks,

$$Er_p = w_1 EX_1 + w_2 EX_2 + \cdots + w_n EX_n = \sum_{k=1}^{n} w_k EX_k, \qquad (6.10)$$

where E denotes mathematical expectation. Similarly, the variance of the portfolio return $\sigma_{r_p}^2$ can be computed through the variances of the stock returns and their covariances,

$$\sigma_{r_p}^2 = w_1^2 \sigma_{X_1}^2 + w_2^2 \sigma_{X_2}^2 + \cdots + w_n^2 \sigma_{X_n}^2 + \sum_{i \neq j} w_i w_j \text{cov}(X_i, X_j),$$

in which the last term appears because we have to sum up the covariances between all pairs of stock returns. There is a more compact way of writing down the expression for $\sigma_{r_p}^2$ using matrix notation,

$$\sigma_{r_p}^2 = w' \Sigma w, \tag{6.11}$$

in which $w = (w_1, \ldots, w_n)$ is the vector of portfolio weights and Σ is the covariance matrix of stock returns,

$$\Sigma = \begin{pmatrix} \sigma_{X_1}^2 & \sigma_{12} & \cdots & \sigma_{1n} \\ \sigma_{21} & \sigma_{X_2}^2 & \cdots & \sigma_{2n} \\ \vdots & \vdots & \ddots & \vdots \\ \sigma_{n1} & \sigma_{n2} & \cdots & \sigma_{X_n}^2 \end{pmatrix},$$

in which σ_{ij}, $i \neq j$, is the covariance between X_i and X_j, $\sigma_{ij} = \text{cov}(X_i, X_j)$. As a result, we obtain that the portfolio return has a normal distribution with mean given by equation (6.10) and variance given by equation (6.11).

The standard deviation is the scale parameter of the normal distribution and the mean is the location parameter. Due to the normal distribution properties, if $r_p \in N(Er_p, \sigma_{r_p}^2)$, then

$$\frac{r_p - Er_p}{\sigma_{r_p}} \in N(0, 1).$$

Thus, because of the properties (6.7) and (6.8) of the VaR, the 99% portfolio VaR can be represented as

$$VaR_{0.01}(r_p) = q_{0.99}\sigma_{r_p} - Er_p \tag{6.12}$$

where the standard deviation of the portfolio return σ_{r_p} is computed from equation (6.11), the expected portfolio return Er_p is given in (6.10), and $q_{0.99}$ is the 99% quantile of the standard normal distribution.

Note that $q_{0.99}$ is a quantity independent of the portfolio composition, it is merely a constant which can be calculated in advance. The parameters that depend on the portfolio weights are the standard deviation of portfolio returns σ_{r_p} and the expected portfolio return. As a consequence, VaR under the assumption of normality is symmetric even though, by definition, VaR is centered on the left tail of the distribution; that is, VaR is asymmetric by construction. This result appears because the normal distribution is symmetric around the mean.

The approach of RiskMetrics can be extended for other types of distributions. Lamantia et al. (2006a) and Lamantia et al. (2006b) provide such extensions and comparisons for Student's t- and stable distributions.

The Historical Method The *historical method* does not impose any distributional assumptions; the distribution of portfolio returns is constructed from historical data. Hence, sometimes the historical simulation method is called a *nonparametric method*. For example, the 99% daily VaR of the portfolio return is computed as the negative of the empirical 1% quantile of the observed daily portfolio returns. The observations are collected from a predetermined time window such as the most recent business year.

While the historical method seems to be more general as it is free of any distributional hypotheses, it has a number of major drawbacks.

1. It assumes that the past trends will continue in the future. This is not a realistic assumption because we may experience extreme events in the future, for instance, which have not happened in the past.
2. It treats the observations as independent and identically distributed (i.i.d.), which is not realistic. The daily returns data exhibits clustering of the volatility phenomenon, autocorrelations and so on, which are sometimes a significant deviation from the i.i.d. assumption.
3. It is not reliable for estimation of VaR at very high confidence levels. A sample of one year of daily data contains 250 observations, which is a rather small sample for the purpose of the 99% VaR estimation.

The Hybrid Method The *hybrid method* is a modification of the historical method in which the observations are not regarded as i.i.d. But certain weights are assigned to them depending on how close they are to the present. The weights are determined using the *exponential smoothing* algorithm. The exponential smoothing accentuates the most recent observations and seeks to take into account time-varying volatility phenomenon.

The algorithm of the hybrid approach consists of the following steps:

1. Exponentially declining weights are attached to historical returns, starting from the current time and going back in time. Let $r_{t-k+1}, \ldots, r_{t-1}, r_t$ be a sequence of k observed returns on a given asset, where t is the current time. The i-th observation is assigned a weight

$$\theta_i = c^* \lambda^{t-i},$$

where $0 < \lambda < 1$, and $c = \frac{1-\lambda}{1-\lambda^k}$ is a constant chosen such that the sum of all weights is equal to one, $\sum \theta_i = 1$.

2. Similarly to the historical simulation method, the hypothetical future returns are obtained from the past returns and sorted in increasing order.

3. The VaR measure is computed from the empirical c.d.f. in which each observation has probability equal to the weight θ_i.

Generally, the hybrid approach is appropriate for VaR estimation of heavy-tailed time series. It overcomes, to some degree, the first and the second deficiency of the historical method but it is also not reliable for VaR estimation of very high confidence levels.

The Monte Carlo Method In contrast to the historical method, the *Monte Carlo method* requires specification of a statistical model for the stocks returns. The statistical model is multivariate, hypothesizing both the behavior of the stock returns on a stand-alone basis and their dependence. For instance, the multivariate normal distribution assumes normal distributions for the stock returns viewed on a standalone basis and describes the dependencies by means of the covariance matrix. The multivariate model can also be constructed by specifying explicitly the one-dimensional distributions of the stock returns, and their dependence through a copula function.

The Monte Carlo method consists of the following basic steps:

Step 1. *Selection of a statistical model.* The statistical model should be capable of explaining a number of observed phenomena in the data such as heavy-tails, clustering of the volatility, and the like, which we think influence the portfolio risk.

Step 2. *Estimation of the statistical model parameters.* A sample of observed stocks returns is used from a predetermined time window, for instance the most recent 250 daily returns.

Step 3. *Generation of scenarios from the fitted model.* Independent scenarios are drawn from the fitted model. Each scenario is a vector of stock returns that depend on each other according to the presumed dependence structure of the statistical model.

Step 4. *Calculation of portfolio risk.* Compute portfolio risk on the basis of the portfolio return scenarios obtained from the previous step.

The Monte Carlo method is a very general numerical approach to risk estimation. It does not require any closed-form expressions and, by choosing a flexible statistical model, accurate risk numbers can be obtained. A disadvantage is that the computed portfolio VaR is dependent on the generated sample of scenarios and will fluctuate a little if we regenerate the sample. This side effect can be reduced by generating a larger sample. An illustration is provided in the following example.

Suppose that the daily portfolio return distribution is standard normal and, therefore, at Step 4 of the algorithm we have scenarios from the standard normal distribution. Under the assumption of normality, we can use the approach of RiskMetrics and compute the 99% daily VaR directly from formula (6.12). Nevertheless, we will use the Monte Carlo method to gain more insight into the deviations of the VaR based on scenarios from the VaR computed according to formula (6.12).

In order to investigate how the fluctuations of the 99% VaR change about the theoretical value, we generate samples of different sizes: 500, 1,000, 5,000, 10,000, 20,000, and 100,000 scenarios. The 99% VaR is computed from these samples and the numbers are stored. We repeat the experiment 100 times. In the end, we have 100 VaR numbers for each sample size. We expect that as the sample size increases, the VaR values will fluctuate less about the theoretical value which is $VaR_{0.01}(X) = 2.326, X \in N(0, 1)$.

Table 6.2 contains the result of the experiment. From the 100 VaR numbers, we calculate the 95% confidence interval for the true value given in the third column. The confidence intervals cover the theoretical value 2.326 and also we notice that the length of the confidence interval decreases as the sample size increases. This effect is best illustrated with the help of

TABLE 6.2 The 99% VaR of the Standard Normal Distribution Computed from a Sample of Scenarios. The 95% Confidence Interval is Calculated from 100 Repetitions of the Experiment. The True Value is $VaR_{0.01}(X) = 2.326$.

Number of Scenarios	99% VaR	95% Confidence Interval
500	2.067	[1.7515, 2.3825]
1,000	2.406	[2.1455, 2.6665]
5,000	2.286	[2.1875, 2.3845]
10,000	2.297	[2.2261, 2.3682]
20,000	2.282	[2.2305, 2.3335]
50,000	2.342	[2.3085, 2.3755]
100,000	2.314	[2.2925, 2.3355]

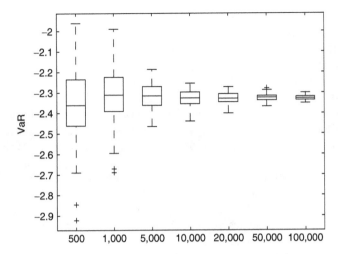

FIGURE 6.3 Boxplot diagrams of the fluctuation of the 99% VaR of the standard normal distribution based on scenarios. The horizontal axis shows the number of scenarios and the boxplots are computed from 100 independent samples.

the boxplot diagrams[6] shown in Figure 6.3. A sample of 100,000 scenarios results in VaR numbers that are tightly packed around the true value while a sample of only 500 scenarios may give a very inaccurate estimate.

This simple experiment shows that the number of scenarios in the Monte Carlo method has to be carefully chosen. The approach we used to determine the fluctuations of the VaR based on scenarios is a statistical method called *parametric bootstrap*. The bootstrap methods in general are powerful statistical methods which are used to compute confidence intervals when the problem is not analytically tractable but the calculations may be quite computationally intensive.

The true merits of the Monte Carlo method can only be realized when the portfolio contains complicated instruments such as derivatives. In this case, it is no longer possible to use a closed-form expression for the portfolio VaR (and any risk measure in general) because the distribution of portfolio

---

[6]A *boxplot*, or a *box-and-whiskers diagram*, is a convenient way of depicting several statistical characteristics of the sample. The size of the box equals the difference between the third and the first *quartile* (75% quantile – 25% quantile), also known as the *interquartile range*. The line in the box corresponds to the median of the data (50% quantile). The lines extending out of the box are called *whiskers* and each of them is long up to 1.5 times the interquartile range. All observations outside the whiskers are labeled outliers and are depicted by a plus sign.

return (or payoff) becomes quite arbitrary. The Monte Carlo method provides the general framework to generate scenarios for the risk-driving factors, then revaluates the financial instruments in the portfolio under each scenario, and, finally, estimates portfolio risk on the basis of the computed portfolio returns (or payoffs) in each state of the world.

While it may seem a straightforward approach, the practical implementation is a very challenging endeavor from both software development and financial modeling point of view. The portfolios of big financial institutions often contain products which require yield curve modeling, development of fundamental and statistical factor models, and, on top of that, a probabilistic model capable of describing the heavy tails of the risk-driving factor returns, the autocorrelation, clustering of the volatility, and the dependence between these factors. Processing large portfolios is related to manipulation of colossal data structures which requires excellent skills of software developers in order to be efficiently performed.

6.4.3 Backtesting of VaR

If we adopt VaR for analysis of portfolio exposure, then a reasonable question is whether the VaR calculated according to any of the methods discussed in the previous section is realistic. Suppose that we calculate the 99% daily portfolio VaR. This means that according to our assumption for the portfolio return (payoff) distribution, the portfolio loses more than the 99% daily VaR with 1% probability. The question is whether this estimate is correct; that is, does the portfolio really lose more than this amount with 1% probability? This question can be answered by backtesting of VaR.

Generally, the procedure consists of the following steps.

Step 1. Choose a time window for the backtesting. Usually the time window is the most recent one or two years.

Step 2. For each day in the time window, calculate the VaR number.

Step 3. Check if the loss on a given day is below or above the VaR number computed the day before. If the observed loss is larger, then we say that there is a case of an *exceedance*. Figure 6.4 provides an example.

Step 4. Count the number of exceedances. Check if there are too many or too few of them by verifying if the number of exceedances belong to the corresponding 95% confidence interval.

If in Step 4 we find out that there are too many number of exceedances, then the VaR numbers produced by the model are too optimistic. Losses exceeding the corresponding VaR happen too frequently. If capital reserves

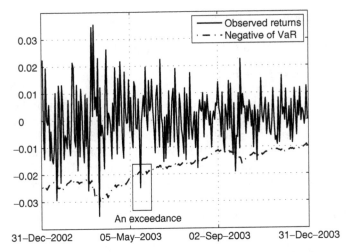

FIGURE 6.4 The observed daily returns of S&P 500 index between December 31, 2002, and December 31, 2003, and the negative of VaR. The marked observation is an example of an exceedance.

are determined on the basis of VaR, then there is a risk of being incapable of covering large losses. Conversely, if the we find out that there are too few number of exceedances, then the VaR numbers are too pessimistic. This is also an undesirable situation. Note that the actual size of the exceedances is immaterial, we only count them.

The confidence interval for the number of exceedances is constructed on the basis of the indicator-type events "we observe an exceedance," "we do not observe an exceedance" on a given day. If we consider the 99% VaR, then the probability of the first event, according to the model, is 1%. Let us associate a number with each of the events similar to a coin tossing experiment. If we observe an exceedance on a given day, then we say that the number 1 has occurred, otherwise 0 has occurred. If the backtesting time window is two years, then we have a sequence of 500 zeros and ones and the expected number of exceedances is 5. Thus finding the 95% confidence interval for the number of exceedances reduces to finding an interval around 5 such that the probability of the number of ones belonging to this interval is 95%.

If we assume that the corresponding events are independent, then there is a complete analogue of this problem in terms of coin tossing. We toss independently 500 times an unfair coin with probability of success equal to 1%. What is the range of the number of success events with 95% probability? Similar questions to this one are discussed in section 4.2 of Chapter 4. In order to find the 95% confidence interval, we can resort to the normal approximation to the binomial distribution. The formula is,

$$\text{Left bound} = N\epsilon - F^{-1}(1 - 0.05/2)\sqrt{N\epsilon(1 - \epsilon)},$$

$$\text{Right bound} = N\epsilon + F^{-1}(1 - 0.05/2)\sqrt{N\epsilon(1 - \epsilon)},$$

where N is the number of indicator-type events, ϵ is the tail probability of the VaR, and $F^{-1}(t)$ is the inverse distribution function of the standard normal distribution. In the example, $N = 500, \epsilon = 0.01$, and the 95% confidence interval for the number of exceedances is $[0, 9]$. Similarly, if we are backtesting the 95% VaR, under the same circumstances the confidence interval is $[15, 34]$.

Note that the statistical test based on the backtesting of VaR at a certain tail probability cannot answer the question if the distributional assumptions for the risk-driving factors are correct in general. For instance, if the portfolio contains only common stocks, then we presume a probabilistic model for stocks returns. By backtesting the 99% daily VaR of portfolio return, we verify if the probabilistic model is adequate for the 1% quantile of the portfolio return distribution; that is, we are backtesting if a certain point in the left tail of the portfolio return distribution is sufficiently accurately modeled. This should not be confused with statistical tests such as the Kolmogorov test or the Kolmogorov-Smirnov test, which concern accepting or rejecting a given distributional hypothesis.

6.4.4 Coherent Risk Measures

Even though VaR has an intuitive interpretation and has been widely adopted as a risk measure, it does not always satisfy the important property that the VaR of a portfolio should not exceed the sum of the VaRs of the portfolio positions. This means that VaR is not always capable of representing the diversification effect.

This fact raises an important question. Can we find a set of desirable properties that a risk measure should satisfy? An answer is given by Artzner et al. (1998). They provide an axiomatic definition of a functional which they call a *coherent risk measure*. The axioms follow with remarks given below each axiom. We denote the risk measure by the functional $\rho(X)$ assigning a real-valued number to a random variable. Usually, the random variable X is interpreted as a random payoff and the motivation for the axioms in Artzner et al. (1998) follows this interpretation. In the remarks below each axiom, we provide an alternative interpretation which holds if X is interpreted as random return.

The Monotonicity Property

Monotonicity. $\rho(Y) \leq \rho(X)$, if $Y \geq X$ in almost sure sense.

Monotonicity states that if investment A has random return (payoff) Y that is not less than the return (payoff) X of investment B at a given horizon in all states of the world, then the risk of A is not greater than the risk of B. This is quite intuitive but it really does matter whether the random variables represent random return or profit because an inequality in almost sure sense between random returns may not translate into the same inequality between the corresponding random profits and vice versa.

Suppose that X and Y describe the random percentage returns on two investments A and B and let $Y = X + 3\%$. Apparently, $Y > X$ in all states of the world. The corresponding payoffs are obtained according to the following equations:

and
$$\begin{aligned} \text{Payoff}(X) &= I_A(1 + X) \\ \text{Payoff}(Y) &= I_B(1 + Y) = I_B(1 + X + 3\%), \end{aligned}$$

where I_A is the initial investment in opportunity A and I_B is the initial investment in opportunity B. If the initial investment I_A is much larger than I_B, then $\text{Payoff}(X) > \text{Payoff}(Y)$ irrespective of the inequality $Y > X$. In effect, investment A may seem less risky than investment B it terms of payoff but in terms of return, the converse may hold.

The Positive Homogeneity Property

Positive homogeneity. $\rho(0) = 0, \rho(\lambda X) = \lambda\rho(X)$, for all X and all $\lambda > 0$.

The positive homogeneity property states that scaling the return (payoff) of the portfolio by a positive factor scales the risk by the same factor. The interpretation for payoffs is obvious—if the investment in a position doubles, so does the risk of the position. We give a simple example illustrating this property when X stands for a random percentage return.

Suppose that today the value of a portfolio is I_0 and we add a certain amount of cash C. The value of our portfolio becomes $I_0 = +C$. The value tomorrow is random and equals $I_1 + C$ in which I_1 is the random payoff. The return of the portfolio equals

$$\begin{aligned} X &= \frac{I_1 + C - I_0 - C}{I_0 + C} = \frac{I_1 - I_0}{I_0}\left(\frac{I_0}{I_0 + C}\right) \\ &= h\frac{I_1 - I_0}{I_0} = hY, \end{aligned}$$

where $h = I_0/(I_0 + C)$ is a positive constant. The axiom positive homogeneity property implies that $\rho(X) = h\rho(Y)$; that is, the risk of the new portfolio will be the risk of the portfolio without the cash but scaled by h.

The Subadditivity Property

Subadditivity. $\rho(X + Y) \leq \rho(X) + \rho(Y)$, for all X and Y.

If X and Y describe random payoffs, then the subadditivity property states that the risk of the portfolio is not greater than the sum of the risks of the two random payoffs.

The positive homogeneity property and the subadditivity property imply that the functional is convex

$$\rho(\lambda X + (1 - \lambda)Y) \leq \rho(\lambda X) + \rho((1 - \lambda)Y)$$
$$= \lambda\rho(X) + (1 - \lambda)\rho(Y),$$

where $\lambda \in [0, 1]$. If X and Y describe random returns, then the random quantity $\lambda X + (1 - \lambda)Y$ stands for the return of a portfolio composed of two financial instruments with returns X and Y having weights λ and $1 - \lambda$ respectively. Therefore, the convexity property states that the risk of a portfolio is not greater than the sum of the risks of its constituents, meaning that it is the convexity property which is behind the diversification effect that we expect in the case of X and Y denoting random returns.

The Invariance Property

Invariance. $\rho(X + C) = \rho(X) - C$, for all X and $C \in \mathbb{R}$.

The invariance property has various labels. Originally, it was called *translation invariance* while in other texts it is called *cash invariance*.[7] If X describes a random payoff, then the invariance property suggests that adding cash to a position reduces its risk by the amount of cash added. This is motivated by the idea that the risk measure can be used to determine capital requirements. As a consequence, the risk measure $\rho(X)$ can be interpreted as the minimal amount of cash necessary to make the position free of any capital requirements,

$$\rho(X + \rho(X)) = 0.$$

The invariance property has a different interpretation when X describes random return. Suppose that the random variable X describes the return of a common stock and we build a long-only portfolio by adding a government bond yielding a risk-free rate r_B. The portfolio return equals

---

[7]This label can be found in Föllmer and Schied (2002).

$wX + (1 - w)r_B$, where $w \in [0, 1]$ is the weight of the common stock in the portfolio. Note that the quantity $(1 - w)r_B$ is nonrandom by assumption. The invariance property states that the risk of the portfolio can be decomposed as

$$\rho(wX + (1 - w)r_B) = \rho(wX) - (1 - w)r_B$$
$$= w\rho(X) - (1 - w)r_B \tag{6.13}$$

where the second equality appears because of the positive homogeneity property. In effect, the risk measure admits the following interpretation: Assume that the constructed portfolio is equally weighted, that is, $w = 1/2$, then the risk measure equals the level of the risk-free rate such that the risk of the equally weighted portfolio consisting of the risky asset and the risk-free asset is zero. The investment in the risk-free asset will be, effectively, the reserve investment.

Alternative interpretations are also possible. Suppose that the present value of the position with random percentage return X is I_0. Assume that we can find a government security earning return r_B^* at the horizon of interest. Then we can ask the question in the opposite direction: How much should we reallocate from I_0 and invest in the government security in order to hedge the risk $\rho(X)$? The needed capital C should satisfy the equation

$$\frac{I_0 - C}{I_0}\rho(X) - \frac{C}{I_0}r_B^* = 0,$$

which is merely a restatement of equation (6.13) with the additional requirement that the risk of the resulting portfolio should be zero. The solution is

$$C = I_0 \frac{\rho(X)}{\rho(X) + r_B^*}.$$

Note that if in the invariance property the constant is nonnegative, $C \geq 0$, then it follows that $\rho(X + C) \leq \rho(X)$. This result is in agreement with the monotonicity property as $X + C \geq X$. In fact, the invariance property can be regarded as an extension of the monotonicity property when the only difference between X and Y is in their means.

According to the discussion in the previous section, VaR is not a coherent risk measure because it may violate the subadditivity property.

An example of a coherent risk measure is the AVaR defined as the average of the VaRs which are larger than the VaR at a given tail probability ϵ. The accepted notation is $AVaR_\epsilon(X)$ in which ϵ stands for the tail probability level. A larger family of coherent risk measures is the family of spectral risk measures, which includes the AVaR as a representative. The spectral risk measures are defined as weighted averages of VaRs. The AVaR and the spectral risk measures will be considered in detail in Chapter 7.

6.5 RISK MEASURES AND DISPERSION MEASURES

In the introduction to this chapter, we remarked that there is a certain relationship between risk and uncertainty. While the two notions are different, without uncertainty there is no risk. Having this in mind, it is not surprising that there are similarities between the axioms behind the deviation measures in section 6.2.5 and the axioms behind the coherent risk measures in section 6.4.4. Both classes, the deviation measures and the coherent risk measures, are not the only classes capable of quantifying statistical dispersion and risk respectively.[8] Nevertheless, they describe basic features of uncertainty and risk and, in effect, we may expect that a relationship between them exists.[9]

Inspecting the defining axioms, we conclude that the common properties are the subadditivity property and the positive homogeneity property. The specific features are the monotonicity property and the invariance property of the coherent risk measures and the translation invariance and positivity of deviation measures. The link between them concerns a subclass of the coherent risk measures called *strictly expectation-bounded risk measures* and a subclass of the deviation measures called *lower-range-dominated deviation measures*. This link has an interesting implication for constructing optimal portfolios, which is discussed in Chapter 8.

A coherent risk measure $\rho(X)$ is called *strictly expectation-bounded* if it satisfies the condition

$$\rho(X) > -EX \qquad (6.14)$$

for all nonconstant X, in which EX is the mathematical expectation of X. If X describes the portfolio return distribution, then the inequality in (6.14) means that the risk of the portfolio is always greater than the negative of the expected portfolio return. A coherent risk measure satisfying this condition is the AVaR, for example.

A deviation measure $D(X)$ is called *lower-range dominated* if it satisfies the condition

$$D(X) \leq EX \qquad (6.15)$$

---

[8] The appendix to this chapter contains an example of a class of risk measures which is more general than the coherent risk measures. This is the class of *convex risk measures*.

[9] The relationship is studied in Rockafellar et al. (2006).

for all nonnegative random variables, $X \geq 0$. A deviation measure that is lower range dominated is, for example, the downside semistandard deviation σ_X^- defined in (6.4).

The relationship between the two subclasses is a one-to-one correspondence between them established through the equations

$$D(X) = \rho(X - EX) \tag{6.16}$$

and

$$\rho(X) = D(X) - E(X). \tag{6.17}$$

That is, if $\rho(X)$ is a strictly expectation-bounded coherent risk measure, then through the formula in (6.16) we obtain the corresponding lower range dominated deviation measure and, conversely, through the formula in (6.17), we obtain the corresponding strictly expectation bounded coherent risk measure.

In effect, there is a deviation measure behind each strictly expectation bounded coherent risk measure. Consider the AVaR for instance. Since it satisfies the property in (6.14), according to the relationship discussed above, the quantity

$$D_\epsilon(X) = AVaR_\epsilon(X - EX)$$

represents the deviation measure underlying the AVaR risk measure at tail probability ϵ. In fact, the quantity $D_\epsilon(X)$, as well as any other lower-range-dominated deviation measure, is obtained by computing the risk of the centered random variable. The definition of AVaR and different calculation methods are provided in Chapter 7.

6.6 RISK MEASURES AND STOCHASTIC ORDERS

In section 5.3 of Chapter 5, we considered stochastic dominance relations. The *second-order stochastic dominance* (SSD), for example, states that X dominates Y with respect to SSD when all risk-averse investors prefer X to Y. Suppose that we estimate the risk of X and Y through a risk measure ρ. If all risk-averse investors prefer X to Y, then does it follow that $\rho(X) \leq \rho(Y)$? This question describes the issue of consistency of a risk measure with the SSD order. Intuitively, a realistic risk measure should be consistent with the SSD order since there is no reason to assume that an investment with higher risk as estimated by the risk measure will be preferred by all risk-averse investors.

Note that monotonicity property of the coherent risk measures implies consistency with *first-order stochastic dominance* (FSD). The condition that $X \geq Y$ in all states of the world translates into the following inequality in terms of the c.d.f.s,

$$F_X(x) \leq F_Y(x), \quad \forall x \in \mathbb{R},$$

which, in fact, characterizes the FSD order.[10] As a result, if all nonsatiable investors prefer X to Y, then any coherent risk measure will indicate that the risk of X is below the risk of Y.

Concerning the more important SSD order, the consistency question is more involved. The defining axioms of the coherent risk measures cannot guarantee consistency with the SSD order. Therefore, if we want to use a coherent risk measure in practice, we have to verify separately the consistency with the SSD order.

DeGiorgi (2005) shows that the AVaR, and spectral risk measures in general, are consistent with the SSD order. Note that if the AVaR, for example, is used to measure the risk of portfolio return distributions, then the corresponding SSD order concerns random variables describing returns. Similarly, if the AVaR is applied to random variables describing payoff, then the SSD order concerns random payoffs. SSD orders involving returns do not coincide with SSD orders involving payoffs, see section 5.3.6 in Chapter 5 for further details.

6.7 SUMMARY

In this chapter, we described different approaches to quantifying risk and uncertainty. We discussed in detail the following dispersion measures:

1. The standard deviation.
2. The mean absolute deviation.
3. The upside and downside semistandard deviations.
4. An axiomatic description of dispersion measures.
5. The family of deviation measures.

We also discussed in detail the following risk measures:

1. The value-at-risk.
2. The family of coherent risk measures.

---

[10]Section 5.3 of Chapter 5 provides more details.

We emphasized that a realistic statistical model for risk estimation includes two essential components:

- A realistic statistical model for the financial assets return distributions and their dependence, capable of accounting for empirical phenomena, and
- A true risk measure capable of describing the essential characteristics of risk.

We explored a link between risk measures and dispersion measures through two subclasses of coherent risk measures and deviation measures. Behind every such coherent risk measure, we can find a corresponding deviation measure and vice versa. The intuitive connection between risk and uncertainty materializes quantitatively in a particular form.

Finally, we emphasized the importance of consistency of risk measures with the SSD order. In the appendix to this chapter, we demonstrate a relationship between probability metrics and deviation measures.

6.8 TECHNICAL APPENDIX

In this appendix, we provide an example of a class of risk measures more general than the coherent risk measures described in the chapter. Then we demonstrate that all symmetric deviation measures are generated from probability metrics.

6.8.1 Convex Risk Measures

In the chapter, we noted that the subadditivity and the positive homogeneity properties of coherent risk measures guarantee that they are convex. The convexity property is the essential feature describing the diversification effect when the random variables are interpreted as portfolio returns. Thus, it is possible to postulate convexity directly and obtain the larger class of *convex risk measures*.

A risk measure ρ is said to be a convex risk measure if it satisfies the following properties.

Monotonicity. $\rho(Y) \leq \rho(X)$, if $Y \geq X$ in almost sure sense.

Convexity. $\rho(\lambda X + (1 - \lambda)Y) \leq \lambda\rho(X) + (1 - \lambda)\rho(Y)$, for all X, Y and $\lambda \in [0, 1]$

Invariance. $\rho(X + C) = \rho(X) - C$, for all X and $C \in \mathbb{R}$.

The remarks from section 6.4.4 concerning the interpretation of the axioms of coherent risk measures depending on whether X describes payoff or return are valid for the convex risk measures as well. The convex risk measures are more general than the coherent risk measures because every coherent risk measure is convex but not vice versa. The convexity property does not imply positive homogeneity. Föllmer and Schied (2002) provide more details on convex risk measures and their relationship with preference relations.

6.8.2 Probability Metrics and Deviation Measures

In this section, we demonstrate that the symmetric deviation measures[11] arise from probability metrics equipped with two additional properties— *translation invariance* and *positive homogeneity*. In fact, not only the symmetric but all deviation measures can be described with the general method of probability metrics by extending the framework. This is illustrated in the appendix to Chapter 9. Stoyanov et al. (2007) provide a more general treatment of similar relationships.

We briefly repeat the definition of a probability semimetric given in section 3.3.1 of Chapter 3 and in the appendix to Chapter 3. The probability semimetric is denoted by $\mu(X, Y)$ in which X and Y are random variables. The properties that $\mu(X, Y)$ should satisfy are the following:

Property 1. $\mu(X, Y) \geq 0$ for any X, Y and $\mu(X, Y) = 0$ if $X = Y$ in almost sure sense.

Property 2. $\mu(X, Y) = \mu(Y, X)$ for any X, Y.

Property 3. $\mu(X, Y) \leq \mu(X, Z) + \mu(Z, Y)$ for any X, Y, Z.

A probability metric is called *translation invariant* and *positively homogeneous* if, besides properties 1, 2, and 3, it satisfies also

Property 4. $\mu(X + Z, Y + Z) = \mu(Y, X)$ for any X, Y, Z.

Property 5. $\mu(aX, aY) = a\mu(X, Y)$ for any X, Y and $a > 0$.

Property 4 is the translation invariance axiom and Property 5 is the positive homogeneity axiom.

Note that translation invariance and positive homogeneity have a different meaning depending on whether probability metrics or dispersion

---

[11]Deviation measures are described in section 6.2.5.

measures are concerned. To avoid confusion, we enumerate the axioms of symmetric deviation measures given in section 6.2.5 of this chapter. A symmetric deviation measure $D(X)$ satisfies the following axioms.

Property 1*. $D(X + C) = D(X)$ for all X and constants $C \in \mathbb{R}$.

Property 2*. $D(X) = D(-X)$ for all X.

Property 3*. $D(0) = 0$ and $D(\lambda X) = \lambda D(X)$ for all X and all $\lambda > 0$.

Property 4*. $D(X) \geq 0$ for all X, with $D(X) > 0$ for nonconstant X.

Property 5*. $D(X + Y) \leq D(X) + D(Y)$ for all X and Y.

We demonstrate that the functional

$$\mu_D(X, Y) = D(X - Y) \tag{6.18}$$

is a probability semimetric satisfying properties 1 through 5 if D satisfies properties 1* through 5*. Furthermore, the functional

$$D_\mu(X) = \mu(X - EX, 0) \tag{6.19}$$

is a symmetric deviation measure if μ is a probability metric satisfying properties 2 through 5.

Demonstration of Equation (6.18)   We show that properties 1 through 5 hold for μ_D defined in equation (6.18).

Property 1. $\mu_D(X, Y) \geq 0$ follows from the nonnegativity of D, Property 4*. Further on, if $X = Y$ in almost sure sense, then $X - Y = 0$ in almost sure sense and $\mu_D(X, Y) = D(0) = 0$ from Property 3*.

Property 2. A direct consequence of Property 2*.

Property 3. Follows from Property 5*:

$$\begin{aligned} \mu(X, Y) &= D(X - Y) = D(X - Z + (Z - Y)) \\ &\leq D(X - Z) + D(Z - Y) = \mu(X, Z) + \mu(Z, Y) \end{aligned}$$

Property 4. A direct consequence of the definition in (6.18).

Property 5. Follows from Property 3*.

Demonstration of Equation (6.19) We show that properties 1* through 5* hold for D_μ defined in equation (6.19).

Property 1*. A direct consequence of the definition in (6.19).

Property 2*. Follows from Property 4 and Property 2:

$$
\begin{aligned}
D_\mu(-X) &= \mu(-X + EX, 0) = \mu(0, X - EX) \\
&= \mu(X - EX, 0) = D_\mu(X)
\end{aligned}
$$

Property 3*. Follows from Property 1 and Property 5. $D_\mu(0) = \mu(0,0) = 0$ and

$$
D_\mu(\lambda X) = \lambda \mu(X - EX, 0) = \lambda D_\mu(X)
$$

Property 4*. Follows because μ is a probability metric. If $D_\mu(X) = 0$, then $X - EX$ is equal to zero almost surely which means that X is a constant in all states of the world.

Property 5*. Arises from Property 3 and Property 4:

$$
\begin{aligned}
D(X + Y) &= \mu(X - EX + Y - EY, 0) = \mu(X - EX, -Y + EY) \\
&\le \mu(X - EX, 0) + \mu(0, -Y + EY) \\
&= \mu(X - EX, 0) + \mu(Y - EY, 0) \\
&= D(X) + D(Y)
\end{aligned}
$$

Conclusion Equation (6.19) shows that all symmetric deviation measures arise from the translation invariant, positively homogeneous probability metrics.

Note that because of the properties of the deviation measures, μ_D is a semimetric and cannot become a metric. This is because D is not sensitive to additive shifts and this property is inherited by μ_D,

$$
\mu_D(X + a, Y + b) = \mu_D(X, Y),
$$

where a and b are constants. In effect, $\mu_D(X, Y) = 0$ implies that the two random variables differ by a constant, $X = Y + c$ in all states of the world.

Due to the translation invariance property, equation (6.19) can be equivalently restated as

$$
D_\mu(X) = \mu(X, EX). \tag{6.20}
$$

As we remarked in the chapter, equation (6.20) represents a very natural generic way of defining measures of dispersion. Starting from equation (6.20) and replacing the translation invariance property by the regularity property of ideal probability metrics given in section 4.4 of Chapter 4, the subadditivity property (Property 5*) of $D_\mu(X)$ breaks down and a property similar to the positive shift property given in the chapter holds instead of Property 1*,

$$D_\mu(X + C) = \mu(X + C, EX + C) \leq \mu(X, EX) = D_\mu(X)$$

for all constants C. In fact, this property is more general than the positive shift property as it holds for arbitrary constants.

BIBLIOGRAPHY

Artzner, P., F. Delbaen, J.-M. Eber, and D. Heath (1998). "Coherent measures of risk," *Mathematical Finance* 6(3): 203–228.

DeGiorgi, E. (2005). "Reward-risk portfolio selection and stochastic dominance," *Journal of Banking and Finance* 29(4): 895–926.

Föllmer, H., and A. Schied (2002). *Stochastic finance: An introduction in discrete time, second revised and extended revision*, Berlin: Walter de Gruyter.

Holton, Glyn A. (2004). "Defining risk," *Financial Analysts Journal* 60(6): 19–25.

Knight, F. H. (1921). *Risk, uncertainty, and profit*, Boston: Houghton Mifflin.

Lamantia, F., S. Ortobelli, and S. T. Rachev (2006a). "An empirical comparison among var models and time rules with elliptical and stable distributed returns," *Investment Management and Financial Innovations* 3(3): 8–29.

Lamantia, F., S. Ortobelli, and S. T. Rachev (2006b). "VaR, CvaR and time rules with elliptical and asymmetric stable distributed returns," *Investment Management and Financial Innovations* 4: 19–39.

Markowitz, H. M. (1952). "Portfolio selection," *Journal of Finance* 7(1): 77–91.

Markowitz, H. M. (1959). *Portfolio selection: Efficient diversification of investments*, New York: John Wiley & Sons.

Rachev, S. T., S. Ortobelli, S. V. Stoyanov, F. J. Fabozzi, and A. Biglova (2007). "Desirable properties of an ideal risk measure in portfolio theory," *International Journal of Theoretical and Applied Finance, forthcoming*.

Rockafellar, R. T., S. Uryasev, and M. Zabarankin (2006). "Generalized deviations in risk analysis," *Finance and Stochastics* 10(1): 51–74.

Stoyanov, S., S. Rachev, and F. Fabozzi (2007). "Probability metrics with application in finance," Technical Report, Department of Econometrics, Statistics and Mathematical Finance School of Economics and Business Engineering, University of Karisrube.

CHAPTER 7

Average Value-at-Risk

7.1 INTRODUCTION

The *value-at-risk* (VaR) measure has been adopted as a standard risk measure in the financial industry. Nonetheless, it has a number of deficiencies recognized by financial professionals. In Chapter 6, we remarked that there is one very important property which does not hold for VaR. This is the subadditivity property which ensures that the VaR measure cannot always account for diversification. There are cases in which the portfolio VaR is larger than the sum of the VaRs of the portfolio constituents. This shows that VaR cannot be used as a true risk measure.

The *average value-at-risk* (AVaR) is a risk measure that is a superior alternative to VaR. Not only does it lack the deficiencies of VaR, but it also has an intuitive interpretation. There are convenient ways for computing and estimating AVaR that allows its application in optimal portfolio problems. Moreover, it satisfies all axioms of coherent risk measures and it is consistent with the preference relations of risk-averse investors.

In this chapter, we explore in detail the properties of AVaR and illustrate its superiority to VaR. We develop new geometric interpretations of AVaR and the various calculation methods. We also provide closed-form expressions for the AVaR of the normal distribution, Student's *t*-distribution, and a practical formula for Lévy stable distributions. Finally, we describe different estimation methods and remark on potential pitfalls.

Besides AVaR, we consider a more general family of risk measures satisfying the axioms of coherent risk measures. This is the class of spectral risk measures which contains AVaR as a special case. In contrast to AVaR, spectral risk measures in general are harder to work with. There are subtle conditions that have to be satisfied in order for spectral risk measures to be a practical concept. Such conditions are stated in the appendix to this chapter.

At the end of the chapter, we note an interesting link between probability metrics and risk measures. Having selected a risk measure, it is possible to find a probability metric which ensures that random variables closer to each other with respect to the probability metric have similar risk profiles.

7.2   AVERAGE VALUE-AT-RISK

In section 6.4.1 of Chapter 6, we noted that a disadvantage of VaR is that it does not give any information about the severity of losses beyond the VaR level. Consider the following example. Suppose that X and Y describe the random returns of two financial instruments with densities and distribution functions such as the ones in Figure 7.1. The expected returns are 3% and 1%, respectively. The standard deviations of X and Y are equal to 10%.[1] The cumulative distribution functions (c.d.f.s) $F_X(x)$ and $F_Y(x)$ cross at $x = -0.15$ and $F_X(-0.15) = F_Y(-0.15) = 0.05$. According to the definition of VaR in equation (6.5), the 95% VaRs of both X and Y are equal to 15%. That is, the two financial instruments lose more than 15% of their present values with probability of 5%. In effect, we may conclude that their risks are equal because their 95% VaRs are equal.

This conclusion is wrong because we pay no attention to the losses which are larger than the 95% VaR level. Figure 7.1 shows that the left tail of X is heavier than the left tail of Y.[2] Therefore, it is more likely that the losses of X will be larger than the losses of Y on condition that they are larger than 15%. Thus, looking only at the losses occurring with probability smaller than 5%, the random return X is riskier than Y. Note that both X and Y have equal standard deviations. If we base the analysis on the standard deviation and the expected return, we would conclude that not only is the uncertainty of X equal to the uncertainty of Y but X is actually preferable because of the higher expected return. In fact, we realize that it is exactly the opposite, which shows how important it is to ground the reasoning on a proper risk measure.

The disadvantage of VaR, that it is not informative about the magnitude of the losses larger than the VaR level, is not present in the risk measure known as *average value-at-risk*. In the literature, it is also called *conditional*

---

[1]In fact, $X = 0.05\sqrt{3}Z + 0.03$, where Z has Student's t-distribution with 4 degrees of freedom and Y has a normal distribution with standard deviation equal to 0.1 and mathematical expectation equal to 0.01. The coefficient of Z is chosen so that the standard deviation of X is also equal to 0.1.

[2]By comparing the c.d.f.s, we notice that the c.d.f. of X is "above" the c.d.f. of Y to the left of the crossing point, $F_X(x) \geq F_Y(x)$, $x \leq -0.15$.

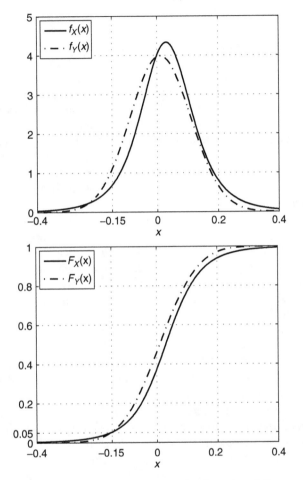

FIGURE 7.1 The top plot shows the densities of X and Y and the bottom plot shows their c.d.f.s. The 95% VaRs of X and Y are equal to 0.15 but X has a thicker tail and is more risky.

value-at-risk[3] or *expected shortfall*, but we will use AVaR because as it best describes the quantity it references.

The AVaR at tail probability ϵ is defined as the average of the VaRs which are larger than the VaR at tail probability ϵ. Therefore, by construction, the AVaR is focused on the losses in the tail which are larger than the

---

[3] This term is adopted in Rockafellar and Uryasev (2002).

corresponding VaR level. The average of the VaRs is computed through the integral

$$A VaR_\epsilon(X) := \frac{1}{\epsilon} \int_0^\epsilon VaR_p(X)dp \qquad (7.1)$$

where $VaR_p(X)$ is defined in equation (6.5) in Chapter 6. As a matter of fact, the AVaR is not well-defined for all real-valued random variables but only for those with finite mean; that is $A VaR_\epsilon(X) < \infty$ if $E|X| < \infty$. This should not be disturbing because random variables with infinite mathematical expectation have limited application in the field of finance. For example, if such a random variable is used for a model of stock returns, then it is assumed that the common stock has infinite expected return which is not realistic.

The AVaR satisfies all the axioms of coherent risk measures. One consequence is that, unlike VaR, it is convex for all possible portfolios which means that it always accounts for the diversification effect.

A geometric interpretation of the definition in equation (7.1) is provided in Figure 7.2. In this figure, the inverse c.d.f. of a random variable X is plotted. The shaded area is closed between the graph of $F_X^{-1}(t)$ and the horizontal axis for $t \in [0, \epsilon]$, where ϵ denotes the selected tail probability. $A VaR_\epsilon(X)$ is the value for which the area of the drawn rectangle, equal to $\epsilon \times A VaR_\epsilon(X)$, coincides with the shaded area which is computed by the integral in equation (7.1). The $VaR_\epsilon(X)$ value is always smaller than $A VaR_\epsilon(X)$. In Figure 7.2, $VaR_\epsilon(X)$ is shown by a dash-dotted line and is indicated by an arrow.

Let us revisit the example developed at the beginning of this section. We concluded that even though the VaRs at 5% tail probability of both random variables are equal, X is riskier than Y because the left tail of X is heavier than the left tail of Y; that is, the distribution of X is more likely to produce larger losses than the distribution of Y on condition that the losses are beyond the VaR at the 5% tail probability. We apply the geometric interpretation illustrated in Figure 7.2 to this example. First, notice that the shaded area in Figure 7.2, which concerns the graph of the inverse of the c.d.f. can also be identified through the graph of the c.d.f. This is done in Figure 7.3, which shows a magnified section of the left tails of the c.d.f.s plotted in Figure 7.1. The shaded area appears as the intersection of the area closed below the graph of the distribution function and the horizontal axis, and the area below a horizontal line shifted at the tail probability above the horizontal axis. In Figure 7.3, we show the area for $F_X(x)$ at 5% tail probability. The corresponding area for $F_Y(x)$ is smaller because $F_Y(x) \leq F_X(x)$ to the left of the crossing point of the two c.d.f.s, which is exactly at 5% tail probability.

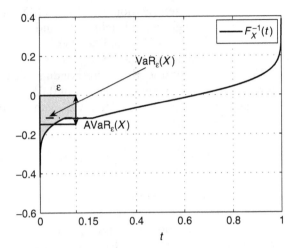

FIGURE 7.2 Geometrically, $AVaR_\epsilon(X)$ is the height for which the area of the drawn rectangle equals the shaded area closed between the graph of the inverse c.d.f. and the horizontal axis for $t \in [0, \epsilon]$. The $VaR_\epsilon(X)$ value is shown by a dash-dotted line.

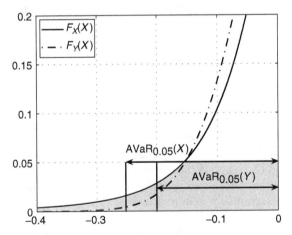

FIGURE 7.3 The AVaRs of the return distributions from Figure 7.1 in line with the geometric intuition. Even though the 95% VaRs are equal, the AVaRs at 5% tail probability differ, $AVaR_{0.05}(X) > AVaR_{0.05}(Y)$.

In line with the geometric interpretation, the $AVaR_{0.05}(X)$ is a number, such that if we draw a rectangle with height 0.05 and width equal to $AVaR_{0.05}(X)$, the area of the rectangle ($0.05 \times AVaR_{0.05}(X)$) equals the shaded area in Figure 7.3. The same exercise for $AVaR_{0.05}(Y)$ shows that $AVaR_{0.05}(Y) < AVaR_{0.05}(X)$ because the corresponding shaded area is smaller and both rectangles share a common height of 0.05.

Besides the definition in equation (7.1), AVaR can be represented through a minimization formula,[4]

$$ AVaR_\epsilon(X) = \min_{\theta \in \mathbb{R}} \left(\theta + \frac{1}{\epsilon} E(-X - \theta)_+ \right) \tag{7.2} $$

where $(x)_+$ denotes the maximum between x and zero, $(x)_+ = \max(x, 0)$ and X describes the portfolio return distribution. It turns out that this formula has an important application in optimal portfolio problems based on AVaR as a risk measure. In the appendix to this chapter, we provide an illuminating geometric interpretation of equation (7.2), which shows the connection to definition of AVaR.

How can we compute the AVaR for a given return distribution? Throughout this section, we assume that the return distribution function is a continuous function, that is, there are no point masses. Under this condition, after some algebra and using the fact that VaR is the negative of a certain quantile, we obtain that the AVaR can be represented in terms of a conditional expectation,

$$ AVaR_\epsilon(X) = -\frac{1}{\epsilon} \int_0^\epsilon F_X^{-1}(t)dt $$
$$ = -E(X|X < -VaR_\epsilon(X)), \tag{7.3} $$

which is called *expected tail loss* (ETL) and is denoted by $ETL_\epsilon(X)$. The conditional expectation implies that the AVaR equals the average loss provided that the loss is larger than the VaR level. In fact, the average of VaRs in equation (7.1) equals the average of losses in equation (7.3) only if the c.d.f. of X is continuous at $x = VaR_\epsilon(X)$. If there is a discontinuity, or a point mass, the relationship is more involved. The general formula is given in the appendix to this chapter.

Equation (7.3) implies that AVaR is related to the conditional loss distribution. In fact, under certain conditions, it is the mathematical expectation of the conditional loss distribution, which represents only one characteristic

---

[4]Equation (7.2) was first studied by Pflug (2000). A proof that equation (7.1) is indeed the AVaR can be found in Rockafellar and Uryasev (2002).

of it. In section 7.9.1 in the appendix to this chapter, we introduce several sets of characteristics of the conditional loss distribution, which provide a more complete picture of it. Also, in section 7.9.2, we introduce the more general concept of higher-order AVaR.

For some continuous distributions, it is possible to calculate explicitly the AVaR through equation (7.3). We provide the closed-form expressions for the normal distribution and Student's t-distribution. In the appendix to this chapter, we give a semi-explicit formula for the class of stable distributions.[5]

1. *The Normal distribution.* Suppose that X is distributed according to a normal distribution with standard deviation σ_X and mathematical expectation EX. The AVaR of X at tail probability ϵ equals

$$AVaR_\epsilon(X) = \frac{\sigma_X}{\epsilon\sqrt{2\pi}} \exp\left(-\frac{(VaR_\epsilon(Y))^2}{2}\right) - EX, \qquad (7.4)$$

where Y has the standard normal distribution, $Y \in N(0, 1)$.

2. *The Student's t-distribution.* Suppose that X has Student's t-distribution with v degrees of freedom, $X \in t(v)$. The AVaR of X at tail probability ϵ equals

$$AVaR_\epsilon(X) = \begin{cases} \dfrac{\Gamma\left(\frac{v+1}{2}\right)}{\Gamma\left(\frac{v}{2}\right)} \dfrac{\sqrt{v}}{(v-1)\epsilon\sqrt{\pi}} \left(1 + \dfrac{(VaR_\epsilon(X))^2}{v}\right)^{\frac{1-v}{2}} & , v > 1 \\ \infty & , v = 1, \end{cases}$$

where the notation $\Gamma(x)$ stands for the gamma function. It is not surprising that for $v = 1$ the AVaR explodes because the Student's t-distribution with one degree of freedom, also known as the *Cauchy distribution*, has infinite mathematical expectation.[6]

Note that equation (7.4) can be represented in a more compact way,

$$AVaR_\epsilon(X) = \sigma_X C_\epsilon - EX, \qquad (7.5)$$

---

[5] Section 4.3.1 in Chapter 4 provides an introduction to stable distributions.

[6] As we remarked, $AVaR_\epsilon(X)$ can be infinite only if the mathematical expectation of X is infinite. Nevertheless, if this turns out to be an issue, one can use instead of AVaR the median of the loss distribution provided that the loss is larger than $VaR_\epsilon(X)$ as a robust version of AVaR. The median of the conditional loss is always finite and, therefore, the issue disappears but at the cost of violating the coherence axioms. Section 7.9.1 in the appendix to this chapter provides more details.

where C_ϵ is a constant which depends only on the tail probability ϵ. Therefore, the AVaR of the normal distribution has the same structure as the normal VaR given in (6.12) in Chapter 6—the difference between the properly scaled standard deviation and the mathematical expectation. In effect, similar to the normal VaR, the normal AVaR properties are dictated by the standard deviation. Even though AVaR is focused on the extreme losses only, due to the limitations of the normal assumption, it is symmetric.

Exactly the same conclusion holds for the AVaR of Student's t-distribution. The true merits of AVaR become apparent if the underlying distributional model is skewed.

7.3   AVaR ESTIMATION FROM A SAMPLE

Suppose that we have a sample of observed portfolio returns and we are not aware of their distribution. Provided that we do not impose any distributional model, the AVaR of portfolio return can be estimated from the sample of observed portfolio returns. Denote the observed portfolio returns by $r_1, r_2, \ldots, r_n$ at time instants $t_1, t_2, \ldots, t_n$. The numbers in the sample are given in order of observation. Denote the sorted sample by $r_{(1)} \le r_{(2)} \le, \ldots, \le r_{(n)}$. Thus, $r_{(1)}$ equals the smallest observed portfolio return and $r_{(n)}$ is the largest. The AVaR of portfolio returns at tail probability ϵ is estimated according to the formula[7]

$$\widehat{\text{AVaR}}_\epsilon(r) = -\frac{1}{\epsilon}\left(\frac{1}{n}\sum_{k=1}^{\lceil n\epsilon\rceil - 1} r_{(k)} + \left(\epsilon - \frac{\lceil n\epsilon\rceil - 1}{n}\right)r_{(\lceil n\epsilon\rceil)}\right) \qquad (7.6)$$

where the notation $\lceil x\rceil$ stands for the smallest integer larger than x.[8] The "hat" above AVaR denotes that the number calculated by equation (7.6) is an estimate of the true value because it is based on a sample. This is a standard notation in statistics.

We demonstrate how equation (7.6) is applied in the following example. Suppose that the sorted sample of portfolio returns is −1.37%, −0.98%, −0.38%, −0.26%, 0.19%, 0.31%, 1.91% and our goal is to calculate the portfolio AVaR at 30% tail probability. In this case, the sample contains

---

[7]This formula is a simple consequence of the definition of AVaR for discrete distributions, see the appendix to this chapter. A detailed derivation is provided by Rockafellar and Uryasev (2002).
[8]For example, $\lceil 3.1\rceil = \lceil 3.8\rceil = 4$.

seven observations and $\lceil n\epsilon \rceil = \lceil 7 \times 0.3 \rceil = 3$. According to equation (7.6), we calculate

$$\widehat{\text{AVaR}}_{0.3}(r) = -\frac{1}{0.3}\left(\frac{1}{7}(-1.37\% - 0.98\%) + (0.3 - 2/7)(-0.38\%)\right)$$

$$= 1.137\%.$$

Formula (7.6) can be applied not only to a sample of empirical observations. We may want to work with a statistical model for which no closed-form expressions for AVaR are known. Then we can simply sample from the distribution and apply formula (7.6) to the generated simulations.

Besides formula (7.6), there is another method for calculation of AVaR. It is based on the minimization formula (7.2) in which we replace the mathematical expectation by the sample average,

$$\widehat{\text{AVaR}}_{\epsilon}(r) = \min_{\theta \in \mathbb{R}}\left(\theta + \frac{1}{n\epsilon}\sum_{i=1}^{n}\max(-r_i - \theta, 0)\right). \qquad (7.7)$$

Even though it is not obvious, equations (7.6) and (7.7) are completely equivalent.

The minimization formula in equation (7.7) is appealing because it can be calculated through the methods of linear programming. It can be restated as a linear optimization problem by introducing auxiliary variables $d_1, \ldots, d_n$, one for each observation in the sample,

$$\begin{aligned}
\min_{\theta, d} \quad & \theta + \frac{1}{n\epsilon}\sum_{k=1}^{n}d_k \\
\text{subject to} \quad & -r_k - \theta \leq d_k, \, k = 1, n \\
& d_k \geq 0, \, k = 1, n \\
& \theta \in \mathbb{R}.
\end{aligned} \qquad (7.8)$$

The linear problem (7.8) is obtained from (7.7) through standard methods in mathematical programming. We briefly demonstrate the equivalence between them. Let us fix the value of θ to θ^*. Then the following choice of the auxiliary variables yields the minimum in (7.8). If $-r_k - \theta^* < 0$, then $d_k = 0$. Conversely, if it turns out that $-r_k - \theta^* \geq 0$, then $-r_k - \theta^* = d_k$. In this way, the sum in the objective function becomes equal to the sum of maxima in equation (7.7).

Applying (7.8) to the sample in the example above, we obtain the optimization problem,

$$\min_{\theta,d} \quad \theta + \frac{1}{7 \times 0.3} \sum_{k=1}^{7} d_k$$

$$\text{subject to} \quad \begin{aligned} 0.98\% - \theta &\le d_1 \\ -0.31\% - \theta &\le d_2 \\ -1.91\% - \theta &\le d_3 \\ 1.37\% - \theta &\le d_4 \\ 0.38\% - \theta &\le d_5 \\ 0.26\% - \theta &\le d_6 \\ -0.19\% - \theta &\le d_7 \\ d_k &\ge 0, k = 1, 7 \\ \theta &\in \mathbb{R}. \end{aligned}$$

The solution to this optimization problem is the number 1.137%, which is attained for $\theta = 0.38\%$. In fact, this value of θ coincides with the VaR at 30% tail probability and this is not by chance but a feature of the problem that is demonstrated in the appendix to this chapter. We verify that the solution of the problem is indeed the number 1.137% by calculating the objective in equation (7.7) for $\theta = 0.38\%$,

$$AVaR_\epsilon(r) = 0.38\% + \frac{0.98\% - 0.38\% + 1.37\% - 0.38\%}{7 \times 0.3} = 1.137\%.$$

Thus we obtain the number calculated through equation (7.6).

7.4 COMPUTING PORTFOLIO AVaR IN PRACTICE

The ideas behind the approaches of VaR estimation can be applied to AVaR. We revisit the four methods from section 6.4.2 of Chapter 6 focusing on the implications for AVaR. We assume that there are n common stocks with random returns described by the random variables $X_1, \ldots, X_n$. Thus the portfolio return is represented by

$$r_p = w_1 X_1 + \cdots + w_n X_n,$$

where $w_1, \ldots, w_n$ are the weights of the common stocks in the portfolio.

7.4.1 The Multivariate Normal Assumption

We noted in section 6.4.2 of Chapter 6 that if the stock returns are assumed to have a multivariate normal distribution, then the portfolio return has a normal distribution with variance $w'\Sigma w$, where w is the vector of weights and Σ is the covariance matrix between stock returns. The mean of the normal distribution is

$$Er_p = \sum_{k=1}^{n} w_k EX_k$$

where E stands for the mathematical expectation. Thus, under this assumption the AVaR of portfolio return at tail probability ϵ can be expressed in closed-form through equation (7.4),

$$AVaR_\epsilon(r_p) = \frac{\sqrt{w'\Sigma w}}{\epsilon\sqrt{2\pi}} \exp\left(-\frac{(VaR_\epsilon(Y))^2}{2}\right) - Er_p$$

$$= C_\epsilon\sqrt{w'\Sigma w} - Er_p, \tag{7.9}$$

where C_ϵ is a constant independent of the portfolio composition and can be calculated in advance. In effect, due to the limitations of the multivariate normal assumption, the portfolio AVaR appears symmetric and is representable as the difference between the properly scaled standard deviation of the random portfolio return and portfolio expected return.

7.4.2   The Historical Method

As we noted in section 6.4.2 of Chapter 6, the historical method is not related to any distributional assumptions. We use the historically observed portfolio returns as a model for the future returns and apply formula (7.6) or (7.7).

The historical method has several drawbacks mentioned in section 6.4.2. We emphasize that it is very inaccurate for low-tail probabilities such as 1% or 5%. Even with one year of daily returns, which amounts to 250 observations, to estimate the AVaR at 1% probability, we have to use the three smallest observations which is quite insufficient. What makes the estimation problem even worse is that these observations are in the tail of the distribution; that is, they are the *smallest* ones in the sample. The implication is that when the sample changes, the estimated AVaR may change a lot because the smallest observations tend to fluctuate a lot.

7.4.3   The Hybrid Method

According to the hybrid method described in section 6.4.2 of Chapter 6, different weights are assigned to the observations by which the more recent observations get a higher weight. The rationale is that the observations far back in the past have less impact on the portfolio risk at the present time.

The hybrid method can be adapted for AVaR estimation. The weights assigned to the observations are interpreted as probabilities and, thus, the portfolio AVaR can be estimated from the resulting discrete distribution according to the formula

$$\widehat{\text{AVaR}}_\epsilon(r) = -\frac{1}{\epsilon}\left(\sum_{j=1}^{k_\epsilon} p_j r_{(j)} + \left(\epsilon - \sum_{j=1}^{k_\epsilon} p_j\right) r_{(k_\epsilon+1)}\right) \qquad (7.10)$$

where $r_{(1)} \leq r_{(2)} \leq \cdots \leq r_{(k_m)}$ denotes the sorted sample of portfolio returns or payoffs and $p_1, p_2, \ldots, p_{k_m}$ stand for the probabilities of the sorted observations; that is, p_1 is the probability of $r_{(1)}$. The number k_ϵ in equation (7.10) is an integer satisfying the inequalities,

$$\sum_{j=1}^{k_\epsilon} p_j \leq \epsilon < \sum_{j=1}^{k_\epsilon+1} p_j.$$

Equation (7.10) follows directly from the definition of AVaR[9] under the assumption that the underlying distribution is discrete without the additional simplification that the outcomes are equally probable. In the appendix to this chapter, we demonstrate the connection between equation (7.10) and the definition of AVaR in equation (7.1).

7.4.4 The Monte Carlo Method

The basic steps of the Monte Carlo method are described in section 6.4.2 of Chapter 6. They are applied without modification. Essentially, we assume and estimate a multivariate statistical model for the stocks return distribution. Then we sample from it, and we calculate scenarios for portfolio return. On the basis of these scenarios, we estimate portfolio AVaR using equation (7.6) in which $r_1, \ldots, r_n$ stands for the vector of generated scenarios.

Similar to the case of VaR, an artifact of the Monte Carlo method is the variability of the risk estimate. Since the estimate of portfolio AVaR is obtained from a generated sample of scenarios, by regenerating the sample, we will obtain a slightly different value. We illustrate the variability issue by a simulation example, similar to the one developed for VaR in section 7.3.6.

---

[9]A formal proof can be found in Rockafellar and Uryasev (2002). The reasoning in Rockafellar and Uryasev (2002) is based on the assumption that the random variable describes losses while in equation (7.10), the random variable describes the portfolio return or payoff.

Suppose that the portfolio daily return distribution is the standard normal law, $r_p \in N(0, 1)$. By the closed-form expression in equation (7.4), we calculate that the AVaR of the portfolio at 1% tail probability equals,

$$AVaR_{0.01}(r_p) = \frac{1}{0.01\sqrt{2\pi}} \exp\left(-\frac{2.326^2}{2}\right) = 2.665.$$

To investigate how the fluctuations of the 99% AVaR change about the theoretical value, we generate samples of different sizes: 500, 1,000, 5,000, 10,000, 20,000, and 100,000 scenarios. The 99% AVaR is computed from these samples using equation (7.6) and the numbers are stored. We repeat the experiment 100 times. In the end, we have 100 AVaR numbers for each sample size. We expect that as the sample size increases, the AVaR values will fluctuate less about the theoretical value, which is $AVaR_{0.01}(X) = 2.665$, $X \in N(0, 1)$.

Table 7.1 contains the result of the experiment. From the 100 AVaR numbers, we calculate the 95% confidence interval reported in the third column. The confidence intervals cover the theoretical value 2.665 and also we notice that the length of the confidence interval decreases as the sample size increases. This effect is illustrated in Figure 7.4 with boxplot diagrams. A sample of 100,000 scenarios results in AVaR numbers, which are tightly packed around the true value while a sample of only 500 scenarios may give a very inaccurate estimate.

By comparing Table 7.1 to Table 6.2 in section 6.4.2 of Chapter 6, we notice that the length of the 95% confidence intervals for AVaR are larger than the corresponding confidence intervals for VaR. This result is

TABLE 7.1 The 99% AVaR of the Standard Normal Distribution Computed from a Sample of Scenarios. The 95% Confidence Interval is Calculated from 100 Repetitions of the Experiment. The True Value is $AVaR_{0.01}(X) = 2.665$.

Number of Scenarios	AVaR at 99%	95% Confidence Interval
500	2.646	[2.2060, 2.9663]
1,000	2.771	[2.3810, 2.9644]
5,000	2.737	[2.5266, 2.7868]
10,000	2.740	[2.5698, 2.7651]
20,000	2.659	[2.5955, 2.7365]
50,000	2.678	[2.6208, 2.7116]
100,000	2.669	[2.6365, 2.6872]

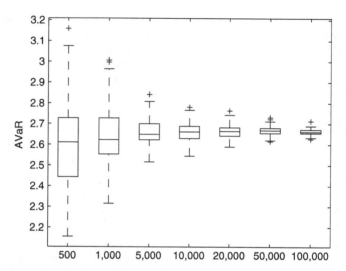

FIGURE 7.4   Boxplot diagrams of the fluctuation of the AVaR at 1% tail probability of the standard normal distribution based on scenarios. The horizontal axis shows the number of scenarios and the boxplots are computed from 100 independent samples.

not surprising. Given that both quantities are at the same tail probability of 1%, the AVaR has larger variability than the VaR for a fixed number of scenarios because the AVaR is the average of terms fluctuating more than the 1% VaR. This effect is more pronounced the more heavy-tailed the distribution is.

7.5   BACKTESTING OF AVaR

Suppose that we have selected a method for calculating the daily AVaR of a portfolio. A reasonable question is how we can verify whether the estimates of daily AVaR are realistic.

In section 6.4.2 of Chapter 6, we considered the same issue in the context of VaR and the solution was to carry out a backtesting of VaR. Essentially, VaR backtesting consists of computing the portfolio VaR for each day back in time using the information available up to that day only. In this way, we have the VaR numbers back in time as if we had used exactly the same methodology in the past. On the basis of the VaR numbers and the realized portfolio returns, we can use statistical methods to assess whether the forecasted loss at the VaR tail probability is consistent with the observed losses. If there are too many observed losses larger than the forecasted VaR, then the model is too optimistic. Conversely, if there are too few losses larger than the forecasted VaR, then the model is too pessimistic.

Note that in the case of VaR backtesting, we are simply counting the cases in which there is an exceedance; that is, when the size of the observed loss is larger than the predicted VaR. The magnitude of the exceedance is immaterial for the statistical test.

Unlike VaR, backtesting of AVaR is not straightforward and is a much more challenging task. By definition, the AVaR at tail probability ϵ is the average of VaRs larger than the VaR at tail probability ϵ. The most direct approach to test AVaR than would be to perform VaR backtests at all tail probabilities smaller than ϵ. If all these VaRs are correctly modeled, then so is the corresponding AVaR.

One general issue with this approach is that it is impossible to perform in practice. Suppose that we consider the AVaR at tail probability of 1%, for example. Backtesting VaRs deeper in the tail of the distribution can be infeasible because the backtesting time window is too short. The lower the tail probability, the larger time window we need in order for the VaR test to be conclusive. Another general issue is that this approach is too demanding. Even if the VaR backtesting fails at some tail probability ϵ_1 below ϵ, this does not necessarily mean that the AVaR is incorrectly modeled because the test failure may be due to purely statistical reasons and not to incorrect modeling.

These arguments illustrate why AVaR backtesting is a difficult problem—we need the information about the entire tail of the return distribution describing the losses larger than the VaR at tail probability ϵ and there may be too few observations from the tail upon which to base the analysis. For example, in one business year, there are typically 250 trading days. Therefore, a one-year backtesting results in 250 daily portfolio returns, which means that if $\epsilon = 1\%$, then there are only two observations available from the losses larger than the VaR at 1% tail probability.

As a result, in order to be able to backtest AVaR, we can assume a certain "structure" of the tail of the return distribution that would compensate for the lack of observations. There are two general approaches:

1. Use the tails of the Lévy stable distributions[10] as a proxy for the tail of the loss distribution and take advantage of the practical semianalytic formula for the AVaR given in the appendix to this chapter to construct a statistical test.

---

[10] Section 4.3.1 of Chapter 4 provides more details on the class of stable distributions and its application as a model in finance.

2. Make the weaker assumption that the loss distribution belongs to the domain of attraction of a maxstable distribution. The behavior of the large losses can then be approximately described by the limit maxstable distribution and a statistical test can be based on it.

The rationale of the first approach is that generally the Lévy stable distribution provides a good fit to the stock returns data and, thus, the stable tail may turn out to be a reasonable approximation. Moreover, from the Generalized Central Limit Theorem,[11] we know that stable distributions have domains of attraction that make them an appealing candidate for an approximate model.

The second approach is based on a weaker assumption. The family of maxstable distributions arises as the limit distribution of properly scaled and centered maxima of i.i.d. random variables. If the random variable describes portfolio losses, then the limit maxstable distribution can be used as a model for the large losses (i.e., the ones in the tail). Unfortunately, as a result of the weaker assumption, estimators of poor quality have to be used to estimate the parameters of the limit maxstable distribution, such as the Hill estimator for example. This represents the basic trade-off in this approach.

7.6   SPECTRAL RISK MEASURES

By definition, the AVaR at tail probability ϵ is the average of the VaRs larger than the VaR at tail probability ϵ. It appears possible to obtain a larger family of coherent risk measures by considering the weighted average of the VaRs instead of simple average. Thus the AVaR becomes just one representative of this larger family which is known as *spectral risk measures*. Acerbi (2004) provides a detailed description of spectral risk measures.

Spectral risk measures are defined as,[12]

$$\rho_\phi(X) = \int_0^1 VaR_p(X)\phi(p)dp, \qquad (7.11)$$

where $\phi(p)$, $p \in [0, 1]$ is the weighting function also known as *risk spectrum* or *risk-aversion function*. It has the following interpretation. Consider a small interval $[p_1, p_2]$ of tail probabilities with length $p_2 - p_1 = \Delta p$. The

---

[11]Section 4.3 of Chapter 4 provides more information on the Generalized Central Limit Theorem.

[12]In fact, the formal definition is more involved. See Acerbi (2004) for further details.

weight corresponding to this interval is approximately equal to $\phi(p_1) \times \Delta p$. Thus, the VaRs at tail probabilities belonging to this interval have approximately the weight $\phi(p_1) \times \Delta p$.

The risk-aversion function should possess some properties in order for $\rho_\phi(X)$ to be a coherent risk measure, it should be:

Positive. $\phi(p) \geq 0$, $p \in [0, 1]$.

Nonincreasing. Larger losses are multiplied by larger weights, $\phi(p_1) \geq \phi(p_2)$, $p_1 \leq p_2$.

Normed. All weights should sum up to 1, $\int_0^1 \phi(p)dp = 1$.

If we compare equations (7.11) and (7.1), we notice that the AVaR at tail probability ϵ arises from a spectral risk measure with a constant risk aversion function for all tail probabilities below ϵ. The left plot in Figure 7.5 illustrates a typical risk-aversion function. The right plot shows the graph of the risk-aversion function yielding the AVaR at tail probability ϵ.

It is possible to obtain formulae through which we can estimate the spectral risk measures from a sample of observations. They are essentially counterparts of (7.6) and (7.7). (See Acerbi and Simonetti (2002) for further details.)

In section 6.4.2 of Chapter 6 and section 7.4 of this chapter, we emphasized that if a sample is used to estimate VaR and AVaR, then there

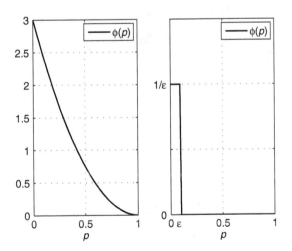

FIGURE 7.5 Examples of risk-aversion functions. The right plot shows the risk-aversion function yielding the AVaR at tail probability ϵ.

is certain variability of the estimates. We illustrated it through a Monte Carlo example for the standard normal distribution. Comparing the results we concluded that the variability of AVaR is larger than the VaR at the same tail probability because in the AVaR, we average terms with larger variability. The heavier the tail, the more pronounced this effect becomes.

When spectral risk measures are estimated from a sample, the variability of the estimate may become a big issue. Note that due to the non-increasing property of the risk-aversion function, the larger losses, which are deeper in the tail of the return distribution, are multiplied by a larger weight. The larger losses (VaRs at lower tail probability) have higher variability and the multiplication by a larger weight further increases the variability of the weighted average. Therefore, larger number of scenarios may turn out to be necessary to achieve given stability of the estimate for spectral risk measures than for AVaR. Ultimately, this is dependent on the choice of the risk-aversion function and the assumed distribution of portfolio return.

In fact, the distributional assumption for the random variable X is very important because it may lead to unbounded spectral risk measures for some choices of the risk-aversion function. An infinite risk measure is not informative for decision makers and an unfortunate combination of a distributional model and a risk-aversion function cannot be identified by looking at the sample estimate of $\rho_\phi(X)$. In practice, when $\rho_\phi(X)$ is divergent in theory, we will observe high variability of the risk estimates when regenerating the simulations and also nondecreasing variability of the risk estimates as we increase the number of simulations. We can regard these effects as symptoms for a bad combination of a statistical model and a risk-aversion function. The appendix to this chapter contains guidelines for avoiding inappropriate choices of a risk-aversion function depending on certain information about the probability distribution of X.

We would like to stress that this problem does not exist for AVaR because a finite mean of X guarantees that the AVaR is well defined on all tail probability levels. The problem for the spectral measures of risk arises from the non-increasing property of the risk-aversion function. Larger losses are multiplied by larger weights which may result in an unbounded weighted average.

7.7   RISK MEASURES AND PROBABILITY METRICS

In Chapter 3, we introduced the notion of probability metrics and remarked that they provide the only way of measuring distances between random quantities. It turns out that a small distance between random quantities does not necessarily imply that selected characteristics of those quantities are close to each other. For example, a probability metric may indicate that two distributions are close to each other and, still, the standard deviations of the two distributions may be arbitrarily different. As a very extreme case, one of the distributions may even have an infinite standard deviation. Thus, if we want small distances measured by a probability metric to imply similar characteristics, the probability metric should be carefully chosen. In section 4.4 of Chapter 4, we described the ideal probability metrics. A small distance between two random quantities estimated by an ideal metric means that the two random variables have similar absolute moments. The technical appendix to Chapter 4 provides more details.

A risk measure can be viewed as calculating a particular characteristic of a random variable. Furthermore, there are problems in finance in which the goal is to find a random variable closest to another random variable. For instance, such is the benchmark tracking problem which is at the heart of passive portfolio construction strategies. Essentially, we are trying to construct a portfolio tracking the performance a given benchmark.[13] In some sense, this can be regarded as finding a portfolio return distribution which is closest to the return distribution of the benchmark. Usually, the distance is measured through the tracking error, which is the standard deviation of the active return.

Suppose that we have found the portfolio tracking the benchmark most closely with respect to the tracking error. Can we be sure that the risk of the portfolio is close to the risk of the benchmark? Generally, the answer is affirmative only if we use the standard deviation as a risk measure. Active return is refined as the difference between the portfolio return r_p and the benchmark return r_b, $r_p - r_b$. The conclusion that smaller tracking error implies that the standard deviation of r_p is close to the standard deviation of r_b is based on the inequality,

$$|\sigma(r_p) - \sigma(r_b)| \leq \sigma(r_p - r_b).$$

The right part corresponds to the tracking error and, therefore, smaller tracking error results in $\sigma(r_p)$ being closer to $\sigma(r_b)$.

In order to guarantee that small distance between portfolio return distributions corresponds to similar risks, we have to find a suitable probability metric. Technically, for a given risk measure we need to find a probability metric with respect to which the risk measure is a continuous functional,

$$|\rho(X) - \rho(Y)| \leq \mu(X, Y),$$

---

[13]Chapter 9 provides more details on the benchmark tracking problem.

where ρ is the risk measure and μ stands for the probability metric. We continue with examples of how this can be done for VaR, AVaR, and the spectral risk measures.[14]

1. **VaR.** Suppose that X and Y describe the return distributions of two portfolios. The absolute difference between the VaRs of the two portfolios at any tail probability can be bounded by,

$$|VaR_\epsilon(X) - VaR_\epsilon(Y)| \leq \max_{p \in (0,1)} |VaR_p(X) - VaR_p(Y)|$$

$$= \max_{p \in (0,1)} |F_Y^{-1}(p) - F_X^{-1}(p)|$$

$$= \mathbf{W}(X, Y),$$

where $\mathbf{W}(X, Y)$ is the uniform metric between inverse distribution functions defined in equation (3.14) in section 3.3.3 of Chapter 3. If the distance between X and Y is small, as measured by the metric $\mathbf{W}(X, Y)$, then the VaR of X is close to the VaR of Y at any tail probability level ϵ.

2. **AVaR.** Suppose that X and Y describe the return distributions of two portfolios. The absolute difference between the AVaRs of the two portfolios at any tail probability can be bounded by,

$$|AVaR_\epsilon(X) - AVaR_\epsilon(Y)| \leq \frac{1}{\epsilon} \int_0^\epsilon |F_X^{-1}(p) - F_Y^{-1}(p)|dp$$

$$\leq \int_0^1 |F_X^{-1}(p) - F_Y^{-1}(p)|dp$$

$$= \kappa(X, Y),$$

where $\kappa(X, Y)$ is the Kantorovich metric defined in equation (3.12) in section 3.3.3 of Chapter 3. If the distance between X and Y is small, as measured by the metric $\kappa(X, Y)$, then the AVaR of X is close to the AVaR of Y at any tail probability level ϵ. Note that the quantity,

$$\kappa_\epsilon(X, Y) = \frac{1}{\epsilon} \int_0^\epsilon |F_X^{-1}(p) - F_Y^{-1}(p)|dp,$$

can also be used to bound the absolute difference between the AVaRs. It is a probability semimetric,[15] giving the best possible upper bound on the absolute difference between the AVaRs.

---

[14]The examples are based on Stoyanov et al. (2007).
[15]The technical appendix to Chapter 3 describes the differences between probability metrics and probability semimetrics.

3. *Spectral risk measures.* Suppose that X and Y describe the return distributions of two portfolios. The absolute difference between the spectral risk measures of the two portfolios for a given risk-aversion function can be bounded by,

$$|\rho_\phi(X) - \rho_\phi(Y)| \leq \int_0^1 |F_X^{-1}(p) - F_Y^{-1}(p)|\phi(p)dp$$

$$= \kappa_\phi(X, Y)$$

where $\kappa_\phi(X, Y)$ is a weighted Kantorovich metric. If the distance between X and Y is small, as measured by the metric $\kappa_\phi(X, Y)$, then the risk of X is close to the risk of Y as measured by the spectral risk measure ρ_ϕ.

7.8 SUMMARY

In this chapter, we considered in detail the AVaR risk measure. We noted the advantages of AVaR, described a number of methods for its calculation and estimation, and remarked some potential pitfalls including estimates variability and problems on AVaR backtesting. We illustrated geometrically many of the formulae for AVaR calculation, which makes them more intuitive and easy to understand.

Besides the AVaR, we considered a more general family of coherent risk measures—the spectral risk measures. The AVaR is a spectral risk measure with a specific risk-aversion function. We emphasized the importance of proper selection of the risk-aversion function to avoid explosion of the risk measure.

Finally, we demonstrated a connection between the theory of probability metrics and risk measures. Basically, by choosing an appropriate probability metric we can guarantee that if two portfolio return distributions are close to each other, their risk profiles are also similar.

7.9 TECHNICAL APPENDIX

We start with a more general view that better describes the conditional loss distribution in terms of certain characteristics in which AVaR appears as a special case. We continue with the notion of higher-order AVaR, generating a family of coherent risk measures. Next, we provide an intuitive geometric interpretation of the minimization formula for the AVaR calculation. We also provide a semianalytic expression for the AVaR of stable distributions and compare the expected tail-loss measure to AVaR. Finally, we comment on the proper choice of a risk-aversion function in spectral risk measures that does not result in an infinite risk measure.

7.9.1 Characteristics of Conditional Loss Distributions

In the chapter, we defined AVaR as a risk measure and showed how it can be calculated in practice. While it is an intuitive and easy to use coherent risk measure, AVaR represents the average of the losses larger than the VaR at tail probability ϵ, which is only one characteristic of the distribution of extreme losses. We remarked that if the distribution function is continuous, then AVaR coincides with ETL, which is the mathematical expectation of the conditional loss distribution. Besides the mathematical expectation, there are other important characteristics of the conditional loss distribution. For example, AVaR does not provide any information about how dispersed the conditional losses are around the AVaR value. In this section, we state a couple of families of useful characteristics in which AVaR appears as one example.

Consider the following tail moment of order n at tail probability ϵ,

$$m_\epsilon^n(X) = \frac{1}{\epsilon} \int_0^\epsilon (F_X^{-1}(t))^n dt, \qquad (7.12)$$

where $n = 1, 2, \ldots$, $F_X^{-1}(t)$ is the inverse c.d.f. of the random variable X. If the distribution function of X is continuous, then the tail moment of order n can be represented through the following conditional expectation,

$$m_\epsilon^n(X) = E(X^n | X < VaR_\epsilon(X)), \qquad (7.13)$$

where $n = 1, 2, \ldots$ In the general case, if the c.d.f. has a jump at $VaR_\epsilon(X)$, a link exists between the conditional expectation and equation (7.12), which is similar to formula (7.23) for AVaR. In fact, AVaR appears as the negative of the tail moment of order one, $AVaR_\epsilon(X) = -m_\epsilon^1(X)$.

The higher-order tail moments provide additional information about the conditional distribution of the extreme losses. We can make a parallel with the way the moments of a random variable are used to describe certain properties of it. In our case, it is the conditional distribution that we are interested in.

In addition to the moments $m_\epsilon^n(X)$, we introduce the central tail moments of order n at tail probability ϵ,

$$M_\epsilon^n(X) = \frac{1}{\epsilon} \int_0^\epsilon (F_X^{-1}(t) - m_\epsilon^1(X))^n dt, \qquad (7.14)$$

where $m_\epsilon^1(X)$ is the tail moment of order one. If the distribution function is continuous, then the central moments can be expressed in terms of the conditional expectation,

$$M_\epsilon^n(X) = E((X - m_\epsilon^1(X))^n | X < VaR_\epsilon(X)).$$

The tail variance of the conditional distribution appears as $M_\epsilon^2(X)$ and the tail standard deviation equals

$$(M_\epsilon^2(X))^{1/2} = \left(\frac{1}{\epsilon} \int_0^\epsilon (F_X^{-1}(t) - m_\epsilon^1(X))^2 dt \right)^{1/2}.$$

There is a formula expressing the tail variance in terms of the tail moments introduced in (7.13),

$$M_\epsilon^2(X) = m_\epsilon^2(X) - (m_\epsilon^1(X))^2$$
$$= m_\epsilon^2(X) - (AVaR_\epsilon(X))^2.$$

This formula is similar to the representation of variance in terms of the first two moments,

$$\sigma_X^2 = EX^2 - (EX)^2.$$

The tail standard deviation can be used to describe the dispersion of conditional losses around AVaR as it satisfies the general properties of dispersion measures given in section 6.2.4 of Chapter 6. It can be viewed as complementary to AVaR in the sense that if there are two portfolios with equal AVaRs of their return distributions but different tail standard deviations, the portfolio with the smaller standard deviation is preferable.

Another central tail moment that can be interpreted is $M_\epsilon^3(X)$. After proper normalization, it can be employed to measure the skewness of the conditional loss distribution. In fact, if the tail probability is sufficiently small, the tail skewness will be quite significant. In the same fashion, by normalizing the central tail moment of order 4, we obtain a measure of kurtosis of the conditional loss distribution.

In a similar way, we introduce the absolute central tail moments of order n at tail probability ϵ,

$$\mu_\epsilon^n(X) = \frac{1}{\epsilon} \int_0^\epsilon |F_X^{-1}(t) - m_\epsilon^1(X)|^n dt. \tag{7.15}$$

The tail moments $\mu_\epsilon^n(X)$ raised to the power of $1/n$, $(\mu_\epsilon^n(X))^{1/n}$, can be applied as measures of dispersion of the conditional loss distribution if the distribution is such that they are finite.

In the chapter, we remarked that the tail of the random variable can be so heavy that AVaR becomes infinite. Even if it is theoretically finite, it can be hard to estimate because the heavy tail will result in the AVaR estimator having a large variability. Under certain conditions it may turn out to be practical to employ a robust estimator instead. The *median tail loss* (MTL) defined as the median of the conditional loss distribution, is a robust alternative to AVaR. It has the advantage of always being finite no matter the tail behavior of the random variable. Formally, it is defined as

$$MTL_\epsilon(X) = -F_X^{-1}(1/2|X < -VaR_\epsilon(X)), \qquad (7.16)$$

where $F_X^{-1}(p|X < -VaR_\epsilon(X))$ stands for the inverse distribution function of the c.d.f. of the conditional loss distribution

$$F_X(x|X < -VaR_\epsilon(X)) = P(X \le x|X < -VaR_\epsilon(X))$$

$$= \begin{cases} P(X \le x)/\epsilon, & x < -VaR_\epsilon(X) \\ 1, & x \ge -VaR_\epsilon(X). \end{cases}$$

In effect, MTL, as well as any other quantile of the conditional loss distribution, can be directly calculated as a quantile of the distribution of X,

$$MTL_\epsilon(X) = -F_X^{-1}(\epsilon/2)$$

$$= VaR_{\epsilon/2}(X), \qquad (7.17)$$

where $F_X^{-1}(p)$ is the inverse c.d.f. of X and ϵ is the tail probability of the corresponding VaR in equation (7.16). Thus MTL shares the properties of VaR. Equation (7.17) shows that MTL is not a coherent risk measure even though it is a robust alternative to AVaR which is a coherent risk measure.

In the universe of the three families of moments that we introduced, AVaR is one special case providing only limited information. It may be the only coherent risk measure among them but the other moments can be employed in addition to AVaR in order to gain more insight into the conditional loss distribution. Furthermore, it could appear that other reasonable risk measures can be based on some of the moments. We believe that they all should be considered in financial applications.

7.9.2 Higher-Order AVaR

By definition, AVaR is the average of VaRs larger than the VaR at tail probability ϵ. In the same fashion, we can pose the question of what happens if we average all AVaRs larger than the AVaR at tail probability ϵ. In fact, this quantity is an average of coherent risk measures and, therefore, is a coherent risk measure itself since it satisfies all defining properties of coherent risk measures given in section 6.4.4 of Chapter 6. We call it $AVaR$ *of order one* and denote it by $AVaR_\epsilon^{(1)}(X)$ because it is a derived quantity from AVaR. In this section, we consider similar derived quantities from AVaR, which we call *higher-order AVaRs*.

Formally, the AVaR of order one is represented in the following way,

$$AVaR_\epsilon^{(1)}(X) = \frac{1}{\epsilon}\int_0^\epsilon AVaR_p(X)dp,$$

where $AVaR_p(X)$ is the AVaR at tail probability p. Replacing AVaR by the definition given in equation (7.1), we obtain

$$AVaR_\epsilon^{(1)}(X) = -\frac{1}{\epsilon}\int_0^\epsilon \left(\int_0^1 F_X^{-1}(y)g_p(y)dy\right)dp$$

$$= -\frac{1}{\epsilon}\int_0^1 F_X^{-1}(y)\left(\int_0^\epsilon g_p(y)dp\right)dy,$$

where

$$g_p(y) = \begin{cases} 1/p, & y \in [0,p] \\ 0, & y > p. \end{cases}$$

and after certain algebraic manipulations, we get the expression

$$AVaR_\epsilon^{(1)}(X) = -\frac{1}{\epsilon}\int_0^\epsilon F_X^{-1}(y)\log\frac{\epsilon}{y}dy$$

$$= \int_0^\epsilon VaR_y(X)\phi_\epsilon(y)dy. \tag{7.18}$$

In effect, the AVaR of order one can be expressed as a weighted average of VaRs larger than the VaR at tail probability ϵ with a weighting function $\phi_\epsilon(y)$ equal to

$$\phi_\epsilon(y) = \begin{cases} \dfrac{1}{\epsilon}\log\dfrac{\epsilon}{y}, & 0 \le y \le \epsilon \\ 0, & \epsilon < y \le 1. \end{cases}$$

The AVaR of order one can be viewed as a spectral risk measure with $\phi_\epsilon(y)$ being the risk aversion function.

Similarly, we define the higher-order AVaR through the recursive equation

$$AVaR_\epsilon^{(n)}(X) = \frac{1}{\epsilon}\int_0^\epsilon AVaR_p^{(n-1)}(X)dp, \tag{7.19}$$

where $AVaR_p^{(0)}(X) = AVaR_p(X)$ and $n = 1, 2 \ldots$ Thus the AVaR of order two equals the average of AVaRs of order one, which are larger than the AVaR of order one at tail probability ϵ. The AVaR of order n appears as an average of AVaRs of order $n - 1$.

The quantity $AVaR_\epsilon^{(n)}(X)$ is a coherent risk measure because it is an average of coherent risk measures. This is a consequence of the recursive definition in (7.19). It is possible to show that AVaR of order n admits the representation

$$AVaR_\epsilon^{(n)}(X) = \frac{1}{\epsilon} \int_0^\epsilon VaR_y(X) \frac{1}{n!} \left(\log \frac{\epsilon}{y} \right)^n dy \qquad (7.20)$$

and $AVaR_\epsilon^{(n)}(X)$ can be viewed as a spectral risk measure with a risk aversion function equal to

$$\phi_\epsilon^{(n)}(y) = \begin{cases} \dfrac{1}{\epsilon n!} \left(\log \dfrac{\epsilon}{y} \right)^n, & 0 \le y \le \epsilon \\ 0, & \epsilon < y \le 1. \end{cases}$$

As a simple consequence of the definition, the sequence of higher-order AVaRs is monotonic,

$$AVaR_\epsilon(X) \le AVaR_\epsilon^{(1)}(X) \le \cdots \le AVaR_\epsilon^{(n)}(X) \le \cdots.$$

In the chapter, we remarked that if the random variable X has a finite mean, $E|X| < \infty$, then AVaR is also finite. This is not true for spectral risk measures and the higher-order AVaR in particular. In line with the general theory developed in section 7.9.6 in this appendix, $AVaR_\epsilon^{(n)}(X)$ is finite if all moments of X exist. For example, if the random variable X has an exponential tail, then $AVaR_\epsilon^{(n)}(X) < \infty$ for any $n < \infty$.

7.9.3 The Minimization Formula for AVaR

In this section, we provide a geometric interpretation of the minimization formula (7.2) for AVaR. We restate equation (7.2) in the following equivalent form,

$$AVaR_\epsilon(X) = \frac{1}{\epsilon} \min_{\theta \in \mathbb{R}} (\epsilon \theta + E(-X - \theta)_+), \qquad (7.21)$$

where $(x)_+ = \max(x, 0)$. Note the similarity between equation (7.21) and the definition of AVaR in (7.1). Instead of the integral of the quantile function in the definition of AVaR, a minimization formula appears in (7.21). We interpreted the integral of the inverse c.d.f. as the shaded area in Figure 7.2.

Similarly, we will find the area corresponding to the objective function in the minimization formula and we will demonstrate that as θ changes, there is a minimal area that coincides with the area corresponding to the shaded area in Figure 7.2. Moreover, the minimal area is attained for $\theta = VaR_\epsilon(X)$ when the c.d.f. of X is continuous at $VaR_\epsilon(X)$. In fact, all illustrations in this section are based on the assumption that X has a continuous distribution function.

Consider first the expectation in equation (7.21). Assuming that X has a continuous c.d.f., we obtain an expression for the expectation involving the inverse c.d.f.,

$$E(-X - \theta)_+ = \int_{\mathbb{R}} \max(-x - \theta, 0)dF_X(x)$$

$$= \int_0^1 \max(-F_X^{-1}(t) - \theta, 0)dt$$

$$= -\int_0^1 \min(F_X^{-1}(t) + \theta, 0)dt.$$

This representation implies that the expectation $E(-X - \theta)_+$ equals the area closed between the graph of the inverse c.d.f. and a line parallel to the horizontal axis passing through the point $(0, -\theta)$. This is the shaded area on the right plot in Figure 7.6. The same area can be represented in terms of the c.d.f. This is done on the left plot in Figure 7.6.

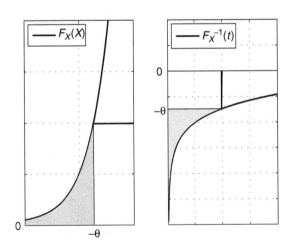

FIGURE 7.6 The shaded area is equal to the expectation $E(-X - \theta)_+$ in which X has a continuous distribution function.

Let us get back to equation (7.21). The tail probability ϵ is fixed. The product $\epsilon \times \theta$ equals the area of a rectangle with sides equal to ϵ and θ. This area is added to $E(-X - \theta)_+$. Figure 7.7 shows the two areas together. The shaded areas on the top and the bottom plots equal $\epsilon \times AVaR_\epsilon(X)$. The top plot shows the case in which $-\theta < -VaR_\epsilon(X)$. Comparing the plot to Figure 7.6, we find out that by adding the marked area to the shaded area we obtain the total area corresponding to the objective in the minimization formula, $\epsilon\theta + E(-X - \theta)_+$. If $-\theta > -VaR_\epsilon(X)$, then we obtain a similar case shown on the bottom plot. Again, adding the marked area to the shaded area we obtain the the total area computed by the objective in the minimization

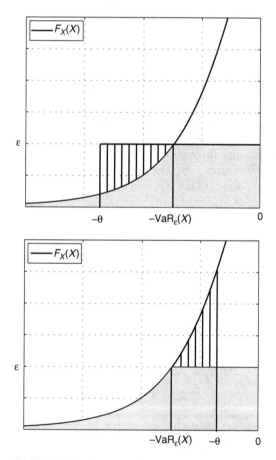

FIGURE 7.7 The marked area is in addition to the shaded one. The marked area is equal to zero if $\theta = VaR_\epsilon(X)$.

formula. By varying θ, the total area changes but it always remains larger than the shaded area unless $\theta = VaR_\epsilon(X)$.

Therefore, when $\theta = VaR_\epsilon(X)$ the minimum area is attained, which equals exactly $\epsilon \times AVaR_\epsilon(X)$. According to equation (7.21), we have to divide the minimal area by ϵ in order to obtain the AVaR. As a result, we have demonstrated that the minimization formula in equation (7.2) calculates the AVaR.

7.9.4   AVaR for Stable Distributions

Section 4.3.1 in Chapter 4 provides an introduction to stable distributions and explains why they represent an appealing model for financial assets return distribution. Working with the class of stable distributions in practice is difficult because there are no closed-form expressions for their densities and distribution functions. Thus, practical work relies on numerical methods.

Stoyanov et al. (2006) give an account of the approaches to estimating AVaR of stable distributions. It turns out that there is a formula that is not exactly a closed-form expressions, such as the ones for the normal and Student's t AVaR stated in the chapter, but is suitable for numerical work. It involves numerical integration but the integrand is nicely behaved and the integration range is a bounded interval. Numerical integration can be performed by standard toolboxes in many software packages, such as MATLAB for example. Moreover, there are libraries freely available on the Internet. Therefore, numerical integration itself is not a severe restriction for applying a formula in practice. Since the formula involves numerical integration, we call it a *semianalytic expression*.

Suppose that the random variable X has a stable distribution with tail exponent α, skewness parameter β, scale parameter σ, and location parameter μ, $X \in S_\alpha(\sigma, \beta, \mu)$. If $\alpha \leq 1$, then $AVaR_\epsilon(X) = \infty$. The reason is that stable distributions with $\alpha \leq 1$ have infinite mathematical expectation and the AVaR is unbounded.

If $\alpha > 1$ and $VaR_\epsilon(X) \neq 0$, then the AVaR can be represented as

$$AVaR_\epsilon(X) = \sigma A_{\epsilon,\alpha,\beta} - \mu,$$

where the term $A_{\epsilon,\alpha,\beta}$ does not depend on the scale and the location parameters. In fact, this representation is a consequence of the positive homogeneity and the invariance property of AVaR. Concerning the term $A_{\epsilon,\alpha,\beta}$,

$$A_{\epsilon,\alpha,\beta} = \frac{\alpha}{1-\alpha} \frac{|VaR_\epsilon(X)|}{\pi\epsilon} \int_{-\bar\theta_0}^{\pi/2} g(\theta) \exp\left(-|VaR_\epsilon(X)|^{\frac{\alpha}{\alpha-1}} v(\theta)\right) d\theta$$

where

$$g(\theta) = \frac{\sin(\alpha(\overline{\theta}_0 + \theta) - 2\theta)}{\sin\alpha(\overline{\theta}_0 + \theta)} - \frac{\alpha\cos^2\theta}{\sin^2\alpha(\overline{\theta}_0 + \theta)},$$

$$v(\theta) = \left(\cos\alpha\overline{\theta}_0\right)^{\frac{1}{\alpha-1}} \left(\frac{\cos\theta}{\sin\alpha(\overline{\theta}_0 + \theta)}\right)^{\frac{\alpha}{\alpha-1}} \frac{\cos(\alpha\overline{\theta}_0 + (\alpha - 1)\theta)}{\cos\theta},$$

in which $\overline{\theta}_0 = \frac{1}{\alpha}\arctan\left(\overline{\beta}\tan\frac{\pi\alpha}{2}\right)$, $\overline{\beta} = -\sin(VaR_\epsilon(X))\beta$, and $VaR_\epsilon(X)$ is the VaR of the stable distribution at tail probability ϵ.

If $VaR_\epsilon(X) = 0$, then the AVaR admits a very simple expression,

$$AVaR_\epsilon(X) = \frac{2\Gamma\left(\frac{\alpha-1}{\alpha}\right)}{(\pi - 2\theta_0)} \frac{\cos\theta_0}{(\cos\alpha\theta_0)^{1/\alpha}}.$$

in which $\Gamma(x)$ is the gamma function and $\theta_0 = \frac{1}{\alpha}\arctan(\beta\tan\frac{\pi\alpha}{2})$.

7.9.5 ETL versus AVaR

The expected tail loss and the average value-at-risk are two related concepts. In the chapter, we remarked that ETL and AVaR coincide if the portfolio return distribution is continuous at the corresponding VaR level. However, if there is a discontinuity, or a point mass, then the two notions diverge. Still, the AVaR can be expressed through the ETL and the VaR at the same tail probability. In this section, we illustrate this relationship and show why the AVaR is more appealing. Moreover, it will throw light on why equation (7.6) should be used when considering a sample of observations.

The ETL at tail probability ϵ is defined as the average loss provided that the loss exceeds the VaR at tail probability ϵ,

$$ETL_\epsilon(X) = -E(X|X < -VaR_\epsilon(X)). \tag{7.22}$$

As a consequence of the definition, the ETL can be expressed in terms of the c.d.f. and the inverse c.d.f. Suppose additionally, that the c.d.f. of X has a jump at $-VaR_\epsilon(X)$. In this case, the loss $VaR_\epsilon(X)$ occurs with probability equal to the size of the jump and, because of the strict inequality in (7.22), it will not be included in the average.

Figure 7.8 shows the graphs of the c.d.f. and the inverse c.d.f. of a random variable X with a point mass at $-VaR_\epsilon(X)$. If ϵ splits the jump of

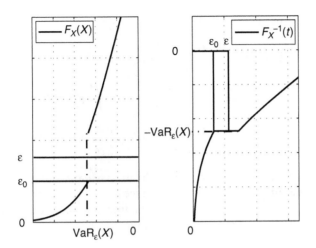

FIGURE 7.8 The c.d.f. and the inverse c.d.f. of a random variable X with a point mass at $-VaR_\epsilon(X)$. The tail probability ϵ splits the jump of the c.d.f.

the c.d.f. as on the left plot in Figure 7.8, then the ETL at tail probability ϵ equals,

$$
\begin{aligned}
ETL_\epsilon(X) &= -E(X|X < -VaR_\epsilon(X)) \\
&= -E(X|X < -VaR_{\epsilon_0}(X)) \\
&= ETL_{\epsilon_0}(X).
\end{aligned}
$$

In terms of the inverse c.d.f., the quantity $ETL_{\epsilon_0}(X)$ can be represented as

$$
ETL_{\epsilon_0}(X) = -\frac{1}{\epsilon_0} \int_0^{\epsilon_0} F_X^{-1}(t)dt.
$$

The relationship between AVaR and ETL follows directly from the definition of AVaR.[16] Suppose that the c.d.f. of the random variable X is as

---

[16] Formal derivation of this relationship can be found, for example, in Rockafellar and Uryasev (2002).

on the left plot in Figure 7.8. Then

$$AVaR_\epsilon(X) = -\frac{1}{\epsilon}\int_0^\epsilon F_X^{-1}(t)dt$$

$$= -\frac{1}{\epsilon}\left(\int_0^{\epsilon_0} F_X^{-1}(t)dt + \int_{\epsilon_0}^\epsilon F_X^{-1}(t)dt\right)$$

$$= -\frac{1}{\epsilon}\int_0^{\epsilon_0} F_X^{-1}(t)dt + \frac{\epsilon - \epsilon_0}{\epsilon}VaR_\epsilon(X),$$

where the last inequality holds because the inverse c.d.f. is flat in the interval $[\epsilon_0, \epsilon]$ and the integral is merely the surface of the rectangle shown on the right plot in Figure 7.8. The integral in the first summand can be related to the ETL at tail probability ϵ and, finally, we arrive at the expression

$$AVaR_\epsilon(X) = \frac{\epsilon_0}{\epsilon}ETL_\epsilon(X) + \frac{\epsilon - \epsilon_0}{\epsilon}VaR_\epsilon(X). \tag{7.23}$$

Equation (7.23) shows that $AVaR_\epsilon(X)$ can be represented as a weighted average between the ETL and the VaR at the same tail probability as the coefficients in front if the two summands are positive and sum up to one. In the special case in which there is no jump, or if $\epsilon = \epsilon_1$, then AVaR equals ETL.

Why is equation (7.23) important if in all statistical models we assume that the random variables describing return or payoff distribution have densities? Under this assumption, not only are the corresponding c.d.f.s continuous, but they are also smooth. Equation (7.23) is important because if the estimate of AVaR is based on the Monte Carlo method, then we use a sample of scenarios that approximate the nicely behaved hypothesized distribution. Even though we are approximating a smooth distribution function, the sample c.d.f. of the scenarios is completely discrete, with jumps at the scenarios the size of which equals the $1/n$, where n stands for the number of scenarios.

In fact, equation (7.6) given in the chapter is actually equation (7.23) restated for a discrete random variable. The outcomes are the available scenarios that are equally probable. Consider a sample of observations or scenarios $r_1, \ldots, r_n$ and denote by $r_{(1)} \le r_{(2)} \le \cdots \le r_{(n)}$ the ordered sample. The natural estimator of the ETL at tail probability ϵ is

$$\widehat{ETL}_\epsilon(r) = -\frac{1}{\lceil n\epsilon \rceil - 1}\sum_{k=1}^{\lceil n\epsilon \rceil - 1} r_{(k)}, \tag{7.24}$$

where $\lceil x \rceil$ is the smallest integer larger than x. Formula (7.24) means that we average $\lceil n\epsilon \rceil - 1$ of the $\lceil n\epsilon \rceil$ smallest observations, which is, in fact, the definition of the conditional expectation in (7.22) for a discrete distribution. The VaR at tail probability ϵ is equal to the negative of the empirical quantile,

$$\widehat{VaR}_\epsilon(r) = -r_{(\lceil n\epsilon \rceil)}. \tag{7.25}$$

It remains to determine the coefficients in (7.23). Having in mind that the observations in the sample are equally probable, we calculate that

$$\epsilon_0 = \frac{\lceil n\epsilon \rceil - 1}{n}.$$

Plugging ϵ_0, (7.25), and (7.24) into equation (7.23), we obtain (7.6), which is the sample AVaR.

Similarly, equation (7.10) also arises from (7.23). The assumption is that the underlying random variable has a discrete distribution but the outcomes are not equally probable. Thus the corresponding equation for the average loss on condition that the loss is larger than the VaR at tail probability ϵ is given by

$$\widehat{ETL}_\epsilon(r) = -\frac{1}{\epsilon_0} \sum_{j=1}^{k_\epsilon} p_j r_{(j)}, \tag{7.26}$$

where $\epsilon_0 = \sum_{j=1}^{k_\epsilon} p_j$ and k_ϵ is the integer satisfying the inequalities,

$$\sum_{j=1}^{k_\epsilon} p_j \leq \epsilon < \sum_{j=1}^{k_\epsilon+1} p_j.$$

The sum $\sum_{j=1}^{k_\epsilon} p_j$ stands for the cumulative probability of the losses larger than the the VaR at tail probability ϵ. Note that equation (7.26) turns into equation (7.24) when the outcomes are equally probable. With these remarks, we have demonstrated the connection between equations (7.6), (7.10), and (7.23).

The differences between ETL and AVaR are not without any practical importance. In fact, ETL is not a coherent risk measure. Furthermore, the sample ETL in (7.24) is not a smooth function of the tail probability while the sample AVaR is smooth. This is illustrated in Figure 7.9. The top plot shows the graph of the sample ETL and AVaR with the tail probability varying between 1% and 10%. The sample contains 100 independent observations on a standard normal distribution, $X \in N(0, 1)$. The bottom plots show the same but the sample is larger. It contains 250 independent observations on a standard normal distribution.

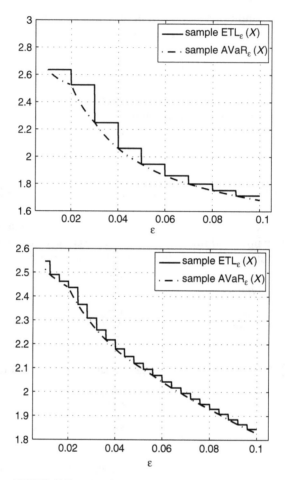

FIGURE 7.9 The graphs of the sample ETL and AVaR with tail probability varying between 1% and 10%. The top plot is produced from a sample of 100 observations and the bottom plot from a sample of 250 observations. In both cases, $X \in N(0, 1)$.

Both plots demonstrate that the sample ETL is a step function of the tail probability, while the AVaR is a smooth function of it. This is not surprising because, as ϵ increases, new observations appear in the sum in (7.24) producing the jumps in the graph of the sample ETL. In contrast, the AVaR changes gradually as it is a weighted average of the ETL and the

VaR at the same tail probability. Note that, as the sample size increases, the jumps in the graph of the sample ETL diminish. In a sample of 5,000 scenarios, both quantities almost overlap. This is because the standard normal distribution has a smooth c.d.f. and the sample c.d.f. constructed from a larger sample better approximates the theoretical c.d.f. In this case, as the sample size approaches infinity, the AVaR becomes indistinguishable from the ETL at the same tail probability.[17]

7.9.6 Remarks on Spectral Risk Measures

In the chapter, we remarked that by selecting a particular risk-aversion function, we can obtain an infinite risk measure for some return distributions. The AVaR can also become infinite, but all distributions for which this happens are not reasonable as a model for financial assets returns because they have infinite mathematical expectation. This is not the case with the spectral risk measures. There are plausible statistical models that, if combined with an inappropriate risk-aversion function, result in an infinite spectral risk measure.

In this section, we provide conditions that guarantee that if a risk-aversion function satisfies them, then it generates a finite spectral risk measure. These conditions can be divided into two groups depending on what kind of information about the random variable is used. The first group of conditions is based on information about existence of certain moments, and the second group contains more precise conditions based on the tail behavior of the random variable. This section is based on Stoyanov (2005).

Moment-Based Conditions Moment-based conditions are related to the existence of a certain norm of the risk-aversion function. We take advantage of the norms behind the classical Lebesgue spaces of functions denoted by

$$L^p([0,1]) := \left\{ f : \|f\|_p = \int_0^1 |f(t)|^p dt < \infty \right\},$$

where $\| \cdot \|_p$ denotes the corresponding norm. If $p = \infty$, then the norm is the essential supremum, $\|f\|_\infty = \mathrm{ess}\sup_{t \in [0,1]} |f(t)|$. If the function f is continuous and bounded, then $\|f\|_\infty$ is simply the maximum of the absolute value of the function.

---

[17]In fact, this is a consequence of the celebrated Glivenko-Cantelli theorem claiming that the sample c.d.f. converges almost surely to the true c.d.f.

The sufficient conditions for the finiteness of the spectral risk measure involve the quantity

$$I_\phi(X) = \int_0^1 |F_X^{-1}(p)\phi(p)|dp \tag{7.27}$$

which is, essentially, the definition of the spectral risk measure but the integrand is taken in absolute value. Therefore,

$$|\rho_\phi(X)| \leq I_\phi(X)$$

and, as a consequence, if the quantity $I_\phi(X)$ is finite, so is the spectral risk measure $\rho_\phi(X)$. Formally, this is a sufficient condition for the absolute convergence of the integral behind the definition of spectral risk measures.

Moment-based conditions are summarized by the following inequalities,

$$C \cdot E|X| \leq I_\phi(X) \leq (E|X|^s)^{1/s} ||\phi||_r \tag{7.28}$$

where $0 \leq C < \infty$ is a constant and $1/s + 1/r = 1$ with $r, s > 1$. Further on, if $r = 1$ or $s = 1$, the second inequality[18] in (7.28) changes to

$$I_\phi(X) \leq \sup_{u \in [0,1]} |F_X^{-1}(u)|, \quad \text{if} \quad r = 1$$

$$I_\phi(X) \leq E|X| \cdot ||\phi||_\infty, \quad \text{if} \quad s = 1. \tag{7.29}$$

As a consequence of equation (7.28), it follows that if the absolute moment of order s exists, $E|X|^s < \infty, s > 1$, then $\phi \in L^r([0, 1])$ is a sufficient condition for $\rho_\phi(X) < \infty$. The $AVaR_\epsilon(X)$ has a special place among $\rho_\phi(X)$ because if $AVaR_\epsilon(X) = \infty$, then $E|X| = \infty$ and $\rho_\phi(X)$ is not absolutely convergent for any choice of ϕ. In the reverse direction, if there exists $\phi \in L^1([0, 1])$ such that $I_\phi(X) < \infty$, then $AVaR_\epsilon(X) < \infty$.

The limit cases in inequalities (7.29) show that if X has a bounded support, then all possible risk spectra are meaningful. In addition, if we consider the space of all essentially bounded risk spectra, then the existence of $E|X|$ is a necessary and sufficient condition for the absolute convergence of $\rho_\phi(X)$.

Conditions Based on the Tail Behavior of X   More precise sufficient conditions can be derived assuming a particular tail behavior of the distribution

---

[18] As a matter of fact, the right-hand side inequalities of both cases can be unified as a consequence of the norm relationship $||fg||_1 \leq ||f||_r ||g||_s$, where $f \in L^r$ and $g \in L^s$ and r and s are conjugate exponents, that is, $1/s + 1/r = 1$ and $1 \leq r, s \leq \infty$. See, for example, Rudin (1970).

function of X. A fairly general assumption for the tail behavior is *regular variation*. A monotonic function $f(x)$ is said to be *regularly varying* at infinity with index α, $f \in \mathcal{RV}_\alpha$, if

$$\lim_{x \to \infty} \frac{f(tx)}{f(x)} = t^\alpha. \tag{7.30}$$

Examples of random variables with regularly varying distribution functions include stable distributions, Student's t-distribution, and Pareto distribution. Thus, it is natural to look for sufficient conditions for the convergence of $\rho_\phi(X)$ in the general setting of regularly varying tails. A set of such conditions is provided next.

Suppose that $\rho_\phi(X)$ is the spectral measure of risk of a random variable X such that $E|X| < \infty$ and $P(-X > u) \in \mathcal{RV}_{-\alpha}$. Let the inverse of the risk spectrum $\phi^{-1} \in \mathcal{RV}_{-\delta}$, if existing. Then

$$\rho_\phi(X) = \infty, \quad \text{if} \quad 1 < \delta \leq \alpha/(\alpha-1)$$

and

$$\rho_\phi(X) < \infty, \quad \text{if} \quad \delta > \alpha/(\alpha-1).$$

The inverse of the risk-aversion function ϕ^{-1} exists if we assume that ϕ is smooth because by assumption ϕ is a monotonic function.

In some cases, we may not know explicitly the inverse of the risk-aversion function, or the inverse may not be regularly varying. Then, the next sufficient condition can be adopted. It is based on comparing the risk-aversion function to a power function.

Suppose that the same condition as above holds, the random variable X is such that $E|X| < \infty$ and $P(-X > u) \in \mathcal{RV}_{-\alpha}$. If the condition

$$\lim_{x \to 0} \phi(x) x^\beta = C$$

is satisfied with $0 < \beta < \frac{\alpha-1}{\alpha}$ and $0 \leq C < \infty$, then $\rho_\phi(X) < \infty$. If $\frac{\alpha-1}{\alpha} \leq \beta < 1$ and $0 < C < \infty$, then $\rho_\phi(X) = \infty$.

This condition emphasizes that it is the behavior of the risk-aversion function $\phi(t)$ close to $t = 0$ that matters. This is reasonable because in this range, the risk-aversion function defines the weights of the very extreme losses and if the weights increase very quickly as $t \to 0$, then the risk measure may explode.

In fact, these conditions are more specific than assuming that a certain norm of the risk-aversion function is finite. It is possible to derive them because of the hypothesized tail behavior of the distribution function of X, which is a stronger assumption than the existence of certain moments.

BIBLIOGRAPHY

Acerbi, C. (2004). "Coherent representation of subjective risk aversion," Chapter 10 in G. Szego (ed.), *Risk measures for the 21st century*, pp. 147–208, Chichester: John Wiley & Sons.

Acerbi, C., and P. Simonetti (2002). "Portfolio optimization with spectral measures of risk," working paper, Abaxbank, Milano.

Pflug, G. (2000). "Some remarks on the value-at-risk and the conditional value-at-risk," In S. Uryasev, (ed.), *Probabilistic Constrained Optimization*: Methodology and Applications, pp., Dordrecht: Kluwer.

Rockafellar, R. T., and S. Uryasev (2002). "Conditional value-at-risk for general loss distributions," *Journal of Banking and Finance* 26(7): 1443–1471.

Rudin, Walter (1970). *Real and Complex Analysis*, New York: McGraw-Hill.

Stoyanov, S. (2005). *Optimal financial portfolios in highly volatile markets*, PhD thesis, University of Karlsruhe.

Stoyanov, S. T., G. Samorodnitsky, S. T. Rachev, and S. Ortobelli (2006). "Computing the portfolio conditional value-at-risk in the α-stable case," *Probability and Mathematical Statistics* 26: 1–22.

Stoyanov, S. T., S. T. Rachev, and F. Fabozzi (2007). "Probability metrics with application in finance," forthcoming in *Journal of Statistical Theory and Practice*.

CHAPTER 8

Optimal Portfolios

8.1 INTRODUCTION

A portfolio is a collection of investments held by an institution or a private individual. Portfolios are constructed and held as a part of an investment strategy and for the purpose of diversification. The concept of diversification is very strong and intuitive. Including a number of assets in a portfolio may greatly reduce portfolio risk while not necessarily reducing performance. Diversification of portfolio risk is, therefore, a key aspect of investment management.

Optimal portfolio selection concerns prudent decision making about the portfolio composition. Basically, the problem of choosing a portfolio is a problem of choice under uncertainty because the payoffs of financial instruments are uncertain. An optimal portfolio is a portfolio that is most preferred in a given set of feasible portfolios by an investor or a certain category of investors.

In Chapter 5, we discussed expected utility theory, which is an accepted theory describing choice under uncertainty. Investors preferences are characterized by utility functions and they choose the venture that yields maximum expected utility. As a consequence of the theory, stochastic dominance relations arise, describing the choice of groups of investors, such as the risk-averse investors. While the foundations of expected utility theory as a normative theory are solid, its practical application is limited as the resulting optimization problems are very difficult to solve. For example, given a set of feasible portfolios, it is hard to find the ones that will be preferred by all risk-averse investors by applying directly the characterization in terms of the *cumulative distribution functions* (c.d.f.s).

A different approach toward the problem of optimal portfolio choice was introduced by Harry Markowitz in the 1950, *mean-variance analysis*

(M-V analysis) and popularly referred to as *modern portfolio theory* (MPT). Markowitz (1952) suggested that the portfolio choice be made with respect to two criteria: the expected portfolio return and the variance of the portfolio return, the latter used as a proxy for risk. A portfolio is preferred to another portfolio if it has higher expected return and lower variance. Not only is M-V analysis intuitive, but it is easy to apply in practice. There are convenient computational recipes for the resulting optimization problems and geometric interpretations of the trade-off between the expected return and variance. Initially, the approach of Markowitz (1952), which he later expanded in his book (Markowitz 1959), generated little interest, but later on the financial community adopted the framework and currently many financial models are built on it.

Even though M-V analysis is an approach different from that of expected utility theory, consistency with the latter is always looked for. For example, if all risk-verse investors identify a given portfolio as most preferred, then is the same portfolio identified by M-V analysis also optimal? Basically, the answer to this question is negative. Generally, M-V analysis is not consistent with *second-order stochastic dominance* (SSD) unless the joint distribution of investment returns is multivariate normal, which is a very restrictive assumption. Alternatively, M-V analysis describes correctly the choices made by investors with quadratic utility functions. Again, the assumption of quadratic utility functions is very restrictive even though we can extend it and consider all utility functions that can be sufficiently well approximated by quadratic utilities.

Another well-known drawback is that in M-V analysis variance is used as a proxy for risk. In Chapter 6, we demonstrated that variance is not a risk measure but a measure of uncertainty. This deficiency was recognized by Markowitz (1959) and he suggested the downside semistandard deviation as a proxy for risk. In contrast to variance, the downside semistandard deviation is consistent with SSD.

M-V analysis can be significantly extended by adopting a true risk measure instead of variance. If the risk measure is consistent with SSD, so is the optimal solution to the optimization problem. Furthermore, the optimization problem is appealing from a practical viewpoint because it is computationally feasible and there are similar geometric interpretations as in M-V analysis. We call this generalization *mean-risk analysis* (M-R analysis).

In this chapter, we describe M-V analysis and its generalization, M-R analysis. We demonstrate how the underlying optimization problems can be simplified if the *average value-at-risk* (AVaR) is selected as a risk measure. In Chapter 6, we discussed an interesting relationship between coherent risk measures and dispersion measures. In this chapter, we show the consequences of this relationship for the efficient frontier generated by M-R analysis.

M-R analysis can also be extended by using a function other than the expected return as a measure of reward. This is demonstrated in the appendix to this chapter, which also provides more details on other topics discussed.

8.2 MEAN-VARIANCE ANALYSIS

The classical mean-variance framework introduced by Markowitz (1952, 1959), and developed further in Markowitz (1987), is the first proposed model of the reward-risk type. The expected portfolio return is used as a measure of reward and the variance of portfolio return indicates how well-diversified the portfolio is. Lower variance means higher diversification level.

The portfolio choice problem is typically treated as a one-period problem. Suppose that at time $t_0 = 0$ we have an investor who can choose to invest among a universe of n assets. Having made the decision, he keeps the allocation unchanged until the moment t_1 when he can make another investment decision based on the new information accumulated up to t_1. In this sense, it is also said that the problem is *static*, as opposed to a *dynamic* problem in which investment decisions are made for several time periods ahead.

The main principle behind M-V analysis can be summarized in two ways:

1. From all feasible portfolios with a given lower bound on the expected performance, find the ones that have the minimum variance (i.e., the maximally diversified ones).
2. From all feasible portfolios with a given upper bound on the variance of portfolio return (i.e., with an upper bound on the diversification level), find the ones that have maximum expected performance.

Whether a portfolio is feasible or not is determined by certain limitations the portfolio manager faces. These limitations can be strategy specific. For example, there may be constraints on the maximum capital allocation to a given industry, or a constraint on the correlation with a given market segment. The limitations can also be dictated by liquidity considerations, for instance a maximum allocation to a given position, constraints on transaction cost or turnover.

8.2.1 Mean-Variance Optimization Problems

We can find two optimization problems behind the formulations of the main principle of M-V analysis. In order to state optimization problems, we introduce the following notation. We will use matrix notation to make the problem formulations concise.

Suppose that the investment universe consists of n financial assets. Denote the assets returns by the vector $X' = (X_1, \ldots, X_n)$ in which X_i stands for the return on the i-th asset. The returns are random and their mean is denoted by $\mu' = (\mu_1, \ldots, \mu_n)$, where $\mu_i = EX_i$. The returns are also dependent on each other in a certain way. The dependence will be described by the covariances between them. The covariance between the i-th and the j-th return is denoted by

$$\sigma_{ij} = \text{cov}(X_i, X_j) = E(X_i - \mu_i)(X_j - \mu_j).$$

Note that in this notation, σ_{ii} stands for the variance of the return of the i-th asset,

$$\sigma_{ii} = E(X_i - \mu_i)^2.$$

The result of an investment decision is a portfolio, the composition of which is denoted by $w' = (w_1, \ldots, w_n)$, where w_i is the portfolio weight corresponding to the i-th instrument. We will consider long-only strategies which means that all weights should be nonnegative, $w_i \geq 0$, and should sum up to one,

$$w_1 + w_2 + \cdots + w_n = w'e = 1,$$

where $e' = (1, 1, \ldots, 1)$. These conditions will be set as constraints in the optimization problem. The return of a portfolio r_p can be expressed by means of the weights and the returns of the assets,

$$r_p = w_1 X_1 + w_2 X_2 + \cdots + w_n X_n = \sum_{i=1}^{n} w_i X_i = w'X. \qquad (8.1)$$

Similarly, the expected portfolio return can be expressed by the vector of weights and expected assets returns,

$$Er_p = w_1 \mu_1 + w_2 \mu_2 + \cdots + w_n \mu_n = \sum_{i=1}^{n} w_i \mu_i = w'\mu. \qquad (8.2)$$

Finally, the variance of portfolio returns $\sigma_{r_p}^2$ can be expressed by means of portfolio weights and the covariances σ_{ij} between the assets returns,

$$\sigma_{r_p}^2 = E(r_p - Er_p)^2$$

$$= \sum_{i=1}^{n} \sum_{j=1}^{n} w_i w_j \sigma_{ij}.$$

The covariances of all asset returns can be arranged in a matrix and $\sigma_{r_p}^2$ can be expressed as

$$\sigma_{r_p}^2 = w'\Sigma w \tag{8.3}$$

where Σ is a $n \times n$ matrix of covariances,

$$\Sigma = \begin{pmatrix} \sigma_{11} & \sigma_{12} & \cdots & \sigma_{1n} \\ \sigma_{21} & \sigma_{22} & \cdots & \sigma_{2n} \\ \vdots & \vdots & \ddots & \vdots \\ \sigma_{n1} & \sigma_{n2} & \cdots & \sigma_{nn} \end{pmatrix}$$

Now we are in position to state the optimization problems. The optimization problem behind the first formulation of the main principle of M-V analysis is

$$\begin{aligned} \min_{w} \quad & w'\Sigma w \\ \text{subject to} \quad & w'e = 1 \\ & w'\mu \geq R_* \\ & w \geq 0, \end{aligned} \tag{8.4}$$

where $w \geq 0$ means that all components of the vector are nonnegative, $w_i \geq 0$, $i = 1, n$. The objective function of (8.4) is the variance of portfolio returns and R_* is the lower bound on the expected performance. Similarly, the optimization problem behind the second formulation of the principle is

$$\begin{aligned} \max_{w} \quad & w'\mu \\ \text{subject to} \quad & w'e = 1 \\ & w'\Sigma w \leq R^* \\ & w \geq 0, \end{aligned} \tag{8.5}$$

in which R^* is the upper bound on the variance of the portfolio return $\sigma_{r_p}^2$.

We illustrate the two optimization problems with the following example. Suppose that the investment universe consists of three common stocks with expected returns $\mu' = (1.8\%, 2.5\%, 1\%)$ and covariance matrix,

$$\Sigma = \begin{pmatrix} 1.68 & 0.34 & 0.38 \\ 0.34 & 3.09 & -1.59 \\ 0.38 & -1.59 & 1.54 \end{pmatrix}.$$

The variance of portfolio return equals

$$\sigma_{r_p} = (w_1, w_2, w_3) \begin{pmatrix} 1.68 & 0.34 & 0.38 \\ 0.34 & 3.09 & -1.59 \\ 0.38 & -1.59 & 1.54 \end{pmatrix} \begin{pmatrix} w_1 \\ w_2 \\ w_3 \end{pmatrix}$$

$$= 1.08w_1^2 + 3.09w_2^2 + 1.54w_3^2 + 2 \times 0.34w_1w_2$$
$$- 2 \times 1.59w_2w_3 + 2 \times 0.38w_1w_3$$

and the expected portfolio return is given by

$$w'\mu = 0.018w_1 + 0.025w_2 + 0.01w_3.$$

It is difficult to imagine how the three stock returns depend on each other by directly looking at the covariance matrix. Covariances are hard to compare because their magnitude depends on how dispersed the random variables are. For this reason, correlations, which are essentially scaled covariances, are a more useful concept. The correlation ρ_{ij} between the random return of the i-th and the j-th asset are computed by dividing the corresponding covariance by the product of the standard deviations of the two random returns,

$$\rho_{ij} = \frac{\sigma_{ij}}{\sqrt{\sigma_{ii}\sigma_{jj}}}.$$

The correlation is always bounded in the interval $[-1, 1]$. The closer it is to the boundaries, the stronger the dependence between the two random variables. If $\rho_{ij} = 1$, then the random variables are positively linearly dependent (i.e., $X_i = aX_j + b, a > 0$); if $\rho_{ij} = -1$, they are negatively linearly dependent (i.e., $X_i = aX_j + b, a < 0$). If the two random variables are independent, then the covariance between them is zero and so is the correlation.

The correlation matrix ρ corresponding to the covariance matrix in this example is

$$\rho = \begin{pmatrix} 1 & 0.15 & 0.23 \\ 0.15 & 1 & -0.72 \\ 0.23 & -0.72 & 1 \end{pmatrix}.$$

The correlation between the third and the second stock return (ρ_{32}) is -0.72, which is a strong negative correlation. This means that if we observe a positive return on the second stock, it is very likely that the return on the third stock will be negative. Thus we can expect that an investment split between the second and the third stock will result in a diversified portfolio.

Suppose that we choose the expected return of the first stock ($\mu_1 = 0.018$) for the lower bound R_*. Optimization problem (8.4) has the following form,

$$
\begin{aligned}
\min_{w_1, w_2, w_3} \quad & \left(\begin{array}{l} 1.08w_1^2 + 3.09w_2^2 + 1.54w_3^2 + 2 \times 0.34w_1w_2 \\ -2 \times 1.59w_2w_3 + 2 \times 0.38w_1w_3 \end{array} \right) \\
\text{subject to} \quad & w_1 + w_2 + w_3 = 1 \\
& 0.018w_1 + 0.025w_2 + 0.01w_3 \geq 0.018 \\
& w_1, w_2, w_3 \geq 0.
\end{aligned}
\tag{8.6}
$$

Solving this problem, we obtain the optimal solution $\tilde{w}_1 = 0.046, \tilde{w}_2 = 0.509$, and $\tilde{w}_3 = 0.445$. The expected return of the optimal portfolio equals $\tilde{w}'\mu = 0.018$ and the variance of the optimal portfolio return equals $\tilde{w}'\Sigma\tilde{w} = 0.422$. There is another feasible portfolio with the same expected return, and this is the portfolio composed of only the first stock. The variance of the return of the first stock is represented by the first element of the covariance matrix, $\sigma_{11} = 1.68$. If we compare the optimal portfolio $\tilde{w}$ and the portfolio composed of the first stock only, we notice that the variance of the return of $\tilde{w}$ is about four times below σ_{11}, which means that the optimal portfolio $\tilde{w}$ is much more diversified.

In a similar way, we consider problem (8.5). Suppose that we choose the variance of the return of the first stock $\sigma_{11} = 1.68$ for the upper bound R^*. Then, the optimization problem becomes

$$
\begin{aligned}
\max_{w_1, w_2, w_3} \quad & 0.018w_1 + 0.025w_2 + 0.01w_3 \\
\text{subject to} \quad & w_1 + w_2 + w_3 = 1 \\
& 1.08w_1^2 + 3.09w_2^2 + 1.54w_3^2 + 2 \times 0.34w_1w_2 \\
& -2 \times 1.59w_2w_3 + 2 \times 0.38w_1w_3 \leq 1.68 \\
& w_1, w_2, w_3 \geq 0.
\end{aligned}
\tag{8.7}
$$

The solution to this problem is the portfolio with weights $\tilde{w}_1 = 0.282, \tilde{w}_2 = 0.69$, and $\tilde{w}_3 = 0.028$. The expected return of the optimal portfolio equals $\tilde{w}'\mu = 0.0226$ and the variance of the optimal portfolio return equals $\tilde{w}'\Sigma\tilde{w} = 1.68$. Therefore, the optimal portfolio has the same diversification level, as indicated by variance, but it has a higher expected performance.

8.2.2 The Mean-Variance Efficient Frontier

In section 8.2.1, we demonstrated how practical optimal portfolio problems can be formulated on the basis of the main principle behind M-V analysis.

We continue the analysis by describing the set of all optimal portfolios known as the *mean-variance efficient portfolios*.

Consider problem (8.4) and suppose that we solve it without any constraint on the expected performance. In this way, we obtain the *global minimum variance portfolio*. It will be the most diversified portfolio, but it will have the lowest expected performance. If we include a constraint on the expected return and start increasing the lower bound by a small amount, the optimal portfolios will become less and less diversified and their expected performance will increase. The portfolio with the highest expected performance also has the highest concentration. It is composed of only one asset, and this is the asset with the highest expected performance.

By varying the constraint on the expected return and solving problem (8.4), we obtain the mean-variance efficient portfolios. Knowing the efficient portfolios, we can easily determine the trade-off between variance and expected performance of the optimal portfolios. This trade-off is known as the *efficient frontier*. The efficient frontier can be obtained not only from problem (8.4) but also from problem (8.5). The difference is that we vary the upper bound on the variance and maximize the expected performance.

The top plot in Figure 8.1 shows the efficient frontier corresponding to the example developed in section 8.2.1. The dot indicates the position of the portfolio with composition $w_1 = 0.8, w_2 = 0.1$, and $w_3 = 0.1$ in the mean-variance plane. It is suboptimal as it does not belong to the mean-variance efficient portfolios. We consider this portfolio as the initial portfolio. The part of the efficient frontier that contains the set of all portfolios more efficient than the initial portfolio can be obtained in the following way. First, we solve problem (8.4) setting the lower bound R_* equal to the expected return of the initial portfolio. The corresponding optimal solution can be found on the efficient frontier by following the horizontal arrow in Figure 8.1. Second, we solve problem (8.5) setting the upper bound R^* equal to the variance of the initial portfolio. The corresponding optimal solution can be found on the efficient frontier by following the vertical arrow in Figure 8.1. The arc on the efficient frontier closed between the two arrows corresponds to the portfolios that are more efficient than the initial portfolio according to the criteria of M-V analysis—these portfolios have lower variance and higher expected performance.

The bottom plot in Figure 8.1 shows the mean-variance efficient portfolios. For each point on the efficient frontier, it shows the corresponding optimal allocation. The top and the bottom plot share the horizontal axis. For example, the optimal solution corresponding to the maximum performance portfolio consists of the second stock only. This portfolio is at the highest point of the efficient frontier and its composition is the first bar on the bottom plot looking from right to left. The black rectangle shows

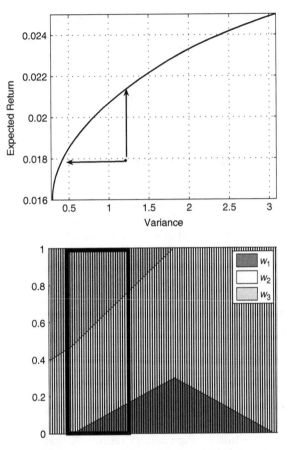

FIGURE 8.1 The top plot shows the efficient frontier in the mean-variance plane. The dot indicates the position of a suboptimal initial portfolio and the arrows indicate the position of the optimal portfolios obtained by minimizing variance or maximizing expected return. The lower plot shows the compositions of the optimal portfolios along the efficient frontier. The black rectangle indicates the portfolios more efficient than the initial portfolio.

the compositions of the more efficient portfolios than the initial portfolio. We find these by projecting the arc closed between the two arrows on the horizontal axis and then choosing the bars below it.

Sometimes, the efficient frontier is shown with standard deviation instead of variance on the horizontal axis. Actually, variance and standard deviation are interchangeable notions in this case. The set of mean-variance efficient portfolios remains unchanged because it does not matter whether we minimize the variance or the standard deviation of portfolio return as any of the two can be derived from the other by means of a monotonic function. Only the shape of the efficient frontier changes since we plot the expected return against a different quantity. In fact, in illustrating notions such as the *capital market line* or the *Sharpe ratio*, it is better if standard deviation is employed.

8.2.3 Mean-Variance Analysis and SSD

In Chapter 5, we discussed stochastic dominance relations resulting from expected utility theory. The *second order stochastic dominance* (SSD) concerns the nonsatiable, risk-averse investors. A venture dominates another venture according to SSD if all nonsatiable, risk-averse investors prefer it. Since portfolios are, essentially, risky ventures, the following consistency question arises. Suppose that a portfolio with composition $w = (w_1, \ldots, w_n)$ dominates another portfolio $v = (v_1, \ldots, v_n)$ according to SSD on the space of returns. Is it true that M-V analysis will identify the portfolio v as not more efficient than w? It seems reasonable to expect that such a consistency should hold,

$$ w'X \succeq_{SSD} v'X \quad \Longrightarrow \quad \begin{cases} v'\mu \leq w'\mu \\ v'\Sigma v \geq w'\Sigma w. \end{cases} $$

However, it turns out that the consistency question has, generally, a negative answer. It is only under specific conditions concerning the multivariate distribution of the random returns X that such a consistency exits. For example, if X has a multivariate normal distribution with mean μ and covariance Σ, $X \in N(\mu, \Sigma)$, other conditions are given in the appendix to this chapter. Thus, the behavior of an investor making decisions according to M-V analysis is not in keeping with the class of nonsatiable, risk-averse investors. Nevertheless, it is possible to identify a group of investors the behavior of which is consistent with M-V analysis. This is the class of investors with quadratic utility functions,

$$ u(x) = ax^2 + bx + c, \ x \in \mathbb{R}. $$

Denote the set of quadratic utility functions by $\mathcal{Q}$. If a portfolio is not preferred to another portfolio by all investors with quadratic utility functions, then M-V analysis is capable of identifying the more efficient portfolio,

$$ Eu(w'X) \geq Eu(v'X), \ \forall u \in \mathcal{Q} \quad \Longrightarrow \quad \begin{cases} v'\mu \leq w'\mu \\ v'\Sigma v \geq w'\Sigma w. \end{cases} $$

The consistency with investors having utility functions in Q arises from the fact that, besides the basic principle in M-V analysis, there is another way to arrive at the mean-variance efficient portfolios. There is an optimization problem that is equivalent to problems (8.4) and (8.5). This problem is

$$\max_{w} \quad w'\mu - \lambda w'\Sigma w$$
$$\text{subject to} \quad w'e = 1$$
$$w \geq 0, \tag{8.8}$$

where $\lambda \geq 0$ is a parameter called the *risk aversion parameter*.[1] By varying the risk aversion parameter and solving the optimization problem, we obtain the mean-variance efficient portfolios. For example, if $\lambda = 0$, then we obtain the portfolio with maximum expected performance. If the risk aversion parameter is a very large positive number, then the relative importance of the variance $w'\Sigma w$ in the objective function becomes much greater than the expected return. As a result, it becomes much more significant to minimize the variance than to maximize return and we obtain a portfolio that is very close to the global minimum variance portfolio.

The objective function in problem (8.8) with λ fixed is in fact the expected utility of an investor with a quadratic utility function,

$$w'\mu - \lambda w'\Sigma w = E(w'X) - \lambda E(w'X - E(w'X))^2$$
$$= -\lambda E(w'X)^2 + E(w'X) + \lambda (E(w'X))^2$$
$$= E(-\lambda(w'X)^2 + w'X + \lambda(E(w'X))^2)$$
$$= Eg(w'X),$$

where the utility function $g(x) = -\lambda x^2 + x + \lambda b$ with b equal to the squared expected portfolio return, $b = (E(w'X))^2$. Since the mean-variance efficient portfolios can be obtained through maximizing quadratic expected utilities, it follows that none of these efficient portfolios can be dominated with respect to the stochastic order of quadratic utility functions.

The fact that M-V analysis is consistent with the stochastic order arising from quadratic utilities, or, alternatively, it is consistent with SSD under restrictions on the multivariate distribution, means that the practical application of problems (8.4), (8.5), and (8.8) is limited. Nevertheless,

---

[1]The parameter λ is also known as a *Lagrange multiplier* after the French mathematician Joseph-Louis Lagrange who developed the method of finding the extrema of a function of several variables subject to one or more constraints.

sometimes quadratic approximations to more general utility functions may be sufficiently accurate, or under certain conditions the multivariate normal distribution may be a good approximation for the multivariate distribution of asset returns. The appendix to this chapter contains an example of a more general approach.

8.2.4 Adding a Risk-Free Asset

If we add a risk-free asset to the investment universe, the efficient frontier changes. In fact, Tobin (1958), Sharpe (1964), and Lintner (1965) show that efficient portfolios with a risk-free asset added to the investment universe is superior to that available to investors without the risk-free asset. The efficient portfolios essentially consist of a combination of a particular portfolio of the risky assets called the *market portfolio* and the risk-free asset. In order to illustrate this result, we take advantage of the efficient frontier in the mean-standard deviation plane.

Suppose that in addition to the risky assets in the investment universe, there is a risk-free asset with return r_f. The investor can choose between the n risky asset and the risk-free one. The weight corresponding to the risk-free asset we denote by w_f which can be positive or negative if we allow for borrowing or lending at the risk-free rate. We keep the notation $w = (w_1, \ldots, w_n)$ for the vector of weights corresponding to the risky assets. If we include the risk-free asset in the portfolio, the expected portfolio return equals

$$Er_p = w'\mu + w_f r_f$$

and the expression for portfolio variance remains unchanged because the risk-free asset has zero variance and, therefore, does not appear in the expression,

$$\sigma_{r_p}^2 = w'\Sigma w.$$

As a result, problem (8.4) transforms into

$$
\begin{aligned}
\min_{w, w_f} \quad & w'\Sigma w \\
\text{subject to} \quad & w'e + w_f = 1 \\
& w'\mu + w_f r_f \geq R_* \\
& w \geq 0, \ w_f \leq 1
\end{aligned}
\tag{8.9}
$$

and the equivalent problems (8.5) and (8.8) change accordingly. The new set of mean-variance efficient portfolios is obtained by varying the lower bound on the expected performance R_*.

The fundamental result on the structure of the mean-variance efficient portfolios states that the optimal portfolios of problem (8.9) are always a combination of one and the same portfolio of the risky assets and the risk-free asset. Changing the lower bound R_* results in different relative proportions of the two. The portfolio of the risky assets is known as the market portfolio and is denoted by $w_M = (w_M, \ldots, w_{Mn})$ in which the weights sum up to one.[2] All efficient portfolios can be represented as

$$r_p = (aw_M)'X + (1 - (aw_M)'e)r_f$$
$$= (aw_M)'X + (1 - a)r_f, \tag{8.10}$$

where aw_M denotes the scaled weights of the market portfolio, a is the scaling coefficient, $1 - a = r_f$ is the weight of the risk-free asset, and we have used that $w'_M e = 1$. The market portfolio is located on the efficient frontier, where a straight line passing through the location of the risk-free asset is tangent to the efficient frontier. The straight line is known as the *capital market line* and the market portfolio is also known as the *tangency portfolio*.

Figure 8.2 shows the efficient frontier of the example in the previous section but with standard deviation instead of variance on the horizontal

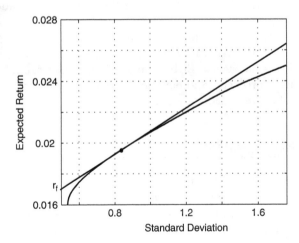

FIGURE 8.2 The capital market line and the mean-variance efficient frontier. The dot indicates the position of the market portfolio.

---

[2]We show how w_M is calculated in the next chapter.

axis. The risk-free rate r_f is shown on the vertical axis and the straight line is the capital market line. A dot indicates the location of the market portfolio, where the capital market line is tangent to the efficient frontier.

It is possible to derive the equation of the capital market line. First, using equation (8.10), the expected return of an efficient portfolio set equals,

$$E(r_p) = aE(r_M) + (1 - a)r_f$$
$$= r_f + a(E(r_M) - r_f),$$

where $r_M = w'_M X$ equals the return of the market portfolio. The scaling coefficient a can be expressed by means of the standard deviation. The second term in equation (8.10) is not random and therefore the standard deviation σ_{r_p} equals

$$\sigma_{r_p} = a\sigma_{r_M}.$$

As a result, we derive the capital market line equation

$$E(r_p) = r_f + \left(\frac{E(r_M) - r_f}{\sigma_{r_M}} \right) \sigma_{r_p} \qquad (8.11)$$

which describes the efficient frontier with the risk-free asset added to the investment universe.

Since any efficient portfolio is a combination of two portfolios, equation (8.10) is sometimes referred to as *two-fund separation*. We remark that a fund separation result such as (8.10) may not hold in general. It holds under the constraints in problem (8.9) but may fail if additional constraints on the portfolio weights are added.

8.3 MEAN-RISK ANALYSIS

The key concept behind M-V analysis is diversification. In order to measure the degree of diversification, variance, or standard deviation, is employed. The main idea of Markowitz is that the optimal trade-off between risk and return should be the basis of financial decision making. The standard deviation of portfolio returns can only be used as a proxy for risk as it is not a true risk measure but a measure of dispersion.[3] If we employ a true

---

[3]The differences between dispersion measures and risk measures are discussed in Chapter 6.

risk measure and then study the optimal trade-off between risk and return, we obtain an extension of the framework of M-V analysis, which we call *mean-risk analysis* (M-R analysis).

The main principle of M-R analysis can be formulated in a similar way to M-V analysis:

1. From all feasible portfolios with a given lower bound on the expected performance, find the ones that have minimum risk.
2. From all feasible portfolios with a given upper bound on risk, find the ones that have maximum expected performance.

A key input to M-R analysis is the particular risk measure we would like to employ. The risk measure is denoted by $\rho(X)$ where X is a random variable describing portfolio return.

8.3.1 Mean-Risk Optimization Problems

We can formulate two optimization problems on the basis of the main principle of M-R analysis. They are very similar to the corresponding mean-variance optimization problems considered in section 8.2.1.

The optimization problem behind the first formulation of the principle is

$$
\begin{aligned}
\min_{w} \quad & \rho(r_p) \\
\text{subject to} \quad & w'e = 1 \\
& w'\mu \geq R_* \\
& w \geq 0
\end{aligned}
\tag{8.12}
$$

The objective function of (8.4) is the risk of portfolio return $r_p = w'X$ as computed by the selected risk measure ρ and R_* is the lower bound on the expected portfolio return. Similarly, the the optimization problem behind the second formulation of the principle is

$$
\begin{aligned}
\max_{w} \quad & w'\mu \\
\text{subject to} \quad & w'e = 1 \\
& \rho(r_p) \leq R^* \\
& w \geq 0,
\end{aligned}
\tag{8.13}
$$

where R^* is the upper bound on portfolio risk.

Mean-risk optimization problems are different from their counterparts in M-V analysis. In order to calculate the risk of the portfolio return $\rho(r_p)$, we need to know the multivariate distribution of the asset returns. Otherwise, it will not be possible to calculate the distribution of the portfolio return and, as a result, portfolio risk will be unknown. This requirement is not so obvious in the mean-variance optimization problems where we only need the covariance matrix as input. Nevertheless, M-V analysis leads to reasonable decision making only under certain distributional hypotheses such as the multivariate normal distribution. Therefore, while it is not obvious from the optimization problem structure, we need to make a certain hypothesis in order for the results to make sense.

The principal difference between mean-risk and mean-variance optimization problems is that the risk measure ρ may capture completely different characteristics of the portfolio return distribution. We illustrate problems (8.12) and (8.13) when the *average value-at-risk* (AVaR) is selected as a risk measure.

AVaR is the main topic of Chapter 7. By definition, AVaR at tail probability ϵ, $AVaR_\epsilon(X)$, is the average of the *value-at-risk* (VaR) numbers larger than the VaR at tail probability ϵ. The formal definition is given in equation (7.1) in Chapter 7. Substituting $AVaR_\epsilon(X)$ for $\rho(X)$ in (8.12) and (8.13), we obtain the corresponding AVaR optimization problems.

The choice of AVaR as a risk measure allows certain simplifications of the optimization problems. If there are available scenarios for assets returns, we can use the equivalent AVaR definition in equation (7.2) and construct problem (7.8) in Section 7.3 of Chapter 7 and substitute problem (7.8) for the risk measure ρ.

Denote the scenarios for the assets returns by $r^1, r^2, \ldots, r^k$ where r^j is a vector of observations,

$$r^j = (r^j_1, r^j_2, \ldots, r^j_n),$$

which contains the returns of all assets observed in a given time instant denoted by the index j. Thus, all observations can be arranged in a $k \times n$ matrix,

$$H = \begin{pmatrix} r^1_1 & r^1_2 & \cdots & r^1_n \\ r^2_1 & r^2_2 & \cdots & r^2_n \\ \vdots & \vdots & \ddots & \vdots \\ r^k_1 & r^k_2 & \cdots & r^k_n \end{pmatrix}, \tag{8.14}$$

in which the rows contain assets returns observed in a given moment and the columns contain all observations for one asset in the entire time period. In this way, the notation $r^1, r^2, \ldots, r^k$ stands for the corresponding rows of the matrix of observations H. We remark that the matrix H may not only be a matrix of observed returns. For example, it can be a matrix of independent and identically distributed scenarios produced by a multivariate model. In this case, k denotes the number of multivariate scenarios produced by the model and n denotes the dimension of the random vector. In contrast, if H contains historical data, then k is the number of time instants observed and n is the number of assets observed.

   Problem (7.8) contains one-dimensional observations on a random variable which, in our case, describes the return of a given portfolio. Therefore, the observed returns of a portfolio with composition w are $r^1 w$, $r^2 w, \ldots, r^k w$, or simply as the product Hw of the historical data matrix H and the vector-column of portfolio weights w. We restate problem (7.8) employing matrix notation,

$$
\begin{aligned}
AVaR_\epsilon(Hw) \;=\; \min_{\theta,d} \quad & \theta + \frac{1}{k\epsilon}d'e \\
\text{subject to} \quad & -Hw - \theta e \leq d \\
& d \geq 0, \theta \in \mathbb{R},
\end{aligned}
\tag{8.15}
$$

where $d' = (d_1, \ldots, d_k)$ is a vector of auxiliary variables, $e = (1, \ldots, 1), e \in \mathbb{R}^k$ is a vector of ones, and $\theta \in \mathbb{R}$ is the additional parameter coming from the minimization formula given in equation (7.2) in Chapter 7. The first inequality in (8.15) concerns vectors and is to be interpreted in a component-by-component manner,

$$
-Hw - \theta e \leq d \qquad \Longleftrightarrow \qquad
\left|
\begin{aligned}
&-r^1 w - \theta \leq d_1 \\
&-r^2 w - \theta \leq d_2 \\
&\ldots \\
&-r^k w - \theta \leq d_k.
\end{aligned}
\right.
$$

   The optimization problem in (8.15) calculates the AVaR of a portfolio with a given composition w. It may seem involved because of the matrix notation, but in fact it has a very simple structure. The objective function is linear and all constraints are linear equalities and inequalities. There are very efficient algorithms for solving problems of this type, which are also called *linear programming problems*. Our goal is to obtain a more simplified version of problem (8.12) in which we minimize portfolio AVaR by changing the portfolio composition w. Employing (8.15) to calculate AVaR, this means that we have to perform an additional minimization with respect to w and, at the same time, adding all constraints existing in problem (8.12). The resulting optimization problem is

$$
\begin{aligned}
\min_{w,\theta,d} \quad & \theta + \frac{1}{k\epsilon}d'e \\
\text{subject to} \quad & -Hw - \theta e \leq d \\
& w'e = 1 \\
& w'\mu \geq R_* \\
& w \geq 0, d \geq 0, \theta \in \mathbb{R}.
\end{aligned}
\tag{8.16}
$$

As a result, problem (8.16) has a more simple structure than (8.12) since the objective function is linear and all constraints are linear equalities or inequalities. In the appendix to this chapter, we provide more details on the numerical difficulties in solving the two problems. It turns out that (8.16) is not always superior as far as the computational burden is concerned.

There is a similar analogue to problem (8.13). It is constructed in the same way, the difference is that AVaR is in the constraint set and not in the objective function. For this reason, we include the objective function of (8.15) in the constraint set,

$$
\begin{aligned}
\max_{w, \theta, d} \quad & w'\mu \\
\text{subject to} \quad & -Hw - \theta e \leq d \\
& w'e = 1 \\
& \theta + \frac{1}{k_\epsilon} d'e \leq R^* \\
& w \geq 0, d \geq 0, \theta \in \mathbb{R}.
\end{aligned}
\tag{8.17}
$$

The structure of the resulting problem (8.17) is more simple than the one of (8.13) and is a linear programming problem.

The method of combining (8.15) with (8.12) and (8.13) may seem artificial and not quite convincing that, for example, the solution of (8.17) and (8.13) with $\rho(r_p) = AVaR_\epsilon(Hw)$ will coincide. However, it can be formally proved that the solutions coincide.[4]

8.3.2 The Mean-Risk Efficient Frontier

Problems (8.12) and (8.13) are the main problems illustrating the principle behind M-R analysis. Varying the lower bound on expected return R_* in (8.12) or the upper bound on portfolio risk R^* in (8.13), we obtain the set of *efficient portfolios*. In a similar way to M-V analysis, plotting the expected return and the risk of the efficient portfolios in the mean-risk plane, we arrive at the mean-risk efficient frontier. It shows the trade-off between risk and expected return of the mean-risk efficient portfolios.

We illustrate the mean-risk efficient frontier with the following example. Suppose that we choose AVaR as a risk measure and the investment universe consists of three stocks in the S&P 500 index—Sun Microsystems Inc. with weight w_1, Oracle Corp. with weight w_2, and Microsoft Corp.

---

[4]Palmquist et al. (2002) give a formal proof that the solutions of (8.12) and (8.13) with $\rho(r_p) = AVaR_\epsilon(Hw)$ coincide with the solutions of (8.16) and (8.17), respectively.

with weight w_3. We use the observed daily returns in the period from December 31, 2002, to December 31, 2003. Thus, the historical data matrix H in equation (8.14) has three columns and 250 rows. Since there are only 250 observations, we choose 40% for the tail probability ϵ in order to have a higher stability of the AVaR estimate from the sample. This means that the risk measure equals the average of the VaRs larger than the VaR at 40% tail probability, which approximately equals the average loss provided that the loss is larger than the VaR at 40% tail probability.[5] The expected daily returns are computed as the sample average and equal $\mu_1 = 0.17\%$, $\mu_2 = 0.09\%$, and $\mu_2 = 0.03\%$ where the indexing is consistent with the weight indexes.

The efficient frontier is shown on the top plot in Figure 8.3. The horizontal axis ranges from about 1.5% to about 2.8%. Thus, the AVaR at 40% tail probability is about 1.5% for the global minimum risk portfolio and about 2.8% for the maximum expected return portfolio. The bottom plot contains the compositions of the efficient portfolios along the efficient frontier. The weight of Sun Microsystems Inc. gradually increases as we move from the global minimum risk portfolio to the maximum expected return portfolio. This is an expected effect because this stock has the highest expected daily return, $\mu_1 = 0.17\%$.

We can estimate the densities of the efficient portfolios and check how they change as we move from the global minimum risk portfolio to the maximum expected return portfolio. The densities of three selected portfolios are plotted in the bottom part of Figure 8.4. The top plot shows the same efficient frontier as the top plot in Figure 8.3 and dots indicate the positions of the three portfolios in the mean-risk plane. Portfolio 1 is the global minimum risk portfolio and its density is very concentrated about the portfolio expected return. Portfolio 2 is in the middle part of the efficient frontier. Its density is more dispersed and slightly skewed to the right. The density of Portfolio 3, which is close to the maximum expected return portfolio, is much more dispersed.

Besides problems (8.12) and (8.13), there exists another, equivalent way to obtain the mean-risk efficient frontier. This approach is based on the optimization problem

$$
\begin{aligned}
\max_{w} \quad & w'\mu - \lambda\rho(r_p) \\
\text{subject to} \quad & w'e = 1 \\
& w \geq 0,
\end{aligned}
\tag{8.18}
$$

---

[5] In fact, 40% of the observations in the sample will be used in the AVaR estimation. section 7.4.4 of Chapter 7 provides more information about stability of AVaR estimation.

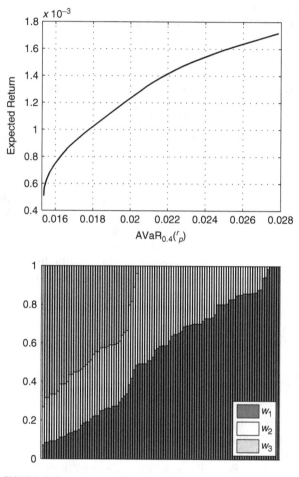

FIGURE 8.3 The top plot shows the efficient frontier in the mean-risk plane. The bottom plot shows the compositions of the optimal portfolios along the efficient frontier. Both plots have the same horizontal axis.

where $\lambda \geq 0$ is a risk-aversion parameter. By varying λ and solving problem (8.18), we derive a set of efficient portfolios that is obtained either through (8.12) or (8.13).

Note that the general shape of the mean-risk efficient frontier in Figure 8.3 is very similar to the shape of the mean-variance efficient frontier in Figure 8.1. Both are increasing functions; that is, the more risk we are ready to undertake, the higher the expected portfolio return. Also,

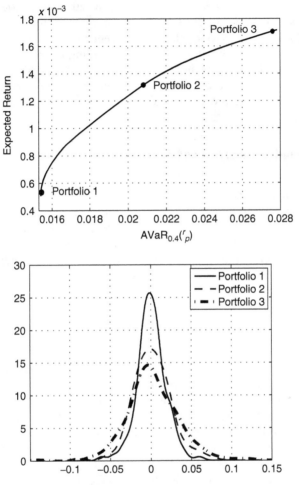

FIGURE 8.4 The top plot shows the efficient frontier with three portfolios selected. The bottom plot shows the densities of the three portfolios computed from the empirical data.

both efficient frontiers have a concave shape; that is, the expected portfolio return gained by undertaking one additional unit of risk decreases. The efficient frontiers are very steep at the global minimum risk portfolio and become more flat close to the maximum expected return portfolio. These common properties are not accidental. It turns out that they are governed by the properties of the risk measure $\rho(X)$, or the standard deviation in the case of M-V analysis. If $\rho(X)$ is convex, then the efficient frontier generated by problems (8.12), (8.13), or (8.18) is a concave, monotonically increasing function. If $\rho(X)$ belongs to the class of coherent risk measures, for example, then it is convex and, therefore, the corresponding efficient frontier has a general shape such as the one in Figure 8.3.[6] In the appendix to this chapter, we consider an even more general setting in which the efficient frontier retains the same shape. Stoyanov et al. (2007) provide a formal proof of the most general case.

8.3.3 Mean-Risk Analysis and SSD

The question of consistency with SSD arises for M-R analysis as well. We considered this question with respect to M-V analysis in section 8.2.3. Suppose that nonsatiable, risk-averse investors do not prefer a portfolio with composition $v = (v_1, \ldots, v_n)$ to another portfolio with composition $w = (w_1, \ldots, w_n)$. If X is a random vector describing the returns of the assets in the two portfolios, then is M-R analysis capable of indicating that the portfolio with return $v'X$ is not less efficient than $w'X$? A reasonable consistency condition is the following one

$$
w'X \succeq_{SSD} v'X \qquad \Longrightarrow \qquad \begin{cases} v'\mu \leq w'\mu \\ \rho(v'X) \geq \rho(w'X). \end{cases} \tag{8.19}
$$

Note that, essentially, it is the risk measure $\rho(X)$ that should be endowed with certain properties in order for (8.19) to hold true.

A fairly general class of risk measures, which we considered in Chapter 6, is the class of coherent risk measures. It turns out that if $\rho(X)$ is a coherent risk measure, then it does not necessarily follow that (8.19) will hold. Nevertheless, for some particular representatives, the consistency condition is true. For instance, if $\rho(X)$ is AVaR or, more generally, a spectral risk measure, then it is consistent with SSD.[7] DeGiorgi (2005) provides more information and a formal proof of this fact.

Since AVaR is consistent with SSD, the set of efficient portfolios, generated for instance by problem (8.12) with $\rho(X) = AVaR_\epsilon(X)$, does not contain a pair of two portfolios w and v such that all nonsatiable, risk-averse investors prefer strictly one to the other, $w'X \succ_{SSD} v'X$. In order to verify that this is the case, assume the converse. If $w'X$ dominates strictly $v'X$ according to SSD, then one of the inequalities in (8.19) is strict. In effect, the

---

[6]Coherent risk measures are a general family of risk measures which we consider in Chapter 6.

[7]These two examples are considered in Chapter 7.

portfolio v cannot be a solution to the optimization problems generating the efficient frontier, which results in a contradiction to the initial assumption. The conclusion is that none of the efficient portfolios can dominate strictly another efficient portfolio with respect to SSD. Therefore, which portfolio on the efficient frontier an investor would choose depends entirely on the particular functional form of the investor's utility function. If the investor is very risk-averse, then the optimal choice will be a portfolio close to the globally minimum risk portfolio and if the investor is risk-loving, then a portfolio close to the other end of the efficient frontier may be preferred.

8.3.4   Risk versus Dispersion Measures

The global minimum risk portfolio can be calculated from problem (8.12) by removing the lower bound on the expected portfolio return. In this way, we solve a problem without any requirements on the expected performance. However, it turns out that even though we remove the constraint, the expected portfolio return may still influence the optimal solution.

Suppose that $\rho(X)$ is a coherent risk measure. Then, changing only the expectation of the portfolio return distribution by adding a positive constant results in a decrease of risk,

$$\rho(X + C) = \rho(X) - C,$$

where C is a positive constant. Thus any coherent risk measure can be represented as

$$\rho(X) = \rho(X - EX) - EX. \tag{8.20}$$

The first term in the difference is completely independent of the expected value of X. As a result of this decomposition, problem (8.12) can be restated without the expected return constraint in the following way,

$$
\begin{aligned}
\max_{w} \quad & w'\mu - \rho(r_p - w'\mu) \\
\text{subject to} \quad & w'e = 1 \\
& w \geq 0,
\end{aligned}
\tag{8.21}
$$

where we have changed the minimization to maximization and have flipped the sign of the objective function. The solution to problem (8.21) is the global minimum risk portfolio and the expected portfolio return $w'\mu$ has a certain impact on the solution as it appears in the objective function.

In contrast, the global minimum variance portfolio in M-V analysis does not share this property. It is completely invariant of the expected returns of the assets in the investment universe. This difference between

M-R analysis and M-V analysis is not to be regarded as a drawback of one or the other. It is one consequence of employing a risk measure in the optimization problem. In spite of the differences between the two, under certain conditions it appears possible to extend the mean-risk efficient frontier by substituting the risk measure for a suitable dispersion measure so that the mean-risk efficient frontier properties become more similar to the properties of the mean-variance efficient frontier. In the appendix to this chapter, we build up a general approach to this question. The current section contains an application of the general approach to the family of coherent risk measures.

In section 6.5 of Chapter 6 we remarked that there exists a connection between a subfamily of the coherent risk measures and a family of dispersion measures. The relationship between the corresponding risk and dispersion measures is the following. Suppose that $\rho(X)$ is a coherent risk measure (i.e., it satisfies the properties in section 6.4.4 of Chapter 6) and, additionally, it satisfies the property $\rho(X) > -EX$. Furthermore, suppose that $D(X)$ is a deviation measure (i.e., it satisfies the properties in Section 6.2.5 of Chapter 6) and, additionally, it satisfies the property $D(X) \leq EX$ for all nonnegative random variables, $X \geq 0$. Under these assumptions, any of the two functionals can be expressed from the other in the following way,

and
$$D(X) = \rho(X - EX)$$
$$\rho(X) = D(X) - EX.$$

Throughout this section, it is always assumed that $D(X)$ and $\rho(X)$ are such that this relationship holds.

Consider the objective function of problem (8.18). Applying the decomposition in equation (8.20), we obtain

$$w'\mu - \lambda\rho(r_p) = w'\mu - \lambda\rho(r_p - w'\mu) + \lambda w'\mu$$
$$= (1 + \lambda)w'\mu - \lambda\rho(r_p - w'\mu)$$
$$= (1 + \lambda)\left(w'\mu - \frac{\lambda}{1 + \lambda}\rho(r_p - w'\mu)\right).$$

Since $\lambda \geq 0$, we can safely ignore the positive factor $1 + \lambda$ in the objective function because it does not change the optimal solution. In effect, we obtain the following optimization problem, which is equivalent to (8.18),

$$
\begin{aligned}
\max_{w} \quad & w'\mu - \frac{\lambda}{1 + \lambda}\rho(r_p - w'\mu) \\
\text{subject to} \quad & w'e = 1 \\
& w \geq 0.
\end{aligned}
\tag{8.22}
$$

We recognize the deviation measure $D(r_p) = \rho(r_p - w'\mu)$ in the objective function. Note that the aversion coefficient is not an arbitrary positive number, $\lambda/(1 + \lambda) \in [0, 1]$, because of the assumption that the risk-aversion coefficient is nonnegative. As a result of this analysis, we can see the parallel between (8.22) and the corresponding problem with a deviation measure,

$$\max_{w} \quad w'\mu - cD(r_p)$$
$$\text{subject to} \quad w'e = 1$$
$$w \geq 0, \qquad\qquad (8.23)$$

where $c \geq 0$ is the corresponding aversion coefficient. The set of optimal portfolios obtained from (8.23) by varying the parameter c contains the set of mean-risk efficient portfolios of (8.22). Furthermore, the efficient frontier corresponding to (8.23) has properties similar to the mean-variance efficient frontier since $D(r_p)$ does not depend on the expected portfolio return.

The optimal portfolios, which appear in addition to the mean-risk efficient portfolios, are obtained with $c > 1$. If $c < 1$, then there is an equivalent $\lambda = c/(1 - c)$ such that the optimal portfolios of (8.22) coincide with the optimal solutions of (8.23).[8] Increasing c, we obtain more and more diversified portfolios. In effect, the left part of the mean-risk efficient frontier gets extended by problem (8.23). Actually, in the mean-risk plane, the extended part curves back because these portfolios are sub-optimal according to M-R analysis while in mean-deviation plane, the efficient frontier is a concave, monotonically increasing function. The difference between the mean-risk and the mean-deviation planes is merely a change in coordinates given by equation (8.20).

The set of optimal portfolios additional to the mean-risk efficient portfolios can be large or small depending on the magnitude of the expected returns of the assets. If the expected returns are close to zero, the set is small and it completely disappears if the expected returns are exactly equal to zero. In practice, if we use daily returns, the efficient portfolios generated by (8.22) and (8.23) almost coincide. Larger discrepancies may appear with weekly or monthly data.

In order to see the usual magnitude of the extension of the mean-risk efficient portfolios by (8.23), we increase five times the expected returns of the common stocks in the example developed in section 8.3.2 keeping every-thing else unchanged.[9] The increase roughly corresponds to the magnitude

---

[8] The case $c = 1$ coincides with the global minimum risk portfolio.

[9] AVaR is a coherent risk measure and satisfies the condition $AVaR_\epsilon(X) > -EX, \epsilon \in (0, 1)$. The corresponding deviation measure is $D(X) = AVaR_\epsilon(X - EX)$. This is noted also in section 6.5 of Chapter 6.

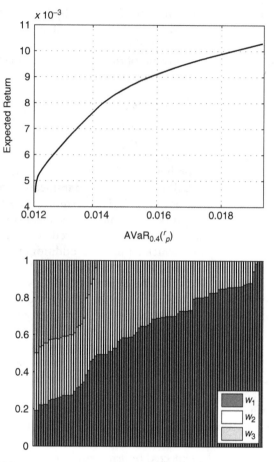

FIGURE 8.5 The top plot shows the efficient frontier in the mean-risk plane. The bottom plot shows the compositions of the optimal portfolios along the efficient frontier. Both plots have the same horizontal axis.

of weekly expected returns. The resulting mean-risk efficient frontier and set of efficient portfolios is given in Figure 8.5. The efficient portfolios generated by problem (8.23) with $D(X) = AVaR_{0.4}(X - EX)$ are shown in Figure 8.6. The rectangle on the bottom plot indicates the optimal portfolios that are additional to the mean-risk efficient portfolios. The upper plot in Figure 8.6 shows the coordinates of the optimal portfolios in the mean-deviation plane. Note the difference between the horizontal axes in Figures 8.5 and 8.6.

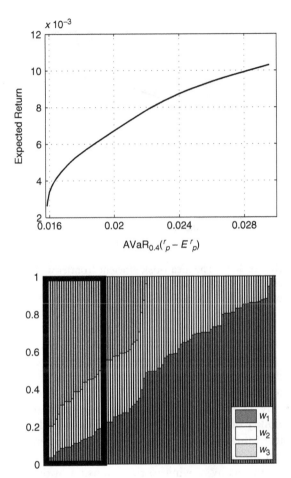

FIGURE 8.6 The top plot shows the efficient portfolios of (8.23) in the mean-deviation plane. The bottom plot shows the compositions of the optimal portfolios. Both plots have the same horizontal axis. The rectangle indicates the portfolios additional to the mean-risk efficient portfolios.

As a next step, we plot the coordinates of the additional portfolios in the mean-risk plane. These portfolios are suboptimal according to M-R analysis and, therefore, the extension of the mean-risk efficient frontier will curve backwards. This is illustrated in Figure 8.7. The portfolios which are indicated by the rectangle on the bottom plot in Figure 8.6 are shown with a dashed line in the mean-risk plane in Figure 8.7. The fact that they are

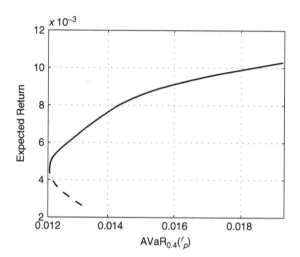

FIGURE 8.7 The mean-risk efficient frontier with the coordinates of the additional optimal portfolios plotted with a dashed line.

sub-optimal has an easy geometric illustration. For any of these portfolios, we can find an equally risky portfolio with a higher expected return, which is on the mean-risk efficient frontier.

If M-R analysis leads to the conclusion that these portfolios are sub-optimal, why do we consider them at all? Suppose that we are uncertain about the reliability of the expected return estimates and we want to minimize the impact of this uncertainty on the optimal solution. Since the means affect the global minimum risk portfolio, we may want to reduce further the effect of the means by moving to the extension of the efficient frontier given by the mean-deviation optimization problem (8.23). The portfolio that appears at the very end of the dashed line in Figure 8.7 is the minimum dispersion portfolio, the composition of which is not influenced by the means at all. In effect, even though the mean-deviation optimal portfolios are sub-optimal, under certain circumstances they may still be of practical interest.

On the basis of the analysis outlined in this section, we can classify all optimal portfolios obtained from the mean-risk optimization problem of the following type

$$\begin{aligned}
\min_{w} \quad & \rho(r_p) \\
\text{subject to} \quad & w'e = 1 \\
& w'\mu = R_* \\
& w \geq 0.
\end{aligned} \qquad (8.24)$$

Note that the expected return constraint in (8.12) is an inequality and in (8.24) it is an equality. This may seem to be an insignificant modification of the initial problem but it results in problem (8.24) being more general than (8.12) in the following sense. The optimal portfolios obtained by varying the bound R_* in (8.24) contain the mean-risk efficient portfolios and, more generally, the mean-deviation efficient portfolios. A more formal argument will be given in the appendix to this chapter but, intuitively, by fixing the expected portfolio return to be equal to R_*, we are essentially minimizing portfolio dispersion. By equation (8.20), the objective function of problem (8.24) can be written as

$$\rho(r_p) = D(r_p) - w'\mu = D(r_p) - R_*,$$

in which R_* is a constant and, therefore, it cannot change the optimal solution. In practice, we are minimizing the dispersion $D(r_p)$.

As a result, the optimal portfolios generated by problem (8.24) by varying R_* can be classified into three groups. Figure 8.8 illustrates the groups. The dark gray group contains the mean-risk efficient portfolios generated by (8.12). They are obtained from (8.24) with high values of R_*. The gray group contains the mean-deviation efficient portfolios produced by problem (8.23) which are not mean-risk efficient. They are obtained from (8.24) with medium values of R_*. Finally, the white set consists of optimal portfolios which are not mean-deviation efficient but solve (8.24). They

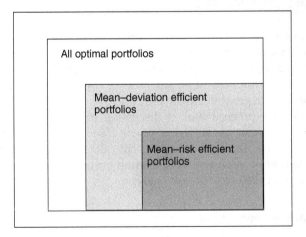

FIGURE 8.8 Classification of the optimal portfolios generated by problem (8.24) by varying the expected return bound R_*.

are obtained with small values of R_*. This set has no practical significance since the portfolios belonging to it have small expected returns and high dispersions.

8.4 SUMMARY

In this chapter, we described M-V analysis and the associated optimal portfolio problems. We discussed the mean-variance efficient frontier and consistency of M-V analysis with the stochastic dominance order of the class of non-satiable, risk-averse investors. In the appendix to this chapter, we remark on the asymptotic validity of quadratic utility functions as reasonable approximations to expected utilities.

Considering a true risk measure instead of standard deviation leads to M-R analysis. The same reasoning leads to the mean-risk efficient frontier which, under certain conditions, is related to a mean-dispersion efficient frontier. As a result of this relationship, we demonstrated that all optimal portfolios can be classified into three groups—mean-risk efficient portfolios, mean-dispersion efficient portfolios that are not mean-risk efficient, and optimal portfolios that are not mean-dispersion efficient.

In the appendix to this chapter, we remark on the numerical difficulties in solving the optimal portfolio problems when AVaR is selected as a risk measure.

8.5 TECHNICAL APPENDIX

We discuss in more detail several topics that are of practical or theoretical value to optimal portfolio problems. We begin with a description of what kind of constraints defining the set of feasible portfolios are typically imposed. They do not depend on whether we consider M-V analysis, M-R analysis, or a more general framework, and are determined by exogenous factors. Next, we proceed with a discussion of how the mean-variance optimization problems are solved in practice and the theoretic plausibility of quadratic utility functions. Then we consider questions concerning the practical solution of mean-risk optimization problems and a generalization of M-R analysis called reward-risk analysis.

8.5.1 Types of Constraints

In the chapter, we noted that M-R analysis concerns feasible portfolios. Whether a portfolio is feasible or not depends on conditions imposed by the portfolio manager.

A risk-averse portfolio manager would not want to see a high concentration of a particular, or any, asset in the portfolio. At the same time, for some of the assets a minimal holding may be required. These two conditions can be implemented by means of *box-type* constraints,

and

$$a_i \leq w_i \leq b_i,$$

$$i = 1, 2, \ldots, n,$$

where a_i is a lower bound and b_i is an upper bound on the weight of the i-th asset. For some assets, the lower bound can simply be zero, $a_i = 0$. For example, suppose there are three assets in the investment universe and we want to invest no more than 60% of the capital in any of them and in asset number 3 to invest at least 10%. This is modeled by the constraints,

and

$$0 \leq w_1 \leq 0.6,$$

$$0 \leq w_2 \leq 0.6,$$

$$0.1 \leq w_3 \leq 0.6.$$

In defining box-type constraints, we have to be careful not to end up with an overly stringent set of constraints. For example, this happens in the above illustration if the upper bound is 20% instead of 60%. Since all weights have to sum up to one, the sum of lower bounds should not be above 1, $\sum_{i=1}^{n} a_i \leq 1$, and the sum of upper bound should not be below 1, $\sum_{i=1}^{n} b_i \geq 1$.

In a similar manner, the portfolio manager may want to impose constraints on certain groupings of assets. Suppose that the investment universe consists of common stocks. Depending on the strategy type, a reasonable condition is a lower and an upper bound on the exposure in a given industry. This is a constraint on the sum of the weights corresponding to all stocks from the investment universe belonging to that industry,

$$a \leq \sum_{i \in I} w_i \leq b,$$

in which I denotes the indices of the common stocks from the given industry.

The general rule that is followed when building constraints is that the resulting set of feasible portfolios should be convex. This is guaranteed if each of the inequalities or equalities building up the constraints define a convex set. Then the set of feasible portfolios is the intersection of these convex sets, which in turn is a convex set.

If the set of feasible portfolios is not convex, then the optimization problem may become hard to solve numerically. An example of a type of constraint that does not lead to a convex set of feasible portfolios is the following. In the previous example, suppose that if an asset is to be included in the portfolio, then it should have at least 10% of the capital allocated to it. This is modeled by the constraints

$$w_1 = 0 \quad \text{or} \quad 0.1 \leq w_1 \leq 0.6,$$

$$w_2 = 0 \quad \text{or} \quad 0.1 \leq w_2 \leq 0.6,$$

and

$$w_3 = 0 \quad \text{or} \quad 0.1 \leq w_3 \leq 0.6,$$

which do not result in a convex set. Problems of this type can be solved by the more general methods of mixed-integer programming and can be very computationally intensive.

The set of feasible portfolios has a simpler structure if it contains only linear inequalities or equalities. In this case, it is said to be *polyhedral*. Every polyhedral set is convex since any linear inequality or equality defines a convex set. A polyhedral set has a simpler structure because its borders are described by hyperplanes, which is a consequence of the fact that the set is composed of linear inequalities or equalities.

8.5.2 Quadratic Approximations to Utility Functions

In the chapter, we remarked that M-V analysis is, generally, inconsistent with SSD. It is consistent with the order implied by investors with quadratic utility functions. The assumption that investors have quadratic utility functions is a significant limitation. Nevertheless, under certain conditions, quadratic utility functions may represent a reasonable approximation of more general types of utility functions. Therefore, there are cases in which the decisions made by investors with quadratic utilities are consistent with the decisions made by larger classes of investors depending on the accuracy of the approximation.

Consider a utility function $u(x)$ and its Taylor series approximation in a neighborhood of the point EX where X is a random variable,

$$u(x) = u(EX) + u'(EX)(x - EX) + \frac{1}{2}u''(EX)(x - EX)^2$$

$$+ \frac{1}{n!}\sum_{k=3}^{\infty} u^{(k)}(EX)(x - EX)^k, \qquad (8.25)$$

where $u^{(k)}(x)$ denotes the k-th derivative of $u(x)$ and x is in a neighborhood of the point EX. We assume that the infinite series expansion is valid for any

$x \in \mathbb{R}$; that is, the infinite power series converges to the value $u(x)$ for any real x. This condition is already a limitation on the possible utility functions that we consider. Not only do we require that the utility function is infinitely many times differentiable but we also assume that the corresponding Taylor expansion is convergent for any real x. Functions satisfying these conditions are called *analytic functions*.

We can calculate the expected utility taking advantage of the expansion in (8.25) which we integrate term by term,

$$Eu(X) = u(EX) + \frac{1}{2}u''(EX)E(X - EX)^2$$

$$+ \frac{1}{n!} \sum_{k=3}^{\infty} u^{(k)}(EX)E(X - EX)^k. \qquad (8.26)$$

The second term vanishes because $E(X - EX) = 0$. As a result, we obtain that the expected utility can be expressed in terms of the derivatives of the utility function evaluated at EX and all moments $m_k = E(X - EX)^k, k = 1, 2, \ldots$ Note that even for analytic utilities $u(x)$, expression (8.26) may not hold. If the random variable X has infinite moments, then (8.26) does not hold. Therefore, a critical assumption is that the random variable X has finite moments of any order.

If $u(x)$ is analytic and the random variable X is such that $m_k < \infty$, $k = 1, 2, \ldots$, then we may choose the first three terms as a reasonable approximation,

$$Eu(X) \approx u(EX) + \frac{1}{2}u''(EX)E(X - EX)^2$$

$$= u(EX) + \frac{1}{2}u''(EX)\sigma_X^2, \qquad (8.27)$$

for the expected utility function. We recognize the moment $\sigma_X^2 = E(X - EX)^2$ as the variance of X. In effect, the expected utility is approximated by the mean and the variance of X. If we consider risk-averse investors, then the utility function $u(x)$ is concave and, therefore, it has a negative second derivative. As a result, the expected utility maximization problem can be linked to M-V analysis.

Samuelson (1970) shows that under certain conditions, the approximation in (8.27) is indeed reasonable. If the choice under uncertainty concerns a very short interval of time and the random variable describes the payoff of a venture at the end of the time period, then under a few regularity conditions the approximation in (8.27) holds. Ohlson (1975) considers weaker conditions under which (8.27) is reasonable.

8.5.3 Solving Mean-Variance Problems in Practice

The main optimization problems behind M-V analysis are (8.4), (8.5), and (8.8). We remark on the type of each of these problems.

In problem (8.4), the portfolio variance is minimized with a constraint on the expected return. The objective function of this problem is quadratic and if the set of feasible portfolios is polyhedral, then the optimization problem is said to be a *quadratic programming problem*. There are efficient numerical methods for solving quadratic problems, which are available in software packages such as MATLAB.

Problem (8.5) has a more simple objective as we maximize the expected portfolio return, which is a linear function of portfolio weights. In the set of feasible portfolios, we include an upper bound on the portfolio variance which results in a quadratic constraint. There are efficient methods for solving such types of problems as well. If all the other constraints are linear, the optimization problems can be formulated as *second order cone programming problems*.[10]

Finally, problem (8.8) is very similar in structure to (8.4). The objective function is also quadratic, the difference from (8.4) is that it has a linear part represented by the expected portfolio return. In effect, (8.8) is a quadratic programming problem.

As far as the computational complexity is concerned, the quadratic and, more generally, the conic programming problems are between the linear optimization problems and the convex optimization problems with nonlinear constraints.

Under certain conditions, it is possible to obtain a closed-form solution to mean-variance optimization problems. In fact, these conditions lead to a simpler problem in which there are no inequality constraints. For example, the optimization problem

$$
\begin{aligned}
\min_{w} \quad & w'\Sigma w \\
\text{subject to} \quad & w'e = 1 \\
& w'\mu = R_{*},
\end{aligned}
\tag{8.28}
$$

which is a simplified analogue of (8.4), allows for a closed-form solution. We have replaced the inequality constraint in (8.4) on the expected portfolio return by an equality constraint and we have removed the requirement that the weights should be nonnegative. As a result, problem (8.28) allows for taking a short position in an asset, which is indicated by a negative weight in the optimal solution.

---

[10]Quadratic programming problems can also be formulated as second order conic problems. Therefore, the conic programing problems are a more general class.

The closed-form solution is obtained by applying the method of Lagrange multipliers, which is as follows. First, we build the corresponding Lagrangian represented by the function

$$L(w, \lambda) = w'\Sigma w + \lambda_1(1 - w'e) + \lambda_2(R_* - w'\mu)$$

in which λ_1 and λ_2 are the Lagrange multipliers. Second, we solve for w the system of equations resulting from the first-order optimality conditions of the Lagrangian,

$$\left| \begin{array}{l} \dfrac{\partial L(w, \lambda)}{\partial w} = 0 \\[2ex] \dfrac{\partial L(w, \lambda)}{\partial \lambda} = 0. \end{array} \right.$$

Since the Lagrangian is a quadratic function of w, the resulting system of equations is composed of linear equations that can be solved for w. As a result, we obtain that the optimal solution can be computed according to the formula in matrix form

$$w = \frac{(C\Sigma^{-1}\mu - B\Sigma^{-1}e)m + A\Sigma^{-1}e - B\Sigma^{-1}\mu}{AC - B^2},$$

where Σ^{-1} stands for the inverse of the covariance matrix Σ, $A = \mu'\Sigma^{-1}\mu, B = e'\Sigma^{-1}\mu$, and $C = e'\Sigma^{-1}e$.

If there are inequality constraints, this approach is not applicable. In this case, the optimization problem is more general and the Karush-Kuhn-Tucker conditions, which generalize the method of Lagrange multipliers, can be applied but they rarely lead to nice closed-form expressions, as the resulting system of equations is much more involved.

8.5.4 Solving Mean-Risk Problems in Practice

The optimization problems arising from M-R analysis have a different structure than the quadratic problems of M-V analysis, which depends on the assumed properties of the risk measure. In Chapter 6, we considered two classes of risk measures introduced axiomatically. Generally, the most important property that determines to a large extent the structure of the optimization problem is the convexity property. It also has a significant practical implication as it guarantees the diversification effect; that is, the risk of a portfolio of assets is smaller than the corresponding weighted average of the individual risks.

Under the general assumption of convexity, problems (8.12), (8.13), and
(8.18) are convex programming problems. In (8.12) and (8.18), the objective
functions are convex functions and, in (8.13), there is a convex function in the
constraint set. Therefore, the three problems can be solved in practice using
the general methods of convex programming. There are commercial solvers
in which such algorithms are implemented. Also, in software packages such
as MATLAB, there are libraries solving numerically convex problems.

Under certain conditions, simplification of the optimization problem
structure is possible for some risk measures. If we choose AVaR as a risk
measure, then the three problems can be reduced to linear optimization
problems provided that future scenarios are available. In the chapter, we
demonstrated that (8.16) and (8.17) correspond to (8.12) and (8.13) and
both (8.16) and (8.17) have linear objective functions and the set of feasible
portfolios is defined through linear inequalities and equalities. As a result,
both problems are linear programming problems, which are significantly
simpler than a convex optimization problem.

However, reducing the convex problem to a linear problem comes at
the cost of increasing the problem dimension. For instance, problem (8.12)
has n variables and $n + 2$ linear constraints, where n denotes the number
of assets in the portfolio. In contrast, the corresponding linear problem
(8.16) has $n + k + 1$ variables and $2k + n + 2$ linear constraints, in which
k denotes the number of scenarios. The dimension and the computational
difficulty of the linear problem then increases with the number of scenarios
because we introduce one auxiliary variable and two constraints for each
scenario. Furthermore, adding more scenarios makes the matrix defining
the linear constraints in the linear programming problem become more
nonsparse. A matrix is called *sparse* if most of the numbers in it are zeros
and the numerical methods for linear programming are more efficient if the
matrix is more sparse. In summary, we are simplifying the problem structure
but we are increasing the problem dimension. As a result, when increasing
the number of scenarios there will be a point at which the two effects will
balance off and there will not be an advantage in solving the linear problem.
In this case, one may consider directly

$$\min_{w} \quad \widehat{\text{AVaR}}_\epsilon(Hw)$$
$$\text{subject to} \quad w'e = 1$$
$$w'\mu \geq R_*$$
$$w \geq 0. \tag{8.29}$$

in which $\widehat{\text{AVaR}}_\epsilon(Hw)$ is the sample AVaR defined in equation (7.6) in
Chapter 7 and H is the matrix with scenarios defined in (8.14). Problem
(8.29) can be solved as a convex programming problem.

In fact, there is another way of viewing problems (8.29) and (8.12) with $\rho(r_p) = AVaR_\epsilon(r_p)$. Suppose that we know exactly the multivariate distribution of the assets returns but we cannot obtain explicitly the AVaR risk measure as a function of portfolio weights. However, we have a random number generator constructed that we can use to draw independent scenarios from the multivariate law. In this situation, we cannot solve (8.12) because we cannot evaluate the objective function for a given vector of portfolio weights. Nevertheless, we can draw a matrix of independent simulations from the multivariate law and compute *approximately* the AVaR for any vector of portfolio weights through the formula of the sample AVaR. Thus, we can solve problem (8.29), or (8.16), which can be viewed as an approximation to (8.12) obtained through the Monte Carlo method. The larger the number of scenarios, the more accurate the approximation. Also, the larger the portfolio, the more simulations we need to achieve a given level of accuracy since the generated vectors are supposed to approximate a distribution in a higher dimensional space. Therefore, the linear problem (8.16) may not be advantageous if higher accuracy is needed or, alternatively, if the portfolio is sufficiently large and there is a target accuracy. If this is the case, one can use (8.29) in which directly the sample AVaR is getting minimized without increasing the problem dimension by including additional variables and constraints.

8.5.5 Reward-Risk Analysis

In M-R analysis developed in the chapter, we consider two criteria as a major determinant of efficient portfolios. They are the expected portfolio return, being a measure of the expected performance, and a risk measure estimating portfolio risk. Instead of the expected portfolio return, we can include a more general functional estimating expected performance. We denote this functional by $v(X)$. Thus we can generalize M-R analysis by considering $v(X)$ and the risk measure $\rho(X)$ as criteria for obtaining efficient portfolios. M-R analysis appears as a special case when $v(X) = EX$. The functional $v(X)$ we call a *reward measure* and the resulting more general analysis is called *reward-risk analysis* (RR analysis).

In this section, we impose several properties on the functional $v(X)$ and explore the resulting optimization problems. Consider the following properties:

1. *Monotonicity.* Suppose that $X \leq Y$ in almost sure sense. It is reasonable to expect that the expected reward of Y will be larger than that of X, $v(X) \leq v(Y)$.

2. *Superadditivity.* We assume that for any X and Y, the following inequality holds:

$$v(X + Y) \geq v(X) + v(Y).$$

That is, the reward of a portfolio is not smaller than the sum of the portfolio constituents rewards. There is an additional stimulus in holding a portfolio.

3. *Positive homogeneity.* The rationale of this assumption is the same as in the case of risk measures.

$$v(hX) = hv(X), \qquad h \geq 0.$$

4. *Invariance property.* Adding a nonrandom term to the portfolio increases the reward by the nonrandom quantity,

$$v(X + C) = v(X) + C,$$

and $v(0) = 0$.

These axioms suggest that the negative of a coherent risk measure is in fact a reward measure; that is, if $v(X) = -\rho(X)$ where $\rho(X)$ is a coherent risk measure, then the above properties hold. For this reason, if $v(X)$ satisfies the properties above, we call it a *coherent reward measure*. The superadditivity and the positive homogeneity properties guarantee that any coherent reward measure is a concave function,

$$v(aX + (1 - a)Y) \geq av(X) + (1 - a)v(Y),$$

where $a \in [0, 1]$. This property, along with the convexity of the risk measure, guarantees nice properties of the resulting optimization problems.

The main principles of RR analysis can be formulated in the same way as for M-R analysis:

1. From all feasible portfolios with a given lower bound on the reward measure, find the portfolios that have minimum risk.
2. From all feasible portfolios with a given upper bound on risk, find the portfolios that provide maximum reward.

The corresponding optimal portfolio problems are the following:

$$\begin{aligned}
\min_{w} \quad & \rho(r_p) \\
\text{subject to} \quad & w'e = 1 \\
& v(r_p) \geq R_* \\
& w \geq 0,
\end{aligned} \qquad (8.30)$$

where R_* is the lower bound on the portfolio reward. Similarly, the the optimization problem behind the second formulation is

$$
\begin{aligned}
\max_{w} \quad & v(r_p) \\
\text{subject to} \quad & w'e = 1 \\
& \rho(r_p) \leq R^* \\
& w \geq 0,
\end{aligned}
\tag{8.31}
$$

where R^* is the upper bound on portfolio risk. Problem (8.30) is a convex optimization problem and (8.31) is reducible to a convex problem by flipping the sign of the objective function and considering minimization. Convex optimization problems are appealing because a local minimum is necessarily the global one. The necessary and sufficient conditions are given by the Karush-Kuhn-Tucker theorem.

In a manner similar to M-R analysis, the optimal solutions obtained from the two problems by varying the limits on the portfolio reward or risk respectively are called *reward-risk efficient portfolios*. The coordinates of the reward-risk efficient portfolios in the reward-risk plane form the *reward-risk efficient frontier*. Stoyanov et al. (2007) prove that the reward-risk efficient frontier is a concave, monotonically increasing function if the reward measure is a concave function, and the risk measure is a convex function. Therefore, the general shape of the reward-risk efficient frontier is the same as the one plotted in Figure 8.3, for example. As a consequence of the Karush-Kuhn-Tucker conditions, the efficient frontier can also be generated by the problem

$$
\begin{aligned}
\max_{w} \quad & v(r_p) - \lambda\rho(r_p) \\
\text{subject to} \quad & w'e = 1 \\
& w \geq 0,
\end{aligned}
\tag{8.32}
$$

where $\lambda \geq 0$ is the risk-aversion parameter, or the Lagrange multiplier.

We demonstrate that the reward-risk efficient portfolios can be derived from a reward-dispersion optimal portfolio problem. Consider the optimization problem (8.32). The objective function is transformed in the following way:

$$
\begin{aligned}
v(r_p) - \lambda\rho(r_p) &= v(r_p) - \lambda\rho(r_p - v(r_p) + v(r_p)) \\
&= (\lambda + 1)v(r_p) - \lambda\rho(r_p - v(r_p)) \\
&= (\lambda + 1)\left(v(r_p) - \frac{\lambda}{(\lambda + 1)}\rho(r_p - v(r_p)) \right).
\end{aligned}
$$

The positive multiplier $\lambda + 1$ does not change the optimal solutions and we can safely ignore it. As a result, we obtain the equivalent optimization problem

$$\max_{w} \quad v(r_p) - \frac{\lambda}{(\lambda + 1)}\rho(r_p - v(r_p))$$
$$\text{subject to} \quad w'e = 1$$
$$w \geq 0, \tag{8.33}$$

where $\lambda \geq 0$ and, as a result, the multiplier $\lambda/(\lambda + 1) \in [0, 1)$. It turns out that the functional $G(X) = \rho(X - v(X))$ is a dispersion measure under the additional condition $\rho(X) \geq -v(X)$, as it satisfies the general properties outlined in section 6.2.4 of Chapter 6, which we illustrate as follows:

Positive shift. $G(X + C) = \rho(X + C - v(X + C)) = G(X)$ for all X and constants $C \in \mathbb{R}$.

Positive homogeneity. $G(0) = \rho(0 - v(0)) = 0$ and $G(hX) = \rho(hX - v(hX)) = hG(X)$ for all X and all $h > 0$.

Positivity. Under the additional condition $\rho(x) \geq - v(x)$, it follows directly that $G(x)$ is positive, $G(x) \geq 0$ for all X, with $G(x) > 0$ for nonconstant X, from the representation

$$G(X) = \rho(X - v(X)) = \rho(X) + v(X).$$

As a result, we can consider the more general reward-dispersion optimal portfolio problem

$$\max_{w} \quad v(r_p) - aG(r_p)$$
$$\text{subject to} \quad w'e = 1$$
$$w \geq 0, \tag{8.34}$$

where $a \geq 0$ and $G(X) = \rho(X - v(X))$. The reward-risk efficient portfolios are obtained from (8.34) with $a \in [0, 1]$. The optimal portfolios obtained with $a > 1$ are in addition to the mean-risk efficient portfolios and are sub-optimal according to RR analysis.

Note that problem (8.34) may not be a convex optimization problem for all values of a because the functional G is, generally, arbitrary as it equals a sum of a convex and a concave functional. However, if $a \in [0, 1]$ then (8.34) is a convex optimization problem because it is equivalent to (8.33).

The purpose of the general framework developed in this section is to demonstrate that the set of efficient portfolios can be obtained from a reward-deviation optimization problem. We showed in Chapter 6 that dispersion measures can be derived from probability metrics. The set of efficient portfolios can then be related to the theory of probability metrics through the reward-dispersion optimization problem.

In the chapter, we showed a special case of this relationship in which the reward measure equals the expected portfolio return and the $\rho(X)$ is a coherent risk measure satisfying $\rho(X) \geq -EX$. Under these conditions, the functional $G(X)$ turns into a deviation measure, which is an example of a dispersion measure, and the corresponding problem (8.34) has better optimal properties.

BIBLIOGRAPHY

DeGiorgi, E. (2005). "Reward-risk portfolio selection and stochastic dominance," *Journal of Banking and Finance* 29(4): 895–926.

Lintner, J. (1965). "The valuation of risk assets and the selection of risky investments in stock portfolios and capital budgets," *Review of Economics and Statistics* February: 13–37.

Markowitz, H. M. (1952). "Portfolio selection," *Journal of Finance* 7(1): 77–91.

Markowitz, H. M. (1959). *Portfolio selection: Efficient diversification of investments*, New York: John Wiley & Sons.

Markowitz, H. M. (1987). *Mean-variance analysis in portfolio choice and capital markets*, New York: Basil Blackwell.

Ohlson, J. A. (1975). "The asymptotic validity of quadratic utility as the trading interval approaches zero," in *Stochastic Optimization Models in Finance, 2006 Edition*, W.T. Ziemba and R.G. Vickson (eds.), pp. 221–234, New York: Academic Press.

Palmquist, J., S. Uryasev, and P. Krokhmal (2002). "Portfolio optimization with conditional value-at-risk objective and constraints," *Journal of Risk* 4(2): 43–68.

Samuelson, P. A. (1970). "The fundamental approximation theorem for portfolio analysis in terms of means, variances and higher moments," *Review of Economic Studies* 37(4): 537–542.

Sharpe, W. F. (1964). "Capital asset prices: A theory of market equilibrium under conditions of risk," *Journal of Finance* 19(3): 425–442.

Stoyanov, S. T., S. T. Rachev, and F. J. Fabozzi (2007). "Optimal financial portfolios," forthcoming in *Applied Mathematical Finance*.

Tobin, J. (1958). "Liquidity preference as behavior toward risk," *Review of Economic Studies* 25: 65–86.

CHAPTER 9

Benchmark Tracking Problems

9.1 INTRODUCTION

An important problem for fund managers is comparing the performance of their portfolios to a benchmark. The benchmark could be a market index or any other portfolio or liability measure in the case of defined benefit pension plans. In general, there are two types of strategies that managers follow: active or passive. An active portfolio strategy uses available information and forecasting techniques to seek a better performance than a portfolio that is simply diversified broadly. Essential to all active strategies are expectations about the factors that could influence the performance of an asset class. The goal of an active strategy is to outperform the benchmark after management fees by a given number of basis points. A passive portfolio strategy involves minimal expectational input and instead relies on diversification to match the performance of some benchmark. In effect, a passive strategy, commonly referred to as indexing, assumes that the marketplace will reflect all available information in the price paid for securities. There are various strategies for constructing a portfolio to replicate the index but the key in these strategies is designing a portfolio whose tracking error relative to the benchmark is as small as possible. Tracking error is the standard deviation of the difference between the return on the replicating portfolio and the return on the benchmark.

In effect, the benchmark tracking problem can be formulated as an optimization problem. Roll (1992) provides a mean-variance analysis of the tracking error; Treynor and Black (1973) also consider a quadratic objective in analyzing tracking error. Besides variance, other researchers, such as Rudolf et al. (1999), consider the first absolute moment and first absolute partial moments as relevant characteristics for the deviation between portfolio returns and benchmark returns, leading to linear optimization problems.

Solving in practice the optimization poses another range of statistical estimation related problems that should be taken into account. For instance, as noted by Pope and Yadav (1994), the presence of serial correlation in tracking error results in a biased estimate of the standard deviation which may lead to wrong rebalancing decisions. This effect is particularly important when working with high-frequency data.

In this chapter, we consider the benchmark tracking problem from a very general viewpoint, replacing the traditional tracking error measures by a general functional satisfying a number of axioms. We call this functional a *metric of relative deviation* because it calculates the relative performance of the portfolio to the benchmark. Our approach is based on the universal methods of the theory of probability metrics. As a result, the optimization problems that arise are a significant generalization of the currently existing approaches to benchmark tracking.

The chapter is organized as follows. We start with a description of the tracking error problem and the axioms defining the metric of relative deviation. Then we provide examples of the new metrics and a numerical example.

9.2 THE TRACKING ERROR PROBLEM

In Chapter 8, we considered the mean-variance analysis, the mean-risk analysis, and the arising optimization problems. These optimal portfolio problems have one feature in common, in that the risk measure, or the dispersion measure, concerns the distribution of portfolio returns without any reference to another portfolio. In contrast, benchmark-tracking problems include a benchmark portfolio against which the performance of the managed portfolio will be compared. As a result, the arising optimization problems include the distribution of the *active portfolio return*, defined as the difference $r_p - r_b$ in which r_p denotes the return of the portfolio and r_b denotes the return of the benchmark. If the active return is positive, this means that the portfolio outperformed the benchmark and, if the active return is negative, then the portfolio underperformed the benchmark.

In the ex post analysis, we observe a specified historical period in time and try to evaluate how successful the portfolio manager was relative to the benchmark. In this case, there are two time series corresponding to the observed portfolio returns and the observed benchmark returns. A measure of the performance of the portfolio relative to the benchmark is the average active return, also known as the *portfolio alpha* and denoted by α_p. Alpha is calculated as the difference between the average of the observed portfolio returns and the average of the observed benchmark returns,

$$\hat{\alpha}_p = \bar{r}_p - \bar{r}_b,$$

where:

$\hat{\alpha}_p$ denotes the estimated alpha.

$\bar{r}_p = \frac{1}{k} \sum_{i=1}^{k} r_{pi}$ denotes the average of the observed portfolio returns $r_{p1}, r_{p2}, \ldots, r_{pk}$.

$\bar{r}_b = \frac{1}{k} \sum_{i=1}^{k} r_{bi}$ denotes the average of the observed benchmark returns $r_{b1}, r_{b2}, \ldots, r_{bk}$.

A widely used measure of how close the portfolio returns are to the benchmark returns is the standard deviation of the active return, also known as *tracking error*. More specifically, when it is calculated using historical observations, it is referred to as the ex post or *backward-looking* tracking error. If the portfolio returns are equal to the benchmark returns in the specified historical period, $r_{pi} = r_{bi}$ for all i, then the observed active return is equal to zero and, therefore, the tracking error will be equal to zero. Intuitively, the closer the tracking error to zero, the closer the risk profile of the portfolio matches the risk profile of the benchmark.

In the ex ante analysis, portfolio alpha equals the mathematical expectation of the active return,

$$\alpha_p = E(r_p - r_b)$$
$$= w'\mu - Er_b, \qquad (9.1)$$

where $r_p = w'X$ in which w denotes the vector of portfolio weights, X is a random vector describing the future assets returns, and $\mu = EX$ is a vector of the expected assets returns. The tracking error equals the standard deviation of the active return,

$$TE(w) = \sigma(r_p - r_b),$$

where $\sigma(Y)$ denotes the standard deviation of the random variable Y. Tracking error in this case is referred to as ex ante or *forward-looking* tracking error.

If the strategy followed is active, then the goal of the portfolio manager is to gain a higher alpha at the cost of deviating from the risk profile of the benchmark portfolio; that is, the manager will accept higher forward-looking tracking error. Thus active strategies are characterized by high alphas and high forward-looking tracking errors.

In contrast, if the strategy is passive, then the general goal is to construct a portfolio so as to have a forward-looking tracking error as small as possible in order to match the risk profile of the benchmark. As a consequence, the alpha gained is slightly different from zero. In effect, passive strategies are characterized by very small alphas and very small forward-looking tracking errors.

In this framework, strategies that are in the middle between the active and the passive ones are called *enhanced indexing*.[1] In following such a strategy, the portfolio manager constructs a portfolio with a risk profile close to the risk profile of the benchmark but not identical to it. Enhanced indexing strategies are characterized by small- to medium-sized forward-looking tracking errors and small to medium-sized alphas.

The optimal portfolio problem originating from this framework is the minimal tracking error problem.[2] Its structure is very similar to the mean-variance optimization problems. The difference is that the active portfolio return $r_p - r_b$ is used instead of the absolute portfolio return r_p. The minimal tracking error problem has the following form:

$$\begin{aligned}
\min_{w} \quad & \sigma(r_p - r_b) \\
\text{subject to} \quad & w'e = 1 \\
& w'\mu - Er_b \geq R_* \\
& w \geq 0,
\end{aligned} \tag{9.2}$$

where R_* denotes the lower bound of the expected alpha. The goal is to find a portfolio that is closest to the benchmark in a certain sense, while setting a threshold on the expected alpha. In this case, the "closeness" is determined by the standard deviation.

By varying the limit R_*, we obtain the entire spectrum from passive strategies (obtained with R_* close to zero), through enhanced indexing (obtained with R_* taking medium-sized values), to active strategies (obtained with R_* taking from medium-sized to large values). The set of the optimal portfolios generated by problem (9.2) is the set of efficient portfolios that, if plotted in the plane of expected alpha versus tracking-error, form the corresponding efficient frontier.

The efficient frontier is illustrated in Figure 9.1. If the investment universe is the same as or larger than the universe of the benchmark portfolio, then the global minimum tracking error is equal to zero. In this case, the optimal portfolio coincides with the benchmark portfolio. The the global minimum tracking error portfolio represents a typical passive strategy. Increasing the lower bound on the expected alpha we enter the

---

[1] In terms of tracking error, Loftus (2000, p. 84), classifies the three strategies for equity portfolio strategies as follows: indexing, 0 to 20 basis points, 50 to 200 basis points, and active management, 400 basis points and greater.

[2] Throughout the rest of this chapter, we drop the term "forward-looking" to describe the type of tracking error because we are dealing with the portfolio selection process.

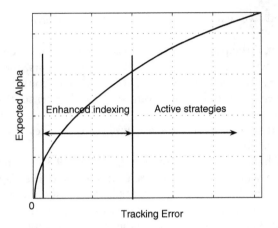

FIGURE 9.1 The efficient frontier generated
from the minimal tracking error problem. The
passive strategies are positioned to the left of
enhanced indexing strategies.

domain of enhanced indexing. Increasing further R_* leads to portfolios that
can be characterized as active strategies.

In Chapter 6, we remarked that a serious disadvantage of the standard
deviation is that it penalizes in the same way the positive and the negative
deviations from the mean of the random variable. Therefore, the tracking
error treats in the same fashion the underperformance and the outperformance, while our attitude toward them is asymmetric.[3] We are inclined to
pay more attention to the underperformance. This argument leads to the
conclusion that, from an asset management perspective, a more realistic
measure of closeness should be asymmetric.

Our aim is to restate the minimal tracking error problem in the more
general form

$$\min_{w} \ \mu(r_p, r_b)$$
$$\text{subject to} \ w'e = 1$$
$$w'\mu - Er_b \geq R_*$$
$$w \geq 0, \tag{9.3}$$

where $\mu(X, Y)$ is a measure of the deviation of X relative to Y. Due
to this interpretation, we regard μ as a functional that metrizes[4] relative

---

[3] See, among others, Szegö (2004) and the references therein.
[4] We use *metrize* in a broad sense and not in the sense of metrizing a given topological
structure.

deviation and we call it a *relative deviation metric* or simply, *r.d. metric*.

Intuitively, if the portfolio r_p is an exact copy of the benchmark, that is, it contains exactly the same stocks in the same amounts, then the relative deviation of r_p to r_b should be close to zero.[5] The converse should also hold but, generally, could be in a somewhat weaker sense. If the deviation of r_p relative to r_b is zero, then the portfolio and the benchmark are indistinguishable but only in the sense implied by μ. They may, or may not, coincide with probability 1.

The benchmark-tracking problem given by (9.3) belongs to a class of problems in which distance between random quantities is measured. In order to gain more insight into the properties that μ should satisfy, we relate the benchmark-tracking problem to the theory of probability metrics. This is a field in probability theory that studies functionals measuring distances between random quantities. In Chapters 3 and 4, we described the notion of a probability metric and offered many examples of probability metrics and distances.

9.3 RELATION TO PROBABILITY METRICS

As explained in Chapter 3, the theory of probability metrics gives a reasonable axiomatic definition of a probability metric and is constructive in the sense that it explains how to build metrics endued with certain properties.

Generally speaking, as explained in Chapter 3, a functional which measures the distance between random quantities is called a probability metric. These random quantities can be of a very general nature. For instance, they can be random variables (such as the daily returns of equities, the daily change of an exchange rate, etc.) or stochastic processes (such as a price evolution in a given period), or much more complex objects (such as the daily movement of the shape of the yield curve). Needless to say, an arbitrary functional cannot be used to measure distances. The probability metric is defined through a set of axioms; that is, any functional that satisfies these axioms is called a probability metric. The axiomatic structure of probability metrics was introduced in Section 3.3 of Chapter 3. Further remarks are provided in the appendix to Chapter 3.

The ideas in the theory of probability metrics show a great deal of potential for application in the field of finance and the benchmark-tracking problem in particular. As a matter of fact, from the standpoint of the theory of probability metrics, the benchmark-tracking problem given by (9.3) can

---

[5]It would not be equal to zero due to transaction costs.

be viewed as an approximation problem. In it, we are trying to find a random variable r_b in the set of feasible portfolios that is closest to the random variable r_b and the distance is measured by the functional μ. This functional should satisfy the properties stated in Section 3.3 of Chapter 3, or some versions of them, in order for the problem to give meaningful results. Actually, the fact that we are applying these ideas to a specific problem may make it necessary to modify the set of fundamental axioms by changing some of them or adding new ones because the nature of the problem may require it. To this end, let us reexamine the set of properties, Property 1 through Property 3, stated in section 3.3 of Chapter 3 to verify if some of them can be relaxed.

Property 1 and Property 3, we leave intact. The reason is that anything other than Property 1 is just nonsensical and Property 1 together with Property 3 guarantee nice mathematical properties such as continuity of μ. Property 3 alone makes sense because of the interpretation that we are measuring distance. In contrast to Property 1 and Property 3, Property 2 can be dropped. The rationale is that, as we noted, in problem (9.3) the assumption of asymmetry is a reasonable property because of our natural tendency to be more sensitive to underperformance than to outperformance relative to the benchmark portfolio.

Now we turn to more subtle questions that give rise to additional properties. Let us consider two equity portfolios with returns X and Y. Suppose that we convert proportionally into cash $100a\%$ in total of both portfolios where $0 \leq a \leq 1$ stands for the weight of the cash amount. As a result, the two portfolios returns scale down to $(1 - a)X$ and $(1 - a)Y$, respectively. Since both random quantities get scaled down by the same factor, we may assume that the distance between them scales down proportionally. Actually, our assumption will be more general. We assume that the distance scales down by the same factor raised by some fixed power s,

$$\nu(aX, aY) = a^s \nu(X, Y) \text{ for any } X, Y \text{ and } a \geq 0.$$

If $s = 1$, then the scaling is proportional. The reason we presume a more general property is that different classes of r.d. metrics originate and, depending on s, they may have different robustness in the approximation problem. This property we call *positive homogeneity of degree s*. It is similar to the homogeneity property of ideal probability metrics described in Chapter 4.

As a next step, consider an equity with return Z which is independent of the two portfolios returns X and Y. Suppose that we invest the cash amounts into equity Z. The returns of the two portfolios change to $(1 - a)X + aZ$ and $(1 - a)Y + aZ$, respectively, where $0 \leq a \leq 1$ denotes the weight of equity Z in the portfolio. In this way, we introduce a completely independent common factor into the two portfolios. A relevant question is, how does the distance change? Certainly, there is no reason to expect that the distance should increase. It either remains unchanged or decreases. In terms of the functional, we assume the property

$$\nu(X + Z, Y + Z) \leq \nu(X, Y)$$

for all Z independent of X, Y. Any functional ν satisfying this property, we call *weakly regular*, a label we borrow from the probability metrics theory. In fact, this is the weak regularity property of ideal probability metrics described in Chapter 4.[6] If the distance between the two new portfolios remains unchanged for any Z irrespective of the independence hypothesis, then we say that ν is *translation invariant*.

Note that if the positive homogeneity property and the weak regularity property hold, then the inequality

$$\nu((1 - a)X + aZ, (1 - a)Y + aZ) \leq \nu(X, Y), \qquad a \in (0, 1) \tag{9.4}$$

holds as well, and this is exactly the mathematical expression behind the conclusion in the example. While the weak regularity property may seem more confined than postulating directly (9.4), we assume it as an axiom because (9.4) is tied to the interpretation of the random variables as return on investment. Suppose that this is not the case and X, Y denote the random wealth of the two portfolios under consideration and Z denotes random stock price. Furthermore, assume that the present value of both portfolios are equal and that we change both portfolios by buying one share of stock Z. Then the random wealth of both portfolios becomes $X + Z$ and $Y + Z$, respectively, and, because of the common stochastic factor Z, we expect the relative deviation to decrease; that is $\nu(X + Z, Y + Z) \leq \nu(X, Y)$. In effect, it appears that the weak regularity property is the fundamental property that we would like to impose.

In order to state the last axiom, suppose that we add to the two initial portfolios other equities, such that returns of the portfolios become $X + c_1$ and $Y + c_2$, where c_1 and c_2 are some constants. We assume that the distance between the portfolios remains unchanged because it is only the location of X and Y that changes. That is,

$$\nu(X + c_1, Y + c_2) = \nu(X, Y)$$

for all X, Y and constants c_1, c_2. We call this property *location invariance*.

---

[6]Rachev (1991) and Rachev and Rüschendorf (1998) provide more information on the weak regularity property and the application of ideal probability metrics.

As a corollary, this property allows measuring the distance only between the centered portfolios returns. We demonstrate how such a functional v can be constructed, for example, from a given probability metric. Suppose that $\mu(X, Y)$ is a given probability metric and denote by g the mapping

$$g : X \to X - EX.$$

The mapping takes as an argument a random variable with a finite mean and returns as output the random variable with its mean subtracted, $g(X) = X - EX$. The mapping g has the property that shifting the random variable X does not change the output of the mapping,

$$g(X + a) = X - EX = g(X).$$

Let us define the functional v as[7]

$$v(X, Y) = \mu(g(X), g(Y)). \tag{9.5}$$

Thus v calculates the distance between the centered random variables $X - EX$ and $Y - EY$ by means of the probability metric μ. As a consequence, the functional v defined in (9.5) is location invariant,

$$v(X + c_1, Y + c_2) = \mu(g(X + c_1), g(Y + c_2))$$
$$= \mu(g(X), g(Y))$$
$$= v(X, Y).$$

The definition in equation (9.5) can be written in a more compact form without introducing an additional notation for the mapping,

$$v(X, Y) = \mu(X - EX, Y - EY).$$

It may be argued that in practice the expected return of the portfolio is a very important characteristic and it seems that we are eliminating it from the problem. This is certainly not the case because this characteristic, as some others, can be incorporated into the constraint set of the benchmark-tracking problem (9.3). For example, the expected alpha constraint imposes a lower bound on the expected alpha, or the expected outperformance relative to

---

[7]Precisely, the functional v defined in this way is a probability metric only on the subspace of zero-mean random variables where it coincides by construction with the probability metric μ. Generally, v cannot be a probability metric because the location invariance property would imply that v equals either 0 or infinity.

the benchmark. In this chapter, we are not going to examine the possible constraint sets as it is the objective function of the optimization problem which is our main focus.

We are finally in position to define the r.d. metrics:

Any functional μ which is weakly regular, location invariant, positively homogeneous of degree s, and satisfies Property 1 and Property 3.

The construction of the r.d. metrics implies that the structural classification of probability metrics described in Chapter 3 holds for r.d. metrics as well. We distinguish between *compound*, *simple*, and *primary* r.d. metrics depending on the degree of sameness implied by the r.d. metric.

Now let us revisit the classical tracking error and try to classify it. First, it is a special case of the average compound metric given by (3.20) with $p = 2$ and therefore it satisfies Property 1 through Property 3. Of course, this also means it is a compound metric, hence it implies the strongest form of sameness—in almost sure sense. Second, concerning the group of the additional axioms, it is positively homogeneous of degree 1, translation invariant, and satisfies the location invariance property.

In the rest of the chapter, our goal is to give other examples of r.d. metrics, which are substantially different from classical tracking error, and to see their properties in a practical setting.

9.4 EXAMPLES OF r.d. METRICS

In Chapter 6, we discussed a family of dispersion measures called deviation measures. In a way similar to the standard deviation or the first centered absolute moment, $D(X)$ is defined to measure the uncertainty of a random variable.

A deviation measure $D(X)$ can generate a functional that is a reasonable candidate for a measure of distance in the optimization problem (9.3). For example, in the technical appendix to Chapter 6, we demonstrated that

$$\mu_D(X, Y) = D(X - Y) \qquad (9.6)$$

is a translation invariant probability semimetric, homogeneous of degree 1 on condition that D is a symmetric deviation measure. Furthermore, a converse relation holds as well. That is,

$$D_\mu(X) = \mu(X - EX, 0) \qquad (9.7)$$

is a symmetric deviation measure, where μ is a translation invariant probability metric, homogeneous of degree 1. In the appendix to this chapter, we demonstrate that if D is general deviation measure, then μ_D is a r.d. metric. In a similar way, if μ is a r.d. metric, then D_μ is a general deviation measure. As a corollary, all deviation measures turn out to be spawned from the class of translation invariant r.d. metrics with degree of homogeneity $s = 1$.

This relationship already almost completely classifies the functional μ_D arising from the deviation measure D. In order to finish, note that μ_D is a compound metric and therefore it implies the strongest, almost sure sense of similarity. Intuitively, this can be seen by considering an example in which X and Y are independent and identically distributed. Then the difference $X - Y$ is a random variable with nonzero uncertainty, hence $D(X - Y) > 0$.

The functional μ_D significantly generalizes the tracking error but still it belongs to the same categories as the tracking error itself and does not illustrate fully the diversity of the class of r.d. metrics in general. We proceed by providing two r.d. metrics belonging to a completely different category—they both are simple and therefore the sense of similarity they imply is only up to equality of distribution functions.

These functionals are defined through the equations

$$\theta_p^*(X, Y) = \left[\int_{-\infty}^{\infty} (\max(F_X(t) - F_Y(t), 0))^p dt \right]^{1/p}, \ p \geq 1 \qquad (9.8)$$

and

$$\ell_p^*(X, Y) = \left[\int_0^1 (\max(F_Y^{-1}(t) - F_X^{-1}(t), 0))^p dt \right]^{1/p}, \ p \geq 1 \qquad (9.9)$$

where X and Y are zero-mean random variables, $F_X(t) = P(X < t)$ is the distribution function of X and $F_X^{-1}(t) = \inf\{x : F_X(x) \geq t\}$ is the generalized inverse of the distribution function.[8]

The intuition behind (9.9) and (9.8) is the following. Suppose that X and Y represent the centered random return of two portfolios and that their distribution functions are as shown in Figure 9.2. Both functionals measure the relative deviation of X and Y using only the part of the distribution functions, or the inverse distribution functions, that describes losses. For example, a closer look at the left plot in the figure reveals that the difference $F_X(t) - F_Y(t)$ is nonnegative only for negative values of t and, therefore, $\theta_p^*(X, Y)$ essentially uses the information about losses contained in the distribution function. The same holds for the other functional. In the case where $p = 1$, then $\theta_p^*(X, Y)$ calculates the area between the two distribution functions to the left of the origin, which is exactly the same area

---

[8] For a proof that (9.9) and (9.8) are r.d. metrics, see Stoyanov, Rachev, Ortobelli, and Fabozzi (2007).

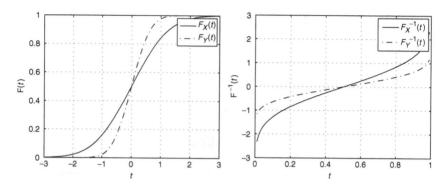

FIGURE 9.2 The distribution functions (left) and the inverse distribution functions (right) of X and Y.

between the inverse distribution functions to the left of $t = 1/2$. It is easy to notice that $\theta_1^*(X, Y) = \ell_1^*(X, Y)$ but this is, generally, not true if $p \neq 1$.

We are not going to illustrate that all defining properties hold for (9.8) and (9.9). A remark on only Property 1 follows as there is a subtle nuance that has to be explained. Clearly, if the two distribution functions coincide, then both (9.9) and (9.8) become equal to zero. We demonstrate that the converse statement holds as well. Suppose that the two r.d. metrics are equal to zero. Then, the distribution functions of the random variables may diverge but only in a very special way,

$$\theta_p^*(X, Y) = 0 \quad \Longrightarrow \quad F_X(t) \leq F_Y(t), \ \forall t \in \mathbb{R}.$$

Figure 9.3 illustrates the inequality. However, this inequality is impossible to hold for r.d. metrics because of the location invariance property; that is, we consider only zero-mean random variables and the inequality between the distribution functions above implies that $EX \leq EY$, hence one of the random variables may have a nonzero mean. As a result, if $\theta_p^*(X, Y) = 0$, then it follows that the c.d.f.s coincide for all values of the argument, $F_Y(t) = F_X(t), \ \forall t \in \mathbb{R}$ and, therefore, the two random variables have identical probabilistic properties. Exactly the same argument applies to $\ell_p^*(X, Y)$.

In summary, we showed that Property 1 holds in a stronger sense for (9.9) and (9.8). Not only does the distance between X and X equal zero, $\mu(X, X) = 0$, but if $\mu(X, Y) = 0$, then for these two cases, because of the location invariance property, it follows that X is equivalent to Y to the extent that their distribution functions coincide. However, there are examples of r.d. metrics for which the location invariance property is insufficient to guarantee this stronger identity property.

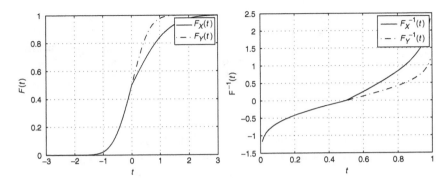

FIGURE 9.3 The distribution functions (left) and the inverse distribution functions (right) of X and Y.

Now we turn to a more practical question. Is is possible to calculate explicitly the r.d. metrics (9.9) and (9.8)? Generally, the answer is negative but in some special cases, this can be done. Suppose that $p = 1$ and that both random variables have the normal distribution, $X \in N(0, \sigma_X^2)$ and $Y \in N(0, \sigma_Y^2)$. Due to the equality $\theta_1^*(X, Y) = \ell_1^*(X, Y)$, it makes no difference which r.d. metric we choose for this calculation. Then, under these assumptions,

$$\ell_1(X, Y) = \int_0^1 (\max(F_Y^{-1}(t) - F_X^{-1}(t), 0))dt$$

$$= \frac{1}{\sqrt{2\pi}} |\sigma_X - \sigma_Y|. \qquad (9.10)$$

Note that (9.10) in this special case is actually a primary metric because it measures the distance between the standard deviations of the portfolio return and the benchmark return. It is because we have restricted our reasoning to the normal distribution only that the simple metric ℓ_1 takes this special form. Otherwise, it is a simple r.d. metric.

Looking more carefully at (9.10), we notice that the symmetry property holds due to the absolute value; that is, in this special case, $\ell_1(X, Y) = \ell_1(Y, X)$. This may appear striking because equation (9.9) is asymmetric by construction, or so it may seem. The symmetry property appears, again, because of the normality assumption—the left and the right tails of the distributions disagree symmetrically in this case. In other words, the particular form of (9.9) *allows for* asymmetry if the corresponding distributions are skewed. If X and Y are symmetric, then this is a fundamental limitation and the potential for asymmetry, granted by the r.d. metric, cannot be exploited.

We can use equation (9.10) to illustrate a point about the relationship between the compound r.d. metrics and the minimal r.d. metrics corresponding to them. One one hand, using very general arguments, basically, only the triangle inequality, we can show that equation (9.10) is related to the tracking error through the inequality

$$|\sigma_X - \sigma_Y| \leq \sigma(X - Y). \tag{9.11}$$

This relationship is true not only when X and Y are normal but in general. Equation (9.11) shows that if the tracking error is zero, then $|\sigma_X - \sigma_Y| = 0$ which, in the normal distribution case, means that $\ell_1(X, Y) = 0$. Conversely, in the normal distribution case one can find two random variables X and Y with $\sigma_X = \sigma_Y$ and, yet, the tracking error can be nonzero, $\sigma(X - Y) \neq 0$, because of the dependence between the two random variables. For example, if they are independent, then $X - Y$ is a random variable with the normal distribution and its standard deviation is strictly positive. In effect, $\ell_1(X, Y) = 0 = |\sigma_X - \sigma_Y|$ means that X and Y have the same probabilistic properties and, nevertheless, the tracking error may be strictly positive. Similar conclusion holds in general, when we consider compound versus simple metrics but an inequality such as (9.11) is guaranteed to hold between compound metrics and the minimal metrics corresponding to them. It is in the normal distribution case that the left side of (9.11) coincides with the minimal metric of the tracking error. More details on minimal metrics are provided in the technical appendix to this chapter.

9.5 NUMERICAL EXAMPLE

We showed that both functionals (9.9) and (9.8) are meaningful objectives in the benchmark-tracking problem. They are very different from the classical tracking error as they are simple metrics and imply a weaker form of sameness. Even if they are both simple, the optimal solutions corresponding to (9.9) and (9.8) will, generally, not be the same if $p \neq 1$. This is understandable as the functionals are not identical. There is one important difference between them concerning Property 4 that we would like to emphasize. The functional $\theta_p^*(X, Y)$ is positively homogeneous of degree $1/p$ while $\ell_p^*(X, Y)$ is positively homogeneous of degree 1 irrespective of the value of p.

In this section, we provide a numerical example. Our goals are:

1. Observe the difference between the optimal solutions of the classical tracking error on the one hand and (9.9) and (9.8) on the other. In this

example, the optimal solution is represented by a portfolio, the empirical c.d.f. of which is closest to the empirical c.d.f. of the benchmark as measured by the corresponding r.d. metric.

2. Examine the effect of the degree of homogeneity in the case of $\theta_p^*(X, Y)$, our expectation being that the higher the degree of homogeneity, the more sensitive $\theta_p^*(X, Y)$ is.

Our dataset includes 10 randomly selected stocks from the S&P 500 universe and the benchmark is the S&P 500 index.[9] The data cover the one-year period from December 31, 2002 to December 31, 2003.

The optimization problem we solve is the benchmark-tracking problem given by (9.3) in which $R_* = 0$ and the objective function $\mu(r_p, r_b)$ is represented by the corresponding empirical counterpart,

$$\hat{\sigma}(r_p - r_b) \tag{9.12}$$

$$\hat{\theta}_p^*(r_{p0}, r_{b0}) \tag{9.13}$$

and

$$\hat{\ell}_p^*(r_{p0}, r_{b0}) \tag{9.14}$$

where the index 0 signifies that the corresponding returns are centered. In the case of tracking error, the sample counterpart $\hat{\sigma}$ is the sample standard deviation. The formula and a short example are provided in section 10.3.2 of Chapter 10. Technical details concerning the calculation of (9.13) and (9.14) are given in the appendix to this chapter.

In the three problems, we start from an equally weighted portfolio and then solve the optimization problems. Therefore, in all cases, our initial portfolio is an equally weighted portfolio of the 10 randomly selected stocks. The constraint set guarantees that the expected return of the optimal portfolio will not be worse than that of the benchmark. For this reason, we compare the inverse distribution functions of the centered returns of the optimal portfolios in order to assess which problem better tracks the benchmark in terms of the distribution function. Note that it makes no difference whether we compare the distribution functions or the inverse distribution functions., the conclusion will not change.

Figure 9.4 compares the inverse distribution functions of the centered returns of the initial portfolio, the optimal portfolio of the classical tracking

---

[9]The stocks are Sun Microsystems Inc., Oracle Corp., Microsoft Corp., Sand Technology Inc., Allegheny Energy Inc., T Rowe Price Group Inc., Allied Capital Corp., EMC Corp./Massachusetts, AMB Property Corp., and Linear Technology Corp.

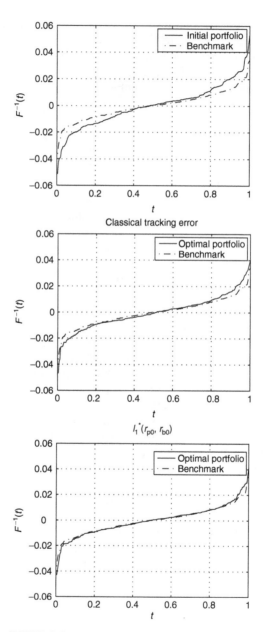

FIGURE 9.4 The inverse distribution functions of the S&P 500 index (the benchmark), equally weighted portfolio (initial portfolio), and the two optimal portfolios.

error problem and the optimal portfolio obtained with objective (9.14) in which $p = 1$. It is obvious that both optimization problems provide solutions that better track the benchmark than the trivial strategy of holding an equally weighted portfolio. Not surprisingly, the functional (9.14) does a better job at approximating the distribution function of the benchmark returns, allowing for asymmetries in the loss versus the profit part. Note that the part of the inverse distribution function of the optimal solution describing losses, the one closer to $t = 0$ is closer to the corresponding part of the inverse distribution function of the benchmark returns, while this is not true for the profit part closer to $t = 1$. Actually, the fact that the inverse distribution function of the optimal solution is above the inverse distribution function of the benchmark returns close to $t = 1$ means that the probability of a large positive return of the optimal portfolio is larger than that of the benchmark.

In order to explore the question of how the degree of homogeneity might influence the solution, we solve the tracking problem with objective (9.13) in which we choose $p = 1$ and $p = 10$. The degree of homogeneity is equal to 1 and 1/10, respectively. We noted already that $\theta_1^*(r_{p0}, r_{b0}) = \ell_1^*(r_{p0}, r_{b0})$ and, therefore, the optimal solutions will coincide. The inverse distribution functions of the returns of the optimal portfolios are shown on Figure 9.5. Apparently, the degree of sensitivity of the objective is directly influenced by the parameter p in line with our expectations. The integrand

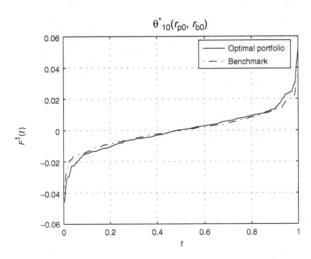

FIGURE 9.5 The inverse distribution functions of the SP 500 index (the benchmark), and the optimal portfolios obtained with (9.13) as objective with $p = 10$.

in the functional (9.13) measures the differences of the two distribution functions and therefore its functional values are small numbers, converging to zero in the tails. Holding other things equal, raising the integrand to a higher power deteriorates the sensitivity of the functional with respect to deviations in the tails of the two distribution functions. This observation becomes obvious when we compare the bottom plot of Figure 9.4 to Figure 9.5.

Generally, the optimization problems involving simple r.d. metrics may not belong to the family of convex problems because the simple r.d. metric may not appear to be a convex function of portfolio weights. Stoyanov, Rachev, and Fabozzi (2007) show that, in particular, this holds for the minimal r.d. metrics. In the appendix to this chapter, we demonstrate that both (9.8) and (9.9) arise as minimal r.d. metrics and, as a consequence, the corresponding optimal portfolio problems are not convex programming problems. Nevertheless, for the purposes of illustration, we obtained the optimal solutions by finding a local minimum starting from the initial portfolio.

9.6 SUMMARY

In this chapter, we considered the problem of benchmark tracking. The classical problem relies on the tracking error to measure the degree of similarity between the portfolio and the benchmark. Making use of the approach of the theory of probability metrics, we extended significantly the framework by introducing axiomatically relative deviation metrics replacing the tracking error in the objective function of the optimization problem. We provided two examples of relative deviation metrics and a numerical illustration of the corresponding optimization problems.

9.7 TECHNICAL APPENDIX

In this appendix, we explore the connections between r.d. metrics and probability metrics and how the theory of probability metrics can be employed to better understand the full variety of questions arising from practical problems such as the benchmark tracking problem. We start with a short note concerning the link between deviation measures and r.d. metrics and proceed with several remarks on the defining axioms. We demonstrate how the notion of the minimal metric applies to r.d. metrics, and, finally, we consider the practical problem of calculating simple r.d. metrics given a sample of observations.

9.7.1　Deviation Measures and r.d. Metrics

In the technical appendix to Chapter 6, we demonstrated that if μ is a translation invariant and positively homogeneous of degree 1 probability metric, then the functional D_μ defined in equation (9.7) is a symmetric deviation measure. In a similar way, if D is a symmetric deviation measure, then the functional μ_D defined in equation (9.6) is a translation invariant and positively homogeneous of degree 1 probability semimetric. Following the arguments, we notice that the symmetry properties of μ and D influence only the symmetry properties of D_μ and μ_D, respectively. Therefore, relaxing the assumption that μ is symmetric (Property 2) results in D_μ being asymmetric as well. As a result, we obtain that if μ is a translation invariant and positively homogeneous of degree 1 r.d. metric, then D_μ is a general deviation measure. In a similar way, if D is a general deviation measure, then μ_D is a translation invariant and positively homogeneous of degree 1 r.d. metric.[10]

9.7.2　Remarks on the Axioms

The appendix to Chapter 3 provides detailed remarks on the axiomatic framework behind probability. Recall that a probability semimetric that does not satisfy the symmetry axiom SYM given in section 3.5.1 is called probability quasisemimetric.

We are in position to illustrate how we can modify a probability metric so that it becomes better suited for the benchmark-tracking problem. Let us choose two classical examples of compound probability metrics—the average compound metric

$$\mathcal{L}_p(X, Y) = (E|X - Y|^p)^{1/p}, \; p \geq 1$$

and the Birnbaum-Orlicz compound metric,

$$\Theta_p(X, Y) = \left[\int_{-\infty}^\infty (\tau(t; X, Y))^p dt \right]^{1/p}, \; p \geq 1,$$

where $\tau(t; X, Y) = P(X \leq t < Y) + P(Y \leq t < X)$. Both $\mathcal{L}_p(X, Y)$ and $\Theta_p(X, Y)$ are ideal because they satisfy the positive homogeinity property and the weak regularity property. Chapter 3 provides more background on these two metrics.

Consider, first, the average compound metric. It satisfies all properties of relative deviation metrics described in the chapter but it is symmetric, a

---

[10] A formal argument is given in Stoyanov, Rachev, and Fabozzi (2007).

property we would like to break. One possible way is to replace the absolute value by the max function. Thus we obtain the asymmetric version

$$\mathcal{L}_p^*(X, Y) = (E(\max(Y - X, 0))^p)^{1/p}, \; p \geq 1. \tag{9.15}$$

In Stoyanov, Rachev, Ortobelli, and Fabozzi (2007), we show that $\mathcal{L}_p^*(X, Y)$ is an ideal quasisemimetric; that is, using the max function instead of the absolute value breaks only the symmetry axiom SYM.

What is the intuition behind removing the absolute value and considering the max function? In the setting of the benchmark-tracking problem, suppose that the random variable X stands for the return of the portfolio and Y denotes the return of the benchmark. Then the difference $Y - X$ can be interpreted as the portfolio loss relative to the benchmark, or the portfolio underperformance. If in a given state of the world, $\omega \in \Omega$, the difference is positive, $Y(\omega) - X(\omega) > 0$, then in this state of the world the portfolio is underperforming the benchmark. In effect, the expectation

$$\mathcal{L}_1^*(X, Y) = E \max(Y - X, 0)$$

measures the average portfolio underperformance. When we minimize $\mathcal{L}_1^*$ in the optimization problem, we are actually minimizing the average portfolio underperformance. The same is idea behind the general case $\mathcal{L}_p^*(X, Y)$. There is additional flexibility in that the power $p \geq 1$ allows increasing the importance of the larger losses by increasing p.

If we consider directly the classical probability metric $\mathcal{L}_1(X, Y)$, then the interpretation in the setting of the benchmark-tracking problem is the following. The absolute difference $|X - Y|$ is either underperformance or outperformance of the benchmark depending on whether the difference $Y(\omega) - X(\omega)$ is positive or negative in a given state of the world $\omega \in \Omega$. Actually, the absolute difference can be decomposed into an underperformance and an outperformance term

$$|X(\omega) - Y(\omega)| = \max(X(\omega) - Y(\omega), 0) + \max(Y(\omega) - X(\omega), 0).$$

If the first summand is positive, then we have outperformance and if the second summand is positive we have underperformance in the corresponding state of the world $\omega \in \Omega$. Therefore, if we minimize $\mathcal{L}_1(X, Y)$ in the benchmark tracking problem, then we minimize *simultaneously* both the portfolio outperformance and underperformance. A similar conclusion holds for the general case $\mathcal{L}_p(X, Y)$.

The same idea, but implemented in a different way, stays behind the asymmetric version of the Birnbaum-Orlicz metric,

$$\Theta_p^*(X, Y) = \left[\int_{-\infty}^{\infty} (\tau^*(t; X, Y))^p dt \right]^{1/p}, \ p \geq 1, \tag{9.16}$$

where $\tau^*(t; X, Y) = P(X \leq t < Y)$. In Stoyanov, Rachev, Ortobelli, and Fabozzi (2007), we show that (9.16) is an ideal quasisemimetric. That is, considering only the first summand of the function $\tau(t; X, Y)$ from the Birnbaum-Orlics compound metric breaks the SYM axiom only.

Let us start by interpreting the integrand—the $\tau^*(t; X, Y)$ function. Just as in the case of the asymmetric version of the average compound metric, suppose that the random variable X represents the return of the portfolio and Y represents the benchmark return. Then, for a fixed value of the argument t, which we interpret as a threshold, the function τ^* calculates the probability of the event that the portfolio return is below the threshold t and, simultaneously, the benchmark return is above the threshold t,

$$\tau^*(t; X, Y) = P(X \leq t < Y) = P(\{X \leq t\} \cap \{t < Y\}).$$

Hence, the function τ^* calculates the probability that the portfolio return is below the benchmark return with respect to the threshold t. As a result, we can interpret $\Theta_p^*(X, Y)$ as a measure of the probability that portfolio loses more than the benchmark. Therefore, in the benchmark-tracking problem, by minimizing $\Theta_p^*(X, Y)$, we are indirectly minimizing the probability of the portfolio losing more than the benchmark.

Interestingly, the special case $p = 1$,

$$\Theta_1^*(X, Y) = \int_{-\infty}^{\infty} \tau^*(t; X, Y) dt$$

allows for a very concrete interpretation. $\Theta_1^*(X, Y)$ is exactly equal to the average underperformance; that is, $\Theta_1^*(X, Y) = \mathcal{L}_1^*(X, Y)$. This statement holds because $\Theta_1^*(X, Y)$ is just an alternative way of writing down the integral behind the expectation in $\mathcal{L}_1^*(X, Y)$.

9.7.3 Minimal r.d. Metrics

Any probability metric is defined on a pair of random variables (X, Y). We noted in section 3.5.1 of Chapter 3 that, depending on the implied equivalence in property ID, we distinguish between three classes of metrics—primary, simple, and compound. The primary metrics imply the weakest form of sameness, only up to equality of certain characteristics. The simple metrics have stronger implications. It is only if the distribution functions of the random variables agree completely that the measured distance between them becomes zero. The compound metrics imply the strongest possible identity—in almost sure sense.

We noted that there are links between the corresponding classes. By including more and more characteristics, we obtain primary metrics that essentially require that the distribution functions of the random variables should coincide; that is, they turn into simple metrics. Also, by minimizing any compound metric on all possible dependencies between the two random variables we obtain a metric that actually depends only on the distribution functions and is, therefore, simple. This is the construction of the minimal metric, which is defined by

$$\hat{\mu}(X, Y) = \inf\{\mu(\widetilde{X}, \widetilde{Y}) : \widetilde{X} \overset{d}{=} X, \widetilde{Y} \overset{d}{=} Y\}.$$

For more information on minimal metrics, refer to section 3.3.5 and the appendix to Chapter 3.

In this section, we verify if minimal r.d. metrics can be constructed in the same manner as minimal probability metrics. It turns out that this is possible and the approach can be used to construct nontrivial examples of simple r.d. metrics such as (9.8) and (9.9).

It is possible to show that, if μ is a functional satisfying properties ID or $\widetilde{\text{ID}}$, TI, or $\widetilde{\text{TI}}$, then $\hat{\mu}$ also satisfies ID or $\widetilde{\text{ID}}$, TI, or $\widetilde{\text{TI}}$.[11] That is, omitting the symmetry property results only in asymmetry in the minimal functional $\hat{\mu}$ and influences nothing else. These are, basically, the results in the proof that $\hat{\mu}$ is a probability (semi)distance. In addition to that, it is easy to check that if positive homogeneity holds for μ, then the same property holds for $\hat{\mu}$ as well. The same holds for the weak regularity.

The construction of the minimal r.d. metric, just as the minimal probability metric, is an important tool because some of the properties above are easy to check for a compound metric and difficult to check for a simple metric. For example, this is the case with the weak regularity property. Therefore, starting with a compound r.d. metric, we are sure that the minimal functional corresponding to it is a simple r.d. metric.

Sometimes, it is possible to calculate explicitly the minimal functional. As explained in the appendix to Chapter 3, this can be done either through the Cambanis-Simons-Stout theorem or through the Frechet-Hoffding

---

[11]Refer to the appendix to Chapter 3 for the definition of these properties.

inequality. Section 3.5.3 provides details on the Cambanis-Simons-Stout result and its application.

Now we will show how the Cambanis-Simons-Stout result is applied to the functional

$$\mathcal{L}_p^*(X, Y) = (E(\max(Y - X, 0))^p)^{1/p}, \; p \geq 1.$$

It is easy to check that $\widetilde{\text{ID}}$, TI, $\widetilde{\text{RE}}$, and Property 4 hold for $\mathcal{L}_p^*(X, Y)$. The previous section provides more details. We identify the function ϕ, $\phi(x, y) = (\max(x - y, 0))^p$. Clearly $\phi(x, x) = 0$ and ϕ is quasi-antitone because $f(x) = (\max(x, 0))^p$, $p \geq 1$ is a nonnegaive, convex function. In effect, the Cambanis-Simons-Stout theorem applies and, therefore, the minimal functional is given by

$$\ell_p^*(X, Y) = \hat{\mathcal{L}}_p^*(X, Y) = \left[\int_0^1 (\max(F_Y^{-1}(t) - F_X^{-1}(t), 0))^p \, dt \right]^{1/p},$$

which is equation (9.9) in the chapter.

Besides the Cambanis-Simons-Stout theorem, there is another method of obtaining explicit forms of minimal functionals via the celebrated Frechet-Hoeffding inequality between distribution functions defined in (3.51) of Chapter 3. See section 3.3 of Chapter 3 for an example. We show how this inequality is applied to the problem of finding the minimal r.d. metric of the Birnbaum-Orlicz quasisemimetric defined in (9.16) by taking advantage of the upper bound.

Consider the following representation of the τ^* function defined in (9.16),

$$\tau^*(t; X, Y) = P(X \leq t, Y < t)$$

$$= P(X \leq t) - P(X \leq t, Y \leq t).$$

This representation is correct because by summing $P(X \leq t, Y > t)$ and $P(X \leq t, Y \leq t)$, the influence of the random variable Y is cancelled out. Now by replacing the joint probability by the upper bound from the Frechet-Hoeffding inequality, we obtain

$$\tau^*(t; X, Y) \geq F_X(t) - \min(F_X(t), F_Y(t))$$

$$= \max(F_X(t) - F_Y(t), 0).$$

Raising both sides of the above inequality to the power $p \geq 1$ and integrating over all values of t does not change the inequality. In effect, we obtain

$$\left[\int_{-\infty}^{\infty} (\max(F_X(t) - F_Y(t), 0))^p \, dt \right]^{1/p} \leq \Theta_p^*(X, Y),$$

which gives, essentially, the corresponding minimal r.d. metric. The left side of the inequality coincides with (9.8) from the chapter, $\theta_p^*(X, Y) = \hat{\Theta}_p^*(X, Y)$.

9.7.4 Limit Cases of $\mathcal{L}_p^*(X, Y)$ and $\Theta_p^*(X, Y)$

There are several interesting limit cases of the two r.d. metrics, which help better understand their behavior. We do not consider all limit cases, but only the most intuitive ones. In line with the setting of the benchmark-tracking problem, in the interpretations in this section we assume that X represents portfolio return and Y represents the benchmark return.

Generally, there are two ways to obtain limit representatives—if we let p approach infinity, or zero. However, we defined both r.d. metrics for $p \geq 1$, and we will slightly change the definitions so that we can see what is going on as $p \to 0$. The slightly extended definitions are,

$$\mathcal{L}_p^*(X, Y) = (E(\max(Y - X, 0))^p)^{1/\min(1, 1/p)}, \ p \geq 0 \qquad (9.17)$$

and

$$\Theta_p^*(X, Y) = \left[\int_{-\infty}^{\infty} (\tau^*(t; X, Y))^p \, dt \right]^{1/\min(1, 1/p)}, \ p \geq 0. \qquad (9.18)$$

Note that the change affects the case $p \in [0, 1)$ and if $p \geq 1$, then we obtain the previous definitions.

As $p \to \infty$, the r.d. metric $\mathcal{L}_p^*(X, Y)$ approaches $\mathcal{L}_\infty^*(X, Y)$ defined as

$$\mathcal{L}_\infty^*(X, Y) = \inf\{\epsilon > 0 : P(\max(Y - X, 0) > \epsilon) = 0\}.$$

This limit case can be interpreted in the following way. $\mathcal{L}_\infty^*(X, Y)$ calculates the smallest threshold so that the portfolio loss relative to the benchmark is larger than this threshold with zero probability. Note that this quasisemimetric is entirely focused on the very extreme loss.

In the other direction, if $p \to 0$, the r.d. metric $\mathcal{L}_p^*(X, Y)$ approaches $\mathcal{L}_0^*(X, Y)$ where

$$\mathcal{L}_0^*(X, Y) = EI\{\omega : \max(Y(\omega) - X(\omega), 0) \neq 0\}$$
$$= P(Y > X).$$

The notation $I\{\omega \in A\}$ stands for the indicator function of the event A, that is, if ω happens to be in A, then $I\{\omega \in A\} = 1$ and otherwise it is equal to zero. This result is self-explanatory, $\mathcal{L}_0^*(X, Y)$ calculates the probability of the event the portfolio to lose relative to the benchmark.

Concerning the Birnbaum-Orlicz quasisemimetric given by (9.18), there is an interesting limit case as $p \to \infty$,

$$\Theta_\infty^*(X, Y) = \sup_{t \in R} P(X \le t < Y).$$

Let us briefly look at the properties of the function $\tau^*(t; X, Y) = P(X \le t < Y)$ in order to see what this limit case calculates. As t decreases to $-\infty$, the sets $\{\omega: X(\omega) \le t\}$ become progressively smaller and at the limit they approach the empty set, $\lim_{t \to \infty}\{\omega: X(\omega) \le t\} = \emptyset$. The same conclusion is valid for the sets $\{\omega: Y(\omega) > t\}$ as t increases to infinity. Since the function $\tau^*(t; X, Y)$ is, essentially, the probability of the intersection of these two events, it follows that $\tau^*(t; X, Y)$ decays to zero as t decreases or increases unboundedly,

$$\lim_{t \to -\infty} \tau^*(t; X, Y) = 0$$

and

$$\lim_{t \to \infty} \tau^*(t; X, Y) = 0.$$

As a result, it follows that the maximum of the function $\tau^*(t; X, Y)$ will not be attained for very small or very large values of the threshold t. Therefore, $\Theta_\infty^*(X, Y)$ is not sensitive to the extreme events in the tail because the threshold t, for which $P(X \le t < Y)$ is maximal, is near the center of the distributions.

Exactly the same effect is present in the minimal quasisemimetric generated by it, $\theta_p^*(X, Y)$. As p increases to infinity, we obtain

$$\theta_\infty^*(X, Y) = \sup_{t \in R}[\max(F_X(t) - F_Y(t), 0)],$$

which is an asymmetric version of the celebrated Kolmogorov metric. Section 3.3 and the appendix to Chapter 3 provide more details on the Kolmogorov metric and its applications. Basically, $\theta_\infty^*(X, Y)$ calculates the maximal difference between the distribution functions, $F_X(t) - F_Y(t)$. Therefore, $\theta_\infty^*(X, Y)$ is not sensitive to the deviations between the two distribution functions in the tails, which describe the probability of extreme events, because as t approaches either of the infinities, the difference $F_X(t) - F_Y(t)$ decays to zero.

9.7.5 Computing r.d. Metrics in Practice

In this section, we state a number of closed-form expressions for some of the r.d. metrics considered in the previous sections and we give examples in the setting of the benchmark-tracking problem. Generally, it is not possible to arrive at a closed-form expression but under additional assumptions for the joint distribution of the pair of random variables, explicit representations can be provided.

Explicit Form of $\mathcal{L}_p^*(X, Y)$ When (X, Y) has Joint Normal Distribution   Suppose that (X, Y) has a centered, bivariate normal distribution. We know that, in this case, the difference $Y - X$ has a zero-mean, normal distribution with standard deviation $\sigma(Y - X)$, $Y - X \in N(0, \sigma^2(Y - X))$. The difference has the same distribution as $\sigma(Y - X)Z$, where $Z \in N(0, 1)$. We use this representation only to calculate the expectation. In effect, we obtain

$$\mathcal{L}_p^*(X, Y) = C_p . \sigma(Y - X), \quad p \geq 1, \tag{9.19}$$

where $C_p = (E(\max(Z, 0))^p)^{1/p}$ is a positive constant that can be explicitly computed.

Note that the parameter p influences the constant C_p only and, therefore, $\mathcal{L}_p^*(X, Y)$ is just a scaled standard deviation of the difference $Y - X$. It turns out that this is not true only under the hypothesis of joint normal distribution. If (X, Y) has a joint elliptical distribution with finite variance, then $\mathcal{L}_p^*(X, Y)$ has, essentially, the form given by (9.19). Certainly, in the elliptical case, one has to ensure additionally that X and Y have finite p-th absolute moment, that is, $E|X|^p < \infty$ and $E|Y|^p < \infty$. Otherwise, $\mathcal{L}_p^*(X, Y)$ may become infinite.

Apparently, the closed-form expression (9.19) can be regarded as typical of the large class of bivariate elliptical distributions in which the joint normal distribution is just a special case. It may seem strange that even though by definition the r.d. metric $\mathcal{L}_p^*(X, Y)$ is asymmetric, equation (9.19) is symmetric. The reason is the elliptical assumption because it implies symmetric distributions of X, Y, and the difference $Y - X$ and, therefore, $\mathcal{L}_p^*(X, Y)$ cannot be asymmetric because of this restrictive assumption.

Let us apply equation (9.19) to the benchmark-tracking problem. To this end, we interpret the random variable X as the portfolio return r_p and the random variable Y as the benchmark return r_b. Concerning the random vector of assets returns, we assume that it follows the multivariate normal, or multivariate elliptical, in order to make sure that the distribution of the portfolio return r_p is normal, or elliptical, for any choice of portfolio weights. As a result, the r.d. metric has the form

$$\mathcal{L}_p^*(r_{p0}, r_{b0}) = C_p . \sigma(r_p - r_b), \quad p \geq 1,$$

which means that $\mathcal{L}_p^*(r_{p0}, r_{b0})$ is just a scaled tracking error. Therefore, the tracking error is the building block of the $\mathcal{L}_p^*(r_{p0}, r_{b0})$ r.d. metric in the multivariate normal, or, more generally, in the multivariate elliptical case. This will not happen under the assumption of a multivariate skewed distribution.

Explicit Form of $\ell_p^*(X, Y)$ When X and Y Have Normal Distribution   The minimal r.d. metric $\ell_p^*(X, Y)$ is simple and, therefore, we do not need a distributional assumption for the pair (X, Y), but only for the marginal laws of X and Y. Suppose that both X and Y have the centered normal distribution, $X \in N(0, \sigma_X^2)$ and $Y \in N(0, \sigma_Y^2)$. Both distributions can be represented as a scaled $N(0, 1)$ distributions and, as a result, we obtain

$$\ell_p^*(X, Y) = C_p.|\sigma_X - \sigma_Y|, \quad p \geq 1, \tag{9.20}$$

where $C_p = (E(\max(Z, 0))^p)^{1/p}$ and $Z \in N(0, 1)$.

In the setting of the benchmark-tracking problem, assume additionally that r follows the multiavriate normal distribution with covariance matrix Σ, $r_0 \in N(0, \Sigma)$. We obtain the explicit formula

$$\ell_p^*(r_0^b, w'r_0) = C_p.|\sqrt{w'\Sigma w} - \sigma(r_b)|, \quad p \geq 1.$$

where w denotes the vector of portfolio weights. In the chapter, we provided the case $p = 1$ in which $C_1 = 1/\sqrt{2\pi}$. Olkin and Rachev (1999) provide a number of related results.

Explicit Forms of $\Theta_p^*(X, Y)$ and $\theta_p^*(X, Y)$ It is much harder to calculate closed-form expressions for $\Theta_p^*(X, Y)$ and $\theta_p^*(X, Y)$ even under additional assumptions for the joint distribution of (X, Y). Nevertheless, for some choices of p, it is possible to link the two r.d. metrics to other classes for which the calculation is not so complicated. For instance, $\Theta_1^*(X, Y) = \mathcal{L}_1^*(X, Y)$ and $\theta_1^*(X, Y) = \ell_1^*(X, Y)$ and we can use the already derived explicit forms.

Estimating r.d. Metrics from a Sample   How can we calculate the simple r.d. metrics (9.8) and (9.9) for a given portfolio with weights $w = (w_1, \ldots, w_n)$ if we have a sample of daily observations for the equity returns and the benchmark returns? Notice that they both involve either the distribution functions of the portfolios returns or the inverse of the distribution functions and these functions we do not know in practice. Therefore, they have to be estimated either directly from the data making no distributional hypotheses or assuming a parametric model and estimating its parameters from the sample.

For example, we may assume that the equity returns and the benchmark returns are jointly distributed according to the multivariate normal distribution. From this hypothesis alone, it follows that the equity returns also have the multivariate normal distribution and, consequently, the return r_p of any portfolio with weights w also has the normal distribution, $r_p \in N(0, w'\Sigma w)$, where Σ is the covariance matrix of the equity returns. As a result, in order to calculate (9.8) and (9.9), we have to estimate the unknown parameters in the first place; that is, the covariance matrix Σ and the variance of the benchmark returns, $\sigma^2(r_b)$. Once we know the estimates $\hat{\Sigma}$ and $\hat{\sigma}^2(r_b)$, we can calculate (9.8) by plugging in the distribution functions of the centered normal distribution with variance equal to the corresponding estimates. Afterwards, in the general case, the integrals can be calculated numerically using an available software package such as MATLAB.

The r.d. metric (9.9) can be calculated, in this case, by taking advantage of the closed-form expression (9.20),

$$\hat{\ell}_p^*(r_{p0}, r_{b0}) = C_p \left| (w'\hat{\Sigma}w)^{1/2} - \sigma(\hat{r}_b) \right|.$$

Note that when $p = 1$, we have the following special case,

$$\hat{\theta}_1^*(r_{p0}, r_{b0}) = \hat{\ell}_1^*(r_{p0}, r_{b0}) = \frac{1}{\sqrt{2\pi}} \left| (w'\hat{\Sigma}w)^{1/2} - \sigma(\hat{r}_b) \right|.$$

Suppose that we do not want to make any distributional hypotheses. Then, the r.d. metrics can be computed through the empirical distribution functions and the empirical inverse distribution functions. Thus, in the case of (9.13), we use

$$\hat{\theta}_p^*(r_{p0}, r_{b0}) = \left[\int_{-\infty}^{\infty} (\max(\widehat{F}_{r_{b0}}(t) - \widehat{F}_{r_{p0}}(t), 0))^p dt \right]^{1/p}, \quad p \geq 1,$$

where $\widehat{F}_X(t) = \frac{1}{n} \sum_{i=1}^{n} I_{\{X_i \leq t\}}$, denotes the empirical distribution function and n is the sample size. The integral can be calculated numerically using an available software package.

The empirical r.d. metric (9.14) can be easily simplified because the stocks in our sample and the index have the same number of observations. In order to give the formula, we introduce additional notation. Let us fix the portfolio weights w, then denote by $r_{p0}^{(1)} \leq r_{p0}^{(2)} \leq \ldots \leq r_{p0}^{(n)}$ the sorted sample of the corresponding observed centered portfolio returns. Similarly, let $r_{b0}^{(1)} \leq r_{b0}^{(2)} \leq \ldots \leq r_{b0}^{(n)}$ be the sorted sample of the observed centered benchmark returns. Then

$$\hat{\ell}_p^*(r_{p0}, r_{b0}) = \left[\frac{1}{n} \sum_{i=1}^{n} (\max(r_{b0}^{(i)} - r_{p0}^{(i)}, 0))^p \right]^{1/p}, \quad p \geq 1.$$

From the point of view of computational burden, minimizing $\widehat{\ell}_p^*(r_{p0}, r_{b0})$ is a lot easier than $\widehat{\theta}_p^*(r_{p0}, r_{b0})$ because the numerical integration adds more complexity to the problem.

BIBLIOGRAPHY

Loftus, John S. (2000). "Enhanced equity indexing," *Chapter 4* in Frank J. Fabozzi *(ed.)*, *Perspectives on Equity Indexing*, Hoboken, NJ: John Wiley & Sons.

Olkin, I., and S. Rachev (1999). "Mass transportation problems with capacity constraings," *Journal of Applied Probability* **36**: 433–445.

Pope, P., and P. Yadav (1994). "Discovering errors in the tracking error," *Journal of Portfolio Management* **21**(2): 27–32.

Rachev, S. T., and L. Rüschendorf (1998). *Mass transportation problems*, vols. 1 and 2, New York: Springer-Verlag.

Rachev, S. T. (1991). *Probability metrics and the stability of stochastic models*, Chichester: John Wiley & Sons.

Roll, R. (1992). "A mean/variance analysis of tracking error," *Journal of Portfolio Management* **18**: 13–23.

Rudolf, M., H-J. Wolter, and H. Zimmermann (1999). "A linear model for tracking error minimization," *Journal of Banking and Finance* **23**(1): 85–103.

Stoyanov, S. T., S. T. Rachev, and F. J. Fabozzi (2007). "Probability metrics with application in finance," *Technical Report, Department of Econometrics, Statistics and Mathematical Finance, School of Economics and Business Engineering*, University of Karlsruhe.

Stoyanov, S. T., S. T. Rachev, S. Ortobelli, and F. J. Fabozzi (2007). "Relative deviation metrics with applications in finance," forthcoming in *Journal of Banking and Finance*.

Szegö, G. (2004). *Risk measures for the 21st century*, Chichester: John Wiley & Sons.

Treynor, J., and F. Black (1973). "How to use security ananlysis to improve portfolio selection," *Journal of Business* **46**(1): 66–86.

CHAPTER 10

Performance Measures

10.1 INTRODUCTION

A key step in the investment management process is measurement and evaluation of portfolio performance. In this step, it is determined whether the portfolio manager has met the goals set by the clients. The criteria for performance evaluation may vary depending on the goals of the client. Usually, the performance of the portfolio is measured with respect to the performance of some benchmark portfolio, which can be a broad-based market index, a specialized index, or a customized index. In recent years, some defined benefit plans have developed liability-driven indexes.

The formula that quantifies the portfolio performance is called a *performance measure*. A widely used measure for performance evaluation is the *Sharpe ratio* introduced by Sharpe (1966). The Sharpe ratio calculates the adjusted return of the portfolio relative to a target return. In essence, it is the ratio between the average active portfolio return and the standard deviation of the portfolio return. In this way, it is a *reward-to-variability ratio* in which the variability is computed by means of the standard deviation.

We noted in Chapter 6 that the standard deviation penalizes both the upside and the downside potential of portfolio return. Therefore, it is not a very appropriate choice as a measure of performance. This deficiency is well recognized and as a result many alternatives to the Sharpe ratio have been proposed in the literature. Some of them are reward-to-variability ratios in which a downside dispersion measure is used in the denominator. One example is the *Sortino ratio*, in which the downside semi-standard deviation is used as a measure of variability.

Other types of performance measures are the *reward-to-risk ratios*. In contrast to the reward-to-variability ratios, these ratios calculate the risk-adjusted active reward of the portfolio. For example, the *Sortino-Satchell ratio* (Sortino and Satchell, 2001) calculates the average active return divided by a lower partial moment of the portfolio return distribution and the *STARR* (Rachev et al., 2006) calculates the average active return divided by average value-at-risk (AVaR) at a given tail probability.

There are examples in which a reward measure is used instead of the average active return. For instance, a one-sided variability ratio introduced by Farinelli and Tibiletti (2002) is essentially a ratio between an upside and a downside partial moment of the portfolio return distribution and the *Rachev ratio* (R-ratio) (Biglova et al., 2004) is a ratio between the average of upper quantiles of the portfolio return distribution and AVaR.

Measuring a strategies performance is an ex post analysis. The performance measure is calculated using the realized portfolio returns during a specified period back in time (e.g., the past one year). Alternatively, performance measures can be used in an ex ante analysis, in which certain assumptions for the future behavior of the assets are introduced. In this case, the general goal is to find a portfolio with the best characteristics as calculated by the performance measure. The performance measure problems of the ex ante type can be related to the efficient frontier generated by mean-risk analysis, and more generally by reward-risk analysis, developed in Chapter 8.

In this chapter, we consider these two types of performance measures and their relationship to the efficient frontier. We provide examples of frequently used performance measures and remark on their advantages and disadvantages. In the appendix to this chapter, the performance measures described in the chapter are classified according to their structure. The properties of the corresponding optimal portfolio problems arising from the ex ante analysis of the generic quasiconcave ratio are explained. Finally, we consider the capital market line in the case of the general reward-risk analysis with a risk-free asset added to the investment universe.

10.2 REWARD-TO-RISK RATIOS

One general type of a performance measure is the *reward-to-risk* (RR) *ratio*. It is defined as the ratio between a reward measure of the active portfolio return and the risk of active portfolio return,

$$RR(r_p) = \frac{v(r_p - r_b)}{\rho(r_p - r_b)}, \qquad (10.1)$$

where

- $r_p - r_b$ is the active portfolio return.
- $r_p = w'X$ denotes the return of the portfolio with weights w and assets returns described by the random vector X.

r_b denotes the return of the benchmark portfolio.

$v(r_p)$ is a reward measure of r_p.

$\rho(r_p)$ calculates the risk of r_p.

Risk measures were described in detail in Chapter 6 and reward measures were described in section 8.5.5 of Chapter 8. The benchmark return r_b can either be a fixed target, for instance 8% annual return, or the return of another portfolio or reference interest rate meaning that r_b can also be a random variable.

In this section, we consider a simpler version of the reward-to-risk ratio in which the reward functional is the expected active portfolio return,

$$RR(r_p) = \frac{E(r_p - r_b)}{\rho(r_p - r_b)}, \qquad (10.2)$$

and the general ratio defined in equation (10.1) is left for the appendix to this chapter.

In the ex post analysis, equation (10.2) is calculated using the available historical returns in a certain period back in time. In this case, the numerator is the average of the realized active return and the denominator is the risk estimated from the sample. The past performance of different portfolios can be compared by the resulting ratios. The portfolio with the highest RR ratio is said to have the best performance in terms of this measure.

In the ex ante analysis, the joint distribution of the portfolio return and the benchmark return is hypothesized. The parameters of the assumed distribution are estimated from the historical data and the RR ratio is calculated from the fitted distribution. In this setting, the portfolio manager is interested in finding a feasible portfolio with highest RR ratio as this portfolio is expected to have the highest return for a unit of risk in its future performance. Formally, this optimization problem is the following:

$$\begin{aligned} \max_{w} \quad & \frac{E(r_p - r_b)}{\rho(r_p - r_b)} \\ \text{subject to} \quad & w'e = 1 \\ & w \geq 0, \end{aligned} \qquad (10.3)$$

where we use the notation introduced in Chapter 8. On condition that the risk measure is a convex function of portfolio weights,[1] the objective

---

[1] If $\rho(X)$ is a coherent risk measure, or a convex risk measure, then it is a convex function of portfolio weights.

function has nice mathematical properties that guarantee that the solution to (10.3) is unique.

In this section, we discuss the relationship of the solution to problem (10.3) with the efficient frontier generated by mean-risk (M-R) analysis. We provide examples of RR ratios and discuss their properties.

10.2.1 RR Ratios and the Efficient Portfolios

The principle of M-R analysis is introduced in section 8.3 of Chapter 8. According to it, from all feasible portfolios with a lower bound on expected return, we find the portfolio with minimal risk. This portfolio represents the optimal portfolio given the constraints of the problem. By varying the lower bound on the expected return, we obtain a set of optimal portfolios that are called *efficient portfolios*. Plotting the expected return of the efficient portfolio versus their risk we derive the *efficient frontier*.

In the following, we demonstrate that the portfolio with maximal RR ratio, that is the solution to problem (10.3), is among the efficient portfolios when the benchmark return is a constant target. If it is the return of another portfolio, then r_b is a random variable and the RR ratio cannot be directly related to the efficient frontier resulting from M-R analysis. Nonetheless, it can be related to the efficient frontier of a benchmark-tracking type of optimal portfolio problem.

For the sake of simplicity, we start the analysis assuming that the benchmark return is equal to zero. In this case, the maximal ratio portfolio is the solution to problem

$$
\begin{aligned}
\max_{w} \quad & \frac{w'\mu}{\rho(r_p)} \\
\text{subject to} \quad & w'e = 1 \\
& w \geq 0,
\end{aligned}
\tag{10.4}
$$

which is derived from (10.3) by setting $r_b = 0$ and making use of the equality $E(r_p) = w'\mu$.

Consider the efficient frontier generated by the optimal portfolio problem (8.12) given in Chapter 8. Suppose that the shape of the efficient frontier is as the one plotted in Figure 10.1; that is, we assume that the risk measure is a convex function of portfolio weights.[2] Each feasible portfolio in the mean-risk plane is characterized by the RR ratio calculated from its coordinates. In fact, the RR ratio equals the slope of the straight line passing through the origin and the point corresponding to this portfolio in

---

[2] Chapter 8 provides more information on how the shape of the efficient frontier depends on the properties of the reward and the risk measures.

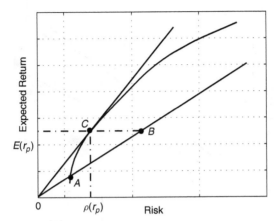

FIGURE 10.1 The efficient frontier and the tangent portfolio.

the mean-risk plane. Moreover, all portfolios having equal RR ratios lie on a straight line passing through the origin. Therefore, the portfolio with the largest RR ratio lies on the straight line passing through the origin, which is tangent to the efficient frontier because it is the line with the largest slope on which there are feasible portfolios. This line is also called the *tangent line*. In Figure 10.1, the portfolio denoted by C has the largest RR ratio. Portfolios A and B have equal RR ratios. Portfolio A is an efficient portfolio since it lies on the efficient frontier and portfolio B is suboptimal because another portfolio exists which is less risky while it has an equal expected return. This is portfolio C, which is also called *ρ-tangent portfolio* to emphasize that it is the tangent portfolio to the efficient frontier generated by a risk measure $\rho(X)$.

This analysis demonstrates that if $r_b = 0$, then the portfolio with the highest RR ratio is one of the efficient portfolios as it lies on the efficient frontier and coincides with the tangent portfolio. As a second case, suppose that the benchmark return is a constant. Then, under the additional assumption that the risk measure $\rho(X)$ satisfies the invariance property

$$\rho(X + C) = \rho(X) - C,$$

where C is a constant, the maximal RR ratio portfolio is a solution to the optimization problem

$$\max_{w} \quad \frac{w'\mu - r_b}{\rho(r_p) + r_b}$$
$$\text{subject to} \quad w'e = 1$$
$$w \geq 0. \tag{10.5}$$

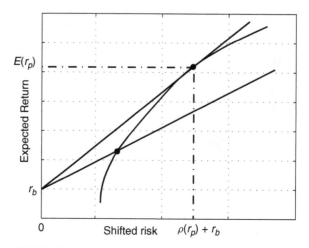

FIGURE 10.2 The efficient frontier and the tangent portfolio in the mean-shifted risk plane.

The additional assumption on the risk measure is satisfied by all coherent risk measures and all convex risk measures which were described in detail in Chapter 6 and, therefore, it is not restrictive.

Consider the efficient portfolios generated by problem (8.12) given in Chapter 8 and the corresponding efficient frontier in which the risk coordinate is replaced by the *shifted risk* defined by the sum $\rho(r_p) + r_b$. The RR ratio of any feasible portfolio is equal to the slope of a straight line passing through the point with zero shifted risk and expected return equal to r_b and the point in the mean-shifted risk plane corresponding to the feasible portfolio. This is illustrated in Figure 10.2. The portfolio with the maximal RR ratio is the tangent portfolio since it is identified by the corresponding straight line with the largest slope. In effect, the portfolio with the highest RR ratio in this case is also an efficient portfolio and it is a ρ-tangent portfolio in the mean-shifted risk plane.

The analysis corresponding to $r_b = 0$ can be obtained as a special case from (10.5). If the benchmark return is equal to zero, then (10.5) is the same as (10.4). Geometrically, starting from $r_b = 0$ and increasing r_b continuously means that we shift the efficient frontier in Figure 10.1 to the right while moving upwards the crossing point between the tangent line and the vertical axis. As a result, the tangent portfolio moves away from the minimum risk portfolio and gets closer to the global maximum expected return portfolio. At the same time, the slope of the tangent line decreases. At the limit, when the benchmark return equals the expected return of the global maximum expected return portfolio, the tangent line becomes parallel to the horizontal axis.

Conversely, starting from $r_b = 0$ and decreasing continuously r_b, we shift the efficient frontier in Figure 10.1 to the left while moving downward the crossing point between the tangent line and the vertical axis. In effect, the tangent portfolio moves toward the minimum risk portfolio. At the limit, when the benchmark return equals the negative of the risk of the global minimum risk portfolio, the tangent line becomes coincident with the vertical axis. The slope of the tangent line in this case is not defined as the RR ratio explodes because the denominator turns into zero. This scenario can be considered as a limit case in which the optimal RR ratio portfolio approaches the global minimum risk portfolio.

In summary, when the benchmark return varies from the negative of the risk of the global minimum risk portfolio to the expected return of the global maximum performance portfolio, the solutions to (10.5) describe the entire efficient frontier. We have tacitly assumed in this analysis that the risk of all feasible portfolios is nonnegative and that ρ is a coherent risk measure that is needed in order for the efficient frontier to have the nice concave shape as plotted in Figure 10.1.

The general case, in which r_b is the return of a benchmark portfolio, is more complicated, and it is not possible to link the solution of (10.3) to the efficient frontier obtained without the benchmark portfolio because r_b is a random variable. Nevertheless, it is possible to simplify the optimization problem at the cost of introducing an additional variable and provided that the risk measure satisfies the positive homogeneity property described in section 6.4.4 of Chapter 6 and a few other technical conditions. Stoyanov et al. (2007) demonstrate that the following problem:

$$\begin{aligned}
\min_{v,t} \quad & \rho(v'X - tr_b) \\
\text{subject to} \quad & v'e = t \\
& E(v'X - tr_b) = 1 \\
& v \geq 0, t \geq 0,
\end{aligned} \qquad (10.6)$$

where $v'X$ denotes the returns of a portfolio with scaled weights and $t \in \mathbb{R}$ is an additional variable, is equivalent to problem (10.3) in the sense that if $(\bar{v}, \bar{t})$ is a solution to (10.6), then $\bar{v}/\bar{t}$ is a vector of weights solving (10.3). This equivalence holds only if the optimal ratio problem (10.3) is well-defined; that is, for all feasible portfolios the risk $\rho(r_p - r_b)$ is strictly positive and there are feasible portfolios with positive mean active return. The equivalent problem (10.6) is discussed in more detail in the appendix to this chapter.

10.2.2 Limitations in the Application of Reward-to-Risk Ratios

The risk of a random variable as calculated by a risk measure may not always be a positive quantity. In Chapter 6, we considered the coherent risk measures, which satisfy the invariance property. The rationale behind the invariance property is the interpretation of the risk measure in terms of capital requirements. Investments with a zero or negative risk are acceptable in the sense that no capital reserves are required to insure against losses. In effect, if a portfolio has risk equal to zero, then its RR ratio is not defined.

This observation has more profound consequences in the ex ante analysis. Suppose that the set of feasible portfolios contains one portfolio with risk equal to zero.[3] Then problem (10.3) becomes unbounded and cannot be solved. In practice, it is difficult to assess whether the set of feasible portfolios contains a portfolio having zero risk. The global minimum risk portfolio and the global maximum return portfolio can be used to construct a criterion. If the former has a negative risk and the risk of the latter is positive, then the feasible set contains a portfolio with zero risk and problem (10.3) is unbounded.

Having a feasible portfolio with a zero risk or a negative risk is not uncommon. For example, if we choose AVaR as a risk measure, $\rho(X) = AVaR_\epsilon(X)$, then for any portfolio with a positive expected return, there exists a tail probability ϵ^* such that $AVaR_{\epsilon^*}(X) = 0$. This is a direct consequence of the definition of AVaR given in equation (7.1) in Chapter 7. AVaR is a continuous nonincreasing function of the tail probability and is not below the negative of the mathematical expectation of the portfolio return distribution. If $\epsilon_1 \leq \epsilon_2$, then

$$AVaR_{\epsilon_1}(r_p) \geq AVaR_{\epsilon_2}(r_p) \geq -E(r_p).$$

Therefore, under these assumptions, if for some small tail probability AVaR is positive, then there exists a tail probability ϵ^* such that $AVaR_{\epsilon^*}(r_p) = 0$. As a result, the AVaR of any portfolio with positive expected return may become equal to zero. It depends on the choice of the tail probability.

A way to avoid the issue of an unbounded ratio is through the *linearized forms of RR ratios*. Intuitively, comparing two investments, if they have

---

[3]In fact for any convex risk measure, if the feasible set of portfolios is convex and there exist a feasible portfolio with negative risk and a feasible portfolio with positive risk, then problem (10.3) is unbounded. This statement holds as, due to the convexity of the risk measure, there exists necessarily a portfolio with risk equal to zero.

equal expected return but different risks, then we prefer the investment with the larger RR ratio. Moreover, if M-R analysis is consistent with second-order stochastic dominance (SSD), then the ratio is also consistent with SSD,[4]

$$w'X \succeq_{SSD} v'X \qquad \implies \qquad \frac{v'\mu - r_b}{\rho(v'X) + r_b} \le \frac{w'\mu - r_b}{\rho(w'X) + r_b},$$

where r_b is a constant benchmark the values of which are in the range discussed in the previous chapter, v and w denote the compositions of the two portfolios, and X stands for the vector of random returns of the assets in the portfolios. The following functional, which is also consistent with SSD, is called a *linearized form of a RR ratio*

$$LRR(w, \lambda) = w'\mu - \lambda\rho(r_p), \tag{10.7}$$

where $\lambda \ge 0$ is a risk-aversion coefficient. The consistency with SSD is a consequence of the corresponding consistency of M-R analysis,

$$w'X \succeq_{SSD} v'X \qquad \implies \qquad LRR(v, \lambda) \le LRR(w, \lambda).$$

In fact, equation (10.7) coincides with the objective function of problem (8.18) in Chapter 8. We remarked in Chapter 8 that by varying λ and solving (8.18), we obtain the efficient frontier. Since the solution to the ratio problem (10.5) is also a portfolio on the efficient frontier, then there exists a particular value of $\lambda = \lambda_{r_b}$ such that using $LRR(w, \lambda_{r_b})$ as the objective function of (8.18), we obtain the portfolio solving the ratio problem (10.5).[5]

The linearized form $LRR(w, \lambda)$ is capable of describing the efficient frontier without any requirements with respect to $\rho(X)$. The risk measure can become equal to zero, or turn negative for a subset of the feasible portfolios, without affecting the properties of $LRR(w, \lambda)$. Therefore, provided that the risk-aversion can be appropriately selected, the linearized form $LRR(w, \lambda)$ can be used as a performance measure.

10.2.3 The STARR

The performance ratio in which AVaR is selected as a risk measure is called *STARR*, which stands for *stable tail-adjusted return ratio*. Rachev

---

[4]Section 8.3.3 of Chapter 8 considers the question of consistency of M-R analysis with SSD.

[5]Note that if the benchmark return is a random variable, then the linearized ratio has the general form $LRR(w, \lambda) = E(r_p - r_b) - \lambda\rho(r_p - r_b)$.

et al. (2006) suggest this name was originally constructed based on the assumption that assets returns follow the stable distribution.[6] In fact, the concept behind STARR can be translated to any distributional assumption. Formally, STARR is defined as

$$STARR_\epsilon(w) = \frac{E(r_p - r_b)}{AVaR_\epsilon(r_p - r_b)}. \tag{10.8}$$

If r_b is a constant benchmark return, then STARR equals

$$STARR_\epsilon(w) = \frac{w'\mu - r_b}{AVaR_\epsilon(r_p) + r_b}. \tag{10.9}$$

Suppose that our goal is ranking the past performance of several portfolios by STARR using a constant benchmark return. The available data consist of the observed returns of the portfolios in the past 12 months. As a first step, the tail probability of AVaR is chosen. The chosen value of ϵ depends on the extent to which we would like to emphasize the tail risk in the comparison. A small value of ϵ, for instance $\epsilon = 0.01$, indicates that we compare the average realized active portfolio return per unit of the extreme average realized losses. In contrast, if $\epsilon = 0.5$, then we compare the average realized active portfolio return per unit of the total average realized loss. In this case, we include all realized losses and not just the extreme ones.

Having selected the tail probability, the empirical AVaR for each portfolio can be calculated using, for example, formula (7.6) given in Chapter 7. The numerator of (10.9) contains the average realized active return of each portfolio, which can be calculated by subtracting the constant benchmark return from the average portfolio return. Finally, dividing the observed average outperformance of the benchmark return by the empirical portfolio AVaR, we obtain the *ex post* STARR of each portfolio. If all empirical AVaRs are positive, then the portfolio with the highest STARR had the best performance in the past 12 months with respect to this performance measure.

In section 10.2.2, we remarked that if a portfolio has a positive expected return, then it is always possible to find a tail probability at which the portfolio AVaR is negative. Alternatively, for a fixed tail probability, the portfolio AVaR can become negative if the expected return of the portfolio is sufficiently high. This can be demonstrated in the following way. In section 6.5 of Chapter 6, we discussed a link between the coherent risk

---

[6]Tokat et al. (2003) provide additional information on the differences between the more general stable distribution framework and the classical Gaussian framework.

measures and dispersion measures according to which an expectations bounded coherent risk measure can be decomposed into two parts, one of which is a measure of dispersion and the other is the mathematical expectation. In the case of AVaR, this means that the first term in the decomposition

$$AVaR_\epsilon(r_p) = AVaR_\epsilon(r_p - Er_p) - Er_p$$

is always non-negative. As a result, if the expected portfolio return is sufficiently high, then portfolio AVaR can turn negative at any tail probability.

In practice, the empirical AVaR at tail probability $\epsilon \leq 0.5$ is very rarely negative if it is calculated with daily returns. One reason is that the expected portfolio daily return is very close to zero. However, negative portfolio AVaRs at tail probability $\epsilon \leq 0.5$ can be observed with monthly returns. In this case, the portfolios performance cannot be directly compared by ranking with respect to STARRs because a negative AVaR results in a negative STARR. In effect, the portfolio with a negative STARR appears at the bottom of the table in which the portfolios are sorted in a decreasing order by their STARRs. It is among portfolios with very poor performance even though a negative AVaR signifies an exceptional performance.

As a consequence, if it turns out that there are portfolios with negative empirical AVaRs, then all portfolios should be divided into two groups and a different ordering should be applied to each group. The first group contains the portfolios with nonpositive AVaRs and the second group contains the portfolios with strictly positive AVaRs. We can argue that the portfolios in the first group have a better performance than the portfolios in the second group on the grounds that a negative risk implies that no reserve capital should be allocated. Even thought their risk is negative, the portfolios in the first group can be ranked. The smaller the risk is, the more attractive the investment. Thus, *smaller* STARRs indicate better performance. Note that STARRs of the portfolios in the first group are necessarily negative because of the inequality,

$$AVaR_\epsilon(r_p) \geq -Er_p,$$

valid at any tail probability. This inequality implies

$$0 \leq -AVaR_\epsilon(r_p) \leq Er_p,$$

meaning that if the portfolio AVaR is negative, then the portfolio expected return is positive. As a result, if the portfolio AVaR is negative, then the portfolio STARR is negative as well. Thus smaller STARRs in this case mean larger STARRs in absolute value. In contrast, the portfolios in the second group should be ranked in the usual way. Larger STARRs imply better performance.

The need to resort to a different ordering for the portfolios with negative AVaR stems from the fact that STARR is not defined when AVaR is equal to zero. In section 10.2.2, we noted that this difficulty can be avoided by adopting a linarized form of the ratio. According to (10.7), the linearized STARR is defined as

$$LSTARR(w) = E(r_p) - \lambda A VaR_\epsilon(r_p), \qquad (10.10)$$

where $\lambda \geq 0$ is the risk-aversion parameter. The linearized STARR does not have a singularity at AVaR equal to zero and one and the same ordering can be used across all portfolios. Higher LSTARR indicates better performance.[7]

In the ex ante analysis, the problem of finding the portfolio with the best future performance in terms of STARR is

$$\max_w \quad \frac{E(r_p - r_b)}{A VaR_\epsilon(r_p - r_b)}$$
$$\text{subject to} \quad w'e = 1$$
$$w \geq 0. \qquad (10.11)$$

According to (10.6), this problem can be reduced to a simpler optimization problem provided that all feasible portfolios have a positive AVaR of their active return and that there is a feasible portfolio with a positive expected active return. Under the additional assumption that the benchmark return is a constant, the simpler optimization problem becomes

$$\min_{v,t} \quad A VaR_\epsilon(v'X) + tr_b$$
$$\text{subject to} \quad v'e = t$$
$$v'\mu - tr_b = 1$$
$$v \geq 0, t \geq 0. \qquad (10.12)$$

This optimization problem can be solved by any of the methods discussed in section 8.3 of Chapter 8 and in the appendix to Chapter 8. For example, if there are available scenarios for the assets returns, then AVaR can be linearized and we can formulate a linear programming problem solving (10.12). Basically, combining equation (8.15) in Chapter 8 with

---

[7]Tokat et al. (2003) provide further details.

problem (10.12) we derive the linear programming problem

$$
\begin{aligned}
\min_{v,\theta,d,t} \quad & \theta + \frac{1}{k\epsilon} d'e + tr_b \\
\text{subject to} \quad & -Hv - \theta e \le d \\
& v'e = t \\
& v'\mu - tr_b = 1 \\
& v \ge 0, \, d \ge 0, \, t \ge 0, \, \theta \in \mathbb{R},
\end{aligned}
\tag{10.13}
$$

in which we use the notation introduced in section 8.3 of Chapter 8.

10.2.4 The Sortino Ratio

The Sortino ratio is defined as the ratio between the expected active portfolio return and the semistandard deviation of the underperformance of a fixed target level s. If r_b is a constant return target, the ratio is defined as

$$
SoR_s(w) = \frac{w'\mu - r_b}{(E(s - r_p)_+^2)^{1/2}},
\tag{10.14}
$$

where the function $(x)_+^2 = (\max(x, 0))^2$. The fixed target s is also called the *minimum acceptable return level*. For example, it can be set to be equal to r_b, $s = r_b$. In effect, the function in the denominator, which is constructed on the basis of a lower partial moment, is a proxy for portfolio risk. However, it is not a risk measure in the sense of coherent risk measures or convex risk measure discussed in Chapter 8.

In the ex post analysis, the Sortino ratio can be calculated as the ratio between the average realized active return and the sample semistandard deviation,

$$
\hat{\sigma}^-(s) = \sqrt{\frac{1}{k} \sum_{i=1}^{k} \max(s - r_i, 0)^2},
$$

where $r_1, r_2, \ldots, r_k$ is the sample of observed portfolio returns. As a result, the empirical Sortino ratio equals

$$
\widehat{SoR}_s(w) = \frac{\bar{r} - r_b}{\hat{\sigma}^-(s)},
$$

where $\bar{r} = \frac{1}{k} \sum_{i=1}^{k} r_i$ is the average realized portfolio return and the "hat" denotes that the formula is an estimator.

In the ex ante analysis, the optimal Sortino ratio problem is given by

$$
\begin{aligned}
\max_{w} \quad & \frac{w'\mu - r_b}{(E(s - r_p)_+^2)^{1/2}} \\
\text{subject to} \quad & w'e = 1 \\
& w \geq 0.
\end{aligned}
\tag{10.15}
$$

Under certain technical conditions discussed in the appendix to this chapter, it is possible to formulate a simpler optimization problem. If there are available scenarios for the assets returns, the simpler problems take the following form,

$$
\begin{aligned}
\min_{v,t,d} \quad & d'Id \\
\text{subject to} \quad & tse - Hv \leq d \\
& v'e = t \\
& v'\mu - tr_b = 1 \\
& v \geq 0, t \geq 0, d \geq 0.
\end{aligned}
\tag{10.16}
$$

where I denotes the identity matrix and the other notation is consistent with the notation in problem (10.13). We only remark that the matrix H contains the scenarios for the assets returns, e is a vector composed of ones, $e = (1, \ldots, 1)$, and d is a set of additional variables, one for each observation. As a result, e and d are vectors, the dimension of which equals the number of available observations.

The simpler problem (10.16) is a quadratic programming problem because the objective function is a quadratic function of the variables and the constraint set is composed of linear equalities and inequalities.

10.2.5   The Sortino-Satchell Ratio

The Sortino-Satchell ratio is a generalization of the Sortino ratio in which a lower partial moment of order $q \geq 1$ is used as a proxy for risk. If r_b is a constant benchmark return, the Sortino-Satchell ratio is defined as

$$
SSR_s(w) = \frac{w'\mu - r_b}{(E(s - r_p)_+^q)^{1/q}}
\tag{10.17}
$$

where $(x)_+^q = (\max(x, 0))^q$, and q denotes the order of the lower partial moment and the other notation is the same as in the Sortino ratio. The Sortino ratio arises from the Sortino-Satchell ratio if $q = 2$.

In the ex post analysis, the Sortino-Satchell ratio is estimated as the ratio of the sample estimates of the numerator and the denominator,

$$
\widehat{SSR}_s(w) = \frac{\bar{r} - r_b}{\hat{\sigma}_q^-(s)},
$$

where $\hat{\sigma}_q^-(s)$ denotes the estimate of the denominator,

$$\hat{\sigma}_q^-(s) = \left(\frac{1}{k}\sum_{i=1}^{k}\max(s - r_i, 0)^q\right)^{1/q}. \tag{10.18}$$

In the ex ante analysis, the optimal Sortino-Satchell ratio problem is given by

$$\begin{aligned}\max_{w} \quad & \frac{w'\mu - r_b}{(E(s - r_p)_+^q)^{1/q}}\\ \text{subject to} \quad & w'e = 1\\ & w \geq 0.\end{aligned} \tag{10.19}$$

which, following the same reasoning as in the Sortino ratio, can be reduced to a simpler form under the same conditions as in the Sortino ratio. The simpler problem is

$$\begin{aligned}\min_{v,t,d} \quad & \sum_{i=1}^{k} d_i^q\\ \text{subject to} \quad & tse - Hv \leq d\\ & v'e = t\\ & v'\mu - tr_b = 1\\ & v \geq 0, t \geq 0, d \geq 0.\end{aligned} \tag{10.20}$$

where the notation is the same as in the Sortino ratio, and $d = (d_1, \ldots, d_k)$ are the additional variables. Thus, the objective function contains the sum of the additional variables raised to the power q.

If the selected order of the lower partial moment is $q = 1$, then problem (10.20) is a linear programming problem since the objective function is a linear function of the variables and the constraint set is composed of linear equalities and inequalities. If $q = 2$, then (10.20) is a quadratic programming problem.

10.2.6   A One-Sided Variability Ratio

Farinelli and Tibiletti (2002) propose a one-sided variability ratio that is based on two partial moments. It is different from the Sortino-Satchell ratio because portfolio reward is not measured by the mathematical expectation but by an upper partial moment. The ratio is defined as

$$\Phi_{r_b}^{p,q}(w) = \frac{(E(r_p - r_b)_+^p)^{1/p}}{(E(r_b - r_p)_+^q)^{1/q}}, \tag{10.21}$$

where $p \geq 1$, $q \geq 1$ are the orders of the corresponding partial moments and r_b denotes the benchmark return. Thus, if the portfolio return is above r_b, it is registered as reward and if it is below r_b, it is registered as loss.

In the ex post analysis, the ratio defined in (10.21) is computed by replacing the numerator and the denominator by the estimates of the mathematical expectation. The estimators can be based on (10.18).

Concerning the ex ante analysis, the optimal $\Phi_{r_b}^{p,q}(w)$ ratio problem does not have nice properties such as the optimal portfolio problems based on STARR or the Sortino-Satchell ratio. The reason is that the ratio is a fraction of two convex functions of portfolio weights and, as a result, the optimization problem involving the performance measure given in (10.21) may have multiple local extrema.

10.2.7 The Rachev Ratio

The Rachev ratio is a performance measure similar to the performance measure defined in (10.21) in that it uses a reward measure which is not the mathematical expectation of active portfolio returns. In contrast, the Rachev ratio is constructed on the basis of AVaR. The reward measure in the Rachev ratio is defined as the average of the quantiles of the portfolio return distribution that are above a certain target quantile level. The risk measure is AVaR at a given tail probability. Formally, the definition is

$$RaR_{\epsilon_1,\epsilon_2}(w) = \frac{AVaR_{\epsilon_1}(r_b - r_p)}{AVaR_{\epsilon_2}(r_p - r_b)} \qquad (10.22)$$

where the tail probability ϵ_1 defines the quantile level of the reward measure and ϵ_2 is the tail probability of AVaR.

Even though AVaR is used in the numerator, which is a risk measure, the numerator represents a measure of reward. This is demonstrated by

$$AVaR_{\epsilon_1}(X) = -\frac{1}{\epsilon_1}\int_0^{\epsilon_1} F_X^{-1}(p)dp$$

$$= \frac{1}{\epsilon_1}\int_{1-\epsilon_1}^1 F_{-X}^{-1}(p)dp,$$

where $X = r_b - r_p$ is a random variable that can be interpreted as benchmark underperformance and $-X$ stands for the active portfolio return. As a result, the numerator in the Rachev ratio can be interpreted as the average outperformance of the benchmark provided that the outperformance is larger than the quantile at $1 - \epsilon_1$ probability of the active return distribution. Thus there are two performance levels in the Rachev ratio. The quantile at ϵ_2 probability in the AVaR in the denominator and the quantile at $1 - \epsilon_1$

probability in the numerator. If the active return is below the former, it is counted as loss and if it is above the latter, then it is registered as reward. The probability ϵ_2 is often called *lower tail probability* and ϵ_1 is known as *upper tail probability*. A possible choice for the lower tail probability is $\epsilon_2 = 0.05$ and for the upper tail probability, $\epsilon_1 = 0.1$. An empirical example is provided in Biglova et al. (2004).

In the ex post analysis, the Rachev ratio is computed by dividing the corresponding two sample AVaRs, which can be calculated by any of the methods discussed in section 7.3 of Chapter 7. Since the performance levels in the Rachev ratio are quantiles of the active return distribution, they are relative levels as they adjust according to the distribution. For example, if the scale is small, then the two performance levels will be closer to each other. As a consequence, the Rachev ratio is always well-defined.

In the ex ante analysis, optimal portfolio problems based on the Rachev ratio are, generally, numerically hard to solve because the Rachev ratio is a fraction of two AVaRs, which are convex functions of portfolio weights. In effect, the Rachev ratio, if viewed as a function of portfolio weights, may have many local extrema. In the appendix to this chapter, we consider in more detail performance measures of this type, which are also called *nonquasiconcave performance measures*.

10.3   REWARD-TO-VARIABILITY RATIOS

Another general type of performance measures are the reward-to-variability (RV) ratios. They are defined as the ratio between the expected active portfolio return and a dispersion measure of the active portfolio return,

$$RV(r_p) = \frac{E(r_p - r_b)}{D(r_p - r_b)}, \qquad (10.23)$$

where

$r_p - r_b$ is the active portfolio return.

r_p denotes the portfolio return.

r_b denotes the return of the benchmark portfolio.

$D(r_p)$ is a dispersion measure of the random portfolio return r_p.

Dispersion measures are axiomatically introduced in section 6.2.4 of Chapter 6. The benchmark return r_b can either be a fixed target, the return of another portfolio, or a reference interest rate.

In a way similar to the RR ratios, we distinguish between application of RV ratios in the ex post and the ex ante analysis. In the ex post analysis, equation (10.23) is calculated using the available historical returns in a certain period back in time. In this case, the numerator is the average of the realized active return and the denominator equals the sample dispersion. For example, if $D(X)$ is the standard deviation, then the denominator equals the sample standard deviation of the active return. A practical example is given in section 10.3.2.

In the ex ante analysis, the joint distribution of the portfolio return and the benchmark return is hypothesized. The parameters of the assumed distribution are estimated from the historical data and the RV ratio is calculated from the fitted distribution. In this setting, the portfolio manager is interested in finding a feasible portfolio with highest RV ratio as this portfolio is expected to have the highest return for a unit of variability in its future performance. Formally, this optimization problem is the following

$$
\begin{aligned}
\max_{w} \quad & \frac{E(r_p - r_b)}{D(r_p - r_b)} \\
\text{subject to} \quad & w'e = 1 \\
& w \geq 0,
\end{aligned}
\tag{10.24}
$$

where we use the notation introduced in Chapter 8. On condition that the dispersion measure is a convex function of portfolio weights,[8] the objective function has nice mathematical properties which guarantee that the solution to (10.3) is unique.

We can consider a simpler version of the optimization problem (10.24), which arises in the same fashion as the simpler version (10.6) of the optimal RR ratio problem. Since the dispersion measure is nonnegative for any random variable by definition, the only necessary assumption for the RV ratio to be well-defined is that it does not turn into zero for a feasible portfolio. This can happen, for example, if the benchmark portfolio itself is a feasible portfolio and can be replicated. In this case, the dispersion measure equals zero because the active portfolio return is zero in all states of the world. Suppose the dispersion measure is strictly positive for any feasible portfolio, it satisfies the positive homogeneity property, and there is a feasible portfolio with positive active return. Under these assumptions, we can consider the simpler optimization problem,

$$
\begin{aligned}
\min_{v,t} \quad & D(v'X - tr_b) \\
\text{subject to} \quad & v'e = t \\
& E(v'X - tr_b) = 1 \\
& v \geq 0, t \geq 0,
\end{aligned}
\tag{10.25}
$$

---

[8]If $D(X)$ is a deviation measure, then it is a convex function of portfolio weights.

in which we use the same notation as in problem (10.6). If $(\bar{v}, \bar{t})$ is a solution to (10.25), then $\bar{v}/\bar{t}$ is a vector of weights solving (10.24) and, in this sense, the two are equivalent.

In this section, we consider the relationship between the solution to problem (10.24) and the efficient portfolios of M-R analysis if the risk measure is an expectation bounded coherent risk measure and the dispersion measure $D(X)$ is the underlying deviation measure. It turns out that there is a close relationship between the solutions to the optimal RV ratio problem (10.24) and the optimal RR ratio problem (10.3). The link between coherent risk measures and deviation measures is described in more detail in section 6.5 of Chapter 6. Finally, we provide several examples of widely used RV ratios.

10.3.1   RV Ratios and the Efficient Portfolios

Suppose that the risk measure ρ in the M-R analysis is a coherent risk measure satisfying the additional property $\rho(r_p) > -Er_p$. In section 6.5 of Chapter 6, we discussed that in this case the risk measure can be decomposed into

$$\rho(r_p) = D(r_p) - Er_p$$

where $D(r_p) = \rho(r_p - Er_p)$ is a measure of dispersion called a deviation measure. In section 8.3.4 of Chapter 8, we demonstrated that, under these assumptions, all optimal portfolios generated by problem (8.24) can be divided into three groups. The smallest group contains the mean-risk efficient portfolios generated, for example, by problem (8.12). These efficient portfolios can also be obtained by varying the constant benchmark return in the optimal RR ratio problem (10.5). The middle group contains the mean-deviation efficient portfolios generated by problem (8.23) in which the deviation measure is the dispersion measure underlying the risk measure ρ. They contain the mean-risk efficient portfolios and can be visualized in the mean-deviation plane as in the example in Figure 8.6.

It can be demonstrated that the mean-deviation efficient portfolios can be obtained from the corresponding optimal RV ratio problem by varying the constant benchmark return. We apply the reasoning developed in section 10.2.1 directly assuming that $r_b \neq 0$. Since deviation measures are by definition translation invariant, that is, they satisfy the property

$$D(X + C) = D(X)$$

for any constant C, the optimal RV ratio problem can be formulated as

$$\max_{w} \quad \frac{w'\mu - r_b}{D(r_p)}$$
$$\text{subject to} \quad w'e = 1$$
$$w \geq 0 \qquad\qquad (10.26)$$

when r_b is a constant benchmark. Therefore, as a consequence of the reasoning in section 10.2.1, the portfolio yielding the maximal RV ratio is positioned on the mean-deviation efficient frontier where a straight line passing through the point with expected return equal to r_b and deviation equal to zero is tangent to it. This is illustrated in the top plot in Figure 10.3. The slope of any straight line passing through the point $(0, r_b)$ on the vertical axis is equal to the RV ratios of the portfolios lying on it. The tangent line has the largest slope among all such straight lines with feasible portfolios lying on them.

In contrast to the geometric reasoning in the optimal RR ratio problem, changing the benchmark return does not affect the position of the mean-deviation efficient frontier because the deviation measure does not depend on it. Therefore, by increasing or decreasing continuously r_b, we only change the position of the reference point on the vertical axis through which the straight line passes. For instance, decreasing the benchmark return to $r_b^1 < r_b$, we obtain a new tangent line and a new tangent portfolio shown on the bottom plot in Figure 10.3. The geometric intuition suggests that decreasing further r_b, we obtain portfolios closer and closer to the global minimum deviation portfolio. As a result, with the only exception of the global minimum deviation portfolio, any mean-deviation efficient portfolio can be obtained as a solution to the optimal RV ratio problem when the benchmark return varies $r_b \in (-\infty, r_b^{max}]$ in which r_b^{max} denotes the expected return of the global maximum expected return portfolio.

Since the mean-risk efficient portfolios are only a part of the mean-deviation efficient portfolios, then, as a corollary of the geometric reasoning, we obtain the following relationship between the optimal RR ratio and RV ratio problems. The solution to problem (10.5) coincides with the solution to problem (10.26) on condition that $r_b \in [-\rho^{min}, r_b^{max}]$ where $\rho^{min} > 0$ denotes the risk of the global minimum risk portfolio. The condition $\rho^{min} > 0$ guarantees that the risk of all feasible portfolios is strictly positive and, therefore, the RR ratio is bounded. If $r_b < -\rho^{min}$, then the optimal RV ratio portfolio does not belong to the mean-risk efficient frontier but belongs to the mean-deviation efficient frontier.

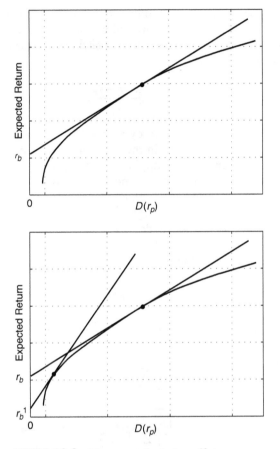

FIGURE 10.3 The mean-deviation efficient frontier and the tangent portfolio. Reducing the benchmark return, we obtain a new tangent portfolio without changing the efficient frontier.

10.3.2 The Sharpe Ratio

The celebrated Sharpe ratio arises as a RV ratio in which the dispersion measure is represented by the standard deviation, $D(r_p - r_b) = \sigma(r_p - r_b)$. Formally, it is defined as

$$IR(w) = \frac{E(r_p - r_b)}{\sigma(r_p - r_b)} \qquad (10.27)$$

when the benchmark return is a random variable. In this case, the Sharpe ratio equals the mean active return divided by the tracking error and is also known as the *information ratio* (IR). If the benchmark return is a constant, then the Sharpe ratio equals

$$SR(w) = \frac{w'\mu - r_b}{\sigma_{r_p}}. \tag{10.28}$$

The Sharpe ratio was introduced by Sharpe (1966) as a way to compute the performance of mutual funds. In the following, we provide an example illustrating how the Sharpe ratio is applied in the ex post analysis. Table 10.1 contains observed monthly returns of a portfolio. Assume that the monthly target return is a constant and equals 0.5%. In order to compute the Sharpe ratio, we have to calculate the average realized monthly active return and divide it by the sample standard deviation of the portfolio return. The average active return can be calculated by subtracting the target return of 0.5% from the average portfolio return,

$$\frac{1}{4}(1.2 - 0.1 + 1.4 + 0.3) - 0.5 = 0.2.$$

The sample standard deviation $\hat{\sigma}$ is calculated according to the formula

$$\hat{\sigma} = \sqrt{\frac{1}{k-1} \sum_{i=1}^{k} (r_i - \bar{r})^2}$$

$$= \sqrt{\frac{1}{k-1} \sum_{i=1}^{k} r_i^2 - \frac{k}{k-1} \bar{r}^2}, \tag{10.29}$$

where $r_1, r_2, \ldots, r_k$ denote the observed portfolio returns and $\bar{r}$ stands for the average portfolio return. In statistics, $\hat{\sigma}$ is called an *unbiased estimator* of the standard deviation. Making use of equation (10.29) for $\hat{\sigma}$, we calculate

$$\hat{\sigma} = \sqrt{\frac{1}{3}(1.2^2 + 0.1^2 + 1.4^2 + 0.3^2) - \frac{4}{3}0.7^2} = 0.716,$$

TABLE 10.1   Realized Monthly Returns of a Hypothetical Portfolio.

	Jan	Feb	Mar	Apr
Realized return (%)	1.2	−0.1	1.4	0.3

where $\bar{r} = 0.7$ is the average monthly return. Finally, the ex post Sharpe ratio of the portfolio equals

$$\hat{SR} = \frac{\bar{r} - 0.5}{\hat{\sigma}} = \frac{0.2}{0.716} = 0.2631.$$

In the ex ante analysis, the portfolio manager is looking for the portfolio with the best future performance in terms of the Sharpe ratio. The corresponding optimization problem is

$$\max_{w} \quad \frac{w'\mu - r_b}{\sigma_{r_p}}$$
$$\text{subject to} \quad w'e = 1$$
$$w \geq 0, \qquad\qquad (10.30)$$

which, according to the general reasoning behind optimal RV ratio problems, can be reduced to the following simpler problem:

$$\min_{v,t} \quad \sigma(v'X)$$
$$\text{subject to} \quad v'e = t$$
$$v'\mu - tr_b = 1$$
$$v \geq 0, t \geq 0, \qquad\qquad (10.31)$$

where the objective function $\sigma(v'X)$ is the standard deviation of the portfolio with scaled weights v and t is an additional variable. In Chapter 8, we remarked that it makes no difference whether the standard deviation or the variance of portfolio returns is minimized as far as the optimal solution is concerned. This holds because variance is a nondecreasing function of standard deviation and, therefore, the portfolio yielding the minimal standard deviation subject to the constraints also yields the minimal variance. In effect, problem (10.31) can be formulated in terms of minimizing portfolio variance,

$$\min_{v,t} \quad v'\Sigma v$$
$$\text{subject to} \quad v'e = t$$
$$v'\mu - tr_b = 1$$
$$v \geq 0, t \geq 0, \qquad\qquad (10.32)$$

where Σ is the covariance matrix of the portfolio assets returns.

The optimization problem (10.32) is a quadratic programming problem because the objective function is a quadratic function of the scaled portfolio weights and all functions in the constraint set are linear. As far as the structure of the optimization problem is concerned, (10.32) is not more difficult to solve than the traditional quadratic mean-variance problem (8.4) given in Chapter 8. In fact, the only difference between the two is the additional variable t in (10.32) but this does not increase significantly the computational complexity.

10.3.3 The Capital Market Line and the Sharpe Ratio

In section 8.2.4 of Chapter 8, we discussed the mean-variance analysis when there is a risk-free asset added to the investment universe. In this case, the mean-variance efficient frontier is a straight line in the mean-standard deviation plane, which is called the *capital market line*. Moreover, the mean-variance efficient portfolios turn out to be a combination of the risk-free asset and a portfolio composed of the risky assets known as the *market portfolio*. This is a fundamental result on the structure of the mean-variance efficient portfolios known as the *two-fund separation theorem*, which is also at the heart of the *Capital Asset Pricing Model* (CAPM). In this section, we demonstrate that the market portfolio is the portfolio yielding the maximal Sharpe ratio in the universe of the risky assets with the benchmark return equal to the risk-free return, and we provide an interpretation of the optimal value of the additional variable t in problem (10.32).

Consider problem (8.9) in section 8.2.4 of Chapter 8, which represents the optimal portfolio problem behind the mean-variance analysis with a risk-free asset. In order to make a parallel with (10.32), we restate problem (8.9) but with an equality constraint on the expected return rather than an inequality constraint,

$$\min_{\omega, \omega_f} \quad \omega' \Sigma \omega$$
$$\text{subject to} \quad \omega'e + \omega_f = 1$$
$$\omega'\mu + \omega_f r_f = R_*$$
$$\omega \geq 0, \ \omega_f \leq 1, \tag{10.33}$$

where:

ω_f stands for the weight of the risk-free asset r_f.

ω denotes the weights of the risky assets.

R_* denotes the bound on the expected portfolio return.

Σ stands for the covariance matrix between the risky assets.

Changing the inequality constraint to equality does not change the optimal solution if the target expected return is not below the risk-free rate,

$R_* \geq r_f$. Conversely, if the target expected return is below the risk-free rate, then (10.33) is an infeasible problem. Our assumption is $R_* > r_f$ because in the case of equality, the optimal portfolio consists of the risk-free asset only.

The weight ω_f of the risk-free asset in the portfolio can be a positive or a negative number. If ω_f is negative, this means that borrowing at the risk-free rate is allowed and the borrowed money is invested in the market portfolio. In this case, it is said that we have a *leveraged portfolio*. Leveraged portfolios are positioned on the capital market line, illustrated in Figure 8.2 in Chapter 8, to the right of the tangency portfolio. The efficient portfolios to the left of the tangency portfolio have a positive weight for the risk-free asset.

We can express the weight of the risky assets in the whole portfolio by means of the weight of the risk-free asset. The weight of the risky assets equals $1 - \omega_f$, which is a consequence of the requirement that all weights should sum up to 1. We introduce a new variable in (10.33) computing the weight of the risky assets, $s = 1 - \omega_f$, which we substitute for ω_f. Thus problem (10.33) becomes

$$
\begin{aligned}
\min_{\omega, s} \quad & \omega' \Sigma \omega \\
\text{subject to} \quad & \omega' e = s \\
& \omega' \mu - s r_f = R_* - r_f \\
& \omega \geq 0, \; s \geq 0.
\end{aligned} \tag{10.34}
$$

There are many similarities between the optimal Sharpe ratio problem (10.32) and (10.34). In fact, if $r_b = r_f$, then the only difference is in the expected return constraint. Not only do these two problems look similar but their solutions are also tightly connected. Denote by $(\overline{\omega}, \overline{s})$ the optimal solution to (10.34). Since by assumption $R_* - r_f > 0$, it follows that

$$
\overline{v} = \frac{\overline{\omega}}{(R_* - r_f)}
$$

and

$$
\overline{t} = \frac{\overline{s}}{(R_* - r_f)} \tag{10.35}
$$

represent the optimal solution to problem (10.32). According to the analysis made for the generic optimal RV ratio problem (10.25), we obtain that the weights $\overline{w}$ of the portfolio yielding the maximal Sharpe ratio are computed by

$$
\overline{w} = \overline{v}/\overline{t} = \overline{\omega}/\overline{s} = \overline{\omega}/(1 - \overline{\omega}_f). \tag{10.36}
$$

On the other hand, if $(\overline{\omega}, \overline{s}) = (\overline{\omega}, 1 - \overline{\omega}_f)$ is the optimal solution to (10.33), then the weights of the market portfolio w_M are calculated by

$$
w_M = \overline{\omega}/(1 - \overline{\omega}_f).
$$

As a result, the market portfolio is a portfolio solving the optimal Sharpe ratio problem (10.30) with $r_b = r_f$.

From a geometric viewpoint, the link between the two problems becomes apparent by comparing the top plot in Figure 10.3 and Figure 8.2 in Chapter 8. The tangent line in Figure 10.3 coincides with the capital market line in Figure 8.2 if the benchmark return is equal to the risk-free rate.

Finally, formula (10.35) provides a way of interpreting the optimal value $\bar{t}$ of the additional variable t used to simplify the optimal Sharpe ratio problem in (10.32). The optimal value $\bar{t}$ equals the weight of the risky assets in an efficient portfolio obtained with a risk-free rate $r_b = r_f$ and a limit on the expected return R_*, divided by the positive difference $R_* - r_f$. Note that this ratio remains one and the same irrespective of the value of the limit on the expected return R_* and, therefore, is a characteristic of the efficient portfolios.

In the appendix to Chapter 8, we gave a closed-form expression of the solution to a type of mean-variance optimization problems. Taking advantage of the approach described there, it is possible to derive a closed-form solution to the mean-variance problem with a risk-free asset (10.33) and also to the optimal Sharpe ratio problem (10.30) through the simplified problem (10.32) by removing the inequality constraints on the weights of the assets. Thus the optimal solution to problem

$$\min_{\omega, \omega_f} \quad \omega' \Sigma \omega$$
$$\text{subject to} \quad \omega'e + \omega_f = 1$$
$$\omega'\mu + \omega_f r_f = R_*$$

is given by

$$\bar{\omega} = \frac{R_* - r_f}{(\mu - r_f e)' \Sigma^{-1} (\mu - r_f e)} \Sigma^{-1} (\mu - r_f e)$$

$$\bar{\omega}_f = 1 - \frac{R_* - r_f}{(\mu - r_f e)' \Sigma^{-1} (\mu - r_f e)} (\mu - r_f e)' \Sigma^{-1} e, \qquad (10.37)$$

where Σ^{-1} denotes the inverse of the covariance matrix Σ. In a similar way, the optimal solution to

$$\max_{w} \quad \frac{w'\mu - r_b}{\sigma_{r_p}}$$
$$\text{subject to} \quad w'e = 1$$

is given by

$$\bar{w} = \frac{\Sigma^{-1}(\mu - r_b e)}{(\mu - r_b e)' \Sigma^{-1} e}. \qquad (10.38)$$

In this simple case, the relationship in formula (10.36) between the solution to the optimal Sharpe ratio problem and the mean-variance problem with a risk-free asset is straightforward to check using formula (10.37) and formula (10.38).

10.4 SUMMARY

In this chapter, we discussed performance measures from the point of view of the ex post and ex ante analysis. We distinguish between reward-to-risk and reward-to-variability ratios depending on whether a risk measure or a dispersion measure is adopted in the denominator of the ratio. A number of performance measures used in the literature are provided as examples and, where possible, the optimal portfolio problems behind the ex ante analysis are simplified.

The appendix to this chapter considers a general approach to classifying performance measures in a structural way. We describe the general optimal quasiconcave ratio problem and the arising simpler optimization problems on condition that certain technical properties are met. Finally, we give an account of nonquasiconcave ratios and demonstrate that the two-fund separation theorem holds for the general reward-risk analysis when a risk-free asset is added to the investment universe.

10.5 TECHNICAL APPENDIX

In this appendix, we demonstrate that as far as the ex ante analysis is concerned, the Rachev ratio can be viewed as an extension of STARR. We also introduce another extension of STARR, which we call the *robust STARR*. Next, we develop a structural classification of performance measures in terms of the properties of the corresponding reward and risk, or dispersion, measures respectively. The performance measures discussed in the chapter are categorized according to the theory developed.

10.5.1 Extensions of STARR

In this section, we revisit the problem of finding the maximal STARR portfolio. We demonstrate that the Rachev ratio can be viewed as an extension of STARR. Furthermore, we show that a new performance measure extending STARR can be derived.

Consider the definition of STARR given in (10.8). In order to keep notation simpler, we denote the active portfolio return by $X = r_p - r_b$.

STARR can be represented as

$$STARR_\epsilon(w) = \frac{EX}{AVaR_\epsilon(X)}$$

$$= \frac{-\epsilon AVaR_\epsilon(X) + \int_\epsilon^1 F_X^{-1}(p)dp}{AVaR_\epsilon(X)}$$

$$= -\epsilon + (1 - \epsilon)\frac{\frac{1}{1-\epsilon}\int_\epsilon^1 F_X^{-1}(p)dp}{AVaR_\epsilon(X)}. \qquad (10.39)$$

The numerator in the ratio is the average active return provided that it is larger than the VaR at tail probability ϵ. In fact, the fraction can be recognized as the Rachev ratio with $\epsilon_1 = 1 - \epsilon$ and $\epsilon_2 = \epsilon$,

$$RaR_{1-\epsilon,\epsilon}(w) = \frac{\frac{1}{1-\epsilon}\int_\epsilon^1 F_X^{-1}(p)dp}{AVaR_\epsilon(X)}.$$

As a consequence, the portfolios maximizing STARR also maximize the $RaR_{1-\epsilon,\epsilon}(w)$ as the former is a positive linear function of the latter which is the main conclusion in (10.39). Thus from the standpoint of the ex ante analysis, STARR and $RaR_{1-\epsilon,\epsilon}(w)$ can be regarded as equivalent performance measures. The more general Rachev ratio appears when $1 - \epsilon$ is replaced by an arbitrary probability ϵ_1.

The representation in (10.39) provides a way of obtaining another generalization of STARR, which we call the *robust STARR* and abbreviate by RobS.[9] It is defined as

$$RobS_{\delta,\epsilon}(w) = \frac{\frac{1}{\delta-\epsilon}\int_\epsilon^\delta F_X^{-1}(p)dp}{AVaR_\epsilon(X)}, \qquad (10.40)$$

where $\delta \geq \epsilon$ is an upper tail probability. The numerator can be interpreted as the average active return between VaR at tail probability ϵ and the quantile at upper tail probability δ. Since the extreme quantiles are not included, the numerator can be viewed as a reward measure which is a robust alternative of the mathematical expectation. A reasonable choice for δ is, for example, $\delta = 0.95$. The optimal STARR portfolios appear from the optimal $RobS_{\delta,\epsilon}(w)$ portfolios when $\delta = 1$.

Taking advantage of the same approach as in the derivation of the representation in (10.39), it is possible to obtain that the optimal $RobS_{\delta,\epsilon}(w)$

---

[9] Stoyanov (2005) provides a formal treatment of the robust STARR and the related optimal portfolio problems.

portfolios also maximize the ratio,

$$RobS^*_{\delta,\epsilon}(w) = \frac{-AVaR_\delta(X)}{AVaR_\epsilon(X)},$$ (10.41)

which means that (10.41) is equivalent to (10.40) as far as the ex ante analysis is concerned. The formula in (10.41) turns out to be a more suitable objective function than (10.40). In effect, the optimal robust STARR problem is

$$\begin{aligned} \max_{w} \quad & \frac{-AVaR_\delta(r_p - r_b)}{AVaR_\epsilon(r_p - r_b)} \\ \text{subject to} \quad & w'e = 1 \\ & w \geq 0. \end{aligned}$$ (10.42)

With respect to the classification developed in Section 10.2, the robust STARR is a quasiconcave performance measure that can be optimized through a linear programming problem.

10.5.2 Quasiconcave Performance Measures

In this section, we consider the RR ratio optimization problem of the general form

$$\begin{aligned} \max_{w} \quad & \frac{v(w'X - r_b)}{\rho(w'X - r_b)} \\ \text{subject to} \quad & w'e = 1 \\ & w \geq 0, \end{aligned}$$ (10.43)

where:

X is a random vector describing the return of portfolio assets.

v is a reward measure.

ρ is a risk measure.

r_b is return of a benchmark portfolio.

Depending on the properties assumed for the reward measure and the risk measure, the optimization problem can be reduced to a simpler form. This section is based on Stoyanov et al. (2007) and Rachev et al. (2007). While we consider RR ratios, the theory developed can be applied to RV ratios as well since we are discussing general properties, which may hold for both risk and dispersion measures.

We start with a few comments on the general properties of problem (10.43), which is also called a *fractional program* because the objective function is a ratio. First, in order for the objective function to be bounded, we have to assume that the denominator does not turn into zero for any feasible portfolio. For this reason, we assume that the risk of the active portfolio return is positive for all feasible portfolios. This assumption is crucial. If it does not hold, then the optimization problem does not have a solution.

Second, without loss of generality, we assume that the reward measure is positive for all feasible portfolios. This may be regarded as a restrictive property. But if it does not hold, then we can consider the optimization problem only on the subset of the feasible portfolios for which $v(w'X - r_b) \geq \epsilon > 0$. The portfolios with negative reward can be safely ignored because the optimal solution can never be among them on condition that there are feasible portfolios with positive reward.

In summary, the basic assumptions for all feasible portfolios are the following:

$$v(w'X - r_b) > 0$$

and

$$\rho(w'X - r_b) > 0. \tag{10.44}$$

If they are satisfied, then we can consider either problem (10.43), in which we maximize the RR ratio, or problem

$$
\begin{aligned}
\min_{w} \quad & \frac{\rho(w'X - r_b)}{v(w'X - r_b)} \\
\text{subject to} \quad & w'e = 1 \\
& w \geq 0,
\end{aligned}
\tag{10.45}
$$

in which we minimize the inverse ratio. Under the basic assumptions in (10.44), the portfolios solving problem (10.43) also solve problem (10.45).

The portfolio yielding the optimal ratio in (10.43) can also be interpreted as a tangent portfolio, which is similar to the corresponding interpretation when the benchmark is a constant target. If r_b is a random variable, then the efficient frontier is generated by an RR analysis with a reward measure v and a risk measure ρ, which are considered on the space of active portfolio returns.[10] The efficient portfolios are obtained by solving optimization problem (10.43) but changing the objective function to

$$f(w) = v(w'X - r_b) - \lambda\rho(w'X - r_b)$$

where $\lambda \geq 0$ is the risk-aversion parameters. By varying λ and solving the optimization problem, we obtain the set of efficient portfolios. The

---

[10]R-R analysis is discussed in the appendix to Chapter 8.

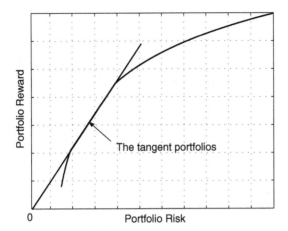

The tangent portfolios

FIGURE 10.4 The efficient frontier may have a linear section which may result in nonunique tangent portfolios.

portfolio yielding the maximal ratio appears as a tangent portfolio to the efficient frontier in the reward-risk plane. The benchmark return is taken into account by considering the risk and the reward of the active portfolio returns. In effect, the tangent line identifying the tangent portfolio passes through the origin. Figure 10.4 shows a case in which the tangent portfolio is not unique.

Quasiconcave Fractional Program If the reward functional is a concave function of portfolio weights and the risk measure is a convex function of portfolio weights, then the objective function of (10.43) is quasiconcave and the objective function of (10.45) is quasiconvex. If the reward measure satisfies the properties given in the appendix to Chapter 8 and ρ is a coherent risk measure, then they are a concave and a convex function respectively. Quasiconcave and quasiconvex functions have nice optimality properties which are similar to the properties of the concave and convex functions, respectively. For example, if the objective function of (10.45) is quasiconvex then there exists a unique solution. The differences from the convex functions can be best illustrated if the function has a one-dimensional argument. A quasiconvex function has one global minimum and is composed of two monotonic sections. In contrast to convex functions, the monotonic sections may not be strictly monotonic; that is, the graph may have some "flat" sections that make the optimization a more involved affair. Generally, an optimization problem with a quasiconvex function can be decomposed into a sequence of convex feasibility problems. The sequence of feasibility problem can be obtained using the set

$$
W_t = \left\{ w : \begin{array}{l} \rho(w^T r - r_b) - t\mu(w^T r - r_b) \le 0 \\ w^T e = 1 \\ w \ge 0 \end{array} \right\},
$$

where t is a fixed positive number. For a given t, the above set is convex and therefore we have a convex feasibility problem. A simple algorithm based on bisection can be devised so that the smallest t is found, t_{min}, for which the set is nonempty, Stoyanov et al. (2007) provide more details. If t_{min} is the solution of the feasibility problem, then $1/t_{min}$ is the value of the optimal ratio and the portfolios, in the set

$$
W_{t_{min}} = \left\{ w : \begin{array}{l} \rho(w^T r - r_b) - t_{min}\mu(w^T r - r_b) \le 0 \\ w^T e = 1 \\ w \ge 0 \end{array} \right\},
$$

are the optimal portfolios solving the fractional problem (10.45). The same set of portfolios also solve problem (10.43).

Convex Programming Problem   Suppose that the reward measure is a concave function of portfolio weights and the risk measure is a convex function of portfolio weights. In addition, suppose that both functions are positively homogeneous,

$$
v(hX) = hv(X)
$$

and

$$
\rho(hX) = h\rho(X)
$$

where $h > 0$. In this case, we can formulate two convex optimization problems equivalent to (10.43) and (10.45), respectively. The equivalent convex problems are obtained through the substitutions $t^{-1} = \rho(w'X - r_b)$ and $t^{-1} = v(w'X - r_b)$ for the former and the latter problem, respectively, and then setting $v = tw$. As a result, we obtain the problems

$$
\begin{aligned}
\max_{v,t} \quad & v(v'X - tr_b) \\
\text{subject to} \quad & v'e = t \\
& \rho(v'X - tr_b) \le 1 \\
& v \ge 0, t \ge 0
\end{aligned}
\tag{10.46}
$$

and

$$
\begin{aligned}
\min_{v,t} \quad & \rho(v'X - tr_b) \\
\text{subject to} \quad & v'e = t \\
& v(v'X - tr_b) \ge 1 \\
& v \ge 0, t \ge 0.
\end{aligned}
\tag{10.47}
$$

The equivalence with (10.43) and (10.45), respectively, is the following. Suppose that the pair $(\bar{v}_1, \bar{t}_1)$ is an optimal solution to (10.46). Then $\bar{w}_1 = \bar{v}_1/\bar{t}_1$ is a portfolio yielding the maximal ratio in (10.43). The quantity $1/\bar{t}_1$ is equal to the risk of the optimal portfolio. Furthermore, if we denote by v_{max} the value of the objective function of (10.46) at the solution point $(\bar{v}_1, \bar{t}_1)$, then v_{max} is equal to the value of the optimal ratio, that is, the optimal value of the objective function of problem (10.43). As a consequence, $v_{max}/\bar{t}_1$ equals the reward of the optimal portfolio.

In a similar way, if the pair $(\bar{v}_2, \bar{t}_2)$ is an optimal solution to (10.47), then $\bar{w}_2 = \bar{v}_2/\bar{t}_2$ is an optimal solution to (10.45) and, therefore, to (10.43). Denote by ρ_{min} the value of the objective function of (10.47) at the solution point $(\bar{v}_2, \bar{t}_2)$. Then $1/\rho_{min}$ is equal to the value of the optimal ratio, that is, the optimal value of the objective function of problem (10.43). In addition, $1/\bar{t}_2$ is the reward and $\rho_{min}/\bar{t}_2$ is the risk of the optimal portfolio.

The portfolios $\bar{w}_1$ and $\bar{w}_2$ may not be the same because there may be many portfolios yielding the unique maximum of the fractional program (10.43). Geometrically, this case arises if the efficient frontier has a linear section and the tangent line passes through all points in the linear section. This case is illustrated in Figure 10.4.

As a subcase in this section, suppose that both the risk and the reward measures satisfy the invariance property described in section 6.4.4 of Chapter 6 and the appendix to Chapter 8, respectively,

$$v(X + C) = v(X) + C$$

and

$$\rho(X + C) = \rho(X) - C. \tag{10.48}$$

where C is an arbitrary constant. Under these assumptions and a few additional technical conditions given in the appendix to Chapter 8, we can associate an optimal RV ratio problem that is equivalent to (10.43) in the sense that both problems have coincident optimal solutions. Consider the following transformations of the objective function of (10.45),

$$
\begin{aligned}
\frac{\rho(w'X - r_b)}{v(w'X - r_b)} &= \frac{\rho(w'X - r_b - v(w'X - r_b)) - v(w'X - r_b)}{v(w'X - r_b)} \\
&= \frac{\rho(w'X - r_b - v(w'X - r_b))}{v(w'X - r_b)} - 1.
\end{aligned} \tag{10.49}
$$

In the appendix to Chapter 8, we demonstrated that the functional in the numerator

$$\rho(w'X - r_b - v(w'X - r_b))$$

can be a dispersion measure and, therefore, the ratio on the right-hand side is the inverse of a RV ratio. On the basis of equation (10.49) and the relationship between (10.45) and (10.43), we arrive at the conclusion that the optimal RV ratio problem

$$\max_{w} \quad \frac{v(w'X - r_b)}{\rho(w'X - r_b - v(w'X - r_b))}$$

$$\text{subject to} \quad w'e = 1$$

$$w \geq 0, \tag{10.50}$$

has the same solution as the optimal RR ratio problem (10.43).

A special example of an optimal ratio problem belonging to the category of convex programming problems is when the reward measure coincides with the mathematical expectation. In this case, the objective function of (10.43) and the reward constraint in (10.43) turn into linear functions. We only provide the corresponding version to (10.43) since the reward constraint can be an equality rather than an inequality,

$$\min_{v,t} \quad \rho(v'X - tr_b)$$

$$\text{subject to} \quad v'e = t$$

$$E(v'X) - tE(r_b) = 1$$

$$v \geq 0, t \geq 0. \tag{10.51}$$

In the case of a linear reward measure, the relationship between the optimal RV ratio problem (10.50) and the optimal RR ratio (10.43) explains the relationship between the RR ratios based on the expectations bounded coherent risk measures and the corresponding RV ratios based on deviation measures, which is discussed in this chapter.

Recall that the assumptions made for ρ in this section are that it should be positive for all feasible portfolios, convex, and positively homogeneous. Generally, these properties alone do not imply that ρ is a risk measure. For example, any deviation measure satisfies them as well. As a consequence, the established relationship between (10.43) and (10.51) holds if there is a deviation measure in the denominator. Consider, for instance, the optimal Sharpe ratio problem (10.30) discussed in the chapter. The standard deviation in the denominator is a convex, positively homogeneous function of portfolio weights. The simpler convex programming problem, which is the analogue of (10.51), is problem (10.31). It turns out that it can be further simplified to the quadratic programming problem (10.32) because of properties specific to the standard deviation.

Another optimal portfolio problem falling into this category is the problem of maximizing the Sortino-Satchell ratio defined in the Chapter. The functional in the denominator is

$$\rho(w'X - r_b) = (E(s - (w'X - r_b))_+^q)^{1/q} \tag{10.52}$$

where $(x)_+^q = (\max(x,0)^q)$, s is the minimum acceptable return level, and $q \geq 1$ is the order of the lower partial moment. Assuming that the portfolio weights sum up to 1, it turns out that this is a convex function of portfolio weights. In order to demonstrate this property, we consider (10.52) in the next more suitable form,

$$g(w) = (E(w'Z)_+^q)^{1/q} \tag{10.53}$$

where $Z = se - X + r_b e$ and $e = (1, \ldots, 1)$. In the demonstration, we refer to the celebrated Minkowski inequality. Consider a portfolio w_λ, which is a convex combination of two other portfolios; that is, $w_\lambda = \lambda w_1 + (1 - \lambda)w_2$. Then

$$
\begin{aligned}
g(w_\lambda) &= (E((\lambda w_1 + (1 - \lambda)w_2)'Z)_+^q)^{1/q} \\
&\leq (E(\lambda(w_1'Z)_+ + (1 - \lambda)(w_2'Z)_+)^q)^{1/q} \\
&\leq (E(\lambda w_1'Z)_+^q)^{1/q} + (E((1 - \lambda)w_2'Z)_+^q)^{1/q} \\
&= \lambda(E(w_1'Z)_+^q)^{1/q} + (1 - \lambda)(E(w_2'Z)_+^q)^{1/q} \\
&= \lambda g(w_1) + (1 - \lambda)g(w_2).
\end{aligned}
$$

The first inequality follows because of the convexity of the max function and in order to obtain the second inequality, we apply the Minkowski inequality. As a result, the function $g(w)$ is a convex function of portfolio weights.

In addition to the convexity property, the function $g(w)$ is also positively homogeneous, $g(hw) = hg(w)$, $h > 0$. Therefore, the problem of maximizing the Sortino-Satchell ratio can be reduced to a problem of the type (10.51). The particular form of the simpler problem is

$$
\begin{aligned}
\min_{v,t} \quad & E(ts - v'X + tr_b)_+^q \\
\text{subject to} \quad & v'e = t \\
& E(v'X) - tE(r_b) = 1 \\
& v \geq 0, t \geq 0,
\end{aligned}
\tag{10.54}
$$

which is obtained after raising the objective function to the power $q \geq 1$. This transformation does not change the optimal solution points.

If there are scenarios available for the assets returns and the benchmark return, then (10.54) can be further reduced to a more simple problem. In this case, the objective function is the estimator of the mathematical expectation and, therefore, it is a sum of maxima raised to the power q. The maxima are either positive or zero and can be replaced by additional variables following the method of linearizing a piecewise linear convex function, which is used also in the linearization of AVaR described in section 8.3 of Chapter 8. In this reasoning, we consider the argument of the max function $ts - v'X + tr_b$ as a random variable, the scenarios of which are obtained from the scenarios of the assets returns and the benchmark return. As a result, we derive the optimization problem

$$
\min_{v,t,d} \sum_{i=1}^{k} d_i^q
$$

$$
\text{subject to} \quad
\begin{aligned}
& tse - Hv + th_b \leq d \\
& v'e = t \\
& v'\mu - tEr_b = 1 \\
& v \geq 0, t \geq 0, d \geq 0,
\end{aligned}
\qquad (10.55)
$$

where $h_b = (r_b^1, \ldots, r_b^k)$ is a vector of the observed returns of the benchmark portfolio.

From the point of view of the optimal portfolio problem structure, there are two interesting cases. If $q = 1$, then (10.55) is a linear programming problem. This is not surprising because in this case the objective function in (10.54) is the expectation of the maxima function. If $q = 2$, then (10.55) is a quadratic programming problem. In this case, the objective function can be represented in matrix form as

$$
\sum_{i=1}^{k} d_i^2 = d'Id,
$$

where I stands for the identity matrix.

Reductions to Linear Programming Problems   Suppose that the reward measure is a concave function of portfolio weights and the risk measure is a convex function of portfolio weights, and that both functions are positively homogeneous. In addition to these properties, which were the basic assumptions in the previous section, suppose that both v and ρ can be approximated by piecewise linear functions. Then, the convex optimization problems (10.46) and (10.46) can be further simplified to linear programming problems. It is also often said that, in this case the convex problem allows for a linear relaxation.

A problem belonging to this category is the optimal STARR problem discussed in the chapter. It arises when $\rho(X) = AVaR_\epsilon(X)$ and the reward measure is the mathematical expectation. On condition that there are scenarios for the assets returns and the benchmark return, AVaR can be approximated by a piecewise linear function on the basis of which the convex optimization problem can be simplified to a linear programming problem. This method is described in Section 8.3 of Chapter 8 and can be directly applied to (10.51) by considering the argument of the risk measure $v'X - tr_b$ as a random variable the scenarios of which are obtained from the scenarios of the assets returns X and the benchmark return r_b.

Another problem in this category is the optimal robust STARR problem formulated in (10.42). The reward measure is the negative of AVaR at a certain upper tail probability and, therefore, it is a concave function of portfolio weights. The risk measure is AVaR. Both the reward measure and the risk measure can be linearized by means of the approach in Section 8.3 of Chapter 8. In the case of the robust STARR, the analogue of the convex problem (10.47) is

$$
\begin{aligned}
\min_{v,t} \quad & AVaR_\epsilon(v'X - tr_b) \\
\text{subject to} \quad & v'e = t \\
& AVaR_\delta(v'X - tr_b) \geq 1 \\
& v \geq 0, t \geq 0.
\end{aligned}
\tag{10.56}
$$

The linear relaxation of the convex optimization problem (10.56) is

$$
\begin{aligned}
\min_{(v,t,\theta_1,d,\theta_2,g)} \quad & \theta_1 + \frac{1}{k\epsilon}d'e \\
\text{subject to} \quad & -Hv - \theta_1 \leq d \\
& \theta_2 + \frac{1}{k\delta}g'e \leq 1 \\
& -Hv - \theta_2 \leq g \\
& v'e = t \\
& v \geq 0, \ t \geq 0, \ d \geq 0, \ g \geq 0 \\
& \theta_1 \in \mathbb{R}, \ \theta_2 \in \mathbb{R},
\end{aligned}
\tag{10.57}
$$

where the auxiliary variables θ_1 and d are because of the linearization of the risk measure and the auxiliary variables θ_2 and g are because of the linearization of the reward measure. The remaining notation is explained in detail in section 8.3 of Chapter 8. Stoyanov (2005) provides formal arguments proving that (10.56) can be reduced to the linear programming problem (10.57).

10.5.3 The Capital Market Line and Quasiconcave Ratios

In section 10.3.3, we considered the capital market line generated by mean-variance analysis with a risk-free asset added to the investment universe and the optimal Sharpe ratio problem. We demonstrated that the market portfolio, which is a key constituent of the efficient portfolios, yields the maximal Sharpe ratio with a constant benchmark return equal to the return on the risk-free asset. It turns out that this property is not valid only for the mean-variance analysis and the Sharpe ratio but also for the more general case of reward-risk analysis and the corresponding optimal quasiconcave ratio problem under certain technical conditions. The necessary general technical conditions are stated in the opening part of section 10.2 with the additional requirements that the reward measure and the risk measure are positively homogeneous and they satisfy the invariance property given in (10.48). Under these conditions, the optimal quasiconcave ratio problem (10.43) can be reduced to the convex problem

$$
\begin{aligned}
\min_{v,t} \quad & \rho(v'X) + tr_b \\
\text{subject to} \quad & v'e = t \\
& v(v'X) - tr_b \geq 1 \\
& v \geq 0, t \geq 0.
\end{aligned}
\tag{10.58}
$$

In this section, we demonstrate that the two-fund separation theorem is valid for the efficient portfolios generated by reward-risk analysis with a risk-free asset added to the investment universe. Similar to the Sharpe ratio, the market portfolio appears as a solution to the optimal reward-to-risk ratio problem (10.43).

The optimal portfolio problem behind reward-risk analysis with a risk-free asset is given by

$$
\begin{aligned}
\min_{\omega,\omega_f} \quad & \rho(\omega'X) - \omega_f r_f \\
\text{subject to} \quad & \omega'e + \omega_f = 1 \\
& v(\omega'X) + \omega_f r_f \geq R_* \\
& \omega \geq 0, \omega_f \leq 1,
\end{aligned}
\tag{10.59}
$$

where:

ω denotes the weights of the risky assets.

ω_f stands for the weight of the risk-free asset.

r_f denotes the return on the risk-free asset.

R_* denotes the bound on the expected portfolio return.

Negative values of ω_f are interpreted as borrowing at the risk-free rate with the borrowed funds invested in the risky assets. Also, we assume that the lower bound on the expected return is larger than the risk-free rate, $R_* > r_f$.

We substitute the variable ω_f for $1 - s$ where s calculates the total weight of the risky assets in the portfolio. In effect, we derive the following optimization problem, equivalent to (10.59):

$$
\begin{aligned}
\min_{\omega, s} \quad & \rho(\omega'X) + sr_f - r_f \\
\text{subject to} \quad & \omega'e = s \\
& v(\omega'X) - sr_f \geq R_* - r_f \\
& \omega \geq 0, s \geq 0.
\end{aligned}
\tag{10.60}
$$

There are many similar features between the optimal ratio problem (10.58) and (10.60). Denote the optimal solution of (10.60) by $(\overline{\omega}, \overline{s})$. The optimal solution to (10.58) equals

$$
\overline{v} = \frac{\overline{\omega}}{(R_* - r_f)}
$$

and

$$
\overline{t} = \frac{\overline{s}}{(R_* - r_f)}.
\tag{10.61}
$$

Formula (10.61) holds because scaling the optimal solution $(\overline{\omega}, \overline{s})$ with the positive factor $1/(R_* - r_f)$ makes the resulting quantities feasible for problem (10.58). Furthermore, scaling the objective function of problem (10.60) by the same factor does not change the optimal solution point.

Note that both $\overline{v}$ and $\overline{t}$, being an optimal solution to (10.58), do not depend on R_* because R_* is not a parameter in (10.58). Therefore, the vector $\overline{v}$ and the scalar $\overline{t}$ can be regarded as characteristics of the efficient portfolios generated by (10.59).

According to the analysis made for the generic optimal RR ratio problem (10.43), we obtain that the weights $\overline{w}$ of the portfolio yielding the maximal RR ratio are computed by

$$
\overline{w} = \overline{v}/\overline{t} = \overline{\omega}/\overline{s} = \overline{\omega}/(1 - \overline{\omega}_f).
\tag{10.62}
$$

As a consequence, the optimal RR ratio portfolio $\overline{w}$ is a fundamental ingredient in all portfolios in the efficient set generated by (10.59). The weights of the risky assets in the efficient portfolios are proportional to it and can be computed according to the formula $\overline{\omega} = \overline{w}(1 - \overline{\omega}_f)$. As a result, the optimal RR ratio portfolio represents the market portfolio and the returns of any reward-risk efficient portfolio with a risk-free asset can be expressed as

$$
\overline{\omega}X + \overline{\omega}_f r_f = (1 - \overline{\omega}_f)\overline{w}X + \overline{\omega}_f r_f,
$$

where $r_M = \overline{w}X$ stands for the return of the optimal RR ratio portfolio.

The approach behind the derivation of the capital market line in the case of mean-variance analysis described in section 8.2.4 of Chapter 8 can be applied for the more general reward-risk analysis. We obtain that the equation for the capital market line is

$$v(r_p) = r_f + \left(\frac{v(r_M) - r_f}{\rho(r_M) + r_f} \right) (\rho(r_p) + r_f), \qquad (10.63)$$

where r_p denotes the return of the efficient portfolio. Equation (10.63) suggests that the capital market line coincides with the tangent line to the efficient frontier in the reward-shifted risk plane.

10.5.4 Nonquasiconcave Performance Measures

Not all RR ratios and RV ratios belong to the class of the quasiconcave performance measures described in the previous section. Examples include the one-sided variability ratio defined in (10.21) and the Rachev ratio described in the Chapter which are ratios of a convex reward measure of portfolio weights and a convex risk measure. Other examples include the generalized Rachev ratio, the Gini-type ratio, and the spectral-type ratio discussed in Rachev et al. (2007).

Since these performance measures are not quasiconcave functions of portfolio weights, there may be multiple local extrema and, therefore, any numerical method based on convex programming will find the closest local maximum which may not be the global one. Nevertheless, for some of the nonquasiconcave performance measures, it could be possible to find a method yielding the global maximum. For example, in the case of the Rachev ratio, it is possible to find a mixed-integer programming problem finding the global maximum of the Rachev ratio. Stoyanov et al. (2007) provide further details.

In this section, we provide a definition of the generalized Rachev ratio as it includes several of the ratios discussed in the chapter as special examples. The generalized Rachev ratio is defined as

$$GRaR^{\delta,\gamma}_{\alpha,\beta}(w) = \frac{AVaR^{\delta}_{\alpha}(r_b - r_p)}{AVaR^{\gamma}_{\beta}(r_p - r_b)}, \qquad (10.64)$$

where α and β denote tail probabilities, and δ and γ are powers generalizing the AVaR concept,

$$AVaR^{\delta}_{\alpha}(X) = \left(\frac{1}{\alpha} \int_0^{\alpha} \left[\max(-F_X^{-1}(p), 0) \right]^{\delta} dp \right)^{1/\delta},$$

in which $\delta \geq 1$ and X stands for the random variable which in this case can be the active portfolio return $X = r_p - r_b$ or the negative of it $X = r_b - r_p$. If $\delta = 1$, then the quantity $AVaR_\alpha^\delta(X)$ coincides with AVaR,

$$AVaR_\alpha^1(X) = AVaR_\alpha(X),$$

if $\alpha \leq F_X(0)$. As a consequence of this equality, the Rachev ratio appears as a special example of the generalized Rachev ratio,

$$GRaR_{\alpha,\beta}^{1,1}(w) = RaR_{\alpha,\beta}(w),$$

when α and β are sufficiently small.

Furthermore, choosing appropriately the tail probabilities, the generalized Rachev ratio generates a scaled one-sided variability ratio $\Phi_{r_b}^{p,q}(w)$ described in the chapter. Suppose that $\alpha_1 = P(r_b - r_p \leq 0)$ and $\beta_1 = P(r_p - r_b \leq 0)$. Then, on condition that the active return is an absolutely continuous random variable,

$$GRaR_{\alpha_1,\beta_1}^{p,q}(w) = C.\Phi_{r_b}^{p,q}(w),$$

where $C = \beta_1^q / \alpha_1^p$ is a positive constant.

10.5.5 Probability Metrics and Performance Measures

In Chapters 3 and 4, we described the notion of a probability metric and offered many examples of probability metrics and distances. Concerning the problem of evaluating the performance of a given portfolio, the ideas behind the theory of probability metrics can be applied in the construction of general families of performance measures.

For example, consider the following general ratio,

$$GR_{\alpha,\beta,M}^{\delta,\gamma}(w) = \frac{AVaR_{\alpha,M}^\delta(r_b - r_p)}{AVaR_{\beta,M}^\gamma(r_p - r_b)}, \qquad (10.65)$$

where

$$AVaR_{\alpha,M}^\delta(X) = \left(\frac{1}{\alpha} \int_0^\alpha \left[\max(-F_X^{-1}(p), 0) \right]^\delta dM(p) \right)^{\min(1,1/\delta)} \qquad (10.66)$$

in which $\delta > 0$ and all notation is the same as in formula (10.64) and the function $M(p)$ satisfies the properties of a cumulative distribution function (c.d.f.) of a random variable defined in the unit interval.

There are a few interesting special cases of (10.66). If $M(p)$ is the c.d.f. of the uniform distribution in $[0, 1]$, then (10.66) coincides with the generalized Rachev ratio given in (10.64). As a next case, suppose that $M(p)$ is the c.d.f. of the constant α, which is the tail probability in (10.66). Under this assumption, the integral equals the value of the integrand function at $p = \alpha$. As a result, we can obtain a performance measure represented by a scaled ratio of two VaRs,

$$GR_{\alpha,\beta,M}^{1,1}(w) = C\frac{VaR_\alpha(r_b - r_p)}{VaR_\beta(r_p - r_b)},$$

where $C = \beta/\alpha$ is a positive constant.

Furthermore, taking advantage of the underlying structure of the performance measure in (10.65), we can derive the next two limit cases. Suppose that $\delta \to \infty$ and $\gamma \to \infty$ and that $M(p)$ is a continuous function. Under these conditions and using the properties of the inverse c.d.f.,

$$GR_{\alpha,\beta,M}^{\infty,\infty}(w) = \frac{VaR_0(r_b - r_p)}{VaR_0(r_p - r_b)},$$

where $VaR_0(X)$ denotes the smallest value that the random variable X can take. Thus, the performance measure $GR_{\alpha,\beta,M}^{\infty,\infty}(w)$ is in fact the ratio between the maximal outperformance of the benchmark and the maximal underperformance of the benchmark. This quantity does not depend on the selected tail probabilities and the form of the continuous c.d.f. $M(p)$.

At the other limit, suppose that $\delta \to 0$ and $\gamma \to 0$. Then, using the properties of the inverse c.d.f., we derive the ratio

$$GR_{\alpha,\beta,M}^{0,0}(w) = \frac{\beta M(\alpha)}{\alpha M(\beta)},$$

the properties of which are driven by the assumptions behind the c.d.f. $M(p)$.

The general ratio defined in formula (10.65) can be regarded as an illustration of how the theory of probability metrics can be employed in order to obtain general classes of performance measures encompassing other performance measures as special cases. The properties of the general performance measure obtained in this fashion can be studied using the methods of the theory of probability metrics.

BIBLIOGRAPHY

Biglova, A., S. Ortobelli, S. T. Rachev, and S. T. Stoyanov (2004). "Different approaches to risk estimation in portfolio theory," *Journal of Portfolio Management* **31** (Fall): 103–112.

Farinelli, S., L. Tibiletti (2002). "Sharpe thinking with asymmetrical preferences," *working paper, University of Turin.*

Rachev, S. T., D. Martin, B. Racheva-Iotova, and S. T. Stoyanov (2006). "Stable *etl* optimal portfolios and extreme risk management," forthcoming in *Decisions in Banking and Finance,* New York: Springer/Physika.

Rachev, S. T., S. Ortobelli, S. T. Stoyanov, F. J. Fabozzi, and A. Biglova (2007). "Desirable properties of an ideal risk measure in portfolio theory," forthcoming in *International Journal of Theoretical and Applied Finance.*

Sharpe, W. F. (1966). "Mutual funds performance," *Journal of Business* **January,** 119–138.

Sortino, F. A., and S. Satchell (2001). *Managing downside risk in financial markets: theory, practice and implementation,* Oxford: Butterworth Heinemann.

Stoyanov, S. T. (2005). *Optimal financial portfolios in highly volatile markets,* PhD thesis, University of Karlsruhe.

Stoyanov, S. T., S. T. Rachev, and F. J. Fabozzi (2007). "Optimal financial portfolios," forthcoming in *Applied Mathematical Finance.*

Tokat, Y., S. T. Rachev, and E. Schwartz (2003). "The stable non-Gaussian asset allocation: A comparison with the classical Gaussian approach," *Journal of Economic Dynamics and Control* **27**: 937–969.

Index

Printed in the USA
CPSIA information can be obtained
at www.ICGtesting.com
LVHW022138220923
757465LV00009B/15